The **REAL** Book
of **Real Estate**

The **REAL** Book
of **Real Estate**

REAL EXPERTS. **REAL** STORIES. **REAL** LIFE.

Robert Kiyosaki

Vanguard Press
A Member of the Perseus Books Group

Published by Vanguard Press

Designed by Anita Koury
Set in 10.5 point Mercury

Library of Congress Cataloging-in-Publication Data
The real book of real estate : real experts, real advice, real success stories/Robert Kiyosaki.
    p. cm.
  Includes index.
  ISBN 978-1-59315-532-2
1. Real estate investment. 2. Real estate business. I. Kiyosaki, Robert T., 1947–
HD1382.5.R33 2009
333.33—dc22

                   2009008346

ISBN 13: 978-1-59315-532-2

Vanguard Press books are available at special discounts for bulk purchases in the United States by corporations, institutions, and other organizations. For more information, please contact the Special Markets Department at the Perseus Books Group, 2300 Chestnut Street, Suite 200, Philadelphia, PA 19103, or call (800) 810-4145, extension 5000, or e-mail special.markets@perseusbooks.com.

10 9 8 7 6 5

"I'm not a genius. I'm just a tremendous bundle of experience."

—DR. R. BUCKMINSTER "BUCKY" FULLER

From left to right: Dr. R. Buckminster "Bucky" Fuller at eighty-six years old with Robert Kiyosaki in 1981. Buckminster Fuller was an American architect, author, designer, futurist, inventor, and visionary. Recognized as one of the most accomplished Americans in history, he dedicated his life to a world that worked for all things and all people.

Contents

Acknowledgments

For years I have been an advocate for financial education. While many other financial advisors are telling people what they should invest in, I have been telling people to invest in themselves—to invest in their own knowledge. That is what I have done, and it has made me rich. I have also been telling people to surround themselves with great teachers who are actively practicing what they preach. The creation of this book was made possible because of the people I consider my teachers. Each one has a lifetime of experience and a lifetime of knowledge. And each one knows the importance of continual learning.

The contributors to this book generously gave of their time and their talent so that you could see the possibilities, avoid the pitfalls, and understand the methods of building wealth through real estate. They have recollected their great achievements, and they have revealed their painful failures. I thank them for their openness. The lessons we learn from our own mistakes and the mistakes of others are the most powerful.

These people are not only my advisors, but they are also my friends. Together we have been through the ups and downs of the real estate cycle, ridden each wave, and made money doing it. These are the friends I run my ideas and my deals by. And because they are friends, I know that they will give me their honest opinions. I thank them for that, too.

I'd also like to thank Jan Ayres and Kathy Heasley of Heasley & Partners, Inc., who took this book from ideas on a flip chart to a finished manuscript. Special thanks to Rhonda Shenkiryk of The Rich Dad Company and Charles McStravick of Artichoke Design for their work on the book's cover. Finally, thank you to my wife, Kim, who more than twenty years ago said yes to a guy with no money and a lot of ideas.

Introduction: A Note from Robert Kiyosaki
Why a Real Book of Real Estate

There are four reasons why I think a real book of real estate is important at this time.

First, there will always be a real estate market. In a civilized world, a roof over your head is as essential as food, clothing, energy, and water. Real estate investors are essential to keeping this vital human need available at a reasonable price. In countries where investing in real estate is limited or excessively controlled by the government, such as it was in former Communist Bloc countries, people suffer, and real estate deteriorates.

Second, there are many different ways a person can participate and prosper with real estate. For most people, their only real estate investment is where they live. Their home is their biggest investment. During the real estate boom from 2000 to 2007, many amateurs got involved with flipping houses—buying low and hoping to sell higher. As you know, many flippers flopped and lost everything. In true investor vocabulary, flipping is known as speculating or trading. Some people call it gambling. While *flipping* is one method of investing, there are many, more sophisticated, less risky ways to do well with real estate. This book is filled with the knowledge and experiences of real, real estate investors—real estate professionals who *invest* rather than flip, speculate, trade, or gamble.

Third, real estate gives you control over your investments, that is, *if* you have the skills. In the volatile times of early 2009, millions of people were losing trillions of dollars simply because they handed over control of their wealth to other people. Even since the middle of 2008, the great Warren Buffett's fund, Berkshire Hathaway, has lost 40 percent of its value! Millions of people have lost their jobs, which means they had no control over their own employment either. The real, real estate professionals in this book have control over both their businesses and investments. They will share their good times and the bad times with you. They will share what they have learned *while* learning to control their investments and their financial destiny. The learning process is continual.

And, finally, here's my real reason for this book. I am sick and tired of financial experts giving advice on real estate, especially when they do not actually invest in real estate. After my book *Rich Dad Poor Dad* came out, I was on a television program with a financial author and television personality. At the time, in 1999, the stock market was red hot with the dot-com boom. This financial expert, who was a former stockbroker and financial planner, was singing the praises of stocks and mutual funds. After the stock market crashed in 2001, this man suddenly resurfaced with a new book on real estate, portraying himself as a real estate expert. His real estate advice was beyond bad. It was dangerous. Then the real estate market crashed and he dropped out of sight again. The last time I saw him, he had written a book on investing in solar energy and was claiming to be a green entrepreneur. If he were to write a book about what he really does, his new book would be about raising bulls . . . and selling BS.

There are other financial "experts" who know nothing about real estate, yet they speak badly about real estate and say it is risky. The only reason real estate is risky for them is because they know nothing about investing in it. Instead, they recommend saving money and investing in a well-diversified portfolio of mutual funds—investments which I believe are the riskiest investments in the world, especially in this market. Why do they recommend investing in savings and mutual funds? The answer is obvious: Many of these professionals are endorsed by banks, mutual fund companies, and the media. It's good business to plug your sponsors' businesses and products.

Commissioning this book gives the public its first chance to learn from real, real estate investors, friends, and advisors—people who have been through the ups and the downs and who walk their talk. This book gives them the opportunity to share the spotlight with the many media financial "experts" and speak the truth. These real estate experts are true pros, and you're about to move beyond the media hype. I hope you are ready. *The Real Book of Real Estate* is the *real* deal.

TOM WHEELWRIGHT

CHARLES LOTZAR

WAYNE PALMER

ROSS MCCALLISTER

CRAIG COPPOLA

GARRETT SUTTON

BERNIE BAYS

PART 1

The Business of Real Estate

The Business of Real Estate

Tom Wheelwright is a rare combination of CPA, real estate investor, and teacher. He has the ability to take the complex and often boring subject of tax and tax law and make it into something that's simple enough for a person like me to understand.

Tom understands the tax code. He actually enjoys reading the tax code, and because he is such a student of it, he understands this lengthy document better than anyone I know. Most CPAs focus on a very small part of the tax code. They focus on the part that lets you and most Americans defer taxes until retirement—the code relating to IRAs, 401(k)s, and other so-called retirement plans. Tom also pays close attention to the other, much lengthier part of the code that shows you how to reduce or eliminate your taxes permanently. The difference between Tom and other CPAs is that Tom understands the purpose of the tax code. It's not just a set of rules. It's a document that when followed is designed to reward certain behaviors through lowering or eliminating taxes. Does your CPA see the tax code this way?

I consider Tom to be a very moral and ethical man. He is very religious, raised in the Mormon faith. While I am not Mormon, I do share many of the values of the Mormon religion—values such as tithing, giving at least 10 percent to spiritual matters, and dedicating a number of years as a missionary. While I have never *been a religious missionary, I have spent nearly ten years as a military missionary: a Marine Corps pilot in Vietnam, serving my country.*

One important lesson I have learned from Tom and others of the Mormon faith is the saying, "God does not need to receive, but humans need to give." This reminds me of the importance of being generous. It is my opinion that greed rather than generosity has taken over the world. Every time I meet someone who is short of money, or if I am short of money, I am reminded to be generous and to give what I would like to get. For example, if I want money, I need to give money. Having been out of money a number of times in my life, I have had to remind myself to give money at times when I needed money the most. Today I make a point of donating regularly to charities and causes that are dear to my heart. My opinion is, if I cannot personally work at a cause near to my heart, then my money needs to work there for me. Going further, if I want kindness, then I need to give more kindness. If I want a smile, then I need to first give a smile. And if I want a punch in the mouth, then all I have to do is throw the first one.

I asked my friend Tom Wheelwright to be a part of this book not only because he is a smart accountant—a team player that anyone who wants to be rich needs to add to his his team—but also because he comes from a generous and sound philosophical background.

Tom is a smart CPA who is an advocate of investing in real estate. Why? Because he knows that tax laws reward real estate investors more than they reward stock investors. He is a great teacher, a generous man, and, most importantly, a friend I respect.

—ROBERT KIYOSAKI

I was one of the fortunate few growing up. Unlike much of the rest of the world—people who have been told to save their pennies and invest in mutual funds—my parents taught me to invest in real estate and business. My father had a printing business, and my mother handled their real estate portfolio.

So, it was natural that once I had received my education, both formal and work related, I opened my own business. (I had a lot of education before I finally opened my own business—a master's degree in professional accounting, thirteen years of experience with international accounting firms, as well as experience as the in-house tax advisor to a Fortune 1000 company. I was a little slow to realize the power of business.) When I started my accounting firm, I did it like most people: I worked all hours of the day and rarely took a vacation.

When I did take a vacation, I still took calls from clients and colleagues. After all, business never rests, so why should I?

Several years into my business, we had experienced significant growth, but I was still working day and night and never taking a real vacation. And outside of my business, I had no substantial assets. That's when I read *Rich Dad Poor Dad* and first met Robert Kiyosaki. He helped me realize that I was thinking about business all wrong. It was not about how *hard* I worked, but rather about how *smart* I worked.

Like many of you, my first real experience with Robert was at a Rich Dad seminar. There I was, sitting next to my business partner, Ann Mathis, and her husband, Joe. Robert was talking about a subject near and dear to my heart—the tax benefits of real estate. Out of the blue, Robert asked me to come up to the front of the room to explain the tax benefits of depreciation, introducing me as his "other accountant."

I had come to learn about Robert Kiyosaki and Rich Dad only a few months earlier. One of my good friends, George Duck, had become the chief financial officer at Rich Dad and had introduced us. I'm not sure who was more nervous that first time I went on stage, Robert or me. Can you imagine putting an accountant on stage? Robert had no idea that I had spent my life teaching in one capacity or another, but he took the chance and put me up there anyway. This began a long and inspiring relationship between us, and it really launched my journey toward financial freedom.

I remember one of the first times Robert and I worked together. He used me as "muscle." That's right, he used his accountant as his muscle. Robert had been asked by a reporter to give an interview for the business section of the *Arizona Republic*. The primary topic was how Robert could claim that he routinely received 40 percent returns on his investments.

I went as the authoritative backup to Robert's ideas. After all, someone might not believe a marketing genius (i.e., Robert) when he says he gets these levels of returns, but who wouldn't believe an accountant? When it comes to investing, numbers are everything, and who better to support the numbers than someone who spends his life documenting, reviewing, and analyzing them?

That was one of the first opportunities I had to explain the benefits of the leverage that comes from real estate. Not long before, I had started my own real estate investing. You would think that with parents who were real estate investors, that I, too, would become a real estate investor. I had even spent my career helping real estate investors and developers reduce their tax burdens.

Not so. I didn't actually begin investing in real estate until after the first time I played Robert's game, CASHFLOW 101®. This game had a powerful impact on me. I saw, with my own eyes, the power of leverage in real estate. The game was so powerful that the next day after playing the game, I called one of my clients who had been investing in real estate for several years and asked him to meet with me to show me how I could begin my own real estate investing.

And then I began making serious changes to my business. My partner, Ann, a systems genius, created the systems, policies, and procedures in our firm so we could focus on *running* the business and not *working in* the business. It took a few years, but eventually we were able to step away from working for hourly professional fees and instead supervise and grow a business that worked without us.

Now, I can take three weeks off each year with no e-mail or phone access, as I did just recently when I took my oldest son on a trip to the châteaux region of northern France. I didn't have to worry about my accounting firm or my real estate investments while I was gone because they were both running without my daily attention.

TIP Real estate investing is a business and should be run like a business.

Robert talks a lot about the CASHFLOW Quadrant, with each labeled as E, S, B, and I. He emphasizes that we need to move out of the E (employee) and S (self employed) quadrants and into the B (business) and I (investor) quadrants. I have learned to take this one step further. That is, to move all I-quadrant investing into the B quadrant.

Think about what you could do with the time you would have if you didn't have to worry about tenants, repairs, and cash flow. How would it feel to eliminate the frustration that comes from constantly watching your real estate investments and worrying about if a tenant might call you in the middle of the night with a problem? You can eliminate all of this stress and free up hundreds of hours of your time simply by running your real estate investments as a B-quadrant business.

FIGURE 1.1 I've learned to take the quadrant a step further and free up hundreds of hours of my time simply by running my real estate investments like a B-quadrant business.

It's really not that difficult. You simply have to *start acting like a business* and apply fundamental business principles to your real estate investing.

Business Principle No. 1: Strategy

Every business has to have a plan. Your real estate investing business is no different. A strategy is simply a systematic plan of action designed to accomplish specific goals. There are seven simple steps to creating a successful strategy.

Step 1: Imagine

Begin your strategy with goals. Imagine where you would like your real estate investing to take you. It may be a white sand beach in the Caribbean, unlimited time with your family, or working for your favorite charity. My favorite places in the world are Hawai'i, France, Arizona, and Park City, Utah. So my dream is to own a house in each of these locations.

Don't be afraid of being too aggressive. These are your dreams, after all, not some number that is artificially imposed by a financial advisor. Our clients frequently have dreams of financial freedom in as few as five to ten years. And with a good strategy in place, anyone can be financially free in less than ten years if they just *start by applying* these few basic business principles to their real estate investing. So far, after six years of investing, I now have houses in Hawai'i, Arizona, and Park City. France is on the agenda for next year. Pretty aggressive goals, but I have been able to reach them in six short years by applying basic business principles to my real estate and business.

Step 2: Financial Goals

Determine what it will take to realize these dreams in terms of wealth and cash flow. And commit to a date for accomplishing this goal. Then write down what you currently have available in terms of investable assets less the liabilities. This is your current wealth (also called net worth).

Step 3: Cash Flow Target

Of course, you will need to figure out the amount of wealth that it will take in order to create your desired cash flow. A simple rule of thumb for calculating this number is to multiply your desired cash flow by twenty. For me, I needed $5 million in order to create an after-tax cash flow of $250,000 each year.

STEP 4: CURRENT WEALTH

Once you have your dream firmly in mind, the next step is to identify where you are today. When considering where you are today, list only your real assets, that is, those that are available to invest. Don't list your car or your jewelry. But do list the amount of equity in your home if it can be made available for investing through a home equity loan. Here is an example of what I mean:

TABLE 1.1

Liquid:	Long-Term:
Savings	Loans
Stocks & Bonds	Real Estate
Mutual Funds	Oil & Gas
CDs	Business
Other	Intellectual
Other	Other
Sub-Total:	Sub-Total:

These first four steps are the essence of a process referred to as "dreamlining," and I will use a simple illustration to show you what I mean. Here is what my dreamline looked like when I first met Robert and started down my road to financial freedom.

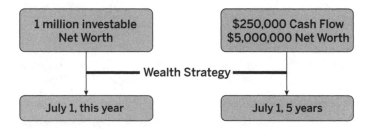

FIGURE 1.2 Tom's "Dreamline" When He First Met Robert Kiyosaki

STEP 5: VISION, MISSION, AND VALUES

After you have your dreamline in place, you can make a plan to reach those dreams. This plan should include your vision, mission and values, the type of real estate you will specialize in buying, and the criteria you use for choosing your real estate investments.

At this point, you may be wondering if I have truly lost my mind. After all, aren't vision, mission, and value statements only for true businesses? Exactly! And your real estate investments are a true business. At least they should be if you are going to reach your dreams in the shortest amount of time possible and with the least amount of work.

When creating your vision, remember that this represents your focus for the future, that is, what you want your life to look like when everything is in place. Your mission is simply a statement of how you are going to go about your investing business. And your values are the values that you insist everyone you work with in real estate share with you.

Tom's Personal
Vision, Mission, and Values

Vision. My vision for financial freedom means having the time and resources to do what I want, when I want. I know I have reached financial freedom when I can travel anytime I desire, spend quality time with family and friends, and go on missions for my church.

Mission. My mission to reach financial freedom is to invest in highly appreciating single-family homes by researching foreclosures, borrowing from banks and sellers, holding properties for five to ten years, and obtaining tax leverage through depreciation.

Values. My values are these: abundance—recognizing that there are plenty of resources and real estate deals to go around; caring—being kind and expressing gratitude; learning—taking the time to grow and improve my real estate knowledge; and respect—treating others the way I want to be treated.

STEP 6: INVESTMENT NICHE

Once you have your vision, mission, and values in place, you can begin looking at what type of real estate makes sense for you. Every successful business owner knows that you are always most successful when you focus your attention on something you enjoy doing and for which you have a natural ability. At my company, ProVision, we have a variety of tools we use to help people figure out which type of real estate they will enjoy the most—multifamily, commercial, industrial, raw land or single-family homes. My personal investment niche remains highly appreciating single-family homes.

STEP 7: CRITERIA

The final step in your strategy—determining your investment criteria—is something that few people take time to do. And yet, if you can determine your investment criteria as part of your strategy, you can avoid a lot of headaches, stress, and wasted time. You can also avoid making costly mistakes. And you will save a considerable amount of time and energy, enabling you to focus on only those investments that meet your criteria. As an example, here are my personal investment criteria:

TABLE 1.2 Tom's Personal Investment Criteria

Criteria	Decision
Minimum appreciation	10%
Minimum rate of return	50%
Cash flow or cash on cash return	-0-
Price range	$200,000-$600,000
Maximum amount of investment/deal	$80,000
Maximum time commitment	5 hours per month
Location of investment	Western U.S.
Price as a % of value	85%

You may be asking why you need to spend so much time and effort developing a strategy. We teach our ProVision clients about the importance of strategy by playing CASHFLOW 101® with them in a very specific way. If you have played the game, you realize that, on average, it will take two and a half hours. We instruct our clients that their team (the players at their table) must spend the first thirty minutes developing a strategy to win the game. This strategy includes the type of assets they will invest in and their criteria for investing. All members of their team, though playing as individuals, must follow the strategy precisely.

The result is astonishing. Each player gets out of the Rat Race and wins the game in less than two hours. So even though they have spent an enormous percentage of their allotted time developing their strategy (roughly 20 percent), they finish substantially earlier than they would have without their strategy. This happens every time, so long as each team member adheres to the strategy.

BUSINESS PRINCIPLE NO. 2: TEAM

Just as every good business has a strategy, every successful business owner has a very carefully chosen team of individuals and companies to help him/her succeed. Your team will add considerable leverage to your investing. You can take advantage of your team members' time, talents, contacts, knowledge, and resources.

TIPS FOR BUILDING A TEAM

Plan. Think carefully about what skills you need on your team. For example, you are going to need an attorney, an accountant, a banker, at least one property manager, and others. Decide on the skill sets you need before you decide on which people will fill those roles.

Referrals. The best team members almost always come as a referral from someone you trust. But make sure the person referring is also a real estate investor and is knowledgeable about your situation and needs. A trusted advisor, such as an attorney, accountant, mentor or wealth coach, can be a good source of referrals.

Agreements. Make sure you have good, clear agreements in place with each of your team members so they know what is expected of them and what they can expect from you.

Before we leave the concept of a team, let me give you my personal experience with developing a real estate team. Anyone who knows me realizes that I spend most of my day growing my business. This doesn't leave me much time for real estate investing. But I love real estate investing and understand completely the importance of it in my wealth strategy.

I estimate the time I spend each week on real estate to be no more than one hour. Yet, I make in excess of $100,000 per month through my real estate investing, all because I have developed a great team and applied the other business principles we are talking about in this chapter. This brings me to our next principle: accounting.

BUSINESS PRINCIPLE NO. 3: ACCOUNTING

You may wonder if I include accounting as a basic principle of business because of my accounting background. While I have to admit to a natural bias in favor of good accounting, I believe that if you were to ask one hundred successful business owners if good accounting (including good reporting) were critical to their business, at least ninety-five of them would agree.

Why? Because good accounting leads to good reporting, and good reporting leads to good decisions. If you don't have the information you need, how are you going to make good decisions, such as when you should sell a piece of real estate or how to know if your portfolio is producing the desired results?

Great entrepreneurs understand the purpose of accounting. Here are a few of my personal keys to great accounting.

KEY NO. 1: PURPOSEFUL ACCOUNTING

Accounting should never be done solely (or even mainly) to satisfy the IRS or other regulators. Accounting's primary purpose should be to provide accurate and useful information so that you can make the best decisions. Poor investors think that the only reason to keep records is so their accountant can prepare their tax return at the end of the year.

This is a huge mistake. Good accounting is critical to good decision making. Without current, accurate numbers, how are you going to make the decision to buy, sell, or refinance your property? And how will you know which property is doing well and which is doing poorly? You won't even know if your property manager is doing a good job or not.

Several years ago, Ann and I purchased a group of fourplexes in Mesa, Arizona. The price was good based on the information we had at the time. We kept

Real Life Story: My Team Took Care of It All

So how do I make time for real estate? You guessed it—I have a terrific team. They are so good, in fact, that the only time I have to spend is to quickly review reports, make decisions (which are pretty easy, since I have very well-defined investment criteria), and sign documents. I remember one time recently when I was speaking to my team leader and he informed me that a tenant had vacated a house unexpectedly and not turned off the water. My team leader, who is not the property manager, drops by all of my houses on a regular basis and noticed that the tenant had left. He rushed into the house only to discover that the pipes had broken (this was in Utah in the dead of winter), and the house was flooded. The cost of repair was in the neighborhood of $50,000.

My team leader immediately took action. After turning the water off, he called the property manager and the insurance agent. He arranged for the repair company to renovate the property, made sure the insurance accepted the claim (before spending any money), and went after the property manager and tenant for any damages not paid for by the insurance company. I did not have to worry about a thing. And I probably spent only thirty minutes total dealing with this mess (signing authorizations and talking to my team leader).

very close track of the cash flow and the income from these properties. But after a year or so, it became clear to us that these properties were not going to generate positive cash flow in the near future. At the same time, we noticed that cap rates (see Principle No. 4, p. 17) were going down. So, based on our numbers, we sold the fourplexes. Because of the decrease in cap rates, we were able to make a significant profit, and we stopped losing money each month.

KEY NO. 2: ACCURATE BOOKKEEPING

While good accounting should go far beyond mere bookkeeping, it begins with accurate and appropriate bookkeeping entries. Accurate bookkeeping is the basis for creating useful reports and analysis.

Bookkeeping is merely the process of entering the results of transactions into a record that can be used for reporting and analysis. I suggest to most of my clients that they outsource their bookkeeping to their accountant or some other professional bookkeeping service. For those who want to do it themselves, I recommend using a very simple accounting software program, such as Quickbooks.

KEY NO. 2A: CHART OF ACCOUNTS

Begin by setting up a chart of accounts (this is just a list of the accounts you are going to use to classify your receipts and expenditures). The accounts you use should be those that make the most sense to you. For example, one person may list printer paper as an office supply while another may list it in the more general category of office expense. It's simply a matter of how detailed you want your reporting to be. Just remember that if you did not create an account for it, you cannot create a report for it.

TIP **Here's a little trick for you: You don't have to create a separate chart of accounts for every property. Instead, you can create a "class" for each property. This allows you to do all of the bookkeeping for your real estate business in one Quickbooks "company" while creating the detail and report options that you need in order to understand what is happening with each property.**

If you need help setting up your chart of accounts, ask your accountant/ CPA—a critical member of your team—to lend you a hand. This person should be happy to help, and can do this fairly quickly for you.

KEY NO. 2B: DETAILED DATA ENTRY

Once you have your chart of accounts set up, you are ready to begin entering your data. Remember that you need to enter the details of every transaction. Most transactions will have some cash involved, so if you enter the details every time you receive or spend money, you probably will catch 98 percent of your transactions. Some transactions don't have cash involved, such as recording depreciation expense. These are done through journal entries. Since you will likely have some journal entries to do, I will give you a brief explanation of how to do these.

Understand that every transaction has two sides to it for accounting purposes; a debit side and a credit side (think left and right so the total of the left side always equals the total of the right side). Expenditures are always a debit to the expense, income, or asset account (left side), and a credit to cash (right side). Receipts are always a credit to an income, expense, or liability account (left side), and a debit to cash (right side). To increase an expense or an asset, you debit that account, and to increase income or a liability, you credit that account.

KEY NO. 2C: JOURNAL ENTRIES

When you enter a receipt or an expenditure into Quickbooks, the software automatically creates both the debit and the credit. But sometimes you will need to make a correction or adjustment to your books when there has not been a cash transaction. You do this with a journal entry. When you make a journal entry, you simply enter both a credit and a debit. Let's use our depreciation journal entry as an example, since everyone has to make this journal entry at least once a year:

Debit to Depreciation Expense in the amount of depreciation calculated for the period (usually based on tables provided by the Internal Revenue Service or your accountant). See page 26 for more details about the Magic of Depreciation.

Credit to Accumulated Depreciation in the same amount (this account is an offset to the asset account for the asset you are depreciating, such as a building).

See? It's simple.

KEY NO. 3: CONSISTENCY

Learn to use the correct accounts, and use the same accounts for all similar receipts and expenditures. If you decide to put paper costs into office supplies, *always* put purchases of paper into office supplies. Don't put them into the office supply account one month and the office expense account the next month.

KEY NO. 4: FREQUENCY

Do your bookkeeping no less than once a week. Two problems happen when you get behind. First, it becomes overwhelming, and you will tend to continue putting it off until the end of the year when it becomes urgent for your tax returns. This creates the second problem: Not having up-to-date bookkeeping means you cannot get good reports to make good decisions.

KEY NO. 5: ONLINE BANKING

Personally, I do my bookkeeping every Friday morning. It takes me less than one hour because I use the systems that are available to me, such as online banking and automatic bill pay. Quickbooks will automatically classify all of my online banking to the right accounts with a few clicks of the mouse. I actually find it quicker to do the bookkeeping myself using these systems than if I were to use an outside bookkeeper (I tried that once and found it took me more time to correct the bookkeeping than if I just did it myself using online banking).

The next principle I'm going to share with you is how to get good reports from your bookkeeping software. If you review these reports each month, you will be able to make good decisions about your real estate business quickly and effectively.

BUSINESS PRINCIPLE NO. 4: REPORTING

All successful entrepreneurs understand the importance of managing their business by metrics. Metrics is simply a measurement of the day-to-day results of the business. Sometimes these measurements are raw numbers, such as cash flow. Other times they take the form of ratios. And still other times these measurements are comparisons, either to a previous period, to targets, or industry averages.

TIP If you don't know your numbers, you don't know your business.

REPORT NO. 1: STATEMENT OF CASH FLOWS

Let's start with the king of all raw numbers: cash flow. Unfortunately, it's rare that a real estate investor has a clear picture of his/her true cash flow. You should know the cash flow from each property as well as the overall cash flow for your real estate business.

There is a tendency among real estate investors to believe that all they need to know about cash flow is the difference in their bank account from the beginning of the month to the end of the month. But the real key to using cash flow as a tool is to understand where the cash came from and where it went. A standard accounting report that you can use to figure this out is the Statement of Cash Flows. This report, though rarely used among real estate investors, is the most important report of all.

It begins with operating income. Operating income includes rents minus normal cash expenses, including repairs, maintenance, and management fees. It then details nonoperating items such as financing transactions and investing transactions. Financing transactions include any money that flows to or from your business because of loans. These include your mortgage payments as well as any loans you take out or money you put it. Investing transactions include any money that flows to or from your business because of investing activities. These include down payments on properties and cash from the sale of a property.

The end result is the increase or decrease in the amount of cash you have at the end of the period (month, quarter, or year) compared to what you had at the beginning of the period. This report makes it clear how much of your positive or negative cash flow is coming from operations versus other activities, such as financing or investing. Wouldn't it be great to know this and be able to

TABLE 1.3 Tom's Statement of Cash Flow

Property A	Oct - Dec
OPERATING ACTIVITIES	
Net Income	-6,706.40
Adjustments to reconcile Net Income to net cash provided by operations:	
Escrow Accounts	-174.40
Security Deposits	800.00
Net cash provided by Operating Activities	-6,080.80
INVESTING ACTIVITIES	
Accumulated depreciation	6,790.00
Accumulated amortization	18.00
Net cash provided by Investing Activities	6,808.00
FINANCING ACTIVITIES	
Mortgage Payable	-258.34
Net cash provided by Financing Activities	-258.34
Net cash increase for period	468.86

find out this information at any time? Table 1.3 is an example of a statement of cash flows for one of my properties. I pulled this report directly from my Quickbooks.

This report tells me several things about this property. First, it tells me there was positive cash flow. Second, it tells me that there was a loss for tax purposes (net income was negative), producing additional cash flow for me through depreciation. Third, it tells me that I paid down my mortgage by $258, which is an additional benefit to me. If all I knew was that my cash had increased by $468 for the period, I would never have learned these other important benefits from this property and may have thought the property wasn't doing too well.

REPORT NO. 2: RATIO ANALYSIS

While raw numbers are helpful to know, serious analysis of your real estate business comes from ratios and comparisons. A list of the most common ratios used to analyze your results is found in Table 1.4.

TIP Two of the most important ratios are the cap rate on your properties and your return on investment (ROI).

TABLE 1.4 Most Common Ratios Used to Analyze Property Results

Ratio	Numerator	Denominator	Tells You
Cap rate	Net Operating Income	Property Value	How much the property is earning
ROI	Annual increase in value plus income	Cash invested	Total return
Cash on Cash return	Net cash from investment after taxes	Cash invested	Cash return
Current ratio	Current assets	Current liabilities	Ability to pay liabilities
Debt/equity ratio	Total debt	Net Equity	Leverage
Return on assets	Net operating income	Total assets	Profitability
Debt coverage	Net operating income	Annual debt service	Ability to service debt from cash flow
Loan to value (LTV)	Debt	Value of Property	Leverage
Internal Rate of Return (IRR)	Complex formula		Average annual return on investment

Ratio No. 1: Cap Rate

Your cap rate (or capitalization rate) is simply your net operating income divided by the value of your property. Remember that this figure represents the value of the property, not the cost of the property. Let's look at an example. Suppose your property produces $10,000 per month in rent, or $120,000 for the year. And suppose your operating expenses (remember, this doesn't include mortgage interest or principal payments, or depreciation) are $70,000. This means that your net operating income (NOI) is $50,000. If your property is worth $500,000, then your cap rate is 10 percent.

TIP You can use this information to make decisions. Let's suppose that you have a loan on the property with a 7 percent interest rate. If your cap rate goes below 7 percent, then you need to think about selling the property. Why? Because now you have what is called "negative leverage." Negative leverage occurs when your return is less than you are paying on your loan. At this point, it is actually costing you money to borrow because the cap rate is lower than your borrowing rate.

When Ann and I sold our fourplexes in Mesa, the cap rate had dipped down around 5 percent. The interest rate on our mortgage was 6.5 percent. So we were now into negative leverage. On top of that, we had negative cash flow. So it was time to sell the properties. And we did so at a substantial profit because we watched the cap rate. When we purchased the properties, the cap rate was around 10 percent. Though our net operating income never increased, our property value doubled simply because of the cap rate decreasing from 10 percent to 5 percent.

Ratio No. 2: ROI

Another ratio we review is Return on Investment, or ROI. This ratio tells us how a property is doing overall. It's critical to review this ratio on a regular basis. I know several investors who calculate expected ROI when buying a property but never again. Like the cap rate, your ROI can tell you if you should be holding on to the property or if you need to do something different with the property.

For example, one of my criteria for investing is an after-tax return of at least 30 percent. This includes cash flow from the property and the appreciation on the property plus my tax benefits from the property and principal reduction on my mortgage. A few years ago, I bought a property in Utah that looked like it would have an ROI of 35 percent over a five-year period. But it turned out that the property was very difficult to rent, so the ROI was less than expected. Once it was clear the ROI was going to fall below my 30 percent requirement, I sold the property and found another property that better fit my investment criteria. It should be obvious to you by now that a lot depends on coming up with the appropriate investment criteria. Many of your decisions will be based on these.

Working through your numbers and applying them to your criteria is where another member of your team—your wealth coach—will be critical. Everyone should have a coach for his/her business. Your coach should be someone well versed in real estate and in overall wealth strategies. Go to www.ProVision Wealth.com/wealthstrategies.asp for more information on wealth coaching.

REPORT NO. 3: COMPARISON REPORTS

The third type of reporting is comparison reporting. Comparison reports take the actual data from your real estate business and compare it to some other data, such as industry standards, past performance, or expected/budgeted performance. Let's suppose that when you bought your property, you expected that it would appreciate 10 percent per year. Suppose the actual appreciation is 15 percent.

Your appreciation report should show you not only your current appreciation, but also your expected appreciation and perhaps the average appreciation in the market. This gives you a good idea of how you are doing compared to the market and to your own expectations and whether you might want to consider buying more property in that market or selling what you have so you can buy other property that better meets your criteria.

Can you see how important it is to have good reports? It's not just the raw data you want; it's also the ratios and the comparisons. One of my biggest complaints about many property managers is that they produce terrible reports. Typically, they give you only the raw data, and frequently even that is impossible to understand. Let me show you the type of report my property manager gives me.

While it doesn't give me any analysis, at least it gives me the data in a way I can create my own analysis. I can see immediately that I have positive cash flow, which meets my criteria. I now need to take this information and put it into my reporting system (Quickbooks or something similar), and from that system I can create reports that give me cap rates, ROI, and other analyses.

TABLE 1.5 Real Life Example of a Good Property Report

Property Address	Lease Rate: $1200/mo
Rent Collected:	$1200.00
Less 8% Management Fee:	$96.00
Expenses-HOA Fee:	$105.00
Amount to Owner	**$999.00**
Mortgage Payment:	$987.90
March 2009 Cashflow:	$11.10 +
April 2009 Projection:	$999.00

Business Principle No. 5: Taxes

If you want to make an immediate impact on the return on your real estate, you need to pay close attention to tax laws.

TIP The fastest way to increase your ROI on a property is to take advantage of the tax laws in place to encourage real estate investment.

The single biggest expense for most people is taxes. In the United States, which is routinely considered to be a low-tax country, the average business owner earning $100,000 pays more than 50 percent of his earnings to the government in some form of taxes. These include income taxes, property taxes, transfer taxes, sales taxes, employment taxes, and excise taxes, not to mention estate taxes.

Some ancient civilizations equated a 50 percent tax to being in bondage. Yet here we are in the twenty-first century paying more than 50 percent of our income in taxes and accepting this as okay. The good news is that if you are in business, and particularly if that business is real estate investment, you can easily lower this rate from 50 percent to 20 or 30 percent. In fact, many of our clients at ProVision who are serious real estate investors legally pay no income tax at all.

Think about what you could do with the extra money you would have if you reduced your income taxes by even 20 or 30 percent. How much more real estate could you buy? How much faster would your portfolio grow? I once calculated that someone in the 30 percent tax bracket could double his investment portfolio over seven years if he simply maximized his tax benefits from real estate and reinvested these savings into his portfolio.

When I tell people that they can legally reduce their income tax by 30 percent or more, they are immediately skeptical. They think I must be getting my clients into some tax shelter. They are correct. That tax shelter is real estate investing. And it doesn't matter whether it is residential, commercial, or industrial property. In the United States and many other countries, real estate is a highly favored investment under the tax laws.

TIP In the United States and many other countries, real estate is a highly favored investment under the tax laws.

So let's talk about what you can do to receive the maximum tax benefit from your real estate. We will focus on the laws of the United States, but keep in mind that many other countries have similar laws. So even if you don't invest in the United States, these tax reduction principles may apply to your real estate investments in Canada, Europe, or other areas of the world. Here are five ways to reduce your income tax by 30 percent or more.

TIP NO. 1: TAX STRATEGY

What? A tax strategy? Didn't we just talk about creating a business strategy for our real estate earlier in this chapter? And now we are going to create a tax strategy? That's right. A tax strategy: a systematic plan of action for permanently reducing or eliminating income taxes.

A good tax strategy is like a good business strategy in many ways. You have to look at the big picture, including not only your real estate but also any other businesses and investments you own. And you have to look at it from a long-term perspective. My personal tax strategy includes aspects relating to my two sons. One of my sons, Sam, works in both of my businesses and wants to be involved for many years to come. My other son, Max, has no interest in business and wants to write children's books. So my tax strategy keeps my sons' interests in mind. They both own parts of my business, but I have to structure their ownership differently, since one is actively involved and the other is not.

Many of our clients work together as a couple on their business. My wife, on the other hand, has no interest in business per se and is interested in helping me only with the speaking part of my business (she is a wonderful speaker and entertainer). So my tax strategy cannot, for example, include my wife as a real estate professional.

TIP A good tax strategist could really help here. So, another team member for you is a tax advisor who specializes in tax strategies.

Your tax strategy needs to be a plan that you can readily accomplish without making life too complicated. Of course, a good tax strategist could really help here. So, another team member for you is a tax advisor who specializes in tax strategies.

TIP NO. 2: ENTITY STRUCTURE

Which type of entity should you use? Should you use a limited liability company (LLC), a corporation, or a partnership? Or should you avoid using an entity at all? In some countries, where there is not a lot of litigation, you may not need a separate entity for your real estate. But in the United States, where 95 percent of lawsuits worldwide are filed, the proper entity is essential. Let's look at a quick overview of the tax entities available in the United States.

While every person's situation is different, let me give you a few pointers about which entity you may want to consider for holding your real estate investments. From an asset protection standpoint (discussed in detail in another chapter of this book), LLCs are frequently the best entity to use. One of the great things about LLCs is that they don't have any tax consequence. You can elect to tax an LLC anyway you want. An LLC can be treated as a sole proprietorship, a partnership, an S corporation, or a C corporation.

For most real estate rental properties, you will want to be taxed either as a partnership or a sole proprietorship. Don't make the mistake of putting your real estate rentals into an S corporation or a C corporation. This could spell disaster if you ever have to take the property out of the corporation to refinance it; you will be taxed as if the corporation sold the property to you at its fair market value. I had someone in my office recently who owned his investment property in an S corporation. We estimated the tax cost of refinancing to be in the neighborhood of $250,000 simply because of the entity structure.

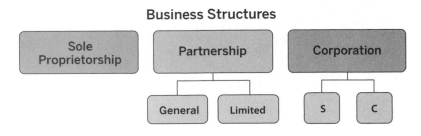

FIGURE 1.3 Overview of Entities

TIP Don't make the mistake of putting your real estate rentals into an S corporation or a C corporation. This could spell disaster if you ever have to take the property out of the corporation to refinance it; you will be taxed as if the corporation sold the property to you at its fair market value.

If you are a real estate dealer or developer, you may want to consider S corporation taxation. This includes those of you who want to fix and flip properties. The reason? You can significantly lower your social security taxes by owning your property in an S corporation. And since you probably won't need to distribute the property out of the company except when you sell it, you won't have the bad income tax consequences I spoke of earlier.

TIP NO. 3: TRAVEL, MEALS, AND ENTERTAINMENT

Remember that the United States and most other countries tax only the net income from a business. So any expenses that you can treat as deductible expenses lower your income tax. The most overlooked deductions in the real estate business are travel, meals, and entertainment expenses. The rule in the United States for meals and entertainment is that if you discuss business before, during, or after the meal or entertainment and the discussion is necessary and ordinary for your business, then you get to deduct the cost of the meal or entertainment.

I'm not talking about going to dinner with your real estate agent or your accountant (though I'm sure they would appreciate it). I'm talking about going to dinner or a sporting event with your partner. For most of you, your business partner in real estate is your spouse. My experience with business owners is that when they go to dinner with their spouses they almost always talk about business. And if you and your spouse are working on the real estate business together, I can virtually guarantee that you are talking about your real estate every time you go out to eat.

My wife and I eat out once or twice a week on average. I cannot even remember the last time we had dinner out and did not discuss business. These discussions are essential to our success as business owners, even though she does not maintain a very active role in any of our businesses. She has a perspective, though, that I find extremely useful as I make business decisions.

So stop paying for your meals out of your personal bank account, and start paying for them from your real estate business bank account.

Travel is a little more difficult to deduct, but not much. If you are traveling within the United States, you simply have to prove that your primary reason for the trip was business. You prove this by showing that you spent more than

50 percent of each eight-hour workday discussing or working on your real estate investment business. This could include your annual meeting or you could simply be investigating real estate opportunities in that location.

We had one client who applied these principles and ended up with a $1 million deal. He really liked to travel to New Mexico. Knowing that he had to look at real estate to deduct his travel expense, he set up a meeting with a local real estate agent to review land development opportunities in his vacation spot. He ended up finding a deal that netted him $1 million. And, of course, he got to deduct his travel expenses.

TIP NO. 4: DEPRECIATION

After Robert and I met with the *Arizona Republic* journalist to discuss 40 percent returns, we walked across the street to have lunch at a local restaurant. Robert asked me what I thought about depreciation. I told him I thought it was like magic. Where else can you get a tax deduction for something you didn't pay for and that is appreciating in value? Yet that is exactly what happens with depreciation in the United States, Canada, and many other countries. Here's how it works:

Say you pay $500,000 for a house that you are going to rent. You put $100,000 of your own money into the house, and the bank loans you $400,000. You get a deduction for a portion of the cost of the house each year—not just a portion of your $100,000, but of the entire purchase price. Let me show you the calculation for U.S. tax purposes.

Let's estimate that 20 percent (or $100,000) of the cost of the house was for the land. Even the IRS recognizes that land does not wear out, so we don't get to depreciate the land. But we do get to depreciate the remaining $400,000. At a minimum for residential property, we should get a deduction of 3.636 percent or $14,545 each year. And that's assuming that the entire $400,000 is allocated to the building. You can increase this deduction by doing what's called a cost segregation or chattel appraisal.

Briefly, here is what happens in a cost segregation. Your accountant or his engineer goes through your property and segregates (on paper) everything that could easily be removed from the building and is not necessary for its basic operation from the building itself. Those items that can be removed are called personal property or chattels. Personal property can be depreciated at 20 percent or more per year.

In our case, let's suppose that $100,000 of costs is segregated from the building. This would increase our annual depreciation deduction from $14,545 to

$30,900—more than double. So while our property appreciates, we still get a tax deduction for depreciation of more than $30,000. This is the best of all deductions, since there is no cash outlay involved other than the down payment on the property.

So if our cash flow is $30,900 or less, we will not pay any income tax on our monthly cash flow. And if our cash flow is less than our depreciation, then we create a tax loss from the property that we can use (with proper planning) to offset income from other sources. This is the primary reason many real estate investors are able to reduce their income tax by 30 percent or more and why some real estate investors pay no income tax at all. See how this can increase your return on investment?

TIP NO. 5: DOCUMENTATION

Last but not least, let's talk briefly about the importance of properly documenting our real estate transactions and expenses. Without good documentation, the IRS has the right to disallow your deductions. What a waste of good deductions! We have already discussed the most important form of documentation— good accounting.

In addition, there are other forms of documentation you must keep. For travel, meals, and entertainment, you must keep receipts, and you must note who you were with, where you went, what you discussed, the date of the event, and why you incurred the expense. For automobile deductions, you need to maintain a log of business versus personal miles driven. And for your entities, you need to write down minutes that detail all of your meetings and major transactions.

Documentation is not the most fun part of real estate, but it's not too difficult if you just take a few minutes a week to take care of it. Stay on top of it. If you don't know exactly what you need to document, consult with your tax preparer. Remember that if it isn't documented, then you probably cannot prove to the IRS that it was a legitimate deduction.

So there you have it—five easy opportunities to reduce your income taxes while making tons of money in your real estate business. Now you can see why smart business owners include tax planning as one of their keys to success. Applying these basic principles to your real estate business will enable you to build enormous wealth in a very short time. Remember to begin with a strategy, add a team, maintain good accounting, regularly review your reports, and minimize your taxes by creating a long-term tax strategy. The sooner you begin treating your real estate investing as a real business, the sooner you can stop working so hard and start reaping the profits that are there for all good real estate investors.

Ways to Learn More

ProVision Wealth Strategy U—a free resource at www.ProVisionWealth.com/WealthStrategyU

ProVision Business Start-up Kit—a series of five training modules on starting up your real estate business. Includes courses on bookkeeping, year-round tax planning, entity structuring, and setting up a business.

ProVision School of Wealth Strategy—a monthly subscription to comprehensive training materials on building wealth. Includes courses on creating your wealth vision, building your wealth team, and designing your personal wealth strategy.

ProVision School of Tax Strategy—a monthly subscription to comprehensive training materials on permanently reducing taxes. Includes courses on designing your family tax strategy, involving your children in your real estate business, and getting the greatest tax benefits out of your real estate.

For more than twenty-five years, **Tom Wheelwright** has strategically developed innovative tax, business, and wealth strategies for sophisticated investors and business owners across the United States and around the world, resulting in millions of dollars in profits. His goal is to teach people how to create a strategic and proactive approach to wealth that creates lasting success. As the founder of ProVision, Tom is the innovator of proactive consulting services for ProVision's premium clientele, who on average, pay much less in taxes and earn much more on their investments. He coaches select clients on their wealth, business, and tax strategies; lectures on wealth and tax strategies around the world; and is an adjunct professor at Arizona State University.

2

A Real Estate Attorney's View of Assembling and Managing Your Team

I first met Chuck Lotzar in 2001 or so when he was a senior partner in a national law firm. At Chuck's former law firm, I delivered a presentation to approximately ten attorneys that covered my rich dad's philosophy on money, wealth creation, and wealth management. Chuck seemed to be the only one out of the ten who understood or was interested in what I was saying.

In 2003, Kim and I used Chuck to finalize one of our biggest real estate investments. It was a zero-down deal that would put more than $30,000 a month net income in our pockets. If not for Chuck, this deal could have been our biggest nightmare. He found irregularities that most people, including most lawyers, would have missed. On top of that, after the deal was closed, Chuck offered to give us a discount on some of his firm's legal fees since he felt his firm did not work as effectively as it could have. Needless to say, we told him to bill us in full and keep the money. He had more than earned it.

In 2007, Chuck again came to our rescue, this time as our personal attorney against our former business partner. The lawsuit was the worst, most vile event in Kim's and my life. If not for Chuck, I do not know where Kim and I would be today.

The good news is that Chuck Lotzar has turned out to be far more than our real estate attorney. Through Chuck's guidance, the Rich Dad Company has emerged stronger, better staffed, and much more profitable. Personally, I have emerged more *mature, wiser, and less of a hothead, which is a miracle. Chuck has not only made Kim and me vastly richer; we have become better entrepreneurs and investors.*

The lesson again is this: It is often through our worst deals with the worst people that the best people emerge.

—ROBERT KIYOSAKI

I know attorneys see the world differently than most people. A working relationship isn't just a working relationship; it ideally should be a contract between two parties with built-in protections, limitations, and provisions, just in case the relationship goes south. A piece of real estate isn't just a piece of property; it's an asset that brings with it the need for appropriate entity structure, identification of risk, allocation of risk, mitigation of risk and liabilities, and a host of other legal protections and caveats associated with its development, management, and eventual sale.

I know you're thinking life is easier when you are not an attorney. You're probably right! But for me life as an attorney and particularly a real estate attorney is full of the excitement, the challenges, and the accomplishments that can come only from working with people so that they sleep well at night, have their family fortunes protected, and bring their dreams to life. It's a profession that keeps me continually learning, which I love. Real estate is a dynamic field that keeps every day at the office new and fresh.

The likelihood that you are reading the chapter written by an attorney first is slim, so I'll assume you've read at least a few chapters before mine. If you have, you've probably noticed that there are a number of references in them to team members: the professionals it takes to make a real estate deal actually happen. Many of the contributors list the types of team members that they need in the type of real estate work that they do and how they have helped.

Well, I will echo their beliefs. Team members are the deciding factors in spelling success or disaster for a real estate project. In my practice, I have seen teams that operate seemingly effortlessly and others that are clumsy and doomed to failure. So how do you assemble one that works effortlessly, and avoid the kinds that are disasters waiting to happen? The answer is, you can't. You can only try to do your best and know that the reality of your team—particularly as you are just starting out—will fall somewhere in the middle of those two extremes. Your job will be to assemble and manage a group of pros that makes its way progressively more efficient to close every deal you do.

My perspective on teams and team members is different from the views of many in this book because I am *one* of those team members. Many of the others in this book are the investors who drive the team. They delegate to team members who advise them. I'm the one they delegate to and who advises them on how to lead the team. That gives me a slightly different perspective. Combine that with my attorney's perspective and you have a chapter with three primary purposes:

1. To tell you who you need on your team and how to know you have a winner.
2. To identify known risks and make sure that they are properly allocated among other writing parties, including the members of your team.
3. To establish performance measures and deadlines, and to follow up to make sure that each of those performance measures and deadlines are met in a timely manner.

See, this is where my lawyer's mentality comes into play. I know your team will not be perfect, no matter how perfectly you follow this book's directions, how well you interview potential team members, or how ironclad their references were. Life and real estate deals are not that cut and dried. So what do you do? Well, quite simply, you do your best on the front end, and you attempt to protect yourself on the back end.

THREE RULES OF THE GAME

Before you say to yourself, "This team thing seems like more trouble than it is worth. For my project, I'll keep it simple and do most of the work I need alone. I'll keep the team small—as small as possible—and that will minimize my problems," understand that it is very hard to do anything in real estate alone. It is a team sport and as such, I have assembled my Three Rules of the Game.

Nowhere else will your team come into play more than when it is time to perform your due diligence. It's a necessary part of every real estate deal, and with the right team it can be your best friend and actually a lot of fun because you often find the hidden gems that can signal great opportunity. On the other hand, it can be the beginnings of a vivid nightmare you are living because you are the proud owner of a "problem-property," thanks to a team that missed something big during due diligence. Again, the first camp is the place to be.

You'll recall that the due diligence period is usually not less than sixty days in length. Its purpose is to discover any problems and opportunities with a property to determine whether you want to go through with the transaction, and if so with what specific stipulations. It's also designed to allocate and alleviate risk among various parties: the buyer, the seller, the lender, and the various third-party professionals on your team.

Chuck's Three Rules of the Game

Rule No. 1: Talent pays for itself. Accept that hiring a capable and talented real estate team to complete your transaction is in your best interest. Although there will be costs up front, your investment should more than pay for itself over time.

Rule No. 2: You are hiring folks' brains; let them use their brains to solve your problems. Allow teammates to give you their honest and complete assessment of any transaction given the circumstances presented—you want to know all of the problems so that you can craft solutions and quantify the costs of obtaining those solutions. Unfortunately, in some instances you will learn that the cost of continuing with the transaction outweighs the opportunity to be achieved, and you are forced to stop so as to prevent yourself from throwing good money after bad.

Rule No. 3: It is better to hire someone with outstanding judgment and wisdom than a person who has merely completed similar types of transactions.

As I mention in rule number two, when it comes to due diligence, you want a team that will be willing to learn the truth about the property and tell you the brutal facts. If your baby is ugly, you need professionals and advisors who aren't going to be afraid to tell you the truth to your face—before the acquisition takes place. So let's delve into the team members and their roles from a fellow team member and a lawyer's perspective.

Consider these your core team members, the ones you'll need for virtually every real estate deal you do. I believe that people generally fall into two categories: those who are relationship oriented and those who are transaction oriented. Although I have a law practice based on the ability to successfully complete transactions, I am a relationship-oriented person who generally seeks out other teammates who are also relationship oriented. I am willing to work with other teammates who are transaction oriented, but I do so recognizing that their ability and willingness to step up to solve a problem is limited, especially after the transaction closes.

REAL ESTATE ATTORNEY

Notice how I wrote *real estate attorney*, not just *attorney*. That's the first tip I will give you right up front. Real estate transactions are significantly different from other transactions, so it is critical to hire an attorney who understands and is experienced in real estate. Contract attorneys without real estate experience are not good enough.

The reason I am so emphatic here is because a good real estate attorney can take a lot of the pressure off you by acting as the quarterback and taking responsibility for coordinating the entire team. A good attorney is strong, experienced, and at the same time self-confident enough to know when he or she needs your input or help from a third party. There are times when a real estate transaction will have nuances that your lead real estate attorney—no matter how experienced—may not have ever encountered before. You don't want your attorney learning on your transaction; you want an attorney with a network of people, inside or outside the firm, that he or she can call on to bridge any gaps.

Often a good real estate attorney can be the master of the due diligence budget and calendar and keep all the other team members on track and on time with their deliverables. That means you'll want your attorney on board early, right at the very start, to handle the early documents, such as the term sheet or the letter of intent, to make sure that the allocation and assignment of risks are thoughtfully documented for closing.

Real Life Story

Every real estate opportunity is different, and it's the truly unique ones that sometimes cause your teams to expand beyond your expectations, even into the realm of the unbelievable.

Too often real estate investors become successful based on their ability to overcome numerous problems, and they become insensitive to the weight of certain problems that would otherwise thwart a transaction. I recall one group of clients who were prolific real estate investors. Although they were astute business people who accomplished a number of successful transactions in sequence, their history of success impeded their ability to walk away from a bad deal, even when they knew that there would be insufficient equity in a transaction and visible and invisible deferred maintenance issues with the heating and cooling system for the apartment complex, which needed replacement and caused the buildings to settle in the ground by more than one foot! No matter how successful you have been in the past, you need to replicate good habits for the diligence and closing with each new transaction.

Most often, however, your team will be highly predictable and consist of several core members. You will find that the more you work with them, the better you will all work together, which will increase your efficiency.

A good real estate attorney can be your greatest ally. I frequently find myself providing ideas and advice that will enhance my clients' transactions and their businesses as a whole. At our firm, we approach projects from a business-owner's perspective. Business owners want us to tell them the things that are standing in their way, of course. But they also want us to come up with innovative ways to transcend the problems and get the deal done. If you have an attorney who seems to be pointing out all the problems without posing solutions, that's a sign that you may need another attorney. If you have an attorney who conducts himself or herself in a manner that makes you uncomfortable, e.g., rudeness, or overly passive or overly aggressive under the circumstances, then that's another sign that you may need another attorney.

Specifically, it's our job to read and analyze all documentation, including third-party reports, title and survey, purchase and sale agreements, and loan documents. Sometimes, we may be requested to draft these documents along with corporate entity documents when dealing with equity investments and partnerships.

Hiring a Real Estate Attorney?
What to Look For, and What to Watch Out For

What to Look For

- Portability of past knowledge, wisdom, and judgment
- Availability of time to do the work
- An understanding of professional limitations
- Openness to engaging the assistance of other lawyers or law firms
- A willingness and ability to work as a team player
- Experience in various forms of real estate transactions
- Experience with complex finance structuring of real estate transactions
- Demeanor and approach to the practice of law, e. g., that's part gentleman, part pit bull
- The support of the law firm—how deep is the bench?

What to Watch Out For

- Any past malpractice claims
- Any past Bar complaints
- Experience with contracts, business, and litigation, but not in relation to real estate
- A personality and/or demeanor incompatible with the client's personality and/or demeanor

Your attorney can either bill you hourly for his or her work or provide a soft estimate for the scope of work. Should the scope of work exceed the estimate, the additional work is billed at the hourly rate. Another payment method is hourly against a hard estimate. These agreements generally have a large contingency built in for unforeseen events that is payable at closing. This type of contract can put the attorney and the client at odds. You want your attorney to find the unexpected—that can save you in a real estate transaction—but if you are worried that the work of searching for the unexpected will cost you more money, you may be thwarting your own success. In the best instances, the fruits of the deal, or the savings in terms of money and/or risk, a contingent fee that changes which party is in control will more than pay for any attorney fees. Many of our clients feel we have more than earned our fees, and that's ideally what both sides want.

Over the years I have focused a good portion of my law practice working on contingent-fee matters related to large revenue bond financings and tax credit projects. Whenever I have a contingent fee, I want to be the person with the most control over the ability to advance and close the transaction. However, a lawyer's compass needs to be completely aligned with the interest of his client, regardless of his fee arrangement.

How to Construct an Effective Engagement Letter

Most members of your team will require an engagement letter before beginning work. They may provide one, or you can. To protect yourself, make sure the following points are included:

• Spell out scope of work, particularly the roles of each party.
• Specify the nature and timing of payment, including timing of service and due date.
• Define the particulars of termination for both the contractor and you.
• Be specific on needs (software) and deliverables (eight copies of plans, etc.) due to cost and which party will bear the cost.
• Disclose conflicting relationships.
• Identify and allocate known risks.
• Dispute resolution.
• Limit liability.

REAL ESTATE BROKERS

Real estate brokers are important team members because they are the genera-
tors of opportunities. They can decide who sees a property that is coming online first and can be the bearers of great opportunities. What it takes is a broker
who understands the importance of relationships and working as part of a team.

On the other hand, many brokers are transactional, living and dying by their
fees, which naturally results in an eat-what-you-kill mentality. They will indis-
criminately pose opportunities that are nothing more than distractions because
they do not fit your business goals. What you really want is a real estate broker
who looks out for your best interest, understands your needs, and seeks out opportunities that match them. That adds value.

Beyond this, the true role of a real estate broker is to bring a willing buyer
and willing seller together, not necessarily to ensure his or her client gets the
best deal. But the good ones do both. They work to execute the best possible
transaction for their client from start to finish.

Sometimes a real estate broker will perform what is known as dual representation, which means the same broker will represent both the buyer and the
seller. On the surface, this may seem like an opportunity to save some money in
commissions; after all, typical transactions have two brokers who must share

---

Real Life Story: How to Know Your Real Estate Broker Is Looking Out for You

The dual brokerage relationship does not trouble me when I see sophisticated
parties on both sides of a transaction. The broker frequently has problems
when there is a mismatch of sophistication among the parties. I have had many
conversations with brokers who had dual agency relationships that they regretted
once problems arose.

I have found that the best real estate brokers have the clients' interests at heart.
The best example I can give relates to my good friend and client, Craig Coppola,
who was acting as my real estate broker in my attempt to buy an office building for
my law firm. Although I had my heart set on buying a particular building, Craig was
a good friend and professional broker who looked me in the eye and told me that it
was not in my best interest to act and that I needed to be patient as the market was
trending downward. Clearly, Craig's advice was in my best interest and not in his
short-term interest since no commission would be paid.

the commissions. But dual representation can be tricky, and in the very least it requires full disclosure of all known facts and circumstances to avoid conflicts of interests.

While most people in business recognize the need to adjust to market changes, real estate brokers really need to moderate their styles as market conditions fluctuate. During the boom times of the mid 2000s, many real estate brokers, based on the volume of work, became more transactional as they tried to close as many deals as they could. But the best ones knew that booms also create busts, and it's the real pros who maintain relationships during the booms that have business during the down times. The best brokers also know that the height of the market is not the time to buy and provide that level of counsel to investor clients. They are market advisors as well as salespeople who are in it for the long term and know that no deal today is worth the loss of many deals tomorrow. That's the kind of broker you want.

ACCOUNTANT

I have found that almost all business is based on some form of mathematics, and it is important to have accountants who are well versed in the intricacies of real estate. In fact, much of the advice that I gave you with respect to establishing a relationship with a real estate attorney has equal weight to establishing a relationship with an accountant.

I have also found that one of the first folks hired internally by real estate investors is an accountant who will be charged with working cooperatively with an outside accounting firm. Frequently, the internal accountant is charged with a substantial amount of responsibility beyond accounting and feels pressure to limit the involvement of the outside accounting firm. If the internal accountant is strong enough, then there will not be problems. Unfortunately, problems frequently do arise based on lack of communication and sophistication.

A strong real estate accountant will understand the effect of changes in deal structure on the various tax attributes such as amortization, depreciation, and losses (which are inevitable during a construction phase since no money is being generated during the development and construction of the project). Additionally, a real estate accountant will know when it is in your best interest to obtain a cost segregation study to identify the component parts of the building(s) so as to allow for an accurate and possibly accelerated application of amortization and depreciation.

ARCHITECT

First of all, special thanks to Greg Zimmerman and Chris Ilg for sharing their knowledge on this subject. Architects are critical members of any real estate team because they have the ability like no one else to provide creativity, innovation, and magic that can transform an ordinary property into a showpiece. They also have the ability to create a lot of expense that sometimes isn't needed at all.

Good architect partners understand that while they may have the ability to turn a property into a project that provides accolades and acclaim, the project objectives may dictate otherwise. The project may require the architect make minor modifications that deliver big results. They are not exciting modifications, and they are often not very dramatic. They may not even be all that rewarding to do, but sometimes that's the nature of the project, and although the design work might be mundane, it can deliver a big payoff for the investors. And that is anything but mundane. While it's more fun to redesign an apartment building to create exciting loft living environments, a profitable, cash-flow-positive project may require only that the architect figure out how to fit a washer and dryer in each existing unit. This is actually one of the biggest challenges faced in the apartment industry. The trend is away from common area laundry rooms, and architects are challenged to make washers and dryers work in small spaces.

Design professionals are a lot like physicians or attorneys. They specialize. While there are excellent neurosurgeons out there, you don't want the neurosurgeon performing your heart surgery. And the attorney who makes a living in divorce court isn't the one you want handling the financial complexities of a real estate transaction. Just the same, you don't want the architect who designs million-dollar homes designing your mini-storage investment property. You want the architect who can design those structures in his or her sleep.

But the biggest reason why you want to work with experienced, specialized architects is because they know the ins and outs. National and local codes change almost daily. Only architects and their firms can keep up with it all. Even the slightest revision to any of the several codes could have a serious impact on a design. As an attorney, I have seen too many investors' projects get caught up in the complicated codes and laws of building, remodeling, and restoring a property. It wastes a lot of time and can get messy. It's never easy to fight city hall, and with the right architect who knows the laws and the regulations, you should not have to.

Let me elaborate on the word *experience*. Architecture is a lifelong endeavor, and it is not unusual for an architect to require years of experience before truly

Experience Is Everything

When you work with an experienced, specialized architect partner, you reap the advantages:

- Design moves along quicker.
- There is not a steep learning curve.
- You get a completed design that works with fewer surprises.
- Plans, although custom, are somewhat field-tested.
- Building is smoother because the plans have commonalities with past projects.
- He knows the ins and outs of building codes.

gaining the amount of competence required to guide the client through a highly specialized project. It's not necessarily just the design aspects that I am talking about. It's the peripheral know-how that cannot be learned in school but can come only from doing things like working through the political process. Working positively and effectively with federal, state, and city employees is a honed skill that only comes over time. And let's not forget the value of a keen sense for anticipating market trends. After all, the work you are hiring from an architect may be happening today, but it needs to be valued by customers for years to come.

Once you interview and select your architectural firm from these perspectives, you can also look at other important requirements like working relationship and costs. I won't elaborate too much on the fact that regardless of how skilled the architect, if that person can't work with the team or with you, you need to keep looking. Relationships are everything, particularly when it comes to the architect. Too often the design side of the project can put off the trades side of the project by being overly demanding about aesthetics and not being open to finding reasonable solutions that don't compromise the look and function of the project. It's extremely important to have a strong and collaborative working relationship between an architect and the general contractor. Forcing the architect or the general contractor to work with an architect or general contractor that they don't work well with leads only to trouble for the property owner.

When it comes to money, be prepared to fully spell out exactly what you are hoping to achieve—your objectives—and how you would like to achieve them. Share your budget both for the design aspects of the project and for how much you plan to put into the building process. You must be concerned at this point with the architect's fees, yes, but also the cost to build out the architect's design.

Again, having been involved in many real estate projects, I have seen architects create designs that are simply too costly to build under the predefined budget and profitability constraints. Those are severe mistakes that can cost time and money. Architects and contractors must communicate to avoid these kinds of problems.

The better the information that you give the architect up front, the more accurate his fee proposal should be. Understandably, it is difficult to have a handle on every issue surrounding a project; things do come up that are unexpected. But there are ways to protect yourself a bit from costs getting out of control. First of all, you may want to begin your working relationship with an architect by putting together an agreement for the due diligence and preliminary design/consulting work. There is nothing wrong with doing this, and as long as both you and the architect understand that further work is contingent on the success and outcomes of the preliminary work, you may find this is the best arrangement.

You can implement this kind of arrangement with either a phased contract or better yet, a time and materials contract with provisions for a subsequent contract using the American Institute of Architects (AIA) form B181, which is a standard agreement between an owner and an architect. You can find this form on the Internet when you search AIA B181. It may serve as a good reference for you.

The benefit of this arrangement is that you can move forward without a huge commitment and no real idea of what can be done. That's handy because most likely at this point, you won't have much idea of what can be done. That's why you need the architect. The benefit to the architect is job security. It's nice to know that if the due diligence is favorable, all further work, including time, designs, and working drawings will be developed in his or her office. That also is excellent incentive for the architect to work harder to find feasible design solutions that fit into the budget for the project. If he or she wants more work, then make the project work.

I've seen this approach work well quite often. One minor, but important, point is that the services you contract with the architect may require the services of other consultants. I recommend contracting with them directly to maintain knowledge and control over the outside service provider's work and progress.

Assuming the project moves forward, and you and the architect have executed the contracts, the next phase is all about communication. The best, most efficient projects I've been associated with have been ones where the design team holds weekly meetings and provides progress plans and updates for review. With so many moving parts to any design project, keeping everyone informed is always a top priority. When well executed, it speeds up the process and delivers far better outcomes.

Once the design and development phase is complete, the construction documents get under way. At this point, it is the architect who should control the consultants and keep the attorneys and lender informed of all progress. As a ring leader for the design and construction side of the project, all information needs to funnel through the architect to maintain control and ensure that no deviation to the schedule, scope, and of course, fees are made without his or her knowledge.

CIVIL ENGINEER

Civil engineers are frequently hired by your architect. They are responsible for locating existing utilities and developing the plans to connect to them or determine if and how to upsize the capacity. American Land Title Association surveys are part of this process, as is obtaining a "will serve" letter from the utility provider, which legally obliges it to serve the particular project with utility service.

Civil engineers are also responsible for such things as drainage, grading requirements, and in cases where canal irrigation is involved, that too. Your architect will inform you when and why a civil engineer is needed for a project.

Your architect will review all contracts for service from not only civil engineers but all related design consultants. And I recommend you allow your real estate attorney to review these documents as well, solely from a legal perspective. By contrast, the architect will review them to make sure the intent of the design is being met and to look for gaps and overlaps with the goal of a seamless scope of service.

You will want to execute the contracts once your real estate attorney and architect have reviewed them and given them the go ahead. Often these contracts contain contingencies or line items in them that are part of the contract, but which could be separately executed or deleted as needed. Your attorney and architect can point these out, but be aware that if these contingencies are executed in the course of work because of requirements in the field, they can and often will cost you more money.

In my experience, civil engineers are not known for adding on unneeded services, but rather omitting services. And it is very difficult as a property owner, particularly if you have not been doing this work for twenty years, to know what the civil engineer should have done until there's a torrential rain and you find half your parking lot is submerged in a murky brown puddle. Then you know more work should have been done regarding drainage. These things happen.

The challenges a civil engineer can solve go beyond the concrete world of grading, utilities, and drainage. I always recommend to my clients that they find civil engineering firms with a lead engineer or representative who is not only knowledgeable of civil engineering but knows how to walk the corridors of city hall. Political savvy is a huge value-added advantage. Knowing the people who matter and then presenting your case before city officials and a crowd of interested citizens without acting and sounding like a civil engineer is a real ace card to hold.

Three Most Common Pitfalls with Civil Engineers

1. Delivering in a timely manner.
2. Plans that do not have sufficient detail to match the existing utilities.
3. Plans that fail to adequately take into consideration the property's topography as it relates to water retention and drainage.

Overcome these problems by holding your civil engineers to incentivized timetables and have your engineer, architect, and your contractor review the drawings with all those involved in advance.

PROFESSIONAL SURVEYOR

We've all seen surveyors standing in the middle of the street, gazing through their transits and taking measurements of the ground. This information is precisely what makes property owners and lenders sleep well at night, knowing that the properties they are considering during the due diligence phase are all that they have been stated to be. And best of all, they report this information with a very official document that bears all the appropriate seals and certifications. It's the real deal, and it becomes a matter of public record.

So what exactly are surveyors looking for, and looking at, through those tiny site scopes? When it comes to most projects, they are confirming or establishing the following:

- Easements. The surveyor is designating or verifying the access into and out of the property.
- Dimension and Location of Property. The surveyor is looking at and marking the property lines to determine the property's exact size and location in respect to other properties.

- Encroachments. The surveyor is looking at the property lines and determining if any structures belonging to another party are within your property line . . . or yours within theirs. This can affect the appraised value of a property and cost money to remediate.
- Location of All Buildings and Improvements. The surveyor is determining the exact placement of all buildings and improvements within the land parcel to assert that they are placed as specified and that they are within the constraints of local building codes.
- Nonvehicular Access. The surveyor is determining the exact placement of any nonvehicular access easements like pedestrian walkways that may exist on the property. These can impact building improvement and building placement plans.
- Traffic Calming Measures. The surveyor is looking at and indicating or planning the location of traffic-calming improvements such as speed humps, median plantings, etc., that slow traffic and improve the environment for residents, pedestrians, and bicyclists.

Of course, every project dictates what your surveyor will need to do, and every piece of land brings its own unique needs, too. In the mountainous, boulder-ridden terrain of Arizona—a state with strict laws related to indigenous plants and natural formations—surveyors indicate the location of every giant saguaro cactus, every palo verde tree, and any rock outcroppings that are to be preserved as natural space.

Ultimately, your title company and the surveyors themselves do not want there to be any gaps between adjacent properties. There are a lot of reasons for this when you think about it. One is ownership. Who is responsible to care and maintain the gap area? A second is liability. Are both owners, one or neither, responsible for a mishap that may take place in between property lines?

Another is property value. It can be really expensive to buy a small piece of land that your project may need in order to be compliant with development requirements related to setbacks, ingress, and egress, etc. Remember, just because you may need additional land to complete your project does not mean that your neighbor has to sell it to you.

HAZARDOUS SUBSTANCE SITE ASSESSMENT ENGINEER

This is a professional you want to bring on very early in the due diligence process because if he or she finds there are hazardous substances on the property, you may want to rethink everything. Your lenders will strongly advise and may even insist upon it. You simply must know the status of the property in terms of hazardous substances. There have been too many cases where—and these are the worst kind—entire housing developments have been built in areas that were later found to be toxic. Love Canal in New York is one of them. Cases that are far less dramatic, but still incredibly expensive, are those where a hazard exists but can be remediated. You never want to find yourself responsible for the first scenario; it is actually quite difficult, given the law and requirements for development and redevelopment today. But in the event of the second case, which is more likely to occur, at least know what kind of remediation costs you are in for.

When selecting an environmental engineer, begin by finding one who is fully accredited in the field. Having a trustworthy relationship with your mortgage banking professional is also key. The mortgage banker will know which environmental engineers are responsive and familiar with the reporting requirements of a broad spectrum of lenders. The lender may have a list of preferred providers that may at times take selection out of the borrower's hands. It is also important that while your environmental engineer is thorough so as to identify actual existing recognized environmental conditions, he does not create unnecessary work by requiring more expensive Phase II reports.

During due diligence, you must contract what is called a Phase I hazardous substance site contamination study. Among the many things the inspector looks at, he or she will perform a visual assessment of the site and surrounding properties; interview the owner, neighbors, occupants; and take a look at the site's history. The goal is to determine if any hazardous materials were ever manufactured, stored, or dumped there. At this stage the inspector doesn't take any samples.

Ideally, you will receive a clean Phase I report and not need any additional testing or a Phase II study in which the inspector takes samples of the discovered hazardous materials. This process can be costly and time-consuming because sometimes just getting the "samples" requires excavation and core drillings.

Interestingly, certain entities in the chain of title may have remediation responsibility should hazardous materials be found. In addition, they have a disclosure responsibility should they know of these hazards during the due diligence period. Lenders obviously are looking for a clean Phase I report so that there is no drag on their ability to seize collateral and liquidate, should the need arise. This action usually requires stepping into the chain of title, and it's best if there are no obstacles due to a history of hazardous materials liability.

Recently, engineers to prepare Phase I and II reports have sought to limit the amount of their liability to property owners by having their engagement letter or contract specify that damages are limited to the amount of fees paid to the engineer. Obviously, limitations of this nature do not afford the property owner the benefit intended when a professional engineer was hired to conduct the Phase I or II investigation and report.

ESCROW OFFICER/TITLE AGENT

The more real estate deals you do, the more you will get to know your escrow officer/title agent. This person acts as a neutral party who is attempting to carry out the express written instructions of the buyer, the seller, the lender(s), and in some cases the real estate brokers. They review and verify all documents and pass the documents along with the funds between the appropriate parties in the transaction. They are there at closing.

Again, my approach to this chapter is from a legal perspective. Where I have seen issues relating to this area is in title insurance. It is the title agent who issues the title insurance policy. Title insurance is insurance covering the past because it protects only against losses arising from events that occurred *prior* to the date of the policy. Coverage ends on the day the policy is issued and extends backward in time for an indefinite period. This is in marked contrast to property or life insurance, which protect against losses resulting from events that occur *after* the policy is issued, for a specified period into the future. A Title policy protects property owners and lenders from monetary losses that could result from ownership of a property's title, which may include fraud, liens against the property, or errors missed during the title search. Title insurance does not prevent loss of marketability due to a title claim, and that is important to know if you are going to assume ownership of a property.

In other words, a title insurance policy does not obligate the title insurance company to make corrections to your property's title if a problem is discovered; rather it simply provides a basis to receive monetary compensation for your loss at a maximum level specified by the title policy limits.

I am frequently surprised by a real estate investor's willingness to accept a title company's offer to "insure over" a known risk because the title insurance does not cure the apparent defect in the title; which may come back to haunt the property owner in the future.

The policy covers only the amount of the loan, so the policy's cost is based on this amount. It is best to obtain both a lender and owner's policy. The coverage extended to the owner is usually referred to as the ALTA policy, which must be based in part on a survey.

The talent associated with escrow and title officers varies widely. For that reason it is important to know who we are dealing with and their approach to solving problems. An effective escrow agent anticipates the demand of the transaction for all parties and is proactive. I am very loyal to escrow and title officers who I know have the capacity to close complex transactions in a timely manner. Unfortunately, I had to kiss a few toads in order to find folks who are keepers!

Mortgage Broker

Selecting your mortgage broker is one of the most important decisions you will make. You want to find a mortgage broker, who like the architect you choose, specializes in your area of investment. You may not know this, but the brokerage industry is a specialty business, and few brokers possess the expertise needed to service all areas of the lending arena. I want a broker who is well versed in not only the execution of the loan but also very in touch with the local trends. If your proposed project is not well suited to the market, your mortgage broker should tell you outright or will facilitate the market telling you. Either way, you'll know because the process will be arduous and most likely not well received by lenders.

Almost anything can trigger lending difficulties. Perhaps the proposed project isn't right for the location. Or maybe the location is right, but the timing isn't right for the project. Sometimes the lender will raise flags because the plan and proposed product didn't go through enough feasibility studies or a satisfactory amount of market research to ensure the project is on target. Any investor who comes to a mortgage broker without having done his or her homework and as a result made the proper adjustments to the plan and design will find the underwriting will stall, and a loan will be next to impossible to attain. That's a failure by the investor.

A failure on the mortgage broker's side can happen, too. A good mortgage broker should guide you to the most appropriate lending vehicle and steer you clear of the ones that are not in your best interest. Too often I have seen or heard of mismatches between a product and the type of loan terms, even when the product has qualified for that kind of loan. A mismatch can impact a lot of things, not the least of which is the pro forma of the property. It can also contribute to reduced profitability. And loan vehicles such as city, local, and federal funding have stringent requirements so their cost-benefit is questionable, unless the fit is just right. Your mortgage broker should be very clear about every loan term so you can take full advantage of them and avoid the pitfalls. If there is something you don't understand, do whatever it takes to clarify it.

You also should ask your mortgage broker what they know about tax credit, HUD financing, and related agencies, and ask them to relate to you the advantages and disadvantages of these financing vehicles. Experience with them in addition to knowledge about them is a real advantage. The last thing you want is a mortgage broker who is learning on the job with your project. Look for a seasoned veteran.

In the absence of a good mortgage broker partner, some real estate attorneys—I am one of them—also specialize in obtaining the most favorable financing vehicles available. It is a service we provide, and I am sure we are not alone. Given that your attorney is looking out for your best interest, he or she will analyze the loan for more than just interest rates and amortization schedules. He or she will read the fine print and the finer points to discover any possible ways a loan, because of its terms, could come back to bite you years later.

INSURANCE AGENT

I won't go into big detail on this one except to make a few points. Have an insurance agent who specializes in real estate and development early on in the process to avoid easily avoidable pitfalls. The lender generally has the specific coverage required for your transaction. You should be able to rely on your insurance broker to easily interpret the requirements and deliver an insurance certificate covering the same within twenty-four hours.

Over the years, as lending has become more oriented to packaging loans for sale in the secondary market, lenders have dictated the types of insurance that must be obtained, as well as the limits that they believe to be appropriate. Your insurance agent should be able to provide you additional insight with respect to the suitability of the proposed forms of coverage applicability of the proposed limits.

There are probably entire agencies in your city or town that offer mostly real estate, construction, and development insurance. There are a number of things, based on your project, that will require insurance of one sort or another. Insurance is all about risk management and the question becomes how much risk you want to assume versus if you should pay a premium to have someone else assume it. If you know in advance the type of insurance you will need, you can factor it into your project budget and determine if the project is feasible and will deliver a solid return with these added costs. If it won't, then you may want to reconsider the project entirely.

1031 EXCHANGE INTERMEDIARY

Every time a client presents me with an opportunity to participate in an IRC Section 1031 transaction, I insist that he or she has his or her accountants run the numbers to determine the effect of paying the taxes versus deferring the tax with an exchange. From my vantage point, the tax savings do not replace the need for a strong real estate transaction for the replacement property. I believe you make money buying real estate; which is best demonstrated when you sell real estate.

Many times, investors are working on a project that will be part of a 1031 Exchange. There's an entire chapter in this book about exchanges, but in a nutshell, a 1031 Exchange occurs when you sell one property and purchase another property under the tax code 1031 and minimize or avoid paying taxes on the gain. Anytime a 1031 Exchange is involved, you should have a qualified intermediary execute it. The reason is simple. If there is any misstep with the procedures of the exchange, you will not qualify and you will end up paying the taxes you were trying to avoid.

You want to know exactly how much the tax is and weigh the pros and cons of the exchange. A good test in my opinion, is asking yourself whether or not you would go forward with the transaction if an exchange was not involved. In other words, would you still consider this opportunity a good investment? Even if you answer yes to this question, I always make sure my client has discussed the exchange with me and his or her tax advisor so the entire plan can be viewed in light of the investor's bigger financial picture.

There are also nontax reasons for exchanges. Here are a few that you may not have considered:

- Exchange from fully depreciated property to a higher value property that can be depreciated.
- Exchange from non-income-producing raw land to improved property to create cash flow.
- Exchange to meet location requirements.
- Exchange from a larger property to several smaller properties, used to divide an estate among several heirs or for retirement reasons.

- Exchange from a tenants-in-common interest in one property to a fee interest in another property.

So what do you look for in a qualified intermediary? Exchangors must feel confident that exchange funds will be safe and available for the successful conclusion of their exchange. It is best to hire a qualified intermediary that, first, comes highly recommended by other real estate investors. You should also do your own due diligence to determine how the intermediary is investing funds it has on hand. Recently, a large intermediary was unable to fulfill its funding obligations because it had invested the bulk of its funds in auction rate securities, which became illiquid overnight! If you cannot understand the nature of the intermediary's underlying investments, then you should not let the intermediary hold your money!

Second, be sure to obtain a written guarantee for the exchange of funds. And, finally, verify that the qualified intermediary has fidelity bond coverage, preferably in the amount of $100 million professional liability insurance and employee theft and dishonesty coverage.

GENERAL CONTRACTORS

Nearly all real estate projects involve some construction or renovation. And for that reason, having a general contractor run the show is a good idea. Unless you are a general contractor yourself, you should never attempt to manage your own construction, no matter how well you think you can do it. If you are an investor, remain an investor.

It should almost go without saying that you want to be very careful which contractor you choose. Your decision will greatly impact the quality of your project. You can get excellent referrals from your architect who may even recommend one particular contractor. And if you have selected the right insurance agency in your city or town, the one that specializes in construction and does the bond work for all the contractors in town, you will be able to get some solid referrals from them as well. Other than that, you can ask your attorney, mortgage brokers, lender, and look around town at the projects that are currently underway. That will give you a good idea of which companies are the most reputable.

No matter how tempting it is to go cheap and hire a small-time player for your "small job," it is never a good idea to hire any contractor who isn't licensed and insured. As an attorney, I will never allow my clients to assume the astronomical risks that they are assuming when working with a contractor or any trades person who is not licensed and insured.

I think it is always a good idea to determine whether or not the general contractor can obtain a performance and payment bond. If you learn that the general contractor is unable to obtain a performance and payment bond, you should find out exactly why that is the case. If the general contractor is involved in its own development activities, bonding companies will frequently shy away from the risk. However, if the general contractor is not involved in development, then bonding companies should be more inclined to underwrite the risk associated with the general contractor's affairs. If a performance and payment bond is obtained, the general contractor will pass the cost on to the developer, which may be significant.

Your general contractor is responsible for carrying out the design plans to the letter, and for managing the trade contractors (subcontractors) who will actually do the work. General contractors seldom actually perform any of the trades themselves; they are simply very experienced project managers who know the process of construction and know the people and the companies that will get the work done. Pick a good contractor and you elevate your chances of having good trades people working on your project. You should look for general contractors who pay their subcontractors and material men in a timely manner and have a systematized manner of obtaining all of the required lien releases. Too often, general contractors who are struggling look to use subcontractors and material men as a form of working capital financing, as a result of the general contractor's failure to pay them in a timely manner. Ask for a list of references who are subcontractors from various trades and material men from various product lines.

How do you know you have a good contractor? First of all, look at their previous projects. Walk through them. Is the quality up to your standards of excellence? You can tell by looking at finishes and details. If the details are shoddy, one can only assume what lies behind the walls hidden from view isn't much better. Second, and perhaps even more important, is ask the tradespeople. Does the contractor pay them on time, or is the company always running way behind on payment? This could be a sign of cash flow problems. Stay as far clear of that as you can. What you don't want is to have construction loan draws that are meant to be buying your building materials going to pay off an old debt on another project.

And speaking of money, building costs—like anything else—can start out in one solar system and end up in a completely differently galaxy if not closely managed right from the time of the initial estimate. To set a price, you'll need a clearly defined budget, a clearly defined scope of work, and a clearly defined schedule.

From my vantage point, I believe that folks starting out in development should look to work with established general contractors who have obtained a performance or payment bond for the project. The additional costs associated with the performance and payment bond are substantially less than the potential downside.

Construction Risks That Can Cost You Money

As an attorney, I'm always concerned about risks, so here are a few that I have encountered, which you'll want to keep within your field of view. It will save you money.

- Poorly defined separation of functions between architect, engineer, and contractor.
- Scope creep that causes a small project to become a big one based on change orders.
- Project acceleration. This may be done as a way to provide an incentive for your contractor to complete your project prior to the original date for purposes of interest savings, favorable material pricing, or changes and deadlines for laws or regulations.
- Poor working relationships between parties that cause a lack of collaboration and inefficiencies.

Keeping your contractors happy is pretty easy. Mostly what they want is to be paid on time. They, in turn, have subcontractors to pay and paying them on time keeps their tradespeople happy. Pay on time and you have a happy worksite. Contractors also tend to take great pride in the work that they do and feel a great sense of accomplishment bringing a building out of the ground. And, finally, they value their relationships with owners, designers, and subcontractors. Work as a team, keeping all these things in good standing, and you'll have a general contractor who will become a valued asset to your real estate investment business.

You can learn more about contractors in Chapter 4, in which Ross McCallister talks about profits from the ground up.

A FEW FINAL WORDS

Any real estate project is all about minimizing financial risk, time risk, design risk, and quality risk. It's about choosing the right people to help you achieve this and working collaboratively all along the way. If you are the type of person who seems to foster adversarial relationships, this will be difficult. That's not to say that there won't be times when being tough will be required. There most definitely will be.

You'll find as you go from simple projects to the more complex that your team will have to function at a higher level with greater cooperation and problem-solving abilities. In all instances, and with every project—big or small—that you do, have a good attorney looking out for your interests. Find the best one you can, and let him or her do the job you deserve.

Charles W. Lotzar is founder of the Lotzar Law Firm, P.C., a diversified practice with representation of clients in commercial and real estate transactions, low-income housing, tax credit financings, administrative proceedings, and various forms of tax-exempt and taxable bond financings. A former senior partner in the national law firm, Kutak Rock LLP, Lotzar is involved in all phases of real estate development, including debt and equity financing. He has extensive experience in dealing with public contracts and issues related to public officials, and he has been involved in bond financings that have an aggregate value in excess of $5 billion. www.lotzar.com

The Way to Exotic Wealth

Wayne Palmer is an artist and a creative genius. However, his creativity is not seen in a painting or heard in the harmony of a song. Wayne's creative genius comes from seeing what cannot be seen: putting a deal together out of the invisible and creating a financial masterpiece.

Wayne is really an alchemist, taking different disciplines such law, taxes, marketing, and design and transforming them into exceptional real estate investments. In other words, it is not the building or the raw land that is the investment. It is the ability to create value out of the elements and forces that surround real estate that gives Wayne his advantage.

Wayne's mastery of creative financing can't be fully described; it must be experienced. As you study Wayne's three chapters in this book, you'll begin to see what I mean by that. You'll begin to understand the difference between Wayne and the rest of the world. Wayne can see a way to make a deal work in less time than it takes most people to pick up a pen and sign their name. And his often simple solutions to financing problems will leave you asking, "Why didn't I think of that?" He has a rare gift that maybe he was born with, and that his lifetime of experience as a real estate developer, certified real estate note appraiser, certified cash flow master broker, and licensed continuing education provider has certainly honed. Wayne is one of kind, and he presents to anyone reading this book an opportunity to see the world of finance in a way that you've never seen it before.

Wayne is a man I trust. If a person is going to be creative, it is imperative that he or she holds him or herself to the highest of legal, ethical, and moral standards, which is Wayne's true strong suit. While he is always pleasant, enthusiastic, and speaks with a smile, his graciousness does not interfere with his straightforward candor. He will tell you what he thinks, even if it means saying that he thinks the deal stinks or that the person representing it is either incompetent or of shady character.

The beauty and power of real estate investing is found in the scope of creativity each property affords the investor. Whenever I am at a dead end, brain dead, and in need of a shot of creativity, Wayne is the person I call.

—ROBERT KIYOSAKI

I sat staring at the envelope with the anticipation of a youngster on Christmas morning. Seeing the title company logo, I had a pretty good idea of what was inside. After months of patient teamwork, the escrow had finally closed. It had required our best collective skills to complete the transaction. I felt a vibration that I knew was part steel on paper and part the tingle of adrenaline as the letter opener glided through the cotton bond. I carefully reached in and removed a single document and unfolded it. It was a proceeds check made payable to my company for $1,175,206.16.

As I paused to savor the victory, my mind wandered back over my thirty years in real estate. How had we come so far? I remembered days in the distant past when lunch money was hard to come by. What was so different about then compared to now? Why was it so relatively easy today to make a million dollars on a single transaction while it had sometimes seemed so difficult to make a living years ago? As I breathed in the magnitude of the moment, one word came to mind, and it wasn't the economy or boom times or anything about having more money. It was simple: formulas.

The word "formula" is rarely used in the real estate industry. We hear about formulas in math and chemistry, but not in real estate. What could a cluster of numerals and digits, strung together with mathematical operatives, possibly have to do with making money? I smiled at the thought, realizing how few people in real estate understand the power of one good formula. I noticed a wave of gratitude flood over me. I felt so lucky to know the formula that had proven to be worth a million dollars.

TIP What could a cluster of numerals and digits, strung together with mathematical operatives, possibly have to do with making money?

A Harvard friend once explained to me that certain truths are too big and too powerful to express, except in the language of mathematics. Even Einstein and his fellow physicist couldn't explain the nature of our universe with mere words, only with equations. Formulas allow us to identify, condense, and use chunks of information that would otherwise be too big to manage.

As I held a $1 million check in my hand, I thought about all that had led up to receiving it. If I were to write a formula to express how that had happened, what would it be? I put the check down on my desk where I could glance at it, and just for fun, I picked up a pad and pen to see if I could create a formula that captured the key elements. Since I didn't major in math, I didn't intend to come up with anything of cosmic significance. I just wanted to know if there was a way to boil it down to one simple and concise expression. After a few failed attempts, scratch-outs, and rearrangements, I looked at what I had scrawled on the paper with a strange sense of satisfaction.

$$W = (\, XO\,(T{+}E)\,)\,/\,K$$

Yes! That was it! My entire career summarized in one inch or less. All of the study, all of the acquired skills, all of the systems I had learned to operate within the "big system" we call real estate were included. I knew I was on to something. I could see that if I could put the essence of my formula in writing, others could save years of struggle by applying the same principles to build their own wealth. That is what I set out to do!

So what exactly does the formula mean?

TIP [W] WEALTH equals [X] EXCHANGE multiplied by [O] OPPORTUNITY multiplied by the sum of [T] TALENT plus [E] EQUITY divided by [K] SPEED/TIME.

Let's look at what each of these variables mean.

W "WEALTH"

What is it? The word clearly has different meanings for different people. Tabloids provide ample examples of the fabulously rich and famous who often appear to live miserable lives in spite of their money. On the other end of the spectrum, I have seen those who barely survive economically but who seem blissfully happy. True wealth, it would seem, is not only about cash in the bank, although most definitions of wealth do include a certain amount of money. I know my own definition of wealth has evolved over time to include freedom, good health, peace of mind, happy relationships, education, recreation, and the ability to serve others. However, for purposes of this chapter and this book, my formula—W = (XO (T+E)) / K—focuses primarily on monetary wealth.

I define monetary wealth as *assets that generate enough cash flow to sustain my chosen lifestyle indefinitely, with minimal time and effort required on my part to manage them.* In Rich Dad terms, it is *getting out of the rat race.* Wealth is an end result, just like the million-dollar check was the end result of one transaction. Becoming wealthy is an overarching goal of the game of business.

I have concluded that one of the great gifts of living in a free society is that everyone has the right to choose what works best for them and how much wealth is enough.

X "EXCHANGE"

Whenever an economic transaction occurs, there is an eXchange of value that takes place. In ancient barter- or commodity-based economies, a cow may have been traded for several bushels of wheat. Milk was traded for eggs. Chickens were traded for hogs, etc. In each of these transactions, it is easy to see the symmetry of the exchange. In currency-based economies, we trade money for goods and services. Regardless, if we look past the symbols of value, such as the animals or the coins, we can see that something else is actually being exchanged. What is the "something else"?

It has been said that energy is everything and everything is energy. With modern scientific tools, such as electron microscopes, we have learned that things are not what they appear to be. What appears to be solid is actually a mass of atoms that each has electrons swirling around the nucleus at astonishing speeds. Each atom that makes up any substance on earth is pure energy. There is relatively as much space between the nucleus and the electrons of the average atom as there is between the earth and the sun. What we see as solid isn't solid at all. We only perceive it as such.

Our perceptions about money are much the same. We have come to think of it as real wealth, but is it real, or is it only the symbol of the energy that constitutes real wealth? I would suggest that the real wealth, or value, that is exchanged in any economic transaction—the "something else"—is not the money but the energy that the exchange of the money causes to move from one place to another. If I use my money to buy oil, it is not the oil that I want but the energy contained in the oil that has value to me. If I exchange my money for food, the value isn't in the food itself but in its ability to provide me with physical energy and perhaps some pleasure in the eating.

The X in our formula represents the eXchange of energy that takes place in a transaction. There are elements of both quantity and quality to each of these exchanges. The element of quantity is easy to see. I pay $2 for a loaf of bread, $3 for a gallon of milk, $4 for a gallon of gas, or $6 for a pound of fish. The aspect of quality is a bit trickier.

It is widely held that nature has ways of balancing its own accounts. If observed closely, true balance—precise equilibrium—is rarely achieved. Rather, balance in nature is somewhat like balancing a teeter totter. It tends to go from one extreme to the other, up and down, being in perfect balance for only a moment in the center of its motion. In the deserts of the Western United States, we have lots of rabbits. From time to time, the population of rabbits may increase to the point that they overrun their habitat. Since nature produces only enough food in the habitat for so many rabbits, and so the weakest starve and die. Or, the coyotes in surrounding areas discover that rabbits are plentiful and come to dine on the bounteous bunnies. The supply of food and the population of rabbits teeters up and down as the energy exchange between rabbits and their environment shifts back and forth, from excess to lack. As human beings, we have the opportunity to rise above the random and seemingly violent balancing found in natural law, by committing ourselves to balancing the energy of our transactions right up front. Unlike rabbits, even pre-schoolers have the ability to learn that by having the heavier person slide closer to the center of the teeter totter, balance can be achieved and a fun give and take established. This is where the quality of the exchange comes into play. If I make sure that I give full value, or in other words, a full measure of energy, in each transaction to which I am a party, I harness the power of nature in providing perpetual abundance. I believe nature is inherently abundant as long as we each choose to balance the energy of our transactions with one another.

So, for purposes of our formula, a fair exchange of energy is simply to consciously give something equal to or greater in value than what one receives. It is a living commitment to the principle of win/win. It is taking pride in the quality of one's contribution. If I give at least as much as I want to receive, nature will balance the scales by seeing that I get full measure in return. If I give extra, I create a vacuum and nature rushes to fill a vacuum, so I set myself up to receive a greater portion. Once this principle of energy eXhange is understood and followed, there can no longer be any lack of any kind. Natural law will see to that.

O "OPPORTUNITY"

Oh, say, can you see? "America is [still] the land of opportunity." In my opinion, this statement is actually truer today than it has ever been. If anyone doubts its validity, I invite them to observe the accomplishments of people immigrating to the United States. They typically come to America with little money, lacking in language skills, and having no background about how Americans do things. Yet, many immigrants build successful businesses, buy nice homes, and end up sending their children to the best schools available, all within a fifteen-to twenty-year period. They seize opportunities and acquire wealth that forever changes their economic standing.

TIP "America is [still] the land of opportunity." In my opinion, this statement is actually truer today than it has ever been. . . . However, I don't believe America is the *only* land of opportunity.

However, I don't believe America is the *only* land of opportunity. Through my travels, studies, and friends, I see tremendous entrepreneurial possibilities in every capitalist country in the world. It is a matter of clear vision and of training ourselves to see things as they are, not as they once were, or as we hope they might be.

I would ask this of anyone doubting the quality of today's opportunities: Are you willing to work as hard, study as long, and sacrifice as much as the immigrants that come to this country do? I think it is an important question because those newcomers are today's competitors, just as the ancestors of most Americans were the newcomers competing for opportunities when they passed through Boston Harbor or Ellis Island. I have no patience for those who stand around whining about things, instead of harvesting the opportunities that are everywhere to be found. Some may cite economic downturns as evidence that the good days are gone. To the contrary, times of economic turbulence may arguably provide greater opportunities to build wealth even faster.

I trust in Buckminster Fuller's concept of "ephemeralization," which paraphrased is to progressively do more with less, faster. The technological revolution we are part of gives us incredible competitive capability and leaves us without excuse. Yes, many things are different now than they were generations ago and may be even more difficult in some ways. However, given all of the advantages we have that our ancestors lacked, I believe we still have the edge. I know I wouldn't want to trade places with them.

Think about the leverage inherent in just a few of our modern conveniences:

Air travel. More than once, I have left Europe in the morning and arrived home in the Rocky Mountains by nightfall, traveling in the comfort of kings. It took my ancestors months of sacrifice and peril to make the same journey by ship.

Cell phones. I am able to talk to anyone from almost anywhere, at minimal expense. I remember the days when I had to get back to my office before I could return calls, act on a thought, or solve a critical problem. Now I can make use of drive time, down time, and spare time as it occurs, with the greatest convenience.

Word-processing software. Decades ago, what constituted a workforce of several secretaries in an office of several hundred square feet is now the size of a book and sits comfortably on my lap. My PC gives me word processing capacity with instant correction, printing, graphics, and even video and sound, if desired. It even surpasses the capacity of entire publishing companies of another era.

Electronic document transfer. When I first started in real estate (1976) there were no fax machines. I put fifty thousand miles a year on my car, just chasing down signatures on documents and delivering them to mortgage companies, title companies, clients, etc. Now I can send a fully executed copy to everyone simultaneously, without ever leaving my desk and without using a single sheet of paper or a thimbleful of gasoline.

The Internet. It is difficult to begin to estimate the value of so much information at one's fingertips. The physical equivalent of the electronic information available on the Internet today would obviously fill the world's libraries and require a staff of several thousand to retrieve when needed. Even then, it would be impossible to match the speeds at which such information is delivered to my computer screen. It is as though all of the knowledge in the world is just a click away. How could our forbearers compete with that?

Consider how only these few tools multiply a person's time, especially when you consider the time, effort, and knowledge it would take to physically reproduce the results one can achieve by using these spectacular tools. We truly live in a time of marvelous opportunities.

As I see it, the biggest challenge in real estate today is to sort through the hundreds of opportunities that are constantly available to determine which ones are the best and which ones truly warrant the allocation of precious time, talent, and capital. My only frustration with "opportunity" is that I cannot possibly invest in all of the good deals I see.

Since opportunity is all around us and the challenge is to sort through the many to find the fabulous few, I believe the most important aspect of the "O" is to become skilled at analyzing opportunity. While this book is full of powerful ideas on how to do just that, here are my basic guidelines in the form of ten questions. (Yes, we literally put every deal through the "Ten Questions" routine!)

Wayne's Opportunity Filter—Ten Questions

1. Is the project in harmony with our major goals and purposes?
2. Are the people involved of good character, and will we likely enjoy working with them?
3. Does the project make sense as explained?
4. Does it promise returns equal to, or better than, our target rates?
5. Do we have, or can we hire, the skill required to successfully complete the project?
6. Do we have, or can we get, the capital needed?
7. Do we have the time to successfully oversee the project?
8. Does it provide at least three acceptable exit strategies?
9. Can we live with the worst case scenario, and is it within our risk profile?
10. Is it a win/win for everyone concerned?

We call this our Opportunity Filter. If we are satisfied with the answers to these ten questions, we will go to the next step and do in-depth underwriting, or "due diligence," as it is called in our industry.

Let's go back to the million-dollar check mentioned at the beginning of this chapter and walk through the project that generated it. As background, the project was a sixty-acre residential development that was only partway through the entitlement process and was in foreclosure. The owners had twenty-four hours to cure the default or they would lose the property, their down payment of nearly $200,000 cash, and more than $3 million in equity.

1. Was the project in harmony with our major goals and purposes? *Yes. We are real estate lenders and developers, and it fit well within our portfolio.*
2. Were the people involved of good character, and would we likely enjoy working with them? *Although we had just met them, their references were positive, and we were willing to give it a go, knowing we could remain lenders only if we chose to do so.*
3. Did the project make sense as explained? *Yes, the proposed lots were in high demand, and the views from the property were exceptional.*
4. Did it promise returns equal to, or better than, our target rates? *Yes. The owners were willing to pay our standard hard-money rates.*

5. Did we have, or could we hire, the skill to do the project? *We saw the owners to be a bit weak in their ability to complete the project, but they had plenty of equity to insure their performance. We were content we had the skills on our team, even if it turned out that they didn't.*

6. Did we have the capital required? *Yes. We had the money on deposit to make the loan and knew we could borrow to complete the improvements, if necessary.*

7. Did we have the time to successfully oversee the project? *Yes. The project was close to home and could be spread across our existing staff, without overloading anyone.*

8. Did it provide at least three acceptable exit strategies? *Yes: (a) get paid off as agreed; (b) complete the project in partnership with the existing owners; or (c) foreclose on the property and sell it or complete the development ourselves.*

9. Could we live with the worst case scenario, and was it within our risk profile? *The answer turned out to be "No," because we discovered the property did not yet have a deeded right of way for access. Although a contract was in place with the neighbor to provide access, it contained no deadline for doing so. This was a deal breaker for us. It threw us outside of our risk profile because we couldn't get title insurance without deeded access to the property.*

10. Is it a win/win for everyone concerned? *No. Because of the problem with the access, it was not a win for us.*

So, how did we solve the problems identified in numbers nine and ten (above)? We renegotiated the terms of our proposed loan agreement with the owners. We knew that we had legal grounds for getting the access from the neighbor. If it took a year longer under the worst case scenario to acquire the access by litigation, we simply needed a way to be compensated for our added exposure. Our solution was this: In addition to our loan fees, and as an offset for our additional risk, the owners agreed to grant us a 35 percent ownership interest in the property.

It took us ten months to acquire the access, at which time we sold the property for a $3.35 million gain. The check in the envelope was our 35 percent share of the net profit.

Sometimes opportunities must be massaged a bit to discover the real gems lurking beneath the surface.

(T+E) "THE SUM OF TALENT AND EQUITY"

This is the mathematics of synergy. One plus one is greater than two. Talent is wasted without equity, and equity tends to dissipate without talent. However, properly combined, T+E equals pure power. While it may be true that *it sometimes takes money to make money*, my experience tells me that of the two, talent or equity, talent is somewhat more important in building and maintaining wealth. For example, who wouldn't want to have the talent of Warren Buffett managing one's equities? Of course, Mr. Buffett is not for hire. I understand it is often difficult to acquire Berkshire Hathaway stock because Buffett's talent has proven so exceptional that the current owners rarely sell their shares. I see that as an undeniable testament to talent. The stock market at large would throw billions of dollars at Mr. Buffett to have him get the results his talent has achieved for his investors.

There is an old adage that states, "When money meets experience, the experience gets the money, and the money gets the experience." I have found that money (or equity) will flock to anyone who demonstrates an ability to protect it and cause it to grow. So, let's consider the value of talent.

T "TALENT"

The *New Oxford American Dictionary* defines talent as aptitude, gift, knack, technique, ability, expertise, capacity, and faculty; strength, forte, genius, skill, and artistry.

It is easy to see that Mr. Buffett has all of these elements of talent on his team. I refer to the Buffett team because in today's business environment, things move too fast and are too technical for any individual to successfully compete against a talented team. I must admit it took me a while to realize this glaring truth. As a self-employed "S," within Rich Dad's CASHFLOW Quadrant®, I took pride in doing everything myself. I remember the day it finally dawned on me that others could actually do some things better than I could. An employee, to whom I had reluctantly delegated a task, not only completed it ahead of schedule, but did it better than I would have done and in a way I would not have considered. I felt a huge weight lift off of my shoulders as I realized that it wasn't all up to me anymore.

Since that glorious day of independence, I have devoted much of my time to building project teams that consist of the best players I can find. Team building became the key for my move from the "S" (self employed) to the "B" (business owner) quadrant (see Robert Kiyosaki's book, *CASHFLOW Quadrant*). The results have been astounding. With an in-house staff of less than ten people and outsourced "partners" of perhaps another dozen, I am now able to manage fifteen companies, nearly six hundred investor accounts, and as many as twenty projects at a time. It sometimes takes my breath away to see how productive our team has become. There are weeks when we close dozens of real estate transactions of one kind or another. I am so proud of my people for the way they produce and for the pride they take in the quality of their work.

Here is a snapshot of the team we assembled for the "million dollar" closing:

1. The previous owners, who became our partners.
2. My business partner, Reed, is our systems guy. I believe every team must have Reed's equivalent to truly excel. He takes care of all of the details required to run our businesses, such as communication systems, information systems, and personnel systems. The genius of his systems organizes our staff to handle every detail of every project and to respond to otherwise impossible deadlines.
3. My support staff, including our receptionist, Lindsey, my administrative assistant, Johanne, Renee who runs our document department, Lincoln, who operates our real estate company, Julie, Dan and Victor in accounting and Lila, our file clerk.
4. Our private investor clients, who, in part, provide the capital we use to fund our loans and acquisitions.
5. Civil engineers to design the proposed subdivision, roads, and utility systems.
6. Lawyers to advise, to draft documents, and to litigate if necessary to secure the needed right of way.
7. Accountants to keep accurate records, establish budgets, and give tax guidance.
8. Title officers to work through issues of boundary lines, easements, legal descriptions, and in resolving the right-of-way issue.
9. City officials, who worked with us to approve our proposed development and who helped formalize the needed right of way.

Each potential investment requires unique talent. I encourage you to learn what is needed for a given project and build a team made up of those who have spent their lives honing exceptional, fundamental skills that qualify them to be part of your team. I don't know who plays on Mr. Buffett's team, but I would wager with confidence that they are people of outrageous talent. After proving the talent of your team, and with a few wins to your record, you, too, should find it relatively easy to attract all of the equity you need to become wealthy.

E "EQUITY"

Definition: value, worth; ownership, rights, and proprietorship (*New Oxford American Dictionary*)

Having said that equity is perishable without talent, let me now say that equity is everything when financing real estate—once one has the talent to activate the equity. Equity leads to net worth on your balance sheet. Equity is the symbol of entrepreneurial wealth. Equity is capital, and understanding the role of equity is a key to raising capital.

I also view equity as paper wealth. Currency is paper. Stock shares are paper. In real estate, the difference between the value of the property and the debt on the property is paper equity. Mortgages are paper assets for those who own the notes and have the rights to receive the payments made by borrowers.

There are two segments of the real estate business where I have learned to use equity in unique ways to achieve outstanding results.

The first is using equity as a tool in the "equity marketing" arena covered in Chapter 22 and the second is real estate paper, or private mortgages. In each of these realms, equity is applied in specific formulas to accelerate the accumulation of personal wealth.

Let's look at the second part of equity—the private paper portion. Private mortgage paper is created by converting the seller's equity into financing for the buyer. A private note comes into existence when a seller "carries back," or in other words, loans equity to a buyer in the form of seller financing or when an owner pledges equity as collateral for money loaned against the property. Since all seller equity is capital, under our definition, seller equity provides one of the most convenient and effective sources of financing for the purchase of the seller's property. Think about it: all seller equity is part of a huge pool of potential financing for the building of your portfolio. Once you know how to use seller financing, it is like having a pre-approved credit line for millions of dollars just waiting to be tapped.

When I purchase real estate, I have trained myself to look to the seller's equity first and foremost for financing. In the overwhelming majority of the properties we have bought over the years, seller financing played some role. Even in the best of markets, when bank financing is plentiful, I prefer to use private financing, for many reasons.

THE BENEFITS OF PRIVATE FINANCING—FOR THE BUYER

1. Negotiable. Whereas banks and mortgage companies usually dictate the terms of their loans, a private note can include any clause the buyer and seller might agree to, such as lower interest rates, alternative collateral, irregular payment schedules to match income fluctuations, and payments tied to the performance of the property or project, to name a few.

2. Always available. Lending goes in cycles, and supplies of mortgage money sometimes dry up. Private financing is always available because there is constant equity in certain properties in the marketplace.

3. Not credit driven. Private financing may be available, even if a credit score is low, income is difficult to verify, or debt ratios are high.

4. No aggregate limit. Once the average borrower has a few loans outstanding, institutional lenders may restrict further borrowing. There is no set limit to what a real estate investor can borrow privately.

5. Flexible loan-to-value ratios. Banks and mortgage companies have set limits on loan-to-value ratios (LTVs), but it is possible to borrow 100 percent of the purchase price of the property from the owner with private financing.

6. A ship for rough seas. In tough times, institutions have historically been rigid in their default and foreclosure procedures. When making payments to a private party who doesn't want the property back, it is possible to re-negotiate terms, extend deadlines, and in general, work together to get through the storm. Equity is preserved for both parties, and in the process, creates another win/win.

These advantages of private financing for the buyer are clear, but I am often asked why sellers would carry back. What's in it for the seller?

BENEFITS OF PRIVATE FINANCING — FOR THE SELLER

1. Providing financing for a buyer in a slow market might make the property sell quicker.

2. By making it easier for the buyer to qualify for financing, sellers often get a higher price for the property.

3. A seller carry-back sale is usually considered an installment sale by the IRS, and any gain on the sale is deferred until the principal portion of the loan is received. Properly structured, an installment sale can push the tax consequences of the sale many years into the future (See Internal Revenue Code Section 453i).

4. The seller earns income from the interest portion of the payment. The rates of interest paid by buyers on private mortgages are usually higher than the rates paid by banks on certificates of deposit. This means that a seller can earn more money on a carry-back loan than he or she could by selling the property for cash and depositing the money in a CD at the bank. This is especially a boon to sellers who are of retirement age. It is as though they convert their home equity into an annuity of sorts.

5. A private note, properly structured, is legal tender. The seller can borrow against the note or use it for a down payment on his next property or even sell it for cash if desired. Selling a note for cash may result in the seller receiving less than the full face amount of the note.

Real Life Story: How Private Financing Can Work for You

As an example, I purchased a condo from a private party who owned the unit free and clear. They agreed to accept a $20,000 down payment and to carry a note of $78,000 at 7.5 percent for twenty years. The monthly principal and interest payment was to be $628.36. I asked for a clause in the note that provided for all payments made in the first year to be allocated to principal, such that the interest rate for the first year of the note was effectively 0 percent. The seller would still receive the same monthly income, while I could prepay as much of the balance as I desired, within twelve months, without interest. However, 7.5 percent interest would begin accruing against the unpaid balance on the first anniversary of the loan. That one simple clause, written into the private note, shortened the amortization of the note from 240 months to 205.68 months, a savings of $21,565.76. You might note that the savings exceeded my down payment. In other words, the zero interest clause was, in essence, an agreement by the seller to rebate my down payment if I paid on the note to maturity.

I trust that now you can see how equity in exchanges and equity in paper, combined with talent, can turbocharge your investment results. I believe this is one of the most important benefits of understanding and using wealth formulas. Unless you were born into money or win the lottery, learning how to harness various forms of equity that currently belongs to someone else, will likely be your fastest road to riches.

Now, before we get to the last part of the formula, let's consider what we have learned so far:

Wealth is our goal—to be wealthy is to get out of the rat race
X stands for the balanced exchange of value and for the context of the real estate exchange marketplace
O is for opportunity that is all around us, all of the time, just waiting to be multiplied by the synergy of
Talent plus
Equity

Looking once again at the million-dollar deal, let's take an inventory of what we had when the borrowers walked into our office with their problem. The property owners were about to lose a chunk of Wealth in foreclosure. We were prepared to provide an eXchange of value using our cash and Equity Marketing formulas. We were presented with an Opportunity to help someone else solve a problem and to profit by doing so. We had the Talent, and they had the Equity to provide safety for our capital. It would seem the stars were all aligned, right? Wrong! There is one more critical element to the formula that I am convinced makes all the difference in today's business environment. I call it the "K" factor.

K "Speed/Time"

In mathematics, a factor is defined as a number or algebraic expression by which another is exactly divisible (*New Oxford American Dictionary*). You may notice that in my wealth formula, the product of everything else is divided by K. K is the last operation that defines the ultimate sum of the wealth. So what could possibly be so important as to warrant this key spot? The K is critical to the equation because to me it represents time multiplied and compressed, as with the metric system K, which is the symbol for kilo, or one thousand. How can I do one thousand times more, a thousand times faster? In other words, SPEED! How much ground can be covered in the least amount of time?

We live in a world where transactional time frames are being condensed and collapsed by the effects of technology. What once took months to accomplish now takes seconds or no measurable time at all. When Benjamin Franklin lived in Paris as the U.S. ambassador to France, he communicated with his family and government through letters. Those letters took up to six months to arrive in the United States by boat from Paris. Today telephone, e-mail, text messaging, and facsimile technologies make such communications instant. We can sometimes do almost everything in almost no time at all. To compete and succeed today, we must prepare to accomplish ever more in ever shorter time frames in every way possible.

Even though all of the stars seemed to be aligned in our million dollar deal, there was one glaring exception. If we couldn't salvage the owner's Wealth by funding the transaction within twenty-four hours, the Opportunity for eXchange of value would expire, and all of the owner's Equity would be lost, regardless of how much Talent we had as a team. The key was the need for speed. Without speed, all else was of no value. Without the K factor, everything that preceded it in the formula was meaningless. Anything divided by zero is zero. What was the key to our speed?

THE KEYS TO SPEED

1. Private capital—the money system. Because we control private capital, there was no need to make a loan application to a bank, order a lengthy appraisal, wait for a meeting of the loan committee, or wade through the rivers of red tape surrounding institutional transactions. In short, we were working in a niche market where their bureaucratic structures knock the banks out of the box. They simply could not compete with us on the basis of speed, and our client was indeed in need of speed.

2. Technology—the mechanical system. Under Reed's direction, our office is wired with high-speed Internet, and we maintain accounts that connect us to all kinds of data sources. These allow us to rapidly download title information, zoning maps, tax rolls, market information, property histories, satellite photos, and demographic data pertinent to our decision-making processes. We can access much of this information instantly or communicate very quickly with others who may be in possession of electronic versions of the data that can be instantly forwarded to us. We can build a loan file in a matter of hours instead of weeks.

3. Talent—the training system. Our staff has a broad scope of talents and disciplines necessary to gather and process information, create documents, communicate with vested parties, and support all others involved in the process. We work as a team. We function as a whole, slicing and dicing the workload and delivering the intended results in dramatically condensed time frames.

4. Relationships—the people system. We consciously invest in people. We do all we can on a day-to-day basis to treat others as we would like to be treated. We make every effort to accommodate others when called upon. We have an absolute rule in our businesses that requires telling the truth and keeping our word to everyone at all times. By making this investment in others, we find that they are there for us when we have a need for speed and they readily respond to our requests. We see these people as extensions of our team's talent and resources. Our network of connected people is one of our greatest assets. We also have an unbreakable rule: No matter what else is right with a transaction, if the people piece is wrong, we walk away. As Robert Kiyosaki so aptly teaches, "You can't do a good deal with a bad partner." The guidelines we have set and hold to in our companies protect the integrity of our teams. Our people abide by such high standards that we rarely need to fire anyone. If the bad guys slip under the radar to find a way onto our team, they soon leave because they are made so uncomfortable by the culture that everyone else upholds. We have zero tolerance for lying, cheating, stealing, gossiping,

petty politics, and sexual harassment. We intend for our business relationships to last for a lifetime and create an environment that is mutually respectful, safe, clean, fun, and productive.

TIP Time is the investor's friend in an appreciating market. As we say, "Appreciation will cover a multitude of investor sins." However in a down market, time is the enemy, and the need for speed, for precision, and for bulletproof decision making becomes even more critical. Speed is often the difference between success and failure, especially in a contracting real estate market.

Many modern tools allow us to cover more ground in less time. I encourage you to use cell phones, computers, e-mail, text messaging, a paperless office, video conferencing, and anything else that gets more out of the time allotted. To illustrate how valuable this can be, one of my favorite tech tools is a digital voice recorder. I keep it in my pocket most of the time. When I have a creative idea or think of something I need to do, I make a quick note of it on the micro recorder. Because I can talk faster than I write, this high tech tool consolidates what would be a scattered pile of sticky notes into one location. I use the recorded notes to compile my daily to-do list. This habit keeps important ideas and tasks from slipping through the cracks. It also reduces my stress levels considerably because my mind is free of all of those details. In addition, I keep an audio journal of important thoughts, events, and new things I learn. It is amazing how valuable some of that information is at a later date, especially when imbued with the emotion of the moment, as captured in my voice. It accelerates the learning process and the implementation of new ideas. Perhaps the most important benefit of all is that it saves so much of my time, which is irreplaceable.

So, there you have it! W = (XO (T+E)) / K. Wealth is XOTEK. To make it easy to remember, say it phonetically. It sounds like "Wealth is exotic." Now you have your first formula for achieving exotic personal wealth.

On a bright spring morning in May, a few days after receiving the million dollar check, I walked down the hall to my office. It was my birthday. I noticed a document taped to the door at eye level. It was a copy of a deposit slip with a printout of my discretionary business account balance. It had been posted there by my accounting staff as a birthday surprise. It showed available funds of $1,217,674.44. All of the bills were paid. There were no strings attached to that money.

It struck me that I had more than a million dollars in cash with which I could do whatever I wanted. I sat down at my desk and again let the full impact of the moment settle in on me. My thoughts were strangely drawn once more to those times in the past when I struggled to learn the secrets of abundance. Of course, I felt joy, peace, gratitude, and a sense of well being, but most of all, I felt vindicated for every effort I had made through years of hard work, tireless study, and the gathering of experiences that collectively prepared me to close million-dollar transactions. A sense of excitement welled up inside of me. I knew it was only the beginning because, now, I had the formula for replicating the same success over and over again.

I glanced at the equation I had scratched on the pad of paper a few days earlier. I felt so utterly blessed. I thought of thousands of other people who are out there in the world, going through the same process I had been through; struggling to find the right combination, the right recipe, the right formula for their own success. I picked up the piece of paper and with a smile, folded it and carefully tucked it in my pocket. I knew it would come in handy soon, when I would have a chance to share it with someone else who was diligently searching for the way to XOTEK Wealth.

WAYS TO LEARN MORE

www.waynelpalmer.com
www.nce1031.com
A soon-to-be-published book on real estate formulas, by Wayne Palmer

Wayne Palmer is widely regarded as a master of the creative structuring of real estate acquisition and financing, using notes and other forms of real estate paper, together with 1031 Equity Marketing formulas. As the owner and manager of National Note of Utah, LC, and several other companies, Wayne is a Certified Real Estate Note Appraiser, Certified Cash Flow Master Broker, a Licensed Continuing Education Provider, and holds the Equity Marketing Specialist (EMS) designation with the National Council of Exchangors. He has been involved in real estate development since 1978 in Utah, Idaho, Arizona, Hawai'i, and Minnesota.

4

Profits from the Ground Up

R oss is Ken McElroy's partner in their business MC Properties. Kim and I are often financial partners with Ken and Ross in a number of their projects and have done very well financially, even in tough economic times.

There are three primary reasons why our investments with Ross do so well. The first reason is that he is a builder. He understands the ins and outs of the construction industry. Second, he is a property manager. This is important because the key to long-term investing in real estate is professional property management. And third, Ross is exceptional at finance by managing the ratios between debt, equity, and expenses. When it comes to real estate investing, he is the complete package. On top of that, he is a great guy. He is fair and honest.

In 2002, when the Tucson apartment market was hot, Ross's background allowed us not only to do well buying existing apartment houses but also building new apartment houses. One of our first investments together was the purchase of an existing apartment complex his company was managing. This gave us an advantage because we knew the numbers were honest—which is important since most pro forma numbers provided by realtors are lies. Second, the property had an additional ten acres of vacant land. Once we bought the existing apartment house, our next step was to begin construction on an additional one hundred units on the vacant land. Then with the increased rents a few years later, Ross refinanced the property, and Kim and I got all of our initial investment money back. This

*means each month we receive a check from the positive cash flow, and Kim and I
have zero invested in the project. If you do the math, this means Kim and I have
an infinite return on our money. In layman's terms, an infinite return is truly
money for nothing . . . every month.*

*This is why Kim and I love being partners with Ross McCallister and Ken
McElroy.*

—Robert Kiyosaki

Perhaps you've already read and maybe even re-read *Rich Dad Poor Dad* by
Robert Kiyosaki, as well as my partner Ken McElroy's book, *The Advanced
Guide to Real Estate Investing*, and now you are ready to take the plunge and invest in real estate on your own. That's probably why you bought this book written by real estate professionals, each of whom have been earning their livings
in real estate for decades.

There are pages in this book that are full of tremendous opportunities and
innovative ways to make money in real estate. But one avenue of investment
you may not have thought of and may want to consider is to develop your own
project from the ground up.

The profits you have heard about from real estate development are mind
boggling, and if you are like most people, the numbers leave you frothing at the
mouth for a piece of the development pie. Yes, there is tremendous profit to be
made from real estate development, but as with any high reward venture there
is also the possibility of tremendous financial losses if you let your emotions
override good judgment, or if you don't know what you are doing.

In this chapter I will outline some of the steps you need to take to evaluate a
development opportunity, steps I've gleaned from my expertise in developing
apartment communities during the past three decades and from some twenty-
plus projects of about four thousand units. And because my experience is primarily in apartment development, that is what we will talk about. However,
these fundamentals apply to any commercial development, such as office or retail, and to any size apartment community, be it four or four hundred units.

For me, development from the ground up is the most exciting way to invest
in real estate. There are few professional accomplishments more rewarding
than to see a project go from conception to reality. And it's even better when
that project produces positive financial results. Yet, with that said, nothing can
be more frustrating than working for years (yes, years!) to start your project
and battling through environmental and governmental regulations, market con-

ditions, financial institutions, and your own continuous questioning about whether all this frustration and risk is worth it. That side of the business is a reality, too, even for those of us who have many projects already under our belts.

I know you can see yourself as the owner of that "perfect" corner lot at Main and Better Main, graced with a structure and a monument sign bearing the name you have been dreaming about for years. Maybe it's (insert your dream name here!) in large letters on the monument sign in the front. You can see all the happy families living there, and you can hear the ka-ching of the cash register as the rents roll in every month. But before you build that sign or take that cash to the bank, let's talk about some of the decisions you must make first before you consider embarking upon this adventure.

TIP The main lesson I have learned in thirty years of apartment development is that each project is unique and different. Each will bring its own set of opportunities and challenges.

Before you call me when you are in the middle of your next development and say, "But Ross, you didn't tell me I would need an environmental impact study on the duck-billed humpback pygmy field mouse!" remember, I did tell you that something always comes up to make your project harder than you thought it would be.

A CLEAR VISION

From the beginning, for any project to be truly successful, you need to have a clear vision of what you want to build and how developing this property meets your own objectives. That means you also need to actually have objectives—or better said, you need a solid understanding what you want this project to achieve. One of the reasons MC Companies—the company Ken and I own—has been successful in development is that we have an infrastructure in place within our firm to develop, construct, manage, and profitably operate multifamily communities. We are careful to select communities large enough to support an on-site staff, earn economies of scale, and that fit within our investment model. We are careful to keep our egos in check and build for the market rather than for our own self esteem.

When we take on a new development, we draw upon each and every one of those disciplines—development, construction, and management—from inception to ensure that we make good decisions in the present because we know they will impact the future. This inclusive team approach is crucial to the successful development and operation of our multifamily communities. If you do not have expertise in all these areas, then it's in your best interest to create a team whose members do have the expertise in each of these fields before you venture into multifamily investments, whether you are building a duplex or four hundred units.

DEVELOP FOR THE LONG TERM

Without exception we build communities with the full intent of operating them once they are done. If the market is strong and the right buyer knocks on our door after the development is complete, we have an alternate option to make money on the investment, but we don't enter a project with this end in mind. It takes many months, or years, from the time we create the vision of our finished community to the time when we collect even a dollar in rent from the first tenant. To predict what the market will be like at the finish line is not always possible. But if you plan to own and operate the project after it is built and use those numbers in your pro forma, you begin with a more solid platform—a better business premise—from which to launch your development, lease it up, and operate the community profitably.

Let's look at the other scenario—from the point of view of building and selling rather than building and operating. What if the market changes from the time that you planned your development to the time it is built and ready for you to operate? If you have not planned on operating it from the beginning, the likelihood of you recognizing the changes, knowing how they affect your project, and then making the necessary adjustments are slim. In the end, you may find yourself holding an obsolete project or one that would require some serious adjustments to fit the new market conditions.

My examples are not entirely hypothetical. In the spring of 2006 the apartment market was hot, and any project completed could be sold for a big profit. Many developers began projects with the idea that they could cash in upon completion with an immediate sale. So, thousands of units were developed and built over the next two years. In 2008, banks had changed their qualification and ratios for loans, and their credit criteria changed dramatically, too. Investor money was not readily available, either. Economic conditions had deteriorated, resulting in higher unemployment and a tight economy. The market for new apartments was, at best, weak. Investors were demanding lower purchase prices to compensate for the slower economy.

Consequently, many developers found themselves sitting on their shiny new properties in a down economy, with cautious investors, reluctant banks, and a weak market for their product. All the assumptions they had made two years prior were based on factors that no longer applied. Because they didn't develop their projects with the idea that they were going to operate them, they created a scenario dependent on a sale and ripe for financial disaster!

Ken and I have avoided this situation because we plan from the start to operate the communities once they are completed, and we make sure all our actions are consistent with our investment objectives. Consequently, we have been able to adjust to market changes and ride out the difficult times, all the while building long-term value.

TIP I don't believe that it is possible to hit a real estate cycle perfectly. If you do, it's luck. Building value from real estate development over the long term takes skill and expertise. It also takes an operator's eye to recognize market shifts and a mind-set that is open to change.

YOUR MARKET NICHE FOCUS

Just as you simply must have your objectives for a development in place, you must decide which market niche your apartment project, or other project, will fill. Here are the basics I consider when looking for a market niche:

- What are the demographics of the area you are considering?
- What is the salary level of the area?
- Is there a college population looking for more off-campus housing, and is that the type of community I want to run?
- Where are the major employment centers?
- Are new businesses and employment being generated in the area?
- What other communities are in the area that a prospective tenant will consider, and are they the same class as the community you are developing, that is, luxury, blue-collar, or subsidized housing?
- What can I build, and how much rent can I charge?
- Will I enjoy owning and managing the community?

In 1999, we took over the development of an eighty-unit townhome community in a town with lots of retirees. Twenty-four units had been built, and only two had sold in more than one year. When we inspected the project, it was obvious why the sales weren't happening. Each unit had two bedrooms with a detached garage. When homeowners came home, they would park in the garage and would have to walk sometimes hundreds of feet through the property to enter their front doors. A review of other competing townhomes for sale in the area revealed they all had attached garages. Homeowners park, get out of their cars, and take a few steps right into their homes. Is it any surprise why an elderly buyer would prefer the competition?

When we took the project over, we bought the two sold units back and converted the entire community to an apartment project, offering it for rent, not to retirees, but to the people who worked in the town. We completed construction of the eighty units, leased the property to full occupancy within six months, and operated the project at a profit until we sold it four years later. That's understanding the niche and developing for it. The original developer of the townhomes clearly did not understand the market niche, which meant he did not understand the buyer.

The most beautiful project imaginable will not rent if it's built in the wrong place. A luxury apartment community may be your dream, but if you build it in a blue collar area, you won't be able to lease the community or be able to charge enough rent to make the economics work. Matching the needs of the community with the project you develop is crucial to your success. Research and know your demographics before you proceed. Only research will give you the perspective that you need before you take another step forward.

WHERE TO BUILD YOUR COMMUNITY

You've most likely heard it before in this book and likely everywhere else: location, location, location. As you are standing on that dusty lot, filled with years of accumulated trash, a couple of homeless camps, and overgrown weeds, envision where the main entrance to your community will be located. Pretend you are driving in and driving out. Look around you. What do you see? If the view is of an industrial complex across the street, a junkyard, or poorly maintained buildings, don't just brush it off. Signs like that generally mean the area isn't going to entice many people to choose your community no matter how beautiful you make it. On the other hand, sometimes negative factors like these can be minimized.

We developed an apartment project on a site where our due diligence revealed that a processing plant was located just half a mile away. The plant took used grease from restaurants and processed it to be reused. When the plant was operating, it stunk to high heaven. But the site was an excellent infill location in a good school district. The clincher was when we discovered that the processing plant was in the midst of implementing rigid pollution-control measures. We were able to pull off a really nice, affordable apartment community in an under-served area with confidence. Research paid off.

While a panoramic view of the mountains or ocean may not be possible, or even relevant to your community plans, don't forget to envision what residents will see and feel coming home. Is it welcoming? Does it feel safe? Would you want to call that home after a long day at work?

Before Beginning a Multifamily Development Project, Ask Yourself These Questions

Lifestyle and Convenience

- Will your community have good exposure to drive-by traffic? Heavy drive-by traffic is a plus when you are trying to attract potential tenants, but possibly a negative for residents concerned about traffic noise. On the other hand, the cutest, most affordable community in town could suffer high vacancy rates if it is located on a street no one can find, even with a blitz of advertising.
- How far from the major thoroughfares will your community be, and how easy is the access to them? Is that important for the type of community you are planning to build?
- How easy will it be for residents to get to work, school, shopping, the movies, etc.?
- Where are the schools in relation to your community? What is the reputation and rating of those schools? What are the transportation options to and from those schools?
- What are the employment opportunities in the area? What mass transit is available to help your residents get to work?
- Is the major downtown area easily accessible?

Social Amenities

- Are parks, movie complexes, theaters, arcades, and sports facilities an acceptable distance from your proposed community?
- What is the "flavor" of the part of town you are considering?
- How does your apartment community plan fit in with the area?

Neighborhood Amenities

- Is shopping in close proximity?
- Is a major grocery store nearby? It matters for those 10 p.m. milk runs.

DEVELOPMENT OF YOUR SITE

By this point, you understand that you must choose a site based on your demographic research. Now consider your site from the development perspective. How easy will bringing the project, literally, out of the ground actually be? This is perhaps the most critical analysis you will need to do, and it is the one that will have the biggest effect on your development costs. Is the site fairly flat, with a minimum of site prep work required? Or does the site have some geographical features that are interesting but challenging?

Flat sites are wonderful, and they typically will allow for the highest density. That is, they allow you to construct the most units per acre. Drainage becomes your biggest concern with flat sites because water will not flow off them without effort. On the other hand, a lovely, hilly piece of land can make for an interesting project. But on the downside, density will be a challenge, and the geography itself can run up the site development and infrastructure costs very quickly. Foundational structures like retaining walls can take a huge chunk of your development budget in the blink of an eye. The point is, each site provides its own set of challenges and opportunities. You need to understand how they affect the number of units you can build and at what costs.

When considering the location of your community, consult with your local governing bodies regarding zoning and other development requirements as soon as you can. Your local government development department can help you determine the required process for gaining permission to develop your project. Be wary, though. I've found cities and counties are notorious for seeing new development as a significant revenue source, and they look for opportunities to solve their problems and budget overruns at your expense. For example, some will make approval of your project contingent upon the city or the town getting concessions from you. You need to understand the law and the regulations, so you know what a government jurisdiction can and cannot legitimately require. Do not take their word as gospel without checking. And most of all, be prepared to do battle on every issue.

Can you tell that I speak from experience? During the approval process for one project we developed, the city initially required us to build a traffic median in the middle of a six lane street—the major highway through town—with the excuse that the median was required to provide safe access to the proposed apartment community. Medians are not cheap! We were going to incur several hundred thousand dollars in off-site expenses that threatened to jeopardize the entire deal. However, after many sleepless nights, a great deal of contemplation, and consultation with our development team, we were able to determine that, although we were required to augment the street improvements to provide safe access, we could do it by slightly redesigning the entrance to the project and re-striping the street, at a cost of only $3,000.

Just as important as knowing how to work with the city or town is knowing how to work with the utility companies. On your to-do list should be checking with the utility companies that will serve your community for availability of their services, hook-up fees, development fees, and monthly service rates. I've seen too many novices get surprised by utility access and hook-up issues. Another often overlooked detail is checking on the possible future infrastructure requirements of your site. For example, if your site is on a heavily traveled two-lane street, and the city decides to widen it to four or six lanes, you will be assessed for your portion of the cost, and you will lose part of your site for the right-of-way. Be prepared for these issues by knowing they can happen up front, then plan your development accordingly.

Oh, and let's not forget the remote possibility, which in some parts of the country isn't that remote, that your site could have archeological or environmental significance. Find out what rules are governing those discoveries in advance of even buying the land. Remember, finding out that your site is the home of those endangered duck-billed humpback pygmy field mice, or the next Machu Picchu, could either kill your development entirely or put it on hold for an indefinite period of time while experts complete expensive studies and develop mitigation plans.

Another tip that every developer must know is the value of checking for any riparian or wetland conditions on the property, as well as drainage, flooding potential, and soil conditions. You don't want your beautiful new community to be in a lake when the summer rains come. And you don't want to find your buildings slowly—or not so slowly—sinking into the ground because of poor soil conditions. When evaluating a site, you must consider all these factors. I know there are quite a number of them, and I can't stress enough that each site has its own nuances. As a developer you must be prepared to spend the money to do a proper evaluation. It's pretty easy to see the cost implications if you don't.

YOUR DEVELOPMENT TEAM

In our company, Ken and I have worked out clear guidelines regarding who will handle which areas of development and management, based on our respective professional backgrounds. At the same time, we constantly consult with each other and make joint decisions.

TIP You do not have the expertise to handle all the development, management, and construction phases for the community you want to build. You need to start by putting together a development team with the strongest expertise in each area you can find.

We're always certain to clarify up front and in writing who will be the team leader and who will make the final decisions. That holds people accountable and gives them ownership. It's fine to use people you know, but this is not the time to give your sister-in-law's cousin his first break in the development business!

YOUR ARCHITECTURAL TEAM

The next person on your team will be your architect. Ideally, this will be someone you have worked with in the past and have traveled a lot of rocky roads together. This person will have the experience and relationships with the governing jurisdiction to guide you through all the government requirements. He or she will also coordinate all the other design professions that you need, and will provide the site plan, design, and building elevations, unit plans, project amenities, and construction drawings with specifications.

Other members of your development team that your architect will coordinate include:

- Mechanical engineer who will design the plumbing and HVAC systems.
- Structural engineer who will design the foundations, the framing requirements, and the roofing system.
- Electrical engineer who will design both the underground electrical systems and the building electrical requirements.
- Civil engineer who will design the grading requirements for your site, including drainage, parking lot, and zoning compliances.

YOUR CONTRACTOR

The contractor will be the guy or gal who is going to take all these drawings, plans, and specifications and construct your community. Think of him/her as translating the two-dimensional plans into three-dimensional buildings, from overseeing the grading of the site all the way through handing over the keys of the finished units. You will want a general contractor licensed in the state in which you are building and who hires only licensed subcontractors in each trade qualified to do the work. Reputation and past performance of the general contractor will be your main guideline for this professional. Once chosen, you will want to have a signed contract between you as the developer/owner and the general contractor that will delineate the terms of the relationships including compensation.

Common Construction Contracts

- **Lump Sum or Fixed Price Contract**—In this type of contract, the contractor agrees to provide specified services for a specific price and receives this sum upon completion of the project or according to a negotiated payment schedule. If the actual costs of labor and materials are higher than the contractor's estimate, his profit will be reduced. If the actual costs are lower, the contractor will get more profit. Either way, the cost to the developer/owner is the same.
- **Cost Plus a Fixed Fee Contract**—In this contract, you as the owner/developer will pay the contractor the actual costs of construction plus a fee to the general contractor. If the actual costs are higher than the estimate, the owner must pay the additional amount. If the actual costs are lower, then the owner gets the savings.
- **Guaranteed Maximum Price Contract**—This contract states the owner/developer will pay for the costs like a Cost Plus contract, but the contractor will guarantee that the costs will not exceed a maximum amount. In the event that actual costs are lower than the estimates, the owner keeps the savings. As costs rise, the owner must pay for the additional costs up to the guaranteed maximum. Thereafter the contractor pays.

THE CONSTRUCTION TEAM

For as important as the general contractor is to the success of any project, understand that the success or failure of your construction relies heavily on the expertise of the entire construction team. I cannot stress enough the importance of hiring a qualified, financially stable contractor who employs a bright project manager, assigns experienced superintendents, and hires excellent tradespeople.

Carefully scrutinize each person who will be involved with the construction of your project; not only is that your prerogative, it's your job. In addition to your general contractor being licensed in the state of your project, he or she must also be fully insured and be bondable. Another tip, and I know, everyone needs to get their start somewhere, but give careful consideration before you agree to allow your general contractor to break in a new superintendent or project manager on your job. His limited experience in the field may cost you money and may even jeopardize the quality of your finished product.

So just who constitutes a construction team? Your team should include a strong project manager. It is this person's responsibility, among other things, to decide which subcontractors will be awarded the contract for the project and to set the construction budget. The project manager studies the plans and specifications submitted by the architectural team and based on his or her experience will often suggest adjustments or changes in the plans. A few choice suggestions made by a perceptive and confident project manager can save you thousands of dollars in the construction budget without affecting the quality or the appearance of the finished product.

Each project has at least one on-site superintendent, based on the size and scope of the project. The superintendent is responsible for the day-to-day operations of all the subcontracting trades who will be working on the project at any given time. Superintendents set the schedule for the trades to ensure the proper flow of work. There is a sequential order to construction; for example, you don't want the painters arriving *before* the drywallers have finished putting up the walls. And you certainly want to make sure all the necessary site work—such as grading, compacting, etc.—is done before the concrete folks come to pour the building pads. This right-on-time kind of scheduling takes a person who has been around the block and knows how long things take to complete. It takes a person who knows what the demand is for the various trades and knows the appropriate lead times. It also takes someone who can forcefully, yet professionally, get you the best treatment from the subs.

Between the subcontractors, superintendents, and the project manager, this construction team is responsible for continued communication with the architect and engineers and for attending to construction methods and details that don't always show up on the drawings, yet become obvious as construction is in progress. They should also be in continual communication with the testing technicians, building inspectors, financial institution inspectors, and, of course, you the owner/developer! Remember, this is your baby, and you cannot deny the fact that you are ultimately responsible for the design and construction pros.

The project manager also has another very vital role, one you will come to appreciate. He or she is the person responsible for keeping a close eye on the construction budget. That involves closely monitoring if or when a particular trade is out of sync with the budget, and making adjustments before the close of the project. This is the person who looks out for your financial interests and communicates with you to discuss any overages. In construction, things often take longer and cost more than originally planned, so having a good project manager with good communication skills is a real plus.

Where does the general contractor make his money? When you get your first glimpse of a construction budget, you'll notice a line item built in for a specified percentage of the overall construction budget for the contractor's overhead and profit. Remember, construction costs are negotiated between you and the contractor, so you need to understand all the components of the construction budget, including direct costs for labor and materials, subcontractors, and general conditions, as well as profit and overhead.

Finally, you are part of the construction team, too. It is up to you to use every means available to make sure that the contractor builds the project correctly and pays his bills.

This includes hiring third party quality-control inspectors; requiring proof of payment for the materials and labor, such as lien waivers; and possibly requiring a payment and performance bond.

YOUR TITLE COMPANY

Title companies have been mentioned several times in this book, and here they are again. Just as they play a role in acquiring existing property, they play a role in new development, too. Here it is their job to hold all monies involved in the transaction of the land transfer in escrow. They also provide a title report and title insurance. The title company can help you by periodically checking to make sure that the contractor is paying his bills and that no liens have been filed against the project by a subcontractor. You don't want to have your buildings almost completed only to find out that there is a lien on the property from an unpaid sub. It happens!

YOUR PROPERTY MANAGEMENT COMPANY

Contrary to what you might think, you'll need a property management company, even before your project breaks ground. It is the property management company that will prepare the market analysis and determine the rents your community can reasonably charge. From there they help you prepare a realistic operating budget. The way management companies make their money is usually based on a percentage of anticipated gross annual rents. Having an experienced property management company has been a true key to our success. The market knowledge and expertise it provides is something we would never dream of doing without.

YOUR FINANCING PARTNER

Unless you are related to Daddy Warbucks or recently won the lottery (if that describes you, let's talk!), you will need to obtain financing for your project. You may qualify for various forms of financing from governmentally controlled financing, to commercial banks, to private money. All are viable and all come with certain requirements.

It is possible to qualify for governmental or commercial bank loans that offer development and construction financing. These lenders historically will lend from 65 percent to 85 percent of the total cost of the project. The credit crunch of 2008 has changed those lending percentages, and developers are required to have more of their own cash in their deal, but regardless of the amount, those capital sources are options. However, governmental or commercial bank lenders will have a first mortgage priority, meaning that in the event of a default, they get paid first. Their interest rates are based on the current market.

Another finance option is securing money from private lenders, meaning individuals wanting to invest in a real estate project as opposed to stocks or bonds. If you have a successful track record and a convincing business plan/sales package for your proposed community, they will lend you the money with the condition that they receive an interest payment as well as a percentage of the profits from the operations of the completed project and any sales proceeds. Although private lenders are typically more expensive than traditional lenders, they are more flexible and may lend you a higher percentage of the project costs.

Given the scope of your project and your financial contacts, your funding may possibly come from a combination of these sources, depending on how you structure the financing. Most of the projects Ken and I work on are structured to obtain a commercial bank loan for approximately 67 percent of the total amount needed for the project, with the remaining 33 percent contributed as the equity, which may come from investors, our own funds, or both.

Your Business Plan

Obtaining financing isn't as easy as strolling into a bank with a good idea. It takes much more than that. In reality, to obtain financing, you will need a business plan. Business plans come in many shapes and sizes, and you can find numerous templates for them all over the Internet. But let me cut to the chase and tell you exactly what banks want to see. This eliminates all the unnecessary fluff that they don't read anyway. Here's what you need to include in your business plan:

- Executive Summary, which explains the purpose of the project and gives a financial summary. You actually can write this first or last, but it's always the first few pages of your plan.
- Property Overview, which includes a description of the site, unit mix, floor plans, site plan, elevations, and pictures of the site.
- Market Overview, which presents neighborhood features, city economics, and the local apartment market.
- Financial Pro Forma, which includes development costs, construction costs, and projected operations income and expenses.
- Developer résumé which highlights your credentials.
- Development team résumés, which highlight the credentials of your architect, engineers, and property managers.

Those are the components lenders care about and are the sections they read. No amount of fluff or page volume will make up for a poor job assembling the details in these sections of the plan. Complete analysis and a realistic business case surrounding that analysis have a better chance of receiving funding. A sketchy plan based on incomplete research and analysis with blue sky projections won't. Not only is this document obviously important in your getting the financing for your project, the exercise of doing it helps articulate and establish your goals and objectives. It is the exercise that helps you determine if your project can ultimately be profitable, and let's face it, you should want to know that as much as the lender does.

Will You Qualify for a Loan?

Ken and I have spent our entire careers building our credit and financial standing, as well as building our network of contacts within banking and investing circles. These bankers and investors know our reputation and qualifications and are willing to entertain a development proposal that we present to them. Our track record and financial strength give banks and investors confidence that we can complete and operate a financially viable project. When searching for financing for your project, whatever your sources, you can count on them scrutinizing your background particularly in these areas:

- What is your financial strength? If you are building the community under the umbrella of a company, what is the financial strength of the entire company?
- What is your development experience? Have you successfully built numerous projects before, or is this your first time at bat? If this is your first development, what attributes and strengths do you have that will put to rest concerns about your experience?
- Have you had one or more previous projects fall through in some way?
- What are the backgrounds, experiences, and strengths of your development team? Are they all solid and strong, or are there any weak links that could potentially cause hesitation from the source of your loan?
- What is the source of the equity you will be bringing to the table for this project? How much of your own money are you willing to invest in the project?

The stronger your answers to each of these questions, the better the terms and rate of loan you will be able to qualify for. A lender will ask these questions regardless of the type of loan you are seeking—a construction loan or a permanent loan. And that leads us to our next subject.

SHORT-TERM LOAN VS. LONG-TERM LOAN

A construction loan is a short-term loan with a term length from six to thirty-six months, depending on the size of your project and construction budget. Construction loans usually have variable interest rates and are interest-only loans. The lending institution holds your project as collateral during the course of the loan. In the event of default, you will lose your property. Construction loans are also typically personally guaranteed by the developer, meaning the bank has recourse to your personal assets in the event of default.

Unlike with other loans, with a short-term construction loan the lender will not hand over to you the full amount of the loan all at once. Rather, you'll receive it in monthly payments based on the percent of completion of your project. This process is called a *draw*, and each month your construction team will submit an application to the lending institution. The lending institution will send out an inspector to verify the work is completed as stated in a workmanlike fashion and that all local government inspections are complete and approved. Only with the inspector's approval will the lender issue that month's draw.

After construction is completed, then you, the developer, will need to obtain a permanent loan. The permanent loan is long-term financing that will require a monthly payment for principal and interest. The proceeds of the permanent loan are used to pay off the short-term construction loan, and possibly repay a portion of your equity. Sometimes, a lender will provide a construction loan that will convert to a permanent loan upon construction completion. This has the advantage of reducing your financing risk. There's always the outside chance that you may have trouble getting long-term financing once the project is done. With a loan of this type, that financing is already in place.

Financing terms can be very complicated. Our company never takes on a loan without thoroughly reviewing the loan documents ourselves, as well as having the documents reviewed by an attorney who specializes in real estate financing. Be sure you understand what you are obligating yourself to.

A FEW FINAL WORDS

You, the developer, will put yourself on the line for the money to fulfill your dream, but you won't see your profit until the project is completed and operational. While the rewards of a well-thought-out and well-constructed project are fantastic in the end, it is a long journey, and there is a lot of risk along the way. The processes I used for building my first home in 1976 for $29,000, and the communities we have built for more than $30 million are basically the same: lots of time, research, due diligence, expenses, and sleepless nights.

By the time we identify a site, analyze the market, hire the professionals, obtain financing, and start construction, we have invested huge amounts of time and money. Every day during the development process a new challenge presents itself. It is a major commitment and financial risk to take on an apartment development, with the prospect of financial reward in the distant future. The development process is complicated and frustrating but also exciting and fun. You cannot anticipate everything, but you can succeed if you approach your project methodically, get the best advice and help, don't cut corners, and never give up! The personal and financial rewards are unsurpassed.

Hang on for a challenging adventure. Watch out for the duck-billed humpback pygmy field mice and all the other bumps in this ride. You are either going to enjoy developing and building a new community as much as I do, or you will find that it isn't your cup of tea. Either way, I wish you much success!

Ross McCallister is a thirty-year industry expert in real estate/development and finance. He is a co-partner of MC Companies and oversees investment analysis, development, construction, financing, business development, and client relations. He is a licensed real estate broker and a licensed general contractor. Ross has developed and constructed more than four thousand apartment units in Arizona and managed condominium conversions in Oregon, Las Vegas, and Arizona valued in excess of $300 million. Prior to founding MC Companies with Ken McElroy, Ross was president of The McCallister Company, a real estate syndication firm and property management company. Ross believes in "giving back" and has served the real estate industry on various boards throughout his career, including the Office of the Governor's Arizona Housing Finance Authority Board.

5

Master Your Universe: Get the Lay of the Land

C ommercial real estate is very different from residential real estate. Craig Coppola is recognized as one of the best commercial real estate brokers in the United States. That is why he is my partner in commercial real estate investments, and we have done extremely well financially.

When Kim and I began our transition from residential to commercial real estate, the first thing we had to do was let go of a residential real estate investor's mindset. We had to see real estate investing through a different set of eyes. If not for Craig's experience, Kim and I might have lost a lot of money paying for our commercial real estate education. Craig is great because he is a tremendous teacher and takes the time to explain what we fail to see.

As an example, Craig's education of Kim and me began with our interest in a beautiful office building in a great location. It was a cute structure, built in the 1980s. The first thing Craig said was that there was not enough parking. He did not even look at the building. Since the 1980s, zoning laws had been passed requiring more parking spaces. If we wanted to improve the building, we would have to tear it down completely and rebuild from the ground up to comply with the new zoning law. The second lesson from Craig on the same building was that "Cute buildings attract cute businesses." He went on to say, "Rent to well-run businesses, not cute people running cute businesses. You'll have fewer headaches and earn more money."

Craig is the best organized person I know. He has his days planned to the minute. He is constantly studying and investing in his personal development—his business—yet time with his family takes the highest priority. Craig is a great family man and natural teacher, and he is priceless as a real estate partner.

—ROBERT KIYOSAKI

People who know me know that when I commit to doing something I generally jump in with both feet. And that is probably an understatement. It's not that I'm foolhardy about it; people would say I'm methodical and possibly relentless. I don't make rash decisions, and I don't give up. That's the way I approach my business goals, my personal goals, and my family goals. People would also say I'm consistent.

One of my passions in life has been baseball. I was an all-state high school and all-conference college player, and I was even drafted and played professionally with the Minnesota Twins organization. But after baseball, I knew I needed something that I could throw myself into 100 percent, something that I would love just as much and that would help me achieve my life goals.

Like so many people, my story of how I entered the real estate profession is a classic friend-of-a-friend story. I won't bore you with the details, but suffice it to say I did my share of dues paying. I didn't mind. My mentality then was no different than it is now and no different than it was playing baseball: Everything I do makes me stronger, smarter, and faster and gives me the only thing I ever ask for in life—an unfair advantage.

Yes, I want an unfair advantage and I do what it takes to get it—ethically. Getting the unfair advantage ethically usually means no shortcuts, lots of homework, discipline, and sacrifice. At least that is how it has been for me. When it pays off, those long days and longer nights of poring over real estate offering Memorandums, market comparables, and property financial data become distant memories that are replaced with cash, which flows into my mailbox on a monthly basis. It's a beautiful thing.

My career in real estate has afforded me spare time to do other things that I love; that was part of my plan when I got into this business. I wanted to be able to spend more time with my family, participate in my kids' lives, and pursue other passions in life such as running, Tai Kwon Do, and of course, baseball.

Today my passion for baseball takes the form of coaching a youth club baseball team—the Arcadia Rat Pack—and I approached that in much the same way I've approached everything else I've set out to do: with a startling amount of research, analysis, planning, and detail all in preparation for intense action. I'm not coaching a pro sports team, but regardless, I had batting lineups (based on who from the opposing team was pitching), training schedules, practice schedules, scouting reports, game strategies, substitution plans, even a plan for who was going to coach first base. Some of the parents, I'm sure, thought I was going a little overboard.

But to me "going overboard" was simply preparing the team to face every challenge in practice so that when those same situations came up in a game, they weren't new. I wanted to give those kids the unfair advantage, ethically. In essence, my role was to put those kids in a position to win.

That included mastering our universe and knowing the lay of the land. What teams were we going to be up against? What were their strengths and their weaknesses? How could we exploit those weaknesses and overcome their strengths? What do we do in a first-and-third situation? What's our bunt defense? How do we handle a "run down"? We studied, strategized, and practiced all this and more. We made it all the way to the state finals and were state runner-ups—that was victory to us. Sixteen wins and three losses. The team played great and came away with better and more confident kids. I want the same for you when it comes to commercial real estate investing. I want you to win! I want you to be the master of your universe before you even think about investing in property.

TIP In real estate, mastering your universe takes the form of knowing intimately your chosen area of city or town, fully understanding and enjoying your preferred type of real estate investment (also known as "asset class"), and being tuned in to the real estate cycle.

In real estate, mastering your universe takes the form of knowing intimately your chosen area of city or town, fully understanding and enjoying your preferred type of real estate investment (also known as "asset class"), and being tuned in to the real estate cycle. Once you've achieved all this, you are in a great position to begin considering properties. Here's your first pitch:

LET'S TAKE A RIDE

Even if you have lived in the same city or town your whole life and feel you know every road and every building, humor me, and still hop in your car and take a ride. This won't be a ride to simply look at buildings; it's a ride to help you look at your town or city with what I like to call "real estate eyes." Actually look-ing at the buildings is a minor thing at this point. This drive will help you to un-derstand the lay of the land—the environment the buildings are sitting in—from many different perspectives. The drive is about location, location, location.

Start your drive with the goal of trying to understand the overall city from a real estate investment perspective. Be observant. What do you think is impact-ing real estate values in one neighborhood or another? Even if you think you know the area in which you want to invest, it's still a good idea to understand what's going on in other areas of your city or town. Those things will play a part in the value of the area you like best.

By now it is probably no surprise to you that I live by my schedule. My days, weeks, months, and years are open to change, but they are highly planned. Whether you are a heavy scheduler or not, if you really look at your life, you'll likely find that we are all creatures of habit. We drive the same way to work and the same way home, day in and day out. Not only do we miss the opportunities on that drive, but we never see the changes that are taking place in the other 90 percent of our community. So the first thing I recommend in order to get the lay of the land and master your universe is to drive a different way to work. If you normally take the highway, then take the residential streets. If you always stop at the same Starbucks for coffee, then go to a different coffee shop. Take in a variety of scenery and people.

TIP Recommendation No. 1: Master your universe by driving a different way at different times to work, and take in the world from a real estate perspective. You'll be surprised by what you see.

Once you think you know an area, travel there at different times of the day. How about evenings, weekends, and at night? Really take the time to see how people live in this area, how it is trafficked. You may be surprised. There are neighborhoods that not only have changed over time, but there are neighbor-hoods that change with the time of day. I've seen parts of town that are "hap-pening" spots during the week and during lunch, but they are absolute ghost towns during the dinner hour and at night. If you're looking for a great building for a daytime business, this area of town could be the right place. But if you're looking for a building for an evening business, look elsewhere. Your goal here is to look at an area and "get it." That means you get what it's about, and you know what is a fit. Once you "get an area," you will begin to be able to see the future. This is a gut response that may be helpful to write down. You'll have an opportunity later to test how right you are when you talk to the experts who will eventually be on your team—appraisers, inspectors, attorneys, brokers, and builders.

LOOK FOR "THE PATH OF GROWTH"

When it comes to understanding the lay of the land, I look for what real estate pros call "the path of growth" in the market. Even in cities that as a whole are not growing, there usually are areas that are. How do you recognize the path of growth when it comes to commercial real estate? Look for the areas where home builders are buying land, where new homes are being constructed, and where elementary schools are being planned and built. City governments are a great resource for this information because they tell you where they are planning to build new facilities and where infrastructure is going in. You can also get good insight from the economic development officials in your city offices. It's always interesting to see which projects they are the most excited about and what they see developing down the road.

TIP Recommendation No. 2: Get to know your city officials and staff. Find out the projects that are underway that they are the most excited about. The more you talk with them, the more you'll come to know where the path of growth really is.

City officials often can be very excited about urban revitalization projects that are underway and often help fund projects that jump-start the process. How exciting it is to think about being part of the solution to violence, crime, and urban blight! But here's my caution: These kinds of projects take time, lots of time. Not only is there the obvious planning, zoning, designing, and entitlement process that must happen; sometimes votes are involved. Then there is the intangible consumer acceptance variable that can take years. In my hometown of Phoenix, there were more than $800 million of revitalization projects built before I considered this area for investment, and the elapsed time to resolve them took more than twelve years. So stay cautious for a very long time because even neighborhoods marked for revitalization may remain in decline for years.

I should point out that some real estate investors make it their entire business to seek out declining neighborhoods. People who specialize in urban revitalization are just one example. That's not my area of interest or expertise, so for my specialty—commercial office space—I stay clear when I see a lot of graffiti or closed businesses. That seems obvious, but you'll be surprised how a quaint historic home that may have been recently rezoned commercial in a troubled neighborhood can still be compelling to emotional investors. These buyers can easily talk themselves into a bad decision by thinking that purchasing this building will be good for the neighborhood, or by telling themselves they will live with the location because the building is so perfect. None of these arguments is good enough. Remember, it's location first, no matter how difficult the dwelling is to pass up.

IT'S TOUGH TO GROW YOUR WAY OUT OF A DOWNHILL SLIDE

The reason I'm such a stickler on this point is that it's really tough to grow your way out of a downhill slide. There's a difference between a declining area and an area that is going to be revitalized. When you get the feel that a neighborhood is going downhill, stay away. If it's on the upswing and that historic building is right in the center of it, don't let your preconceived beliefs about the neighborhood hold you back. There may be an opportunity. Understand they call it *real estate* for a reason. You're looking at the real estate first. That's the key underlying truth to all of this. The building is second.

To me an absolute must is to fully understand where the market is going, not just where it is today. It's all about feel and not getting in too early. What I mean by that is unlike some businesses where speed is everything, there is no need to be on the bleeding edge in real estate. You don't have to be first. You don't want to be first; leave that to the biggest players who can afford the risk. There's plenty of opportunity and money to be made by being second, third, and even twenty-third. Leave the bleeding edge to the big boys. In fact, if you're a small investor who is starting out, never be first.

TIP Recommendation No. 3: Do the homework it takes to fully understand where the market is going, not just where it is at this moment in time. You're investing for the future, so see the future as best you can.

Even though time flies, when it comes to real estate, I've been surprised by how long it takes the future to actually arrive. And if you're in a downhill slide, the future can't happen quick enough, believe me. You may find out that your grand vision for the property isn't two years away; it's actually twenty. This has happened to many real estate investors. The town of Fountain Hills, Arizona, was started by a real estate speculator in the 1970s. He built the world's highest fountain, which is powered by jet engines and shoots a huge plume of water 560 feet into the air. His goal was to attract curious people to the new community that at the time was out in the middle of nowhere. People came and marveled at the fountain, but not enough bought real estate. It took decades for the real estate in Fountain Hills to really take off. Today it is a thriving community, but it took almost thirty years for that to happen.

Is your view of the future too far ahead of the curve? My rule is to take my time and be patient. There's no need for excessive urgency at this point in the process. If there's room for one person to make money in an area, then there's room for more. In fact, I've found there are very few properties that are so special that if you miss them, you miss the deal of the century or even the decade. While those properties do exist, their owners know it and they typically overprice the properties anyway, negating the value of the deal. A good example is the Esplanade and Biltmore Fashion Park, both within the same city block in the highly sought after Camelback Corridor in Phoenix. Those properties are the types that are bought by huge institutions who want trophy properties where the look and the location are more critical than the solidity of the real estate and the return. For example, General Electric bought Hayden Ferry Lakeside in a prestigious area of Tempe, Arizona. MetLife bought the Esplanade in Phoenix. These are called core plus properties and are named such because they create a portfolio of foundation projects that entice other investors who are looking for glamorous investments.

TIP Recommendation No. 4: Real estate investing is about patience. There is no need to rush into an investment in any market.

KEEP YOUR REAL ESTATE EYES OPEN

As you look at neighborhoods, don't overlook the places that you think might be too expensive, too cheap, or that used to be blighted. Neighborhoods change. I know one investor who has made a ton of money improving the looks and performance of less-than-stellar buildings and increasing the property values. It takes a big commitment to do that, but she's doing it. Understand, too, that there are slum lords out there who have made big bucks owning very shabby properties. That's not something I encourage; part of what we can do as investors is create better spaces for all. But with that said, it's a free country.

Everyone always asks this: What are the warning signs of a declining neighborhood? That's easy, and if you go with your feelings, you'll know them instinctively. True story, I was driving one morning, checking out a few neighborhoods I hadn't been through in a while and drove right by a car on blocks with the tires missing. That's the classic bad sign, and there it was in all its glory. Other signs are multiple cars parked in the street at night and a tenant mix in a building that looks fly-by-night or that are in shady businesses. Finally, take a look at the general upkeep. If the properties are unkempt, that's not good either. You may even want to take a look at the police reports to see how much crime happens in the area.

The bottom line is you can modify your building, but you alone can't modify the neighborhood your building sits in. And about that quaint historic building in a seedy part of town: Sure it would make great offices for a trendy design studio, but if your employees are too afraid to work there or stay after hours, how wise was your decision? Open your eyes and think through what you're seeing, and listen to your gut. Write down what you feel—yes, what you feel—about every neighborhood. On the next page is a form that will not only help you know important considerations, but also will give you a place to record your impressions about the area.

TIP Recommendation No. 5: Look for the signs of a declining neighborhood, and don't be in denial about them. Unless you want to specialize in renewal projects, those signs matter.

LET'S TALK BUILDINGS . . . SORT OF

As I mentioned, the actual buildings themselves are practically the last things I look at when I'm getting familiar with a city and its neighborhoods. And even when it comes to a building, I don't initially see the vertical structure; I see the property it's sitting on. Are there enough parking spaces? Is it easy to get into and out of? In other words, does the property have good access? And looking at the building and the site it is sitting on, does it feel right? And can visitors find the location without getting lost?

From there I take a closer look at who is occupying the building. What are the tenants like? Are they quality, established companies or a little on the flakey side? A tenant doesn't have to be The Home Depot or Taco Bell to be acceptable. A local plumbing outfit that's been in a building for ten years is actually a good tenant—I have one like that—particularly when compared to let's say a start-up

Drive Guide – The Neighborhood Environment

Below are the things you need to look for as you drive neighborhoods and look at environments. (Rating scale: 1 is poor, 2 is fair, 3 is average, 4 is good, 5 is very good.) Add comments to right.

Neighborhood Environment: _____ *(list area)*

Border: N_____ / S_____ / E_____ / W_____

(comments)

Overall upkeep	1	2	3	4	5 _____
General condition of buildings	1	2	3	4	5 _____
Quality/condition of cars in area	1	2	3	4	5 _____
Quality of businesses in area	1	2	3	4	5 _____
Traffic patterns	1	2	3	4	5 _____
Area landscape	1	2	3	4	5 _____
Overall visual interest	1	2	3	4	5 _____
Perceived prestige	1	2	3	4	5 _____

Would I buy here?   Yes   No
If yes, what product type? _____
On what street(s) would I own? _____

Your Feelings and Impressions

High points?	Morning	Noon	Night
	_____	_____	_____
	_____	_____	_____

Low points?	Morning	Noon	Night
	_____	_____	_____
	_____	_____	_____

Future Outlook

In 5 years: _____
_____

In 10 years: _____
_____
_____

Other impressions: _____
_____
_____

Questions I need answered: _____
_____
_____

FIGURE 5.1

technology company that no one has ever heard of with millions in venture capital money and a burn rate of a million dollars per month with one customer and no profits. I also consider the tenant's position within their industry, the level of competition, and where the industry is going.

TIP Recommendation No. 6: Consider the building last and look at the location and property it's on first.

One afternoon, a friend called me from her car as she was traveling in a small town some distance from her home. She said, "Hey Craig, I'm looking at a great building here that's all set up for a call center. What do you think?" For me the answer was easy. Call centers are declining in the United States with most companies shipping their operations overseas. I replied, "Unless you're in India right now, I'd pass." Much of this is really common sense and having some knowledge of where the trends are, not just in real estate, but also in the areas of business and life that affect real estate.

The tracking form on the next page is a tool you can use to record your first-glance view and impressions of a property. It's also a great idea to bring along a digital camera so you can take photos of buildings and attach them to the Driving Guide records. Pay special attention to these items and be sure to record your overall impressions as well.

COMMERCIAL ASSET CLASS OPTIONS

One of the most important decisions you as a real estate investor will have to make is in which area of the business you want to specialize. If reading this book tells you anything, it should tell you that there are a lot of ways to make and lose money in the world of real estate. Even within the commercial real estate sector, there are a number of different asset class options. You'll soon discover that they are each quite specialized with plenty of their own nuances and requirements. I believe it's important to see the commercial real estate sector in its entirety so that you get an accurate picture of how it is all interconnected because, even though the different asset classes are unique, they all do work together to create an environment within an area of a city or town. Here are the asset classes complete with descriptions and the risks and the rewards.

TIP Recommendation No. 7: No one can possibly be an expert in every commercial asset class. Choose the one you think you'll enjoy most and specialize in it.

Drive Guide – The Building

Below are the things you need to look for as you drive and look at buildings. You'll want one form for each building you view. (Rating scale: 1 is poor, 2 is fair, 3 is average, 4 is good, 5 is very good.)

Building Name: _____

Building Address: _____

(comments)

Location within area	1	2	3	4	5 _____
Curb appeal	1	2	3	4	5 _____
General condition	1	2	3	4	5 _____
Parking	1	2	3	4	5 _____
Lighting	1	2	3	4	5 _____
Access/entrance and exit	1	2	3	4	5 _____
Tenants	1	2	3	4	5 _____
Ease of finding	1	2	3	4	5 _____
Landscaping	1	2	3	4	5 _____
Fits with your needs/wants	1	2	3	4	5 _____

Your Feelings and Impressions

High points?   Morning   Noon   Night

Low points?   Morning   Noon   Night

Future Outlook

In 5 years: _____

In 10 years: _____

Other impressions: _____

FIGURE 5.2

MULTIFAMILY

The multifamily asset class includes everything from small duplex apartment buildings to entire apartment complexes with eight hundred units or more. The biggest risk in this asset class is oversupply because when people have lots of choices, rents can fall, affecting your property's operating performance and cash flow. Another risk with multifamily is that when interest rates are low, more people can afford to buy homes, so they don't have to rent. That leaves more apartment units vacant and competing for fewer residents. But on the plus side, when lending gets tighter and it becomes harder to qualify for a home mortgage, renting becomes the only option, and the demand for apartment homes increases. Investors have made a lot of money in this area of commercial real estate by buying right and managing efficiently. Like all commercial real estate, the value of a multifamily property increases based on increased operating performance. In other words, buying a property and then managing it and filling up the vacant space better than the previous owner can create an automatic bump in value.

RETAIL

Retail commercial space is something you know probably quite well: shopping centers, strip centers, malls, and stand-alone retailers. The benefit with retail property is that construction costs are high—often tens to hundreds of millions of dollars—making for a high barrier to entry by competitors. This keeps demand usually ahead of supply. As an investor, that's generally a good position to be in. But it's not all blue sky. Economic factors such as reports of inflation, recession, and declining consumer spending trends can trigger retailers to go out of business, and as a building owner you could lose a retail tenant. Competition can also turn a favored retail center into one that is second class. That's what I mean about knowing the lay of the land and seeing the future. You want to know what is coming, not just what is.

COMMERCIAL OFFICE

Office buildings and office condos are one of the largest real estate asset classes. Just look around. We all work somewhere, and offices house many of us daily from eight-to-five. Offices come in many shapes and sizes, so there is diversity and easy entry for new investors. Some offices are former residential buildings converted to office space. Others are conventional office buildings of all shapes and sizes. The benefit of commercial office space is that there is likely something in your town that will fit your budget whether you are a first-time or a seasoned investor and give you plenty of room to grow as you increase your wealth and your level of investment.

INDUSTRIAL

Just like commercial office buildings, industrial spaces tend to have longer leases and lots of options when it comes to investing. There are giant warehouses with upward of five hundred thousand square feet and smaller mixed-use spaces in the neighborhood of three thousand square feet, along with everything in between. Because of the many options available, industrial space is a classic first-time-investor property. One reason for industrial's popularity with first-time investors is that many have their own businesses and need this kind of space.

HEALTH CARE

This asset class in commercial real estate includes not just hospitals, but also nursing homes, medical buildings, and assisted living facilities. The benefit of this class is that recessions and economic downturns don't really affect it much. But it is prone to the ups and downs of the tenant. Medical practices are small businesses. Hospitals are big businesses. And business can fluctuate. Plus, the medical profession is one that is in a state of flux, and it will be so for many years to come. Through my experience in this area I know that not only is it important to have the right tenants in your space, but it's important to have the right *mix* of tenants in your space—the right practices and the right practitioners. Assisted living facilities, on the other hand, rely heavily on good management. Having a reputable management company that specializes in these kinds of communities is a must.

SELF STORAGE

Self storage spaces are those mini-warehouse consumer and commercial facilities that you most likely have seen in your town. You may even have some of your things stored in one of them. They are seemingly recession resistant, and that is a big advantage for you as an investor. Generally, the management is relatively easy. Believe it or not, corporations are actually the biggest users of storage facilities, and every year they pay billions to store excess files, records, and general stuff. The downside is that building self storage facilities is a low-cost proposition. That means it's easy for competitors to break into the market, charge a lower price, and erode your margins. When it comes to self storage, I always make sure there are lots of rooftops nearby as well.

HOSPITALITY

This asset class includes hotels, motels, casinos, bed and breakfasts, resorts, and vacation rentals. And like assisted care facilities, management is important. In general, it is the asset class most closely connected with the health of the economy. In periods of economic decline, travels for business or pleasure are early casualties of cost-cutting and penny-pinching. That affects the number of room nights booked, which means per-night room rates can fall as properties vie for fewer customers. This, in turn, erodes income and profitability, but in markets with a balanced supply-and-demand ratio, hospitality can be very lucrative.

Within each of these asset classes are subcategories. All these options may at first seem overwhelming, but in reality it's this diversity that makes commercial real estate so lucrative and why smart investors specialize. It's this specialization that enables us to have an advantage over other types of investments and over other types of investors who are trying to do it all.

THE ABCS OF COMMERCIAL SPACE

Just as you need to know the various asset classes and some of the nuances of each, it's a good idea to know the four classes of commercial space that refer to the quality of the property. Too often I have seen novice investors duped into believing that an office building is one class, when it is really a lesser class. Class matters because the better the class of building, the higher the rent per square foot. Here are the official class guidelines:

Class A+. Landmark quality, high-rise buildings with a central business district location. These are the best of the Class A buildings.

Class A. Buildings that are one hundred thousand square feet or larger with at least five floors. The construction of these buildings is concrete and steel, and they were built after 1980. Buildings include business/support amenities such as cafés and banks, and they have strong identifiable locations and accesses.

Class B. Renovated buildings in good locations or newer buildings that are smaller in size. These can be wood frame construction in nonprime locations. Most first-time investors invest here.

Class C. Older buildings that are not renovated. They can be of any size, and are in average to fair condition.

Keep these qualifications in mind as you look at properties. They will help you know what you are looking at, and they will also help you recognize false advertising when you see it.

The Real Estate Cycle Revealed

Although you now know there are more kinds of commercial property than you could have imagined, you may still be surprised to learn that their performance over time is cyclical in whole and in part. What I mean by that is that each asset class runs through a cycle. And each asset class's cycle either flows before, flows with, or flows after another asset class's cycle.

For example, you'll find that growth in residential housing will fuel a similar but slightly lagging rise in retail. This pattern makes sense when you consider that new homeowners will want shopping centers, grocery stores, and other conveniences near where they live. The surge in retail then drives growth in the industrial and distribution sectors, so that means warehouse and mixed-use property development grows. Home development also drives some growth in commercial office space, but again commercial lags behind. That's why when housing development slows, it takes a few years for commercial to slow down, too. You've probably noticed that. When the news is reporting real estate declines, new commercial projects are still getting underway. Now you know why.

Real estate is about cycles and the inevitability of them. Once you know that and know how to pay attention to the cycles, you'll know the lay of the land in this regard, too, and you'll be in a position to make the best of the cycle by making the best decisions along the way.

TIP Recommendation No. 8: Understand the real estate cycle and watch for the indicators, and you will seldom be surprised.

Cycles are important, but in reality if you buy right, your real estate will do well, regardless of where in the cycle you bought. But if you are just starting out, buying right may not be as intuitive to you, so understanding the real estate cycle becomes golden knowledge. The following diagram shows the typical commercial real estate cycle and how it affects new construction and vacancy.

Let's walk through each quadrant. In Phase 1, the lower left quadrant, the market is in recovery phase. There is declining vacancy and no new construction. You know the market is in this phase when there is some growth in the market indicated by properties being rented and properties being sold. This uptrend can, and often does, last a long time, years in many cases. That's why I never feel like I need to rush into an investment. I also don't like surprises, so I generally let the bigger guys make the first leaps during this phase. Then I make my moves with solid knowledge that we are solidly in Phase one—the buying phase.

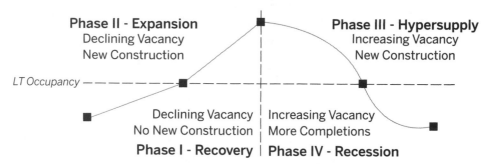

FIGURE 5.3 Market Cycle Quadrants
Used with permission by Glenn R. Mueller, Ph.D.

TIP Recommendation No. 9: Phase 1 in the real estate cycle is the time to buy, and Phase 2 and 3 is the time to sell.

As you'll see in a minute when we talk about Phase 3 and Phase 4, declining markets aren't the time to take vacations. Doing lots of homework during those times will make you smarter and at the ready during a Phase 1 market when it *is* time to buy. When the other guys who bought poorly, or bought in the wrong phase of the market, have thrown in the towel, that's when I buy.

During Phase 2, you see the occupancy rates move below the Long Term Occupancy (LT Occupancy line on the diagram) for your market. (Long Term Occupancy means that owners typically need at least a minimum of five years of term remaining.) Every market is different, but in most cases, vacancy is very healthy when it is below 10 percent. Understand that new construction tends to start when vacancy rates drop below 10 and 15 percent, so during this phase new properties begin to be developed. Again, this phase of the cycle does not last days, weeks, or months. It tends to last a few years, so there is no hurry here. If and when I buy during this phase, I really make sure the numbers work and that the property meets my qualifications. There's no way of knowing exactly where the top of the market is or how long it will last, so caution is the rule. If you're going to sell, Phase 2 is when you do it.

TIP Recommendation No. 10: Phase 3 and Phase 4 are not the times to buy. They are the times to research and target properties to buy when Phase 1 kicks in.

In Phase 3, the market is in obvious decline. The guessing game, however, is how far the market will fall and how long it will take. If you bought in Phase 1, you may have bought yourself some strength. But when you are still seeing new construction underway and occupancy rates increasing above the LT Occupancy for your market, recognize the signs that you are in Phase 3. This is known as "hyper supply." Obviously, I never buy during this phase no matter how badly I want a building. I am simply not willing to ride the wave to the bottom, not knowing how far down bottom is. What's the point when I know that there will be plenty of time for deals that make sense in Phase 1? In fact, I'll be buying at bargain prices the properties others foolishly bought in Phase 3! You'll hear people say that there are buying opportunities in every phase. That is true. But it just depends on how strong your constitution is and how deep your pockets are.

Finally, Phase 4 signals market bottom. But there's good news in Phase 4, too. The darker it gets in Phase 4, the better the buying opportunities will be in Phase 1. So if you're on the buying side, relish Phase 4, and take the time to look at properties. Look a lot, but don't buy a thing. There's no way of knowing the bottom until it makes the turn upward. You'll know you're in Phase 4 when vacancy hits its high well above the LT Occupancy and buildings are no longer under construction. The cranes and bulldozers will be replaced by completed buildings sitting vacant. At this time, I do a lot of research so that when Phase 1 kicks in I have pinpointed some ripe buying opportunities. I have lined up investors and financing and spoken to lots of people and told them that when the turnaround happens, I'll give them a call.

While it is helpful to know that real estate is cyclical and in all cases interconnected by asset class, knowing where you are in a market cycle and predicting where it is going is key. Savvy investors can make money anywhere in the cycle, but it takes great skill and experience to make money on the right side of the line.

Further, understand that all real estate follows this pattern and that some asset classes will follow the curve earlier or later than others. For instance, residential real estate is always the first to decline and the first to rebound. Multifamily follows a little later, and retail and commercial after that. Commercial/industrial is usually the last asset class to emerge from a down market; however it is usually the last to enter it. The more familiar you get with watching the real estate cycles, the better you will get at knowing where you are in them. Commercial real estate, for me, gives me plenty of warning to buy, sell, and hold.

THE LAST WORD ON MASTERY

Well, now you know how critical the lay of the land in terms of neighborhood, asset class, and the real estate cycle is to the success of your real estate investment career. But just like in baseball, there's a huge gap between *knowing* how to hit a home run and *hitting* a home run. That gap, of course, is technique, practice, and unfortunately, failure. Becoming master of your real estate universe will take all of those, too. It did for me. I've lived in Phoenix for more than twenty years, and I still drive around the market with real estate eyes. Things are always changing, and I need to keep up with those changes. I develop new systems to make me more efficient as I analyze properties and deals. And I'm not ashamed to say on my first deal I lost $15,000 and didn't even end up with the property! It never closed. These kinds of things happen to everyone, and they are what separate the serious investors from the novices.

The same goes for baseball. Every time the Arcadia Rat Pack stepped out on the diamond, they expected to win, but they also knew that losing was a possibility. Of course we did everything in our power to increase the odds of winning, but on those occasions when we didn't come out on top, our team learned what didn't work, what we had to do better next time, and what subtleties we missed. We didn't make the same mistakes twice, and that's the benefit of losing: the lessons.

Yes, knowledge is just part of the story. But action is the most critical part. All the information in this chapter and within this book as a whole is only as good as your willingness to take action on it. So make a pact with yourself to become master of your real estate universe. Step up to the plate. That first swing is yours to take.

WAYS TO LEARN MORE

CCIM Institute (Certified Commercial Investment Manager)
SIOR (Society of Industrial and Office Realtors)
CRE (Councilors of Real Estate)
NAIOP (National Association of Industrial and Office Properties)
ULI (Urban Land Institute)
LoopNet.com—a great place to learn about your market and research properties
InvestorWords.com—excellent online glossary of terms

A forthcoming Rich Dad Advisor book: *The ABC's of Commercial Real Estate: Your Guide to Finding, Evaluating, and Purchasing Your First Commercial Property in 9 Weeks or Less,* by Craig Coppola

One of the premier commercial real estate brokers in the United States, **Craig Coppola** has been awarded the Arizona Office Broker of the Year six times in the past thirteen years by the National Association of Industrial and Office Properties. He has completed more than twenty-five hundred lease and sale transactions over the past twenty-three years, totaling a value in excess of $2.5 billion. As founding principal of Lee & Associates Arizona, Craig has earned the top three designations in the real estate industry: CCIM, CRE, and SIOR. Only thirty-five people worldwide hold all three.

6

Garrett SUTTON

10 Rules for Real Estate Asset Protection

*G*arrett and I share a common love: the love of the game of rugby. Although we do not remember each other, we played against each other years ago on opposing teams at the Monterrey Rugby Festival. He played for the Hastings Rugby Club of San Francisco, and I played for the Navy/Marine Corps Flight School team from Pensacola, Florida. Unfortunately, we were not the better team, but it was a great game.

In 2003, Garrett and I traveled to Sydney, Australia, to watch the Rugby World Cup. It is in our humble opinion that we witnessed the greatest game of rugby ever played. It was the final match between England and Australia. For as long as I live, I will always remember that game and feel honored to have been a spectator in the stands as we watched England beat Australia in overtime by a score of twenty to seventeen.

Besides being a rugby player, Garrett is an attorney. He is a very important attorney. He specializes in asset protection, which is a vital area of law because in today's world there are more attorneys who want to steal your assets than there are who want to protect them. One of the reasons why Kim and I can sleep soundly at night is because Garrett is an expert at making sure our assets are protected. This does not mean we are totally protected. This means Garrett has built legal firewalls around different assets. It means we might lose one or two properties, but we will not lose everything.

In today's litigious world, having a Garrett Sutton on your side is vital for anyone who wants to grow rich and get a good night's sleep, too.

—ROBERT KIYOSAKI

As a Rich Dad's Advisor, one of the questions I am most frequently asked is: "How can I protect my real estate?"

In answering this key question, a pattern of repetitive follow-up queries always ensues such that after several years I have been able to distill all of the issues and concerns into what I call the "10 Rules for Protecting Your Real Estate."

By knowing, following, and implementing these ten rules, you will not only properly protect your assets, but you will also avoid the many pitfalls placed in your path by the overpriced asset protection "gurus" and service providers out there who are more interested in your money than your situation. You will have the confidence to say "No" to these people because you will know more than they do.

Your important and easily acquired education lies ahead. Let's begin.

RULE NO. 1: INSURANCE IS NEVER A COMPLETE ASSET PROTECTION STRATEGY

Or: Never let a commissioned salesperson tell you how to protect your assets. At Rich Dad events around the country I am always confronted by the person who asserts that his insurance agent has assured him that asset protection is a hoax and that all that is needed is a good insurance policy. I have to laugh because there are so many instances of insurance companies failing to cover real estate investors and others under the provisions of their policies, that there is a whole area of law named after the situation. It is called "Bad Faith Litigation," as in the bad faith that occurs when insurance companies say they will cover you, collect your premiums, and then, heaven forbid, a claim arises and they find reasons not to cover you.

Never forget that insurance companies have an economic incentive not to cover you. As is clearly obvious, the less they pay out in claims, the more money they make. Also never forget that insurance agents receive a commission on all the policies they sell. So when an insurance agent says that all you need is insurance instead of asset protection, please remember where his incentive lies. It is also important to acknowledge that insurance agents are not licensed to give legal advice. You would have to question the motives of one who would do so.

Real Life Story: The Plight of "Paul"

A client of mine, we'll call Paul, initially believed in the strident assertions of his "insurance professional." Instead of combining insurance with entities for his Aspen, Colorado, fourplex, he obtained only an insurance policy on the mountain property. He held title to the fourplex in his individual name.

Despite the 100 percent insurance protection guarantees of his agent, the policy was very clear that the company would not cover any claims related to an avalanche.

Sure enough, Paul's fourplex was greatly damaged in a swift and freakish avalanche. The insurance company quite correctly refused to cover the claim. Its policy expressly excluded avalanche damage.

Paul was furious at his agent who, besides assuring that the pricey policy covered everything and that no other protection was needed, had never pointed out the very clear policy exclusions. By relying on his agent and not taking any other protective steps, all of Paul's assets were exposed to the avalanche claim.

Paul's problem was completely avoidable. If he had relied on a team of advisors, including an asset protection attorney, the situation where a highly commissioned salesperson got away with giving legal advice would never have occurred.

Given my healthy skepticism of the insurance industry, you would think that I would advocate the exclusive use of asset protection entities without the use of any insurance at all.

TIP Insurance is the first line of defense when protecting assets. The proper use of asset protection strategies is this second line of defense.

But to the contrary, I believe that insurance is the first line of defense when protecting assets. Many insurance companies are forthright in their dealings and will honor their coverage commitments. Others, with the help of a legal nudge, will do the right thing. So I always advocate the reasonable use of insurance as a protection strategy. However, because we know that a certain percentage of insurance companies will use exclusions and find reasons not to cover you, you most certainly need another defense mechanism. The proper use of asset protection strategies is this second line of defense. As we will learn in this section, asset protection is not difficult or expensive, but it is required if you are to succeed at building real estate wealth.

Now that we know that insurance alone will not completely protect us, let's review further ways to *not* protect your real estate before we get to the promised land of beneficial strategies in later rules.

Rule No. 2: The Two Most Common Ways of Taking Title to Your Real Estate Do Not Provide Asset Protection

Or: Why to avoid joint tenancies and tenants in common.

It is indeed ironic that the two most common and popular methods of taking title to your real estate provide you with the least protection. Joint tenancy is one of the most popular forms of holding title because it provides for a right of survivorship. This works such that if one party dies the other joint tenant becomes the sole owner by operation of law, meaning it happens automatically. Joint tenancy is popular with husband and wife couples. If the husband, for example, passes away first, then the wife has complete control of the property without having to go to court or file new deeds.

The problem for real estate investors is twofold. First, joint tenancies offer no asset protection. Suppose Peter, Paul, and Coco own a sixplex as joint tenants. If Paul gets sued, his creditor can reach Paul's joint tenancy interest. Peter and Coco now have a new partner in the sixplex, most likely someone, who after suing their friend and barging their way in, they don't like right off the bat. As well, this new partner can bring a partition lawsuit to force a sale of the property. It can get expensive in legal fees and messy in court.

Secondly, the right of survivorship feature that makes joint tenancies easy and attractive to married couples is the same feature that makes them so scary and abhorrent to investors. Let's take another look at the joint tenancy that holds Peter, Paul, and Coco's sixplex. Suppose Coco were to die in a fashion industry disaster. Her interest in the sixplex is automatically terminated. She can't pass her interest on to her heirs because Peter and Paul, by operation of law, are now the two remaining joint tenants on title.

Savvy investors will not invest with you if you propose taking title as joint tenants. The good ones know that you should never put yourself in a position where someone will benefit from your demise. That's what you are doing with joint tenancies. I will withhold comment on the state of marriage today and why so many knowledgeable spouses continue to use joint tenancies. But for investors it is not the right choice.

TIP Savvy investors will not invest with you if you propose taking title as joint tenants.

Similarly, but with one exception, taking title as tenants in common is not the best course, either. Again, there is no asset protection. In our example, if Peter gets sued, Paul and Coco can find themselves with a new and unwanted partner. Once again, the partner can bring a partition suit to force a sale of the property. As well, if there is a lawsuit involving the property (i.e., a tenant sues over a defective water heater) the individual tenants in common (or individual joint tenants, for that matter) can be held personally responsible. All of their personal assets can be exposed to such a claim. Holding title to any property as individual tenants in common does not make good sense in our very litigious world. In fact, it can make you more of a target.

The one exception for using tenants in common to hold title is when investors take their interest not as exposed individuals but with protected entities. In a TiC situation ("TiC" stands for tenants in common) investors come together from 1031 exchanges or with investment money to buy a large property. The large property is held as a tenancy in common with all the various investors holding their specific TiC interest through a protective entity such as a LLC (limited liability company).

A chart helps to illustrate:

The Difference Between Individual Tenants in Common and Tenants in Common (TiC)

All assets personally exposed to all claims   *Outside assets protected from all claims*

FIGURE 6.1

While I may have let the cat out of the bag (that LLCs are good entities for real estate), it is my belief that most of you may have already known this. Still, there are a few more rules involving what not to use before we get to positive asset protection territory.

Rule No. 3: Never Hold Real Estate in a C Corporation

Or: Fire the professional who even suggests such a thing.

One of the cardinal sins of real estate asset protection is to take title in the name of a C corporation. While there are certainly advantages to using a C corporation in business (which are discussed in my Rich Dad's Advisor book *Own Your Own Corporation*) there is a huge disadvantage to using a C corporation for real estate, which can be expressed in one word: taxes.

As you probably know, C corporations face a double tax. You pay taxes once at the company level and then again when dividends are distributed to shareholders. With an S corporation, LLC, or LP you pay tax only once at the company level. A chart graphically illustrates the difference between double taxation and flow-through taxation.

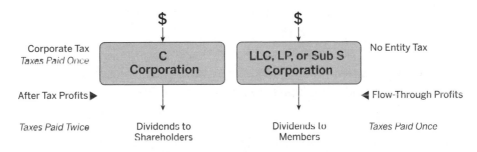

FIGURE 6.2

So what happens when you have a capital gain on the sale of real estate held by a C corporation? You pay a lot more in taxes.

Consider the situation in which a $500,000 long-term capital gain is realized on the sale of real estate held for longer than one year.

As the chart on p. 114 indicates, you will pay $144,500 more in federal taxes by using a C corporation instead of an LLC. Does Uncle Sam want you to use a C corporation? Of course. Will investors likely join your deal if you propose using a C corporation? Probably not. They'll know you don't know what you are doing. Avoid the professional who advises you to use a C corporation to hold any interest in real estate. They just don't know what they are doing—to your later detriment.

C Corporation

$500,000	Gain
–170,000	Less 34% corporate tax *(35% for larger corporations)*
$330,000	
– 49,500	Less 15% tax to shareholder on distributions
$280,500	**Amount after tax**

LLC

$500,000	Gain
– 75,000	Less 15% capital gain tax
$425,000	**Amount after tax**

FIGURE 6.3

TIP Avoid the professional who advises you to use a C corporation to hold any interest in real estate.

We frequently have clients discuss how some asset protection "guru" or other promoter advised them to set up their structure as follows:

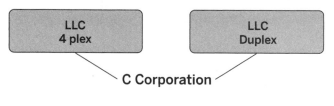

FIGURE 6.4

The rationale is that the two pieces of rental property are owned by the LLCs and each LLC is in turn owned by a C corporation. The gurus will state that all kinds of deductions can be taken with a C corporation. The problem is that, as flow-through entities, the profits flow from the LLCs to a double tax C corporation. You are still in a bad tax position.

If you are intent on using a C corporation in your entity mix (and please be cautious of promoters who overly tout the supposed glorious benefits of the C corporation) a better scenario is the following:

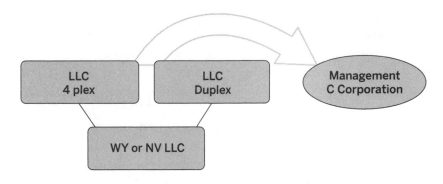

FIGURE 6.5

In the structure above, the title-holding LLCs are held by an asset protecting Wyoming or Nevada LLC, thus providing flow-through taxation throughout the structure. For those desiring the write-offs of a C corporation, a management C corporation is used. Each title-holding LLC pays a management fee to the corporation so their benefits are obtained. But there is no ownership of real estate through the C corporation, thus avoiding the double taxation of profits we had in the first instance.

Please also beware of promoters who would have you set up more entities than you need. The management corporation may provide some benefits in later years when there is plenty of cash flow. But at the start, do you really need one? Probably not. So be very cautious of those promoters who want what is in their best interest and not yours.

RULE NO. 4: OFFSHORE STRATEGIES DO NOT WORK FOR ONSHORE REAL ESTATE

Or: What have you been smoking?

As you have probably noticed, throughout this chapter and in my other writings I have found the need to warn against the slick and salesy gurus and promoters with their incredible claims and come-ons. Certainly some of the most outrageous claims come from the offshore promoters who offer tax savings and absolute privacy. Of course, they never mention the existing United States rules and regulations that do, in fact, run contrary to their claims. In most cases, these people actually live on small Caribbean Islands or in European principalities beyond the reach of U.S. authorities. They can say what they want.

But as a U.S. citizen, can you afford to listen to those who intentionally misrepresent U.S. laws? Of course not.

To further your caution, let's review what can happen when offshore asset protection is used in attempt to protect U.S. real estate.

Real Life Story: John's Bad Day

John was a doctor in California. He had worked hard and paid his taxes. He owned a twenty-unit Roseville apartment building free and clear and a significant brokerage account. He felt as if he were doing well, but the combination of the malpractice and real estate litigation explosion and the ravenous demands of both the IRS and California's notorious state tax collector—the Franchise Tax Board—had led John down the path of considering offshore options.

A promoter from the Caribbean Island of Nevis held a seminar for doctors and dentists in John's hometown. The self-styled asset protection man with glowing testimonials and advanced degrees from schools John had not heard of, laid out a comprehensive and seamless case for using Nevis structures to protect assets. The promoter boldly claimed that by using offshore trusts John could obtain complete privacy and incredible tax savings. His strategy was graphically represented as follows:

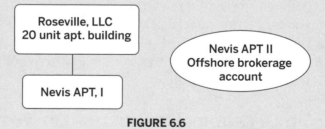

FIGURE 6.6

The promoter indicated that John would not have to pay any taxes. Because the apartment building LLC was owned by the Nevis APT ("asset protection trust"), profits generated from rents could pass offshore without taxes. The domestic LLC would simply file zero return. The promoter further stated that insurance was not needed on the apartment building because it was now in a bulletproof structure. As well, by moving John's significant brokerage account into the second APT, profits could be generated offshore without U.S. or California taxes. Better yet, the monies could be accessed by John, tax free, into the United States by simply requesting the Nevis trustee—who received $3,000 a year for the service—wire the money.

John followed the promoter's advice, paid the $25,000 for setting it all up, and in the first year his financial condition greatly improved. With his assets offshore and no onshore taxes paid, he was doing really well. He wondered why everyone didn't do this. Then, in one day, two problems arose. He was sued for malpractice by a patient and a tenant fell at the apartment building.

When the tenant's claim was made, John informed the claimants that there was no insurance. When the tenant's lawyer indicated they would sue anyway, John calmly replied that the building was owned by a bulletproof offshore asset protection trust.

The lawyer laughed and said John needed to get a local attorney to advise him. When John did so he learned the bitter truth: You can't protect U.S. real estate with offshore entities. The apartment building was located in California and, as such, California courts had jurisdiction. This was the law in all fifty states. The tenant could bring a claim against the LLC, and with no insurance in place, the tenant could reach the entire free-and-clear equity in the apartment building. The fact that the LLC was owned by an offshore APT was of absolutely no consequence and offered zero protection.

John also spoke to his new lawyer about the malpractice claim. As a doctor, John was sued individually. But he felt protected because his brokerage assets were privately all held offshore. This was when the second shoe dropped.

The lawyer explained that if John had followed all the tax reporting requirements associated with offshore entities, a creditor could easily learn what John owned.

John was incredulous. The promoter had assured him that he had bulletproof privacy and asset protection without the requirement of taxes or even tax reporting. The lawyer had seen other professionals lured in before. He presented John with the following chart detailing all the reporting requirements:

TABLE 6.1

IRS Requirement	IRS Rule
U.S. persons must report all gratuitous and nongratuitous transfers to a foreign trust.	Section 6048, Section 1494
Foreign trusts owned by U.S. persons must file an annual tax return on IRS Form 3520-A. U.S. persons are subject to a 5% penalty against the value of offshore assets each year for failure to file.	Sections 671 to 679
U.S. persons receiving offshore distributions, whether taxable or nontaxable, must report them or pay 35% penalty.	Section 6677(a)
Foreign trusts owned by U.S. persons must appoint a U.S. agent so that the IRS may examine offshore records.	Sections 7602 to 7604

CONTINUED

CONTINUED

> John now realized that everything the promoter said was false. Given the IRS rules, there was no privacy, no tax savings, and no bulletproof protection. With the help of his new lawyer, John cleaned up the offshore mess by paying significant IRS penalties and fees. A demand to the Nevis promoter for the $25,000 John was lured into paying for worthless strategies and documents went unanswered.

TIP Offshore strategies do not work for onshore real estate.

RULE NO. 5: LIVING TRUSTS OFFER NO ASSET PROTECTION

Or: Will you please stop listening to these guys?

Many of you have seen the ads touting the significant benefits of living trusts. Invariably, one of the great features mentioned is the ability of these trusts to protect your assets.

While living trusts do offer certain advantages it is very important to clearly recognize the one benefit they do not offer: asset protection.

Let's take a closer look.

Primarily used for estate planning, the key benefit of a living trust is to avoid probate. If you have only a will, or pass without a will, the distribution of your estate is supervised by a local probate court. The probate process is long and time consuming and a matter of public record, meaning that anyone can view the file to see what assets are involved, and perhaps challenge the distribution.

As well, the attorney's fees awarded for probate proceedings can be quite lucrative for the lawyers involved. For example, with a $1 million primary residence passing through a California probate, the court awards a statutorily set attorney's fee of $23,000. An executor is entitled to the same amount. These fees are due, even if the home is fully encumbered by loans, and thus without equity to pay the fees.

The solution is to set up a living trust, which is a trust document allowing you to use an appointed trustee, typically a surviving spouse or other family member, to distribute your assets without the need for probate court assistance or review. The several thousand dollars spent on a living trust can easily save many more thousands of dollars in probate fees.

The living trust also features a great deal of flexibility. It is a revocable trust, meaning you can change its terms and/or beneficiaries at any time. But that also means it does not offer any asset protection. Because it can be easily altered, a judgment creditor can get a court order forcing a transfer of any property from the trust to the litigation party.

Despite this factual lack of asset protection, living trust promoters continue to sell their services as offering such protection. When challenged, they will parse and narrow their overly broad claims to suggest that their living trusts help protect against creditor claims because they avoid the very public probate process. And this is true. But just as deciding not to sunbathe completely in the nude is not the same as the judicious use of sunscreen, avoiding a fully public probate is not the same as proper asset protection. By relying only on the former examples, you are going to get burned.

Asset Protection

Probate Avoidance

FIGURE 6.7

Real Life Story: Mario's Mistake

A client of mine named Mario came to me after titling all of his assets—his house, a rental fourplex, and a significant brokerage account—in the name of his living trust. The formal name for the trust—The Mario T. and Carmen O. Sanchez Revocable Trust dated June 10, 2004—was given to the county recorder and assessor for taking title to the two real estate properties. The Smith Barney broker took the same name for the Sanchez's brokerage account.

Mario indicated that the seminar promoter who set up his living trust assured him that his assets were now fully protected. But now he was being sued by a tenant who fell at the fourplex, and he wanted a second opinion.

It was not pleasant to inform Mario that his assets were not protected. By titling everything in his living trust's name, all of his assets were exposed to the tenant's claim.

When Mario asked if he could re-title everything into a more protective structure, it was even more difficult to explain that it was now too late to do so. Once you've been sued, or even threatened with suit, it is too late for asset protection.

The next question clients always have is: How do they combine the benefit of a living trust's probate avoidance with the necessity of asset protection? The answer is simple, and it is graphically charted in Figure 6.7: The LLC is on title with the county recorder as owning the fourplex. We have asset protection at this level. The living trust owns the membership interests in XYZ, LLC. If both Mario and Carmen die, the living trust document will dictate who owns the LLC without the need for court supervision. At this level we have probate avoidance.

TIP You can't rely on the LLC for probate avoidance, and you can never count on the living trust for asset protection, but in concert you can get both.

Properly structured LLCs and living trusts work well together and complement each other. You can't rely on the LLC for probate avoidance, and you can never count on the living trust for asset protection, but in concert you can get both.

RULE NO. 6: LAND TRUSTS OFFER PRIVACY BUT NOT ASSET PROTECTION

Or: Why privacy is not enough.
For many of the same reasons a living trust offers no asset protection, neither does a land trust offer asset protection. In fact, a land trust is very similar to a living trust. In both, you are transferring assets to a trust administered by a trustee for your benefit.

According to the seminar promoters, the big benefit of a land trust is its privacy. By using a trustee other than yourself, your name can be kept off the chain of title and public records. And while privacy is a good thing in this day and age, it is not a perfect substitute for asset protection.

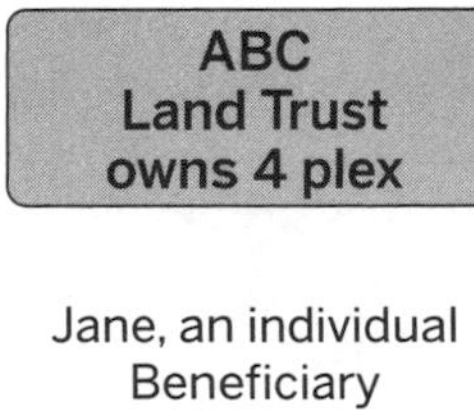

It is important to understand the structure of a land trust in order to appreciate why asset protection is not inherent.

In our chart, Joe is identified on public records as being the trustee, but Jane, as beneficiary, is not anywhere identified. In this manner, privacy can be achieved.

But the land trust, like the living trust, does not protect Jane. If there is a lawsuit involving the fourplex, a judgment rendered is against the ben-

ABC
Land Trust
owns 4 plex

Jane, an individual
Beneficiary

FIGURE 6.8

eficiary. If Jane, as an individual, is the beneficiary, then any judgment is against her personally, and all of her personally held assets are exposed.

There are two better ways to handle it. In example A, we show the beneficiary to be an LLC.

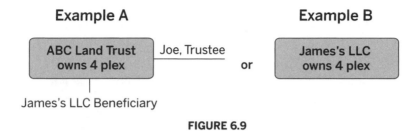

Example A   Example B

ABC Land Trust owns 4 plex — Joe, Trustee

or

James's LLC owns 4 plex

James's LLC Beneficiary

FIGURE 6.9

In this way, a judgment attained against the beneficiary is rendered against a limited liability entity. James's personal assets are not exposed.

Of course, this structure entails setting up two structures—the land trust and the LLC—as well as paying the trustee to serve every year. The same asset protection is attained by just setting up one entity, the LLC, as in example B.

TIP If privacy is important you can certainly have the manager of the LLC be a nominee, a person other than yourself.

If privacy is important you can certainly have the manager of the LLC be a nominee, a person other than yourself. Our firm charges $650 a year for this service. Others may charge more or less. But in this way you can achieve asset protection and privacy, without the need to set up a land trust.

RULE NO. 7: LLCS AND LPS ARE EXCELLENT ASSET PROTECTION ENTITIES

Or: Why you want the charging order.
So, finally at rule seven we are getting to the good stuff. But as I mentioned, there is so much misinformation out there that I felt it was important to first dispel the myths and outright lies. With all that completed, I can now state that LLCs and LPs offer excellent asset protection via the *charging order*.

Before reviewing the charging order, the difference between LLCs and LPs must be explained. With an LP you must have at least one general partner and one limited partner. The general partner, if an individual, is personally responsible for the LP's activities. To encapsulate that unlimited liability you must form a limited liability entity—a corporation or an LLC—to be the general partner. While you are now fully protected, it is important to remember that you have had to form two entities: first, the LP, and then second, a corporation or LLC to be the general partner of the LP. With the LLC you need to form only one entity, the LLC. Everyone is protected within the LLC. While LPs certainly have their place, due to the need for only one entity instead of two, we shall use the LLC example from here on out.

When it comes to protecting your real estate, we must also distinguish between attacks. A chart helps to explain:

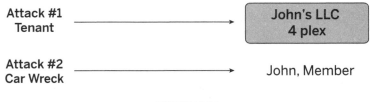

FIGURE 6.10

In Attack No. 1, a tenant sues the LLC over a broken stairway. If successful, the tenant can get what is inside the LLC—the fourplex—subject to any deeds of trusts against the property.

But if the tenant can get the equity in the property, you ask, why even bother with an LLC? Because without the LLC, the tenant could get everything John owns—his house and bank account and everything else. The LLC limits the tenant to just what's in the LLC and shields your outside assets from attack.

In Attack No. 2, John gets in a car wreck, his insurance company won't cover him, and a judgment creditor (the person who won in court; we'll call him Nate) is seeking to get paid. Because the car wreck had nothing to do with the real estate, Nate, the judgment creditor, can't sue John's LLC directly. Instead, Nate must go after John's membership interest in the LLC.

This is where the charging order comes into play. The charging order rule provides that Nate can't take possession of John's membership interest, his ownership in the LLC. If Nate could, he could then sell the fourplex and get paid. (And please note, this is what can happen with a corporation. The judgment creditor gets the shares and takes control and sells all the corporate assets. Nevada, to date, is the only state that has extended charging order protections to corporate shares in corporations with between two and seventy-five shareholders.)

The charging order instead allows Nate to stand in John's shoes as a member and receive distributions.

But what if no distributions are made? Then Nate gets nothing. He has to wait to be paid. But what if money is made, there are taxes due, but no money is distributed to even pay the taxes? This is called phantom income, and is frustrating to creditors. Under the charging order, Nate is standing in John's shoes. So he must pay the taxes on money he did not receive.

Most people do not want to be put in this position, which is why the proper use of LLCs and LPs is an excellent deterrent to frivolous litigation. Not many people want to fight it out in court to not receive any money *and* have to pay taxes on the money they didn't receive. Using LLCs and LPs can be an aid in settlement discussions. They can even prevent a lawsuit from being filed in the first place.

TIP Using LLCs and LPs can be an aid in settlement discussions. They can even prevent a lawsuit from being filed in the first place.

Charging order rules vary from state to state. Nevada and Wyoming have the strongest laws. In those states, the exclusive creditor remedy is the charging order. California has the weakest law. There are two California court cases allowing creditors to pierce through and sell off LLC and LP assets to pay the creditor.

So if you are going to buy property in California or one of the many other states with weak asset protection laws (including Georgia), you have the choice of setting up your LLC or LP in the state where the property is located or forming in Nevada or Wyoming, and then qualifying in the state where the property is located. The process of qualifying involves submitting, for example, the Wyoming LLC papers and appropriate fees to the California secretary of state's office. If properly done it is always granted and keeps you within the law.

But the benefit is that if you get sued as in Attack No. 2, Wyoming or Nevada law applies, not California law. A judgment creditor has to hire a Wyoming or Nevada lawyer to fight a very uphill battle. This is what you want: a very strong reason for predators to leave you alone.

More information on this is found in my book, *How to Use Limited Liability Companies and Limited Partnerships* (SuccessDNA, 2009).

RULE NO. 8: SEGREGATION OF ASSETS IS GOOD

Or: Let's not put all of our eggs in one basket.
Since we've learned that LLCs and LPs are good entities for holding and protecting our real estate, the question then becomes: How many properties do I put in each entity?

This is a judgment call on your part. But consider these scenarios involving Liz, who owns twelve properties:

Scenario #1

LLC 12 properties

Scenario #2

LLC 3 properties	LLC 3 properties	LLC 3 properties	LLC 3 properties

Scenario #3

LLC 1 property	LLC 1 property	LLC 1 property	LLC 1 property
LLC 1 property	LLC 1 property	LLC 1 property	LLC 1 property
LLC 1 property	LLC 1 property	LLC 1 property	LLC 1 property

FIGURE 6.11

In Scenario 1, if a tenant sues over a problem at one property, the other eleven properties are exposed to the attack. In Scenario 2, with three properties in each LLC, only two additional properties are exposed if Liz is sued. Of course, in Scenario 3 with only one property in each LLC, only one property is exposed.

I would never suggest a client hold twelve properties in one LLC. With that many properties, your LLC is a rich target. In my experience, most of my clients choose somewhere between Scenario 2 and 3. As is evident, the best asset protection is obtained through Scenario 3. Only one property is exposed to any one attack.

But some clients don't want to pay the one-time initial set-up fees and continuing annual fees for twelve entities. In a state like California, where the annual fee is $800 per entity, $9,600 a year for twelve entities is rather daunting. So the choice of using one LLC to hold three properties is an option. It is your call. But once again, the fewer properties you hold in each entity, the better protected you will be.

Due to these issues, a new type of LLC is being touted to help reduce the number of LLCs you need to form, called the "Series LLC." Unfortunately, I cannot recommend this new creature. It attempts to place separate properties into separate series under one LLC, as follows:

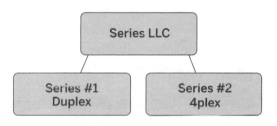

FIGURE 6.12

The supposed benefit is that by setting up one LLC you can independently protect two properties. The idea is that within the Series LLC there is an *internal liabilities shield* whereby a claim against the duplex in Series 1 does not affect the fourplex in Series 2. The problem is there is no guidance whether or not this supposed internal liability shield will be upheld. There are no court cases in the subject, and conceptually the strategy may be difficult for a court to uphold. Can two properties in the same state-chartered entity be protected from each other? As well, what if one series goes bankrupt? Will the other series be protected? No one knows.

The California tax authorities (the very aggressive Franchise Tax Board) have their opinion. If you are going to try and set up one series to hold two properties, they are going to charge you $800 per series, the same as if you had set up two separate LLCs to begin with.

Of course, by setting up two separate LLCs you have the certainty of separateness, rather than hoping that someday a court will miraculously rule that the muddled and imperfect concept of an internal liability shield actually makes sense.

TIP Stay away from promoters who would put you into this untested entity called the Series LLC.

Interestingly, the American Bar Association brought together the nation's brightest lawyers to review LLC developments. After looking at the Series LLC they declined to endorse the whole concept. Stay away from promoters who would put you into this untested entity called the Series LLC.

RULE NO. 9: TRANSFER TITLE INTO YOUR ENTITY

Or: What's the point if you don't?

All right, so you have set up one or more LLCs to protect your real estate. You have the articles properly filed with the state. You have approved and signed the operating agreement governing how the LLC will run. You have signed the minutes of the first meeting and issued the membership certificates. All the important documents are in one binder in a safe place.

And remember, if all these steps are not taken, you are not ready. Beware of promoters who will sell you the articles for just $99 but will not provide you with an operating agreement, meeting minutes, and membership certificates. Our firm charges $695 (or less if you are with Rich Dad) plus state filing fees for the complete package—binder and all—with all your documents prepared and finalized according to your specific needs, along with live phone support through the whole process. You have the certainty of knowing that everything is in order.

TIP You've formed the asset protection entity. The next step is to transfer title to the property into the LLC.

So assuming that everything is in order, now what?

Just because you have your asset protection entity in place, are your real estate assets now protected? No, not yet. You must take the next step, which is to transfer title to the property into the name of the LLC.

You must prepare a grant deed transferring ownership of your fourplex, for example, from John Jones, as an individual, to the Jones Real Estate, LLC.

Several questions arise during this process.

FIGURE 6.13

First, is this a taxable event? Will the IRS or my state taxing authority assess taxes when this happens? The answer is no. This is not a sale of the property—you are not receiving any money in this transaction. Instead, it is a transfer. You are transferring the property from yourself (as an individual) to yourself (your new 100-percent-owned LLC).

The property goes into the LLC at its basis, which is the amount you paid for the property originally. That basis, for tax purposes, remains the same once the property is in the LLC. So, for example, if you paid $250,000 for your fourplex, the basis of $250,000 remains once it is titled in the LLC's name. There is no gain in the transaction, and with no gain there are no capital gain or ordinary income taxes.

If John Jones added new members (owners) into Jones Real Estate, LLC before or after the transfer, there could be a taxable event. Be sure to consult with your advisors prior to any change in ownership.

The next question is: Are there any transfer taxes? The answer is: It depends.

Transfer taxes, a tax based upon the value of the property being transferred, vary from state to state. Many states have an exception to their transfer taxes. If you are transferring the property from yourself as an individual to yourself as an LLC, there is no tax. Check with your local advisors to understand your local rules.

Some states are very tricky, though. In Nevada, you are free to transfer title into your LLC. But if you transfer it from the LLC back to yourself there is a transfer tax. This situation occurs when you are refinancing and the lender wants title to be in your name when the new first deed of trust attaches. Resist the lender's attempts to require this. He will argue that he doesn't have security if title is in the LLC. That is nonsense. With title in the LLC, he will have your personal guarantee for the loan and a first deed of trust against the property, the same as if it was in your individual name. He is equally protected in either situation. Seek out lenders who are enlightened as to asset protection. They do exist.

One state is very costly when it comes to transfer taxes. Pennsylvania charges a 2 percent tax on the value of the property. So if you have a million dollar property with a mortgage of $950,000, you will still pay $20,000 (2 percent of $1 million) for the privilege of holding title in the name of your LLC. Ouch.

The best course in all of this is to take title in the name of your LLC when you first buy the property. With title in the proper entity at the start there is no need for a later transfer, thus no issue of transfer taxes. There are lenders who will let you take title at closing in the name of the LLC (or your LP). You can view the LLCLoan.com Web site for more information.

Speaking of banks and lenders, the next questions is: Will they call the loan if I transfer title? In dealing with clients, I have heard numerous times about the attitude of lenders regarding transferring title into an LLC. In their reptilian mind-set, they feel as if you are trying to hide assets from them and deny them their due. Of course, as mentioned, if the lender has your personal guarantee and a first deed of trust on the property, he is protected whether it is in your name or the LLC's name.

But that logic is lost on the functionaries at most lenders. They will argue that if you make the transfer they will enforce the due-on-sale clause, which states that the loan is due when you sell the property. Of course you haven't sold the property; you transferred it to yourself.

So what do you do?

In my experience it comes down to: Is it better to ask for permission or forgiveness? If you ask most lenders, as if by reflex, they will say no. But if you just go ahead and make the transfer without asking you can always say you are sorry later. The chances are good you will never have such a conversation. In my dealings, the lenders have never called a note. Will you be the first one? I don't know. But as long as you keep making the monthly payments, there is a very good chance that they are not going to call the loan. Why would they want to create such trouble for themselves, especially when they are being paid? If in some bizarre case they do, refinance with a lender comfortable with LLCs. It's not as if you are going to lose your property if they call the note.

But some of you may be overly cautious in this realm, which is fine. If you are willing to spend a little more money, there is another way to skin the cat.

Federal law holds that a lender can't prevent you from transferring title from your individual name to your living trust. Land trusts look like, and can be named like, a living trust. So by forming a land trust and transferring title into it, you may be able to accomplish your goals.

The extra money involved is the preparation of a land trust. Our firm charges $395 for such a document; others may charge more or less. But remember, as discussed in Rules 5 and 6, neither land trusts nor living trusts offer asset protection. So when utilizing this strategy you still need to form that LLC and name the LLC as beneficiary of the land trust.

With the title transferred to the land trust and an LLC as beneficiary of the land trust you may be able to get the protection you need without irrational lender interference.

The only group you do need to notify when you transfer title is your insurance company. It needs to know the policy is in your LLC name and not in your personal name. Otherwise, and this does happen, your friendly insurance company may claim it was insuring you as an individual, not your LLC, and use that as an excuse to deny any coverage in the event of a problem at the property. And while the insurance company may notify the lender of the change in insureds, that usually does not lead to due-on-sale threats.

A final question always arises as to why to use a grant deed instead of a quit claim deed to transfer the title. A quit claim deed merely transfers everything you claim you may own to the next party. A grant deed is a much more affirmative grant of property rights. As such, in many cases, title insurance coverage flows to the next party with a grant deed. Since you are essentially transferring property from yourself to yourself, it makes sense to give yourself the most complete rights you can. Use a grant deed.

RULE NO. 10: DON'T SET UP MORE ENTITIES THAN NECESSARY

Or: Beware of promoters telling you otherwise.
Several years ago I was at a real estate event in San Francisco. A lady approached me after hearing my speech, in which I argued that people should not go overboard and set up more entities than are needed.

I was shocked by her story.

Jane was looking to invest in her first duplex. She had previously attended a seminar on asset protection given by a self-styled asset protection guru. The seminar had been sponsored by a local real estate organization. She trusted that the group would provide her only with competent service providers.

The asset protection guy indicated that she needed the following structure for protection: (See Figure 6.14.)

Jane stated that the man convinced her that for the necessary protection she:

1. Needed the LP to hold her LLC. The LP was then, in turn, owned by the Nevada Asset Protection Trust and the Offshore Asset Protection Trust. These structures gave her extra layers of protection.

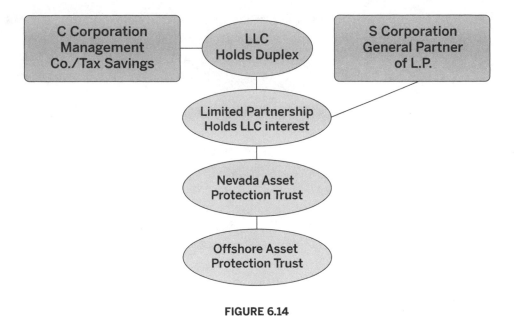

FIGURE 6.14

2. Needed an S corporation to manage the LP in order to achieve necessary asset protection.

3. Needed the C corporation to manage the LLC in order to achieve significant tax savings.

The cost of this structure was $20,000. The annual fees were more than $5,000 to maintain all the entities. Jane was in tears because after spending such a large sum of money for asset protection, she no longer had enough money for the down payment on her duplex.

I told her the truth. She had spent way too much money. The asset protection man's arguments were false. Extra layers of entities do not necessarily provide extra layers of protection. If you aren't making any money yet, you don't really need a C corporation to save on taxes. The structure they created was designed for their profit, not her needs. Jane asked me to give her a chart of what she needed to protect her duplex. It took five seconds to chart her strategy:

FIGURE 6.15

Jane was in shock. She asked how the local real estate group promoter, a person she trusted, could let such a snake in the door to present to them. I told her something that was an open secret in that business. The local promoter in many cases receives 50 percent of what the service provider sells. As such, there is a powerful economic incentive for local promoters to tout the value, integrity, and importance of the service provider, as well as the urgent need for the services offered. In Jane's case, the local promoter may have made as much as $10,000 for doing so.

Jane calculated that fifteen people had signed up for all this and figured the promoter must have cleared a total of $150,000 at the one asset protection event. She was furious and sickened by what had happened. She vowed never to invest in real estate. I tried to counsel her but could not. She had gone through a horrible experience and was adamant that her decision was final.

Do not let Jane's experience be yours. Real estate is an excellent way to build wealth, but at some points during your journey you will need to be able to navigate through shark-infested waters.

Important Tips

- Engage in critical thinking.
- Ask yourself if the "expert" really is such an expert.
- Ask yourself if the services are for your legal benefit or the expert's financial benefit.
- Use healthy skepticism and old-fashioned due diligence.
- Check around, and don't bite at the first supposedly "discounted" offer.

These tips will work out to your advantage.

That said, asset protection, as we have seen, is important. You want to take the necessary steps to protect your real estate assets and your financial future. The correct use of entities will greatly assist you in achieving this goal.

Remember, asset protection is neither overly difficult nor outrageously expensive. And with critical thinking, never allow someone to tell you it is.

Good luck in all your asset-protected real estate investing.

WHERE TO LEARN MORE

www.corporatedirect.com
www.sutlaw.com
www.successdna.com

 **Garrett Sutton** is a Rich Dad's Advisor and is the author of *Own Your Own Corporation*, *The ABC's of Getting Out of Debt*, *The ABC's of Writing Winning Business Plans*, and *How to Buy and Sell a Business*. He is also the co-author of *Real Estate Advantages*. Garrett is an attorney with more than twenty-five years experience in assisting individuals and businesses to determine their appropriate corporate structure, limit their liability, protect their assets, and advance their financial, personal, and credit success goals. He has been featured in the *Wall Street Journal* and the *New York Times*, among others. His firm, Sutton Law Center, has offices in Reno, Nevada; Jackson Hole, Wyoming; and Rocklin, California, and accepts new clients at (800) 700-1430.

Of Marbles and Capital

This book is called The Real Book of Real Estate *because the people I chose to be a part of it are real-life real estate investors. They are not people who just teach real estate and make their money teaching. Wayne like the others who I asked to be part of this book, makes his money doing what he teaches. He is one of the best real estate investors and one of the best finance guys I know. He is, like all of the advisors in this book, doing his own deals while teaching others how to be rich using the same methods and formulas he uses himself. I am always leery of people who give advice and say, "Trust me." Then they don't do what they are telling me to do. Those are not the kind of teachers I want around me. And they are not the kind of teachers who are in this book. This book is real people and real-life real estate strategies that they use to build wealth.*

One of the things I like most about Wayne is how his brain goes into overdrive whenever he sees a roadblock in the way of his or one of his client's goals. When it comes to finance, nothing stops Wayne's creative mind. Obstacles become excuses for Wayne to find innovative ways to get around them.

Wayne is an excellent teacher, and he has taught me more through example and through the deals we do together than even he probably knows. He can take things that are very complex and make them simple so that I can understand them. When I first met Wayne, I could tell from the way he talked and the way he carried himself that he spoke from years of experience, successes, and failures. Life is the best teacher, and that's why Wayne's chapters and the others in this book are so powerful. They are full of stories and experiences that are entertaining and educational. Education should be fun. If it isn't, I'm not interested. Wayne is a great communicator. He has a way of telling a story and teaching a lesson that keeps you wanting more. Read this chapter, and you'll see what I mean.

—ROBERT KIYOSAKI

O n the bookshelf opposite the desk in my office sits an antique jar filled with marbles. It is there to remind me of the importance of capital. As a fourth grader, I didn't call it capital, and I surely didn't realize the role that capital plays in business. I just knew I wanted to play marbles with the other kids, and I couldn't get in the game unless I owned some marbles, or at least one marble.

Coming from a family of modest means, it was out of the question to ask for money for marbles. I accepted that I should expect only a few new toys on my birthday and on Christmas. If I didn't take care of the toys I received twice a year, I would go without or make my own. I made trucks out of scrap lumber, bows and arrows out of whittled sticks, and forts out of haystacks, but I could think of no way to make a marble. Every day I watched with envy as other boys, and a few bold girls, played with those flashing glass spheres on the playground. I studied their techniques and strategies. I ached to get in the game. I had a plan as to how I would approach the game if I could find a way to play, but I was locked out. I had no "taw."

Where I come from, a taw is that one precious marble that each player selects in order to play with the greatest skill. It is the perfect weight. It fits the thumb just so. It is the single marble out of the entire bag that the player feels will give him or her the greatest advantage in a particular game. I knew if I could just find a taw, I could get in the game.

"FIND A TAW!" That was it! I suddenly remembered playing along the side of our home as a five-year-old. While digging in the dirt to build roads for my toy cars, I had unearthed a white marble. Having no value to me at the time, I left it lying in my diggings where I had found it. I wondered if it was still there. I rushed to the barn and grabbed a shovel. I turned up the dirt and carefully chopped through the overturned earth to loosen it. I got down on my hands and knees and sifted through the soil with a spoon. After a few minutes of mining, I felt and heard a click on the end of the spoon. My heart jumped into my throat. I felt a burst of excitement tingling in my temples. I brushed back the soil, and there it was—a somewhat dirty, but perfectly formed, ivory-colored marble.

Something shifted within me at that moment. I felt a rush of freedom and opportunity. I was wild with excitement that I could finally get in the game on the playground. It was as if I had come of age or had been declared worthy to be a real boy. The doors to my future opened wide. I was prepared to be a marble master, or so I thought. Owning my own taw became a right of passage for me.

Suddenly, my jubilation was cut short by a flood of fears that crowded my thoughts. In every game of marbles, like battles in a war, someone wins and someone loses. What if I lose my only marble? Where will I find another one? Who am I to think I could win when the other kids have been playing for months or years? What if I get totally embarrassed? What if I start crying right there in front of the toughest guys and the bravest girls? What will they say about me? What if they make fun of me? I was petrified.

As I clutched the marble in my hand, I realized how critical it was to my game and yet knew I couldn't play without risking it. Finally, I decided that if I must take the chance, I would take the smallest risk possible. I would challenge someone of the lowest skill level. Because I had been watching others play marbles for months, I knew who the champions were and who to avoid. Even if they called me out and teased me for being too chicken to play them, I would refuse to risk my taw on a game I couldn't win. I would play to win by carefully choosing the first games I entered and the opponents I faced.

I took my chances and got in the game. By the end of fourth grade, my shooting skills had improved considerably. I dared to play anyone in the school under the right conditions, and I had a gallon can full of marbles as proof of my progress. They were treasure to me. Each one held a memory, and each had a story of how it had been won. I kept my original white taw safely in a smaller pouch to remind me of how far I had come. It was no longer my best marble for play, but would always be my favorite, for sentimental reasons.

Sometimes when I teach seminars, I ask which of the attendees consider themselves to be capitalists. Almost every hand in the room goes up. Then I ask how many have capital. Most of the hands go down. To play in the game of capitalism, one must own or control some capital. Like marbles, capital is the "taw" that allows us to play the game. Raising capital is a vital skill for anyone who wants to get out of the rat race, as taught by the Rich Dad CASHFLOW game.

TIP Louis Kelso, the father of the Employee Stock Option Plan in the United States said, "The right to life implies the right to earn a good income. When 90 percent of the goods and services are produced by capital workers— people who own capital—as it is in an industrial society like ours, you can't earn a good income without owning capital."

(BILL MOYERS, A WORLD OF IDEAS [NY: DOUBLEDAY, 1990])

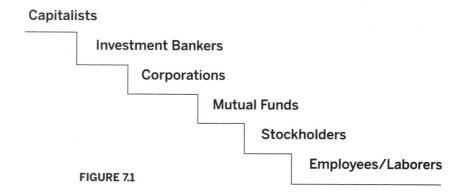

FIGURE 7.1

Robert Kiyosaki expressed the same principle in one of the Rich Dad business schools, showing the hierarchy of the economic food chain:

You may notice that those who work for money are on the bottom of the food chain. They get only crumbs, after everyone else has taken the best returns. Also notice that the capitalists are at the top of the food chain. Everyone works for the capitalists. Capitalists fund all enterprises. The capitalists own and control the majority of the wealth. The biggest returns, the best leverage, and the greatest tax advantages go to the capitalists. The capitalists are also those who take the biggest risks. Still, given a choice, why would anyone want to remain an employee, rather than becoming a capitalist?

Working for money is an arduous way to move up the economic food chain. If you continue to work only for money you will never escape the trap of the rat race. What is the key to economic freedom? It is the ownership or control of capital. If you want to be a capitalist instead of an employee, capital is the key. Capital is your taw. It empowers you to leverage and move ahead faster.

So how does someone who has no capital get started? Where do you go to get your first marble?

There are three basic ways:

1. Save it from your earnings
2. Borrow it from someone else
3. Trade ownership (equity) for capital

Let's look at each of these methods in more detail.

SAVING

Accumulating seed capital by saving money is the long, hard way to get your taw, but it has been proven viable by fledgling capitalists since ancient times. In his classic book *The Richest Man in Babylon*, George S. Clason shares a fable that clearly shows how one can go from the Rich Dad E quadrant (employee) to the S quadrant (specialist/self-employed), and even to the I quadrant (investor), by frugality and sacrifice. In America and other capitalist countries, immigrants prove over and over again that by working hard—sometimes even for subsistence wages—and by saving part of what they earn, individuals or families can rise quickly to capital ownership and wealth. Setting aside a portion of one's labor to accumulate an initial capital stake is within everyone's reach, just as I employed my own labor to dig in the dirt until I found my first marble. However, no matter how much capital you acquire by your own labor, your earnings will always be limited by the hours you can spend at work. Using only the capital you can save from your own earnings means that you will be severely restricted in growth and income.

FIGURE 7.2 Rich Dad CASHFLOW® Quadrant

BORROWING

Back in fourth grade, I may have been able to get into a game of marbles sooner if I had thought to borrow a taw from someone else. But how would I have repaid the debt if I had lost? These are the kinds of risks we must consider when borrowing capital as well. As my grandpa Palmer used to say, "Any damn fool can run into debt, but everyone will crawl out!" In other words, it is easy to go into debt, but not usually so easy to get back out. Borrowing money has consequences, and it is wise to fully consider those consequences before signing for the debt. Under most market conditions, borrowing money is relatively easy for strong investors with viable collateral. Paying it back as agreed will determine the true nature of your character and business skills. If you become good at taking care of Other People's Money (OPM), you will likely have plenty of capital with which to pursue your investment opportunities.

TIP Bad deals chase the money, while the money chases good ones.

The term OPM has become a popular acronym for the concept of raising capital. OPM can refer to borrowed capital as well as equity capital. It is sometimes spoken of with reckless abandon, as though getting others to back your idea is as easy as asking. As simple as some might make it appear, there are proven guidelines and important legalities for qualifying yourself and your project to attract the capital of others. I have often heard this said by lenders: "Bad deals chase the money, while the money chases good ones." In the end, how successful you are at borrowing will be largely determined by the answers to these two questions:

1. How viable is the opportunity?
2. How clear, concise, complete, compelling, and convincing is the communication contained in your loan package?

Let's consider these questions one at a time.

VIABLE OPPORTUNITY

First and foremost, what you propose must be viable—it must make sense. How do we define a viable opportunity? It is something that the average lender could look at and say, "Wow, I believe that will work." The projections of profit are based on reasonably probable outcomes, not on pie-in-the-sky dreams. The assumptions that lead to the bottom line are in harmony with the way things work in the real world. The outcome is not dependent upon anyone turning back the tides or walking on water or otherwise doing things that mere humans have never done before. More importantly, the lender must believe that *you* can do it. Just because Donald Trump did it doesn't mean the average Joe can pull it off. The outcome must be highly likely, given the skills, experience, and resources of your team. Above all, it must be economic, which means it must make money. Why else would a lender risk capital on your idea?

LOAN PACKAGE

Two of our companies do real estate lending. As lenders, we see and hear dozens of loan requests each week. Not long ago I received an e-mail from a would-be borrower that consisted of merely six line items, each with a large number at the end of the line, all totaling $2.44 million. There was nothing else in the e-mail. No borrower information, no outline of the ownership entity, no information about the structure of the proposed loan, no indication of the value of the properties that were to be pledged as collateral. Frankly, such a proposal is an insult to a lender. Underwriters rarely have enough time to sort through the mountains of paper and electronic packages that end up on their desks each day. To have borrowers suppose that, as a lender, I am going to hold their hand, do their work for them, beg for the documents that are needed to underwrite the loan, or spend hours on the phone with them, educating them in the business of borrowing, communicates to me only how naïve, or perhaps lazy, the borrower must be. We do not risk our capital on naïve or lazy people. We prefer hardworking, well-informed, and experienced borrowers. They have a better track record of paying us back. To avoid making a complete fool of yourself, wasting everyone's time, and killing your chances of getting a loan, take the time to compile a complete and easy-to-read loan package. In other words, be prepared!

HOW TO PREPARE A LOAN PACKAGE

At a minimum, a good commercial real estate loan package includes the following twelve items:

1. **A brief Executive Summary:** This is a one-page concise summary of the loan request in outline form. An executive summary typically includes:
   a. Name and contact information of the borrower;
   b. A description of the collateral property (address, type, age);
   c. The requested loan amount; and

d. The proposed terms of the loan (loan to value, interest rate, maturity date, and balloon or call date, if any).

2. **A Table of Contents for the remainder of the package:** This allows the Lender to quickly and conveniently find any information that may be of interest without reading the entire binder. It is also in your best interest to insert tabs at the front of each section to make the package easy to navigate. The more convenient it is to access the information, the more likely it is that your loan proposal will receive full consideration.

3. **Maps:** Include in the map section a state map, a city map, and a plat map of the subject property/site.

4. **Photos:** Include a small group of pictures that give a good idea of the property, its condition, and a sense of the neighborhood.

5. **Appraisal:** If you've had a professional appraisal done on the property, include the full document, or at a minimum, the summary pages. If there is no appraisal, provide some estimation of value, based on cost, comparative market analysis, or a list of comparable sales in the marketplace.

6. **Environmental Study:** Because environmental contamination is almost always an automatic deal killer, it is in your best interest to pay for a Phase One Environmental Report and include it in the package. Such reports are compiled by environmental engineering firms. The only exception may be when the property is known to have had zero exposure to contaminants, such as might likely be the case with raw farm land or mountaintop property.

7. **Operating Statement and/or Projections ("Pro forma"):** The operating statement sets forth the historic annual income and expenses on the property, usually for the past two to three years. This is one of the most important parts of the package so take extra care to make sure you compile and report this information accurately. Perhaps nothing will destroy the credibility of your proposal faster than a misstatement of the income or expenses on the property. The Pro forma is a projection of future income and expenses related to the property. An inaccurate or incomplete Pro forma is evidence that you, the borrower, have not entirely thought through the financial future of the project. That will likely result in the loan being declined.

8. **Borrower Financial Information and Credit:** This section will typically include the balance sheets and income statements on you, the borrower, and Guarantors, as well as tax returns for the prior two years. Each borrower and Guarantor will likely be required to submit a credit report or allow the lender to pull one.

9. **Management Experience:** Make sure that you have a person on your team with the experience to manage the kind of project you are proposing. Include in the loan package a copy of his or her résumé or professional qualifications and experience.

10. **Use of Funds Statement:** The use of funds statement is a one-page (or less) description of how you will use the borrowed funds. If the proposed loan is intended to be a purchase money mortgage, which is a term used to describe any mortgage that is taken out to pay for a property at the time of purchase, also include a statement of the source of the down payment.

11. **Title Report:** Provide a title report on the property from a local title company. Such a report is generally called a PR (Preliminary Report) or a Title Commitment.

12. **Ask in advance about any submission guidelines** your lender might have and if he would prefer to have you submit your package electronically or in hard copy.

Perhaps most importantly, once your loan is approved and closed, pay it back on time. Nothing will enhance your status with lenders or do more to encourage additional funding of your investments than precise performance on your part. I relish the comment Lee Iacocca made when he was chairman of Chrysler Corporation. He said, "We borrow money the old-fashioned way; we pay it back."

EQUITY

Raising equity capital is another matter altogether. First of all, there are very stringent securities laws that govern the raising of capital. *Do not* start soliciting funds for your business without consulting a good lawyer to make sure you are within legal guidelines. The penalties for breaking securities laws can be severe.

Whereas lenders primarily look at collateral values, cash flows, and the strength of the borrower to repay his loans, venture capitalists who may consider investing in your enterprise additionally look to management expertise and a solid business plan. Raising capital for real estate can take on elements of both borrowing and venture capital. When others approach me to be their potential joint venture partner, I want to see all of the information contained in the loan packaging above. Additionally, I must also be satisfied concerning the following:

- Who is providing what to the venture? A real estate investment is made up of two basic parts: money and management. Who will provide the money and in what increments? And who will do the work of managing the project? Some investments require more money than work, and some require more work than money. Our companies generally negotiate to provide debt or equity. We may also sometimes choose to structure a combination of both. As equity investors, or venture capitalists, we will require our potential partners to answer these questions:
- How much capital are we being asked to risk?
- For how long will it be at risk?
- Will our rate of return be based on an interest rate paid periodically, with an equity kicker in the end, or will it be based solely on the upside equity and cash flow?
- What management skills are required to protect the capital and deliver the projected returns?
- Does anyone on the team possess these skills or will they be contracted from outside of the ownership group?
- How much of our time and expertise will be required?
- How will those who contribute their time to the project be compensated? Will they receive money or additional equity in the property?
- What is the order of priority for each team member in the disbursement of funds? Most of the time, a venture is structured to first pay expenses, including interest and personnel costs; second, the costs of sale; third, a payment of the remaining principal balance on the debt; fourth, a return of the initial joint venture (equity) capital; and finally, the disbursement of profits to each partner at the pre-agreed percentages. As sponsors of an opportunity, we sometimes agree to disburse profits to our money partners as a first priority, until they have achieved a predetermined rate of return, with remaining profits going to ourselves or to the group at large.

A Word About Legal Compliance

I have learned just enough about securities laws to know that they are complicated, diverse, and generally unforgiving. Inasmuch as I am not qualified or willing to give anyone legal advice, the only guidance I will venture to suggest is this: Make sure you get competent legal counsel if you are going to ask anyone else to participate in your projects with you. Do not underestimate the seriousness of even unintentional violations of securities regulations. The Securities and Exchange Commission (SEC) is the regulator of securities issues on the federal level in the United States. Each state also has wide-ranging, and sometimes peculiar regulations for the issuance and governance of securities within its respective boundaries. You are well advised to stay in compliance with the rules and regulations they administer, when your venture falls within the definition of a securities transaction.

A Word About Entity Structure

It is critical to consider what legal structure will best serve the ownership group and its purposes. Will it be a corporation, a general partnership, a limited partnership, or a limited liability company? The structure chosen is more important than it may appear on the surface, especially when the tax position of each investor is taken into consideration. Once again, seek competent legal advice in forming the entity that will own and manage the investment. Garrett Sutton's chapter in this book is a great source of information, as is Garrett himself.

If I had been more astute at age ten, perhaps I could have convinced another player to spot me some marbles from his bag, with an agreement to share my winnings with him. In the end, I may have had fewer marbles, or I may have had more. My treasure would clearly have been reduced by the profits I shared with my partner, while on the other hand, getting in the game earlier may have resulted in more winnings over a longer period of time. You will face similar decisions as you decide how you will raise capital.

Regardless of which method you use to capitalize your investments—saving, borrowing, or equity—please consider the following perspective on money. If you use your own capital, it is probably painfully clear that it represents months, perhaps years, of work, sacrifice, and discipline on your part. Until we have a grubstake of our own we are stuck in the rat race. As employees, we trade our time for money. Our time is largely someone else's capital as long as we are stuck in the E quadrant.

TIP In the end, the time we spend on this planet equals life. Most people would agree that a human life is sacred and carries a higher value than almost anything else on earth. Since we trade our time—our very lives—for money or capital, I conclude that capital equals life. If that is the case, then capital, like life, is sacred and should be treated as such.

How much different would the annals of business history read if executives regarded Other People's Money as a sacred trust, akin to life itself? When an investor has worked all of his or her life to accumulate capital, then invests in a venture that is mismanaged or illegally operated and the capital is lost, a very real part of that investor's life is destroyed. For the elderly, in particular, the hours, days, weeks, and years are irreplaceable. Risking your own marbles, your own time, your own life capital, is one thing. Taking upon yourself the moral responsibility of safeguarding someone else's capital is another. I encourage you to approach the use of OPM with this kind of serious moral grounding. There is nothing else you can do that will have a more positive influence on your success. If you conduct yourself with integrity not only in word, but in deed, and keep the capital entrusted to you secure and productive, a time will soon come when you will likely have more capital than you can put to use. As suggested earlier in this chapter, the money will begin to chase you, which is perhaps a crude way of saying that as you respect capital, you will attract capital.

Think of all the capital that exists in the world. Land, minerals, timber, plants, animals, fish, and even some insects and reptiles have capital value. In addition, tools, equipment, machinery, processes, intangibles (such as intellectual assets like software and know-how), and all forms of money and securities represent capital. Various forms of naturally occurring energy, such as solar, wind, tidal, gravitational, geothermal, human labor, and animal labor (horsepower) constitute capital as well.

The reason I ask you to consider this enormous supply of capital is to empower you to overcome any thoughts of scarcity. The more we need the money, the less likely we are to believe that it exists in abundance. Under such circumstances, fear overpowers faith that money is available in ample supply.

TIP Even in difficult economic times, capital is rarely destroyed. It only changes hands or changes forms.

Consider how capital flows around the world. It is mind-boggling to ponder the number of individual transactions that take place every day. From the child buying penny candy at the grocery store, to international banks moving mountains of money, to balancing government currency accounts, there are billions of individual capital flows that take place every day. In its most basic definition, capital is either energy or a symbol of energy. Capital is the energy that flows through each economic transaction, not the money itself. The money is only a symbol of the energy, the value, the increment of human life (time) that is inherent in the underlying asset, process, or function.

When we start to see these countless transactions as flows of economic energy, having real value, instead of as merely the exchange of money, the true nature of capital is revealed. It is not in scarce supply. It is, in fact, infinitely abundant. It is not all locked up in vaults where you cannot get to it. You already possess a great deal of it in your time, your talent, your knowledge, and in your ability to start where you are to increase your stock of capital. One buried marble properly played soon becomes a bag of marbles and perhaps even a barrel. You need not wait for anyone else to begin growing your capital. You already have the power to start where you are to increase your holdings.

What, then, is the trigger that causes capital to flow in each of these individual transactions? I believe it is human emotion that drives each exchange. Commerce is driven by emotions such as need, greed, desire, trust, or confidence. Someone once told me that "emotion" is energy in motion. See if this is true by considering the following: If a person needs an expensive operation to preserve health and life, he will do all in his power to gather the money to pay for it. If someone is hungry, he will move what capital he has to someone who has food for sale. If I believe you can teach me something of value, I may direct some of my personal resources to you for books or seminars or personal coaching. If you decide to visit your grandma in a distant place, you will most likely pay for transportation to get from where you are to where you want to go. Notice how in each of these examples the influence of human desires causes the economic energy (money) to move.

My family once took a chartered bus trip across the United States. As I sat on the bus, gazing out the window, I came to a profound realization. Somewhere in the middle of Nebraska, while seeing farm after farm and wondering about the people who lived on each one, it struck me. I imagined a couple of people living in each farmhouse who had fallen in love and married. Their love brought children into the family. Every day they worked the farm to provide for their loved ones. It was then that I suspected the lyrics to the old song that my dad sang to my mother were true, "Love Makes the World Go 'Round." I realized in that moment that the economy was actually the energy of human love and other human desires that spur us to creation and consumption of various kinds.

As we continued down Interstate 80 on the same bus, I noticed all the trucks passing by me in both directions, carrying the freight produced in the factories and foundries of America. It was then that I first knew that all would be well and that the economy would go on because people would keep falling in love, keep having children, and keep working hard to give them a good life. The trucks would keep running, and capital would continue to be exchanged in countless daily transactions that support the needs and desires of human beings. No force on earth, no government blunder, could bring the real economy to a halt. It was energy in motion and would remain in motion as long as individual human beings had any desires for a better life.

So, since capital exists in abundance all around you, how do you cause it to move from wherever it is now to where you want it to be?

1. **First, establish the mind-set of abundance.** Ask yourself if you are operating from fear or from trust, from doubt or from confidence. Be constantly mindful that there is no shortage of capital and that it is eager to flow to you, if you do what is necessary to attract it and safeguard it. A dear friend of mine shared with me that her family loves blueberries. She had the feeling blueberries were scarce because they were quite expensive at the grocery store. One day she had the chance to take her boys to the country and pick blueberries on a farm. For the same price she paid for a small box at the store, she could buy two big flats from the farmer, and he let them eat all they wanted while they picked. She realized that blueberries were in abundant supply once she had a change of perspective.

2. **Qualify yourself to attract capital flows.** Make a conscious choice to adopt an energy within and around yourself that is harmonious with the energy of the capital you wish to attract. What kind of energy attracts capital? Read on!

3. **Practice full accountability.** Take the committed stand that Gene Kranz, Apollo 13 mission control director (played by the actor Ed Harris in the movie) took during that fated mission. If you saw the movie, you may remember that there was an explosion that damaged the command module while on its journey to the moon, threatening its ability to return to earth. The astronauts had to extend their supplies of oxygen and electricity to survive. On the ground in Houston, Kranz pulled his team together and declared, "We never lost an American in space. We're sure as hell not going to lose one on my watch. Failure is not an option." He demanded that his engineers find a way to bring the crew home safely, using only the resources the astronauts had on board. Capital rushes toward that kind of commitment because complete accountability inspires confidence, creativity, and can-do attitudes. To the total extent of your ability and capacity take personal responsibility to make sure that no one ever loses a nickel on your watch.

4. **Work with integrity.** To me, the meaning of integrity is clear. It is simply to do what you say you will do, when you say you will do it, and to tell the truth

in all things and under all conditions. Integrity is what integrity does. Being reliable will set you apart from most of your competition. People want to do business with those who are dependable.

5. **Disclose.** Provide your potential lenders or investors with all of the information you would want to know if you were in their shoes and were considering placing capital with you.

6. **Establish the habit of over-communicating.** Keep your lenders and investors constantly informed of important details. This attention shows respect and accountability.

7. **Prepare yourself to attract capital flows.** You will notice I differentiate between qualification and preparation. Qualification is about energy, competency and your state of being. Preparation is the act of taking care of the mechanics and the details, where the rubber meets the road. My experience tells me these are the key areas of preparation.

8. **Know your business.** Know a good deal from a bad one. Drive yourself to constantly study and stay abreast of the real estate industry. What are the trends in financing, demographics, product types, customer preferences, building materials and methods, technology, municipal codes, taxation, regulations, and risk management, to name but a few.

9. **Write a business plan.** Create a comprehensive plan that fully explores the risks and responses that will be required to generate a profit.

10. **Have multiple exit strategies.** Do you have enough confidence in your proposed investment, based on solid economic principles and potentially changing conditions, to absolutely believe that you can achieve the projected results? Have you run different scenarios? Do you have multiple exit strategies? If the worst happens, how will you protect the capital that your investors have entrusted to you?

11. **Define and staff up to provide core competencies.** Do you, or does your team, have the skills, the core competencies, needed to fully execute your business plan? If something is lacking, are you realistically addressing it? How will you compensate for the weakness? Will you hire someone with that skill? Will you take on another partner who has the talent? Just imagine trying to drive your car with one flat tire! Your business won't run smoothly if there is a "flat" on the team. An abundance of talent will overcome a multitude of challenges.

12. **Develop a stellar track record.** Protect your reputation by over-performing. If you are just starting out and have no track record, be honest about it, and clearly communicate to potential lenders and investors that you are aware of your lack of experience. Be prepared to show them how you will deal with

any shortfall in your experience. Remember, experience and expertise can be hired, too. Robert Kiyosaki continually emphasizes that he isn't the smartest guy in every situation, so he surrounds himself with those who understand certain things better than he does. I can't think of a time that I was unable to find the talent I needed. People of extreme capability love the game and are usually eager to play with a quality team, even if it is their experience the team must rely upon.

13. **Take care of business.** It has been my experience that my JOB ONE is to fully focus on whatever business I am operating. Businesses don't run themselves. Running a viable business requires the best energy and efforts of the team. Rich rewards are in store for those who give their all to protect business operations and to provide all it takes to prosper and turn a profit.

PROTECT-PROVIDE-PROSPER-PROFIT

When a business does well, everyone wants to be a part of it. Wall Street clamors to buy shares in any enterprise that is producing a healthy return on investment. On the other hand, you have likely seen the statistics that suggest as many as 90 percent of small businesses fail within the first five years. People and companies squander billions of dollars in investment capital on poor business investments. If you want to attract capital to your business, make your business work. Make it profitable. Infuse it with passion and the prospect of continued success. People invest in real estate ventures to make money. If you develop a proven talent for generating solid returns and offer such an opportunity to others with proper disclosures, they will naturally want to be a part of your enterprise.

As you attract the capital of others, no matter how small-scale at first, and take exquisite care of that capital, your investors will spread the word. Others will be knocking on your door to become part of a good thing. It is almost as if the only thing you need to do is to prove your ability to run your company honorably and profitably. If you do that in the face of the corporate corruption that seems to be more and more prevalent, capital will seek a home in your enterprise. However, remember that even when potential investors come to you through referrals, you still have the same responsibility to provide all of the disclosures required by law.

I know these principles work because I applied them to build my own group of companies from zero to millions in assets over a sixteen-year period. What I am sharing with you I have learned from firsthand experience. Business school baloney would have you believe that there is some magical formula, some scientific certainty that makes success in business predictable and fail-safe. Nonsense. There is much value in the average college curriculum, but it is mostly theory. A college degree is the beginning of the journey, not the end. A diploma is only a way of qualifying yourself for a position on a team in the real world where you will work for money.

It is no mistake that the metaphor of war is so often chosen to describe the dynamics of business. Once graduation is over, every student must meet the competition on the corporate battlefield. Out there, no one is taken prisoner. Economically speaking, everyone lives or dies by his own ability to recognize the opportunity, strategize the attack, and execute the plan under the ever-changing conditions of battle. When I started the company National Note in December of 1992, my vision for it was very different than it is today. I originally intended to broker notes to institutional buyers for a commission. That put me squarely in the "S" corner of the Rich Dad CASHFLOW Quadrant. I soon found that many institutional note buyers were often too subjective and sometimes even fickle, I tired of seeing perfectly good proposals turned down for reasons that seemed capricious to me.

With IRA funds of my own and limited money from family, friends, and clients I had known for years, I started buying the notes myself with private capital. I soon realized that I was building assets and equity in my company at a rather rapid rate. My balance sheet was improving dramatically from year-to-year. It wasn't until I read Robert Kiyosaki's book, *The CASHFLOW Quadrant*, that I realized I had become an investor ("I" quadrant), instead of merely self-employed ("S" quadrant).

Years later, while teaching a seminar with Robert, I was stunned to learn that the rapid growth of my company was primarily because I had inadvertently managed to structure it in harmony with the Rich Dad philosophy. Not being sophisticated in any sense of the word, I simply kept my head down and focused on managing my business as best I knew how. Others came to me with various ideas and wanted to be part of National Note. Rather than share equity, I joint-ventured new business opportunities with a few of the best people. These enterprises, funded by National Note, prospered because of my partners' talents and National Note's capital. I split profits with my partners at pre-agreed percentages, as the companies grow and prosper.

Somewhere along the way, something phenomenal started to happen. Those to whom we had been faithfully sending checks each month, with never a delinquency, began to tell their family and friends about us. Our business has grown every year for the past sixteen years and is ten times larger today than it was four years ago. We simply "stuck to our knitting," as the saying goes, and managed the company in such a way as to make it stronger and stronger to assure the safety of the capital entrusted to us.

What is the key to such growth? The very principles I am sharing with you now. By focusing on acquiring quality assets, running our business, telling the truth, making the required disclosures, under-promising, and over-performing, capital continues to be available to our companies.

From among the people who do business with us today, there are dozens of inspiring personal stories of how debts were liquidated, stock market losses recovered, retirements funded, tuition paid, and moms who quit work to stay at home with their babies. These private victories were possible because of the careful deployment of their capital in real estate and real estate paper. For me, seeing our clients achieve such milestones is the most rewarding aspect of being a capitalist.

There is no way I could have known when I was ten years old how important that white marble would become to me. I trust you now understand why I keep a jar of marbles in my office. Growing a business does not need to be difficult or highly technical. By gaining some proficiency in the practice of capitalism, just like learning to shoot marbles, you, too, can build a machine that will crank out profits for you and those who are fortunate enough to be in business with you.

There is no need to gamble or speculate, as so many do when investing. Find a simple system that works, and work it! Attend to your game of marbles. Pick your matches (investments) carefully, and celebrate as treasure fills first a bag, then a barrel, and perhaps even a bank vault. I am astonished at how far our companies have come. What a fabulous experience it is to be a capitalist! What a ride it has been! What a joy it is to look back and relish the journey and to look ahead with eager anticipation of an exciting future!

Now, could it be your turn? Where will you find your "taw"? When will you enter your first game? How long will it take you to acquire more marbles than you ever dreamed possible? Those questions are yours to answer, and the journey ahead is yours to begin. Good luck!

Ways to Learn More

www.waynelpalmer.com
www.nce1031.com
A soon-to-be published book on real estate formulas, by Wayne Palmer

Wayne Palmer is widely regarded as a master in the creative structuring of real estate acquisitions and financing, using notes and other forms of real estate paper, together with 1031 Equity Marketing formulas. His skills come from thirty years of daily practice of his trade, as the owner and manager of National Note of Utah, LC and several other companies. He has been involved in real estate development since 1978, in Utah, Idaho, Arizona, Hawai'i, and Minnesota. By way of industry credentials, Wayne is a Licensed Principal Real Estate Broker, a Certified Real Estate Note Appraiser, a Certified Cash Flow Master Broker, a Licensed Continuing Education Provider, and holds the Equity Marketing Specialist (EMS) designation with the National Council of Exchangors.

8

Bernie BAYS

How to Avoid and Handle
Real Estate Disputes

Bernie Bays has been a friend of mine since the mid-1970s. He is also a fellow marine and rugby team member. If you go over his record, you can tell he is no ordinary marine, but a Force Recon Marine, the toughest of the tough. He is also no ordinary rugby player, playing for USC and for Stanford University on a national championship team. Small wonder he is such a smart and respected real estate attorney.

When I first started out in real estate, my deals were small, and I thought I did not need an attorney. Being naïve, I thought a real estate broker and a good appraiser were enough. On my first investment property—a small one bedroom, one bath condo on the island of Maui—my little dream bubble was popped. A few months after acquiring the property and putting a tenant in it, netting me a whopping $25 a month, the septic system in the condominium complex burst and flooded the apartment. The apartment went empty, I began to lose money, the homeowners told me the septic damage to my unit was my problem, not theirs. My first asset became a liability, and I learned a priceless but expensive lesson about real estate. Hire an attorney before you invest, not after.

Real estate is more than dirt, sticks, bricks, financing, and tenants. Real estate is also law, agreements, boundaries, and disputes. This is why Bernie Bays is not only a friend; he is the real estate attorney I call before investing in Hawai'i.

—Robert Kiyosaki

One unfortunate reality of real estate deals today is that there is always the possibility that you can become involved in a dispute with other participants during the making of the deal. These participants can include sellers, lenders, construction and planning professionals, construction contractors, and buyers. Success in real estate means not only being great at picking properties, managing them well, and eventually selling at the right time, it also means knowing how to minimize the risk of becoming involved in a protracted dispute.

I have been representing clients involved in real estate–related disputes for more than thirty-eight years. During that time, I have observed that some participants in real estate deals are constantly involved in disputes. Others rarely get into disputes and when they do, they usually manage to resolve them relatively quickly. What's the difference between these two groups of people: the ones who seem to get into dispute after dispute and the ones who seldom do? How can you minimize your chances of being involved in a dispute?

Make no mistake about it. Disputes in real estate deals can spoil your party by diverting time, money, other resources, and, most importantly, emotional energy from what you are trying to achieve: a successful real estate deal. There are admittedly a few perverse individuals who occasionally come out ahead by picking fights in a real estate deal. And there are a few people who thrive on the negative emotional energy of disputes, even though they may not really come out ahead. You want to avoid these people in your real estate deals. But it's not always about the people. Sometimes it's the kind of real estate deals that are prone to disputes and you want to avoid those as well.

TIP Disputes in real estate deals can spoil your party by diverting time, money, other resources, and, most importantly, emotional energy from what you are trying to achieve: a successful real estate deal.

My objective here is to give you some simple guidelines so you can reduce your chances of becoming involved in a real estate dispute. I also want to give you some suggestions for how best to handle the disputes that you cannot avoid.

How to Avoid Disputes

The best defense against a dispute is to avoid the dispute altogether. Here's my list of how to keep yourself out of trouble.

WORK WITH A GOOD, EXPERIENCED BROKER

Always work with your own real estate broker on a real estate deal. Do not just work with the seller's real estate broker when you are buying a property. You want to select a broker who has the experience and good sense to look out for your interests rather than simply pushing you to close the deal at hand in order to get a commission. You want a broker who is in it for the long term and knows that there will be other deals to do with you if this one does not work out. You want a trusted broker who will advise you to walk away from the deal if that is the best thing for you to do under the circumstances.

I recently concluded a case for a client who had purchased a development property through the listing broker without using his own broker. My client initially told the broker that he could not buy the property because of the three-unit affordable housing requirement. The broker told my client that if my client would sell him three of the lots in the proposed subdivision at a reduced price, he would construct the affordable housing on the three lots and satisfy the requirement. My client allowed the broker's lawyer to draft the agreement regarding the three lots and proceeded with the purchase of the property. He did not have his own lawyer review the agreement, but instead just trusted the seller's broker. After my client purchased the property, he discovered that the affordable housing requirement for the project was actually five units, not three. Even more shocking, the broker said that he was not obligated to build *any* affordable housing at the site. "That was just something we discussed that I might do if it worked out," the broker said.

The broker then demanded that my client convey the three lots to him at the reduced price and threatened to sue. When my client came to me, we discovered that the agreement drafted by the broker's attorney provided for a sale of the lots to the broker at a reduced price, but said nothing about building the affordable housing.

My client did not have a legal leg to stand on. We were finally able to settle the case by conveying only two of the three lots to the broker. My client was left to satisfy the five-unit affordable housing requirement on his other lots. This case demonstrates how dangerous it is not to have your own broker representing you in a real estate transaction. It also demonstrates how dangerous it is not to have your own lawyer representing you in documenting your agreements, which is what the next section is about.

TIP Do not just work with the seller's real estate broker when you are buying a property. You want a trusted broker who will advise you to walk away from the deal if that is the best thing for you to do.

Consult with a Good, Experienced Lawyer Early and Often

I was giving a speech a few months ago to a group of real estate developers and joked that in real estate deals you should get a lawyer involved "early and often." I was joking, but there is a good deal of truth in what I said. The truth here is that an ounce of prevention in lawyer time spent drafting the deal contracts is worth a pound of cure in the form of costly litigation. So spend a little money on lawyers in the beginning to get clear contracts that protect your interests. It may save you a fortune in litigation costs later on. These are my suggestions to get the most value from your lawyer in a real estate deal:

- Find an experienced real estate attorney you trust and can afford.
- Keep him or her up to speed on pending transactions and request advice early and often.
- Specifically, have your lawyer involved in the preparation of any term sheets or letters of intent, even though they may be nonbinding. This is usually when the buyer and the seller agree upon important deal points that are difficult to change later on.
- Have your lawyer prepare any binding contracts.
- Do not try to save money by allowing the lawyer on the other side to prepare the first draft of the contracts. It is better to spend the money to have your lawyer prepare the first draft. It is often difficult to change a contract drafted by the other side. Once they have prepared and approved it, they tend to become wedded to it.
- Involve your lawyer in your due diligence process for any property you are buying. Skimping on legal due diligence to save money is a bad idea, a false economy. If a property is worth putting under contract, then it is worth spending the money on a thorough due diligence including legal.

TIP The truth here is that an ounce of prevention in lawyer time spent drafting the deal contracts is worth a pound of cure in the form of costly litigation.

Insist on Clear Contracts that Protect Your Interests

I handle real estate litigation that results when real estate deals go bad. Often these cases result from poorly drafted contracts that do not do a good job of protecting the legitimate interests of the parties. For example, I have had two cases in the last year or so where, believe it or not, the contracts really did not require one of the parties to follow through on his commitments to complete the real estate projects that were the subject of those contracts. Clearly the intent of the parties was to execute contracts that were binding, but the contracts they signed did not effectively do the job. In one case, the party financing the development just refused to proceed with the project, even though the market was good and the project would have been profitable. Unfortunately, the contracts did not explicitly require the investor to proceed. The developers had allowed the investor's lawyer to prepare the agreements without hiring their own lawyer, which turned out to be a very costly mistake.

In the other case, the investors gave the developer the money he said he needed to complete the development. Unfortunately the contracts did not really obligate him to finish the project, and the contracts also prevented the investors from replacing the developer, even if he completely failed to finish the project. The lesson here is to insist on clear contracts that obligate the parties to do what they have agreed to do and to have a lawyer represent you who is looking out for your interests and protecting your rights.

You are entitled to contracts that spell out precisely what you expect to happen in the real estate deal; contracts that reduce the uncertainty and keep ambiguity to a minimum. You also want to make absolutely sure the other parties are required to do exactly what you expect them to do when you expect them to do it. Spell out the consequences if the other parties do not do what you expect them to do. By the same token, you also want to know what the consequences will be if you do not or cannot uphold your side of the agreement. A good lawyer can help you define and limit your downside as much as possible in those situations. Later we'll talk about limiting remedies in more detail, but here's some legal advice: If you are not sure you can perform under the terms of the contract, then you should not sign it.

Beyond these words of wisdom, take the time to read and understand the contracts you are going to sign. In doing so, your real estate broker and your lawyer can give you all the help you need. Let them help you identify any risks that others will not perform or that you cannot perform, and make the necessary changes to fix the problems. Don't hesitate to have things explained again if you do not understand. And don't worry about looking stupid. The more you understand, the smarter you will get. The stupid thing is to sign a contract you really do not understand.

TIP You are entitled to contracts that spell out precisely what you expect to happen in the real estate deal; contracts that reduce the uncertainty and keep ambiguity to a minimum. You also want to make absolutely sure the other parties are required to do exactly what you expect them to do when you expect them to do it.

CAREFULLY SPECIFY AND LIMIT REMEDIES IN THE CONTRACT

Much of the uncertainty regarding real estate contracts can be eliminated by clearly specifying remedies. For example, real estate contracts often provide that the seller's only remedy if the buyer defaults is to keep the buyer's deposit. On the other hand, if you are a seller, you want to limit the buyer's remedy to just getting the deposit back and you want to specifically preclude the buyer from getting what is called "specific performance."

"Specific performance" is an equitable remedy that gives the buyer the right to legally compel the seller to sell the property to the buyer upon the terms in the contract. If the buyer is arguably entitled to specific performance, the buyer may have the ability to tie up the seller's property in court for years while the parties litigate their respective obligations under the contract and who did what. This could effectively give the buyer an option on the seller's property for years with only the deposit at risk. This is not where you want to be if you are a seller. If you cannot completely negotiate out specific performance, you want to limit the situations where the buyer is entitled to seek specific performance as much as possible.

TIP "Specific performance" is an equitable remedy that gives the buyer the right to legally compel the seller to sell the property to the buyer upon the terms in the contract. As a seller, if you cannot completely negotiate out specific performance, you want to limit it as much as possible.

Let me share with you a story of how powerful specific performance can be. I represented a large hotel chain in litigation that resulted from the failed sale of a trophy resort hotel in Honolulu. The buyer had failed to perform according to the exact terms of the contract, so my client finally canceled the deal and kept the buyer's $1 million deposit. The buyer had also spent more than $200,000 on a lengthy due diligence before my client canceled the contract. Had I been involved earlier, I would have recommended that my client give the buyer more time to perform and would have carefully positioned the buyer before canceling. But by the time the case got to me, the contract had been canceled, and the buyer had sued. We asked the court for summary judgment without a trial based upon the fact that the buyer had not met the time deadlines provided for in the contract. We got lucky and the federal court gave us summary judgment against the buyer.

After the hearing, I advised the top management of the hotel chain that we had been very lucky to get summary judgment, and that the court's decision might be reversed on appeal. I told them that they did not want a premier hotel tied up for years by the buyer's potential right to specific performance while the appeal got resolved. I recommended that they use this opportunity to settle with the buyer by returning some of the deposit. But warmed by the glow of victory, they refused to offer the buyer anything, and I was reprimanded by a senior partner for spoiling our victory with my dismal predictions about an appeal.

To make a long story short, I left the firm with some of my colleagues to form our own firm, and someone else handled the appeal. Years later, after the hotel had increased 50 percent in value, the appeals court ruled that the buyer should be allowed to proceed with the purchase of the hotel at the original price with full credit for the deposit the seller had retained.

TIP Here are some words of experience:

- Limit the buyer's right to specific performance whenever possible
- Always try to resolve the dispute instead of rolling the dice in litigation

In that case, the seller's failure to limit specific performance and insistence on keeping the buyer's $1 million tied up a premier hotel for years and resulted in the sale of an $80 million hotel for $55 million. Not a good outcome!

AVOID PROBLEM PEOPLE

Do not do real estate deals with people who are likely to be trouble down the road. Some people get into disputes with everyone. You want to do online litigation checks on people you are considering doing business with. If they have been involved in a lot of litigation you want to avoid them. This is also another good reason for you to avoid litigation; so that other people will not avoid doing business with you! Conversely, you want to do business with people who have a history and reputation for working things out when a real estate deal hits a rough spot. You want to have a mutual trust and respect for the other people involved in a real estate deal whenever possible, especially a real estate development project that will go on for several years.

TIP Do online litigation checks on people you are considering doing business with. Avoid litigation so people will do business with you!

Rough spots are sure to come up, and potential disagreements are certain to arise. You want to be involved with people who will work them out with you, not make a mountain out of every molehill. The last thing you want is someone who will blow up your deal in litigation to prove they are right.

AVOID PROBLEM DEALS

Some deals are just more trouble than they are worth. Some deals get more complicated, involved, and difficult as they progress. And the more complicated and difficult the deal becomes, the more likely there are to be disputes later on that will be difficult to resolve. So when the deal gets more and more difficult and the brain damage mounts, you need to ask: Is it worth it? Is this deal so good and so beneficial for you that it is worth the brain damage and risk that is inherent in complex, difficult deals? Some are worth it, and you may want to continue. Most are not, and you will be better off letting those go. Let someone else deal with all the headaches and problems if the potential benefit to you is really not worth the trouble. If the benefit is there and you decide to go ahead, then the help of a good lawyer and the need for clear contracts become doubly important. However, even a good lawyer can do only so much to overcome the risks inherent in a difficult deal.

TIP The more complicated and difficult the deal becomes, the more likely there are to be disputes later on—and problem people and problem deals often go hand in hand.

The purchase of a large ranch that I helped a friend put together several years ago was a deal that was just too difficult and complicated. A limited partnership owned the ranch and the general partner who originally formed the group that owned the ranch had sold his interest to a stranger who had gotten into litigation with the holder of the grazing license. In order to buy the ranch, my friend had to put together another partnership composed of some of the partners in the original partnership that owned the ranch and some new investor partners. We also had to get a federal farm loan, renegotiate the underlying ground lease to extend it to twenty-five years, settle the litigation between the general partner and the licensee, and resolve the disagreements among everyone as to how all this should be done. I was the person responsible for doing all of this. As I look back, the brain damage, work, and stress involved in trying to put this extremely complicated deal together clearly outweighed any gain. The deal finally collapsed of its own weight when the buyer went on a long-planned, month-long family vacation when the deal was supposed to close. Luckily, no one involved got sued; we just wasted a lot of time and money on a deal that was just too difficult and complicated.

Another point to consider is that problem people and problem deals often go hand in hand. Clear contracts can go only so far in controlling problem people in the context of a problem deal. The probability of serious disputes that will be difficult, if not impossible to resolve without litigation goes up exponentially. Some experienced real estate developers and investors would say that no deal is worth going through the brain damage, emotional drain, and risk of problem people and problem deals and would advise you to just walk away from them. I will just say that the problems will be more numerous and much worse than you expect so you need to be sure the deal is really worth it. A few deals are that good, but the vast majority are simply not worth it.

DO A THOROUGH DUE DILIGENCE, INCLUDING LEGAL DUE DILIGENCE

Due diligence is a period of time designated within a contract that allows a buyer to check out the property and the deal before committing to close. Usually the buyer's deposits are refundable until the buyer notifies the seller that the property and the deal are acceptable. At that point, the buyer's deposit "goes hard" (becomes nonrefundable) and the buyer is also usually required to increase the deposit so that the buyer will lose a substantial amount of money if the buyer fails to close. This nonrefundable deposit also gives the seller comfort that the deal will close.

TIP If you are a buyer and you think a deal is worth doing, then it is worth spending the money to do a thorough due diligence, including careful legal due diligence.

If you are a buyer and you think a deal is worth doing, then it is worth spending the money to do a thorough due diligence, including careful *legal* due diligence. If the deal is big, then you need to spend a substantial amount of money to check it out carefully before you agree to close. Many disputes can be avoided if you check out the property and the deal very carefully before you commit to close. If you discover problems or issues at the due diligence stage, you can insist that the contract be amended to fairly deal with the problems you have discovered. If you need more time to complete your due diligence, show the seller the effort you are making and the money you are spending on the deal and ask for an extension of time. You will usually get it if the seller is convinced you are proceeding in good faith. But sometimes the seller won't feel that way.

I recently had a development property in escrow and delayed the legal due diligence to save money. I instead focused a lot of time and money on planning the proposed subdivision and locating an adequate water source for the property. When I finally started the legal due diligence, my lawyers discovered an unusual legal restriction that prevented us from developing the subdivision project we had planned for the property. As a result, all the money we had spent on engineering and land planning was completely wasted.

How to Avoid Real Estate Disputes

Avoid disputes in your real estate deals by doing the following:

• Work with a good, experienced broker.

• Consult with a good, experienced lawyer early and often.

• Insist on clear contracts that protect your interests.

• Carefully specify and limit remedies in the contract.

• Avoid problem people.

• Avoid problem deals.

• Do a thorough due diligence, including legal due diligence.

HOW TO HANDLE REAL ESTATE DISPUTES

Even if you follow the steps I have outlined above, no contract is perfect, and conditions may change in ways that may make the deal more difficult for one or more of the parties. As a result, disputes can arise, even when you have clear contracts with decent people: One party may also just want to try to improve the deal after it is agreed upon. So how do you handle the disagreements that do arise in your real estate deals? The simple answer is that you should always do your best to work it out. In doing this, you may want to consider the following suggestions:

CONSULT WITH A GOOD, EXPERIENCED LITIGATION LAWYER TO AVOID LITIGATION

Strangely enough, a good litigation lawyer knows better than anyone that litigation in real estate deals seldom pays off and also knows the best ways to avoid it. While helping you avoid litigation, an experienced litigation lawyer can also put you in the best position possible if litigation cannot be avoided. He or she can also make sure you do not give up the farm or get bullied by the other parties. There is usually some middle ground between getting pushed around and doing your part to resolve disagreements. A good lawyer can help you find that middle ground.

But here is a fair warning. Litigation lawyers make a lot more money by representing you in litigation than they do in helping you avoid it. Some do not have enough work and may have a financial self interest in prolonging your dispute, or even aggravating it. Some lawyers also are just enamored with the litigation process and get carried away with protecting your position to the point they lose sight of the real objective, which is resolving the dispute for you as quickly and cheaply as possible. You do not want these unbalanced lawyers representing you. You want lawyers helping you who have the experience and good judgment to strike the right balance between protecting your interests and resolving your dispute.

TIP Experience warning: Litigation lawyers make a lot more money by representing you in litigation than they do in helping you avoid it. Choose carefully.

WHEN DISPUTES ARISE, DO WHATEVER YOU CAN TO WORK IT OUT

As I have said, disagreements may occur in real estate deals, even though you have had clear contracts prepared by a good lawyer. Generally, the more complicated the deal and the longer it lasts, the more likely there are to be disagreements. For example, a joint venture agreement to develop a planned community over a ten- to twenty-year period is almost certain to involve a number of disagreements, while the sale of a house in "as is condition" for cash to close in thirty days is much less likely to generate disagreements.

My advice is when disagreements arise, you should do your best to work out the disagreements as soon as possible. This can usually be done by respecting the other party's interests while protecting your own. There is no need to force the other party to live up to the letter of the contract if you can accommodate their legitimate interests without hurting yourself. You are almost always better off giving up a little ground, generating some good will, and resolving the disagreement before it becomes a serious dispute. Here are some suggestions:

- Respect the legitimate interests of the other party, and try to accommodate them whenever you can. There is usually a way to respect the other party's interests while protecting your own. For example, if you are selling a property, and the buyer wants to extend due diligence for thirty days, figure out a way to do it, maybe by getting a cash payment. This point is demonstrated by a case I handled several years ago for a very wealthy client whose name some of you would recognize. He was buying a large oceanfront resort property for development, and the seller refused to extend the time for due diligence in a situation where it was reasonable to do so. The seller's refusal to extend due diligence and abrupt cancellation of the sale precipitated a lawsuit by my client that tied up the seller's property for years and eventually led the seller to sell the property to my client for about $2 million less than the contract price, even though the real estate market had gone up. All this could have been avoided if the seller had just given my client a thirty-day extension for due diligence.

- Generate clear correspondence to the other side with the help of your lawyer. This will often help avoid litigation and, if not, this correspondence will be valuable evidence for you in any litigation.

- You can usually make substantial concessions to resolve disputes and avoid litigation and still come out way ahead. The cost of litigation is always higher than you expect. The case always costs more than you expect and there are hidden costs. The emotional cost of litigation can be overwhelming for many people and the lost time, energy, and opportunities can also be huge and may be more expensive than the direct costs of the lawyers and experts who participate in the case. The adage "avoid litigation at all costs" is only slightly off the mark.

TIP You are almost always better off giving up a little ground, generating some good will and resolving the disagreement before it becomes a serious dispute.

TRY MEDIATION

When you have tried your best and have been unable to settle the dispute directly with the other party, you may want to try mediation. Mediation is an abbreviated dispute resolution process where an experienced professional helps the parties reach a voluntary settlement of their dispute.

A number of years ago when mediation was first used, it had a very high success rate, between 80 and 90 percent. In recent years, the success rate is much lower. Today, the mediation process is only as good as the mediator. Highly skilled, experienced mediators still maintain a high success ratio while less skilled mediators probably succeed in less than half their attempts. Mediation can work when you select the right mediator, and that is probably the most important factor in a successful mediation.

The second most important factor is a mutual desire by the parties to resolve the dispute in the mediation. Mediations used to take place in one day, but today a good mediator may work for as long as one or two months, going back and forth with the parties to resolve a dispute. A good mediator will put in whatever effort it takes to succeed. I was the mediator appointed by the court to resolve a series of interrelated cases that were estimated to use up one year of court time if they were not settled. That mediation lasted several months before I succeeded, but it saved a fortune in lawyers' fees and court time. It was well worth the effort I put into it.

TIP Mediation can work when you select the right mediator and when there is a mutual desire by the parties to resolve the dispute.

Another way to improve the odds for success in mediation is to begin the process with a comprehensive settlement offer that includes all the details of a settlement. You then want to insist that the negotiation of major terms take place within the context of this comprehensive agreement so you will know exactly what you are agreeing to.

Mediation is relatively inexpensive if it is successful and is much better than any other method of formal dispute resolution. However, if it is unsuccessful, then nothing has been accomplished, and the mediation will have been a waste of time and money. Because mediation can be so efficient and effective, many real estate contracts require mediation before arbitration or litigation. I recommend that you include a provision requiring mediation in most contracts.

Several years ago, I represented a client in a case that seemed ripe for mediation. The parties decided to pay a blue ribbon mediator $10,000 for one day, and we all flew to San Francisco to have him mediate the case. Although the mediator was very experienced and had a good reputation, he completely screwed up this mediation and failed to get any concrete settlement offer out of the other side. My client was so anxious to resolve the case that he made repeatedly lower offers to the other side without any counter offer, all contrary to the instructions his business advisor and I gave him repeatedly. The client negotiated against himself throughout the day and reduced his settlement offer from $500,000 (which was a fair deal for the other side) down to something substantially under $100,000, which the arrogant folks on the other side should have jumped at.

The case finally settled years later when the vice president of the real estate title insurance company (who was himself an attorney) called me directly and said we had to settle the case right then. He said that he could no longer take the amount the case was costing. He indicated his lawyer's fees had already exceeded $1 million with no end in sight. I recalled that his attorney had bragged after an earlier hearing in the case that he had "bought a new car" with the fees from the case. The title company finally agreed to pay my client $850,000 in cash to settle a case that could have been settled at the outset for less than $100,000 in the mediation. I estimate the total cost to the title company was well over $2 million, all because it did not accept my client's offer in the mediation. You should avoid making this mistake!

CONSIDER ARBITRATION

If settlement fails and mediation fails, you may want to consider arbitration as an alternative to litigation in court. Arbitration is a trial conducted by an experienced arbitrator paid by the parties instead of a judge or jury who are paid by the federal or state government. Many real estate contracts require arbitration instead of litigation. Where the contract requires arbitration, then the parties are required to resolve the dispute by arbitration, and any court litigation initiated by either party based upon the contract will be dismissed by the court in favor of arbitration under the terms of the contract.

The arbitrator hears the evidence and makes a binding and final decision based upon the evidence and the law. Your ability to appeal a bad decision made by an arbitrator is very limited. Arbitration used to be quicker and cheaper than litigation, but today it is unclear whether there is any net benefit to arbitration over litigation. Because the arbitrator is getting paid and a refusal to hear all evidence may be grounds to upset the arbitration decision, arbitrations can tend to go on forever, can become more expensive than litigation, and may not get the case resolved any quicker.

The quality of arbitrators can also vary greatly with some having difficulty deciding cases correctly. Because the benefits of arbitration are unclear, the trend toward requiring arbitration instead of litigation in real estate contracts has been curtailed to some extent. The arbitration requirement has now been deleted from some real estate contracts in favor of traditional court litigation. For example, the standard real estate "Purchase Contract" used by real estate agents in Hawai'i was recently revised to delete the mandatory arbitration requirement.

To me, arbitration and litigation are now a toss up with no clear-cut advantage to either. If your case is assigned to a good judge that your attorney has confidence in then you should stick with the judge. On the other hand, if your case is assigned to a poor judge and you can agree with the other side on a good arbitrator, then you may want to opt for arbitration. For example, both sides in a court case I handled recently agreed to arbitration instead of going through the litigation process. We selected a very experienced retired judge as the arbitrator, and my client just received a very fair award that the other side has paid in full. In that case, the arbitration was completed promptly and worked out very well for my client.

TIP Arbitrations can tend to go on forever, become more expensive than litigation, and may not get the case resolved any quicker. Because the benefits of arbitration are unclear, the trend toward requiring arbitration instead of litigation in real estate contracts has been curtailed somewhat.

LITIGATION IS YOUR LAST RESORT

If you are unable to resolve the dispute by negotiation or mediation and your contract does not require arbitration, then you are left with litigation. As I said earlier, litigation can be very expensive and emotionally draining. The direct cost—meaning cash—can be very high, and the indirect costs in terms of wasted time and emotional energy can be even higher. But there are also opportunities to resolve the dispute. The court will usually agree upon a request by either party to conduct settlement conferences in an effort to resolve the case early and without the expense of a trial. The court may also appoint a mediator to help settle the case. In my experience, a court-appointed mediator has a better chance of success than one without court backing.

In one case where I was acting as a court-appointed mediator, several of the parties were not even paying their own lawyers or returning their phone calls, much less contributing to a settlement of the case. Because I had been appointed by the court, I was able to get the presidents of those large companies on the phone and get their attention with some direct talk, and eventually I got their cooperation in contributing to a global settlement of a number of complicated interrelated cases.

There may also be opportunities to file motions to decide or limit issues in advance of the trial. However, generally things are not going well if you are embroiled in the litigation process. If you end up there, then you are left with no alternative but to do your best to win with the understanding that it will be very expensive.

A case earlier in my career demonstrates the financial and emotional toll that litigation can take. I recall sitting at the counsel table in court in the morning waiting for the trial to resume. The man on the opposing side was sitting at his table, waiting for his lawyer to arrive. I could not help feeling sorry for him; he looked so dejected. His lawyer had refused to settle the case, and he had been forced to go into this trial that was not going well for him. Things took a turn for the worse when the sheriff came in and served him with a complaint in a separate case that had been filed against him by his own lawyer to collect the fees he was owed. This caused a great deal of dissention between the client and his lawyer who arrived a few minutes later. The dissention lasted through the rest of the trial and probably contributed to the large monetary award the court made against this poor individual. Leaving aside the ethical problems with his lawyer, this graphically demonstrates the emotional and financial cost of litigation.

TIP The direct cost—meaning cash—of litigation can be very high, and the indirect costs in terms of wasted time and emotional energy can be even higher.

NEVER QUIT TRYING TO RESOLVE THE DISPUTE NO MATTER WHERE YOU ARE IN THE PROCESS

Always keep in mind that mediation, arbitration, and litigation are only means to an end: resolving a dispute. No matter where you stand in these processes, you should never quit trying to resolve the case on some basis you can live with. Never quit trying to work things out with the other side. Also never hesitate to take the initiative in trying to settle. Don't worry too much about appearing weak because you have taken the initiative. Only a fool would not want to settle a case if it is at all possible. The other side is probably not having any more fun than you are, and as both sides get progressively more fed up with the time and expense of litigation, they may be more willing to settle. So never stop trying to come up with alternative ways to resolve the dispute.

TIP Don't worry too much about appearing weak because you have taken the initiative to settle. Only a fool would not want to settle a case if it is at all possible.

Several years ago I represented the developer of the only large, new oceanfront hotel developed in Waikiki over the past twenty years. The owners and residents of the condominium apartment building across the street had opposed his project from the beginning through their association of apartment owners. They had contested the shoreline permit required for any oceanfront development in

Hawai'i and had appealed the granting of that permit all the way through the court system. They also contested a number of zoning variances that the developer required for the construction of the hotel. To say that my client had a great deal of animosity toward these people would be an understatement.

I filed a motion in the case to have the variances upheld as a matter of law so that my client could proceed with the construction of the hotel. The argument before the judge went very well. We were well organized and made a clear, compelling presentation using visual aids, while our opposition made a sloppy, disjointed presentation. The judge also appeared receptive to our arguments. To observers in the courtroom, including my client, it looked like we were sure to win. I told my client after the hearing that I thought the judge's positive reaction was because of my favorable relationship with him, and that my intuition was telling me that we were going to lose the motion and the variances that would sabotage his plans for the hotel. My client was not buying it. He was at the hearing, and he was confident we were going to win.

Nevertheless, I started negotiations with the lawyer on the other side for my client to make a cash payment to the condo association in exchange for dropping its opposition to the variances. The association finally agreed to accept $150,000 to drop the case. My client refused, even though this case could sabotage his $100 million hotel project if he lost. He was also infuriated with me for wasting time and showing weakness by negotiating with his enemies. He told me to stop dealing with them and just wait for the judge's favorable decision. I got the judge to postpone his decision and continued to negotiate a reduced amount with the association. The client also rejected that offer and threatened to fire me. I continued to negotiate. Finally, the association agreed to accept $55,000 to settle the case. My client was very angry with me, but I kept calling and recommending that he accept the offer. I pointed out how small the amount was and how much was at stake. He told me never to call again about the offer. I continued to call. He again threatened to fire me. I did not let up, and he finally agreed to accept the offer and paid the $55,000 to settle the case. My client considered it a complete waste of money since he was confident he was going to win.

I went to see the judge after the case was settled, and he told me that he thought all the variances were wrong and that he was going to strike down all of them. Shortly after we settled the case on the variances, we won the appeal on the shoreline permit, and my client was able to proceed with what is now a beautiful oceanfront hotel owned and operated by another one of my clients. So this story had a happy and profitable ending, which is your goal in all real estate deals. The moral here is this: Keep trying to settle, and never take the risk of an adverse court decision if you can avoid it.

So, don't reconcile yourself to trudge down the path of seemingly endless acrimony in litigation if you can get a resolution you can live with. You are almost always better off settling than you will be by taking the risk of an uncertain outcome in litigation. Because of the complication of real estate deals and the limited remedies that can be provided by the court, in many situations a settlement is often a much better resolution for both parties than litigation, even for the "winner." In short, you may not be able to get what you really need from a court decision, even if you win.

How to Resolve Real Estate Disputes

Try to resolve the disputes you cannot avoid by doing the following:

- Consult with an experienced litigation lawyer to avoid litigation.
- When disputes arise, do whatever you can to work it out.
- Try mediation.
- Consider arbitration.
- Litigation is your last resort.
- Never stop trying to resolve the dispute no matter where you are in this process.

CONCLUSION

You are almost always better off settling your disputes in a reasonable, fair way that respects the interests of the other parties while protecting your own than you are having the dispute decided by an arbitrator, a judge, or a jury. And most of all, the best solution is to avoid disputes altogether by going into the right real estate projects, with the right people, the right mind-set, the right contracts, and the right legal representation.

Bernie Bays is a partner in Bays, Deaver, Lung, Rose & Holma, a boutique real estate firm based in Honolulu, Hawai'i, and is one of the few attorneys in Hawai'i who is board certified as a civil trial specialist by the National Board of Trial Advocacy and the Hawai'i Supreme Court. During his thirty-eight year career, Bernie has represented clients in landmark real estate cases before the Hawai'i Intermediate Court, the Hawai'i Supreme Court, and the U.S. Supreme Court. His experience encompasses a broad range of business and real estate cases, including the representation of minority and majority shareholders, corporate proxy fights, antitrust representation of both plaintiffs and defendants, as well as litigation concerning real estate sales, commercial leases, land use problems, rent renegotiations, claims for economic loss and lost profit, property damage, general and limited partner disputes, condominium and subdivision problems, land valuation issues, and condemnation.

PART 2

Your Real Estate Project

Buy by the Acre, Sell by the Foot
Understanding Real Needs, Financial Logic, and Asking Questions

Mel is my neighbor. We met at a neighborhood holiday party. I liked him im-mediately because he is a real estate developer and was a longtime owner of two professional sports teams. There is nothing like sitting in the owner's seat at a Phoenix Suns basketball game. The players, cheerleaders, and the action are much more intense at the court level. Usually I sit higher up and need to use binoc-ulars to see the game.

One of the advantages of having a friend like Mel is that I get to find out where the next growth areas are going to be. Being a land developer, he is operating three-to-ten years out into the future. Not only do his developments expand the city, Mel and his high-profile team are responsible for bringing new life back into down-town urban areas.

Mel is a great neighbor, friend, and a real estate visionary. Whenever I want to know about the future and where to invest, I call Mel Shultz.

—ROBERT KIYOSAKI

Have you ever been driving around your city or town and passed by an open field and wondered if that field might be the only undeveloped land in the area? I asked myself that question many times, and actually found it pretty fascinating. I found it so fascinating, in fact, that the question itself actually jump-started my real estate career, and the discovery became my strategy.

Driving through your city or town can reveal a great deal about real estate. For instance, you may have noticed that houses tend to dot the interiors of most cities and towns while shopping, office, and other commercial properties generally run along the major streets. This all makes sense once you start to notice and make mental notes of how most cities and towns develop.

In the late 1970s, driving around seemed like a good way to find real estate. I didn't own any sophisticated tools other than maps and a car to explore opportunities, although I did buy one of the first giant mobile phones that looked and felt like a brick. Driving along the main streets of my city provided all the options needed to buy property during this time before instant information. When I saw larger parcels that were skipped over by development, yet were right in the path of growth or on the beaten path, it made sense to find out who owned these underserved parcels and inquire about the status. It seems pretty simple and obvious; however, there were ample spots that were ignored by most land buyers and developers. Finding the owners was just one call away to the title company. Once I found the owner's number, I handled it just like I learned in my insurance business training: pick up the phone and meet the prospect. These prospects were slightly different, though. Rather than the buyers I was used to calling, this time I was calling sellers, and I was offering to give people money rather than asking them to write checks.

Hard to believe, but it's always easier to buy something than it is to sell. Think about it. In your own life, you'll find it to be true. The problem is that the owner knows that what they own is valuable, so it's worth holding on to. On the other hand, the owner may not want to go through the process and the risk of investing the time and money it takes to plan and perform feasibility studies, as well as other land-use studies that may be required to develop the property.

Even though real estate can be very tax favorable, the process and final entitlement received on the land may negatively affect the tax status for some owners. We always discuss these kinds of tax issues with our tax advisors to be sure we are never crossing the lines, or if we are, to be fully informed of the negative tax implications. This is a complex part of the equation, and I absolutely recommend finding the best real estate tax counsel before even beginning to zone or make any changes to a piece of real estate. It is just as important to understand the tax and legal aspects at the beginning of a property transaction so you can get off on the right foot, as it is to understand these same implications when selling the property purchased. This cannot be emphasized enough. Talk to professional tax and legal experts.

I regularly hire and talk to CPAs and lawyers before getting too far down the road in real estate. My brother's law practice was the logical entry place for me. It is the oldest law firm in Arizona with expertise in all areas of real estate. I believed from the beginning that a portion of my investment dollars were to be earmarked, first for the land and, second for lawyers and other consultants who could better my chances for success.

The value of a team is self-evident. I always wanted to be the quarterback of our team at school. I knew the position was less about heroics and more about being sure the best support was in front of me. My job then was simply to remember the plays and throw or hand the ball to the best players.

TIP The *Dictionary of Real Estate Terms*, Sixth Edition, defines "entitlement" as this: The right to develop land with government approvals for zoning density, utility installations, occupancy permits, use permits, and streets.

MATCHING MARKET NEEDS WITH PRODUCT CREATION

Just because you buy a hotel doesn't mean it has to stay a traditional hotel. Just because you buy an apartment building doesn't mean it needs to stay an apartment building. Markets change, market needs change, and in order to be successful, you may find you have to change a property from one kind of product to another. Here are a few examples:

Converting a traditional hotel into a timeshare property.
Converting a rental apartment into a for-purchase apartment to the renter or another buyer.

These are examples of matching market needs with product creation. Space that already existed was transformed to create new revenue sources based on market demands.

When it comes to land, changes may involve simply splitting one larger lot into two or more residential lots or changing land permitted for one use to a different use that is usually better economically. Most often this requires the approval of the city or town (municipality) to consent to the proposed use change. This is called rezoning and/or the entitlement process.

Real Life Story: The Education on 32nd Street

In the mid 1970s, I bought a house on about five acres for $240,000. Within a short time, a friend asked if he could buy the home. His intent was to change the zoning from one house per acre to commercial/office use. He offered to pay triple my price with the caveat that the closing had to wait for up to twelve months. He figured it would take that long to convince all the residents on the north and south sides of the property to agree and the city to approve his rezoning plan. This was my first personal experience watching someone change the use (rezoning) of a property. I was in my mid-twenties, and it seemed worth waiting a year to make such a compelling profit.

Time passed; his rezoning was approved, and we closed the deal. This was an early eye opener. Suddenly, it hit me! I could add value by changing the use of the underlying land. I decided this was to be part of my new investment path.

Real Life Story: View from the Mountain

With confidence from my 32nd Street experience, I purchased the twenty-nine-thousand-square-foot McCune Mansion in Paradise Valley, Arizona. The monstrous mansion was built by oil tycoon Walker McCune in the 1960s for more than $3 million. The mansion sat on forty acres of hillside that overlooked the entire city and the spectacular Camelback Mountain. My plan was to change the use from a single home to a resort. The city fought the rezoning, so I decided to go with what they called preferred residential zoning, which included the "hillside ordinance." This is where I truly became a real estate developer and gained firsthand knowledge about the zoning process and lot layout. Each lot building pad had to meet complicated cut-and-fill requirements—how much you could cut into the mountainside and fill back in to create a building pad. I ended up on the committee with real homebuilders rewriting the town ordinances for slope-and-hillside cutting and refilling. In the process, I found a buyer who purchased the mansion for the price I paid for the entire forty acres and mansion. The sale included the mansion and five acres, which I carved out around the house. I then held onto the remaining land, which was now converted into twenty-eight one-acre-plus home sites. The lots sold from $200,000 to $600,000, and I had made my biggest profit yet. I retained one lot to build a home for my family, but the "desert snakes" were not my friends, so I made the decision to sell at a later time. Sales topped $10 million.

My early experience with the mansion on the mountain got me thinking about the economics of the land business. There's a story about Abe Lincoln's farm that makes the point about creative financial engineering better than I could ever make on my own. It seems Abe Lincoln bought his family's farm from his father, Thomas, when cash got a little tight as a way to bail him out. Eventually, after Abe became president and one of the great figures of our country, the friends of the Abe Lincoln Historical Farm near Lerna, Illinois, took on the ownership. It seems the owners of this land had a brilliant idea. They wanted to give people of Illinois and the nation the opportunity to own a tiny piece of American history in an effort to raise money for the owner's family. They planned to sell off small parcels of the estate to interested people. When they parceled out the designated acre, they had more than six million squares to offer the public. The net return on this is not known, but even with a low price for the land parcel, I am sure it was substantial.

This is the ultimate subdivision of land, almost beyond the scope of imagination. But I'm sure it won't be the last ingenious idea. If I had to start over today in the real estate business, what would I do? I can answer that question this way. In the late 1970s we would joke about a wealthy private lender and investor named Bill Levine. We'd say that if he were dropped out of a plane with a parachute on his back in the middle of China and with no money, within a few years he would be one of the wealthiest men in China or wherever else he happened to fall. Some people just seem to know how to create wealth. They are the true financial engineers.

TIP Starting is the hardest part of anything in life.

Starting is the hardest part of anything in life. In the early 1970s I had saved up about $5,000 from my life insurance sales commissions. A real estate firm in my building had several older, unoccupied houses it was trying to unload. Inside these old house bones lay bright red carpeting, purple-painted walls, and linoleum floors from the 1950s. Even the carpet stains were better than the original colors.

The cash requirement to acquire these homes was straightforward: pay closing costs, include a few hundred dollars in commissions, and assume the debt. I thought why not? I soon found that renting these showplaces was not easy because after I had purchased the properties I didn't have enough money to repaint and update the interiors, nor did I have the mechanical skills to do it myself. But somehow, enough renters were willing to take the houses and do their own fix ups. From the cash flow I received, I was able to buy more houses and sell some along the way, accumulating about $10,000 in cash. I didn't like the rent collection process much, so after selling my last house in 1973, I immediately moved on to something a little more sophisticated.

My first office building was just east of 24th Street on Thomas Road in Phoenix, Arizona, as were my second and third buildings. My logic was after buying my first building and not knowing where else to buy, it seemed like a good idea to go next door and buy those buildings, too. If it hadn't been for other opportunities that came my way, I may have just kept buying along the same major road in Phoenix. What did I know? These small office buildings were, for me, where it really all began.

After selling the first building and making $30,000, I began to get some traction. The next two were sold as a package with $130,000 in net profit. A California syndicator was looking for more buildings in Phoenix, and I liked the idea of negotiating the purchase and sale. My strategy was to buy and improve the properties, much like the houses I owned, except this time I wanted to be able to afford to hire contractors. After my house experiences, I learned to set aside cash up front for this purpose. The old painted white brick needed a modern look, so we put in new windows and doors, added beige-colored stucco to the brick exterior, new signage, and a parking lot. This clean, new exterior brought the building back to life. First impressions are lasting.

STARTING OFF WITH REAL ESTATE MATH

Getting started with basic real estate math is helpful to me. There are 43,560 square feet in one acre, and there are 640 acres in a section of land. The question arises regarding land uses and valuations. Commercial land is a higher economic use than a similar size residential-sized lot. In the course of planning, developers study the market demands and the appropriate use of a parcel of land and determine the best land use before buying. The planning and zoning process, which I learned after my house buying experience, incorporates the information learned along with the market demand to create the highest and best use. With that said, consider the math for a parcel of land. It may look something like this:

On the next page is a very simple illustration of buying in bulk at a "per acre" price and converting to a "square foot" price. Usually land owners sell large parcels of unzoned land in areas outside traditional development cores in bulk at a per-acre price. In urban areas, commercial or multifamily property is usually

Buying by the Acre, and Selling by the Foot

This example may help you see the potential of real estate in a new way.

The purchase price of ten acres is $50,000 per acre, or $500,000 total (zoned for ten houses).

The final plan for ten acres may be 250 apartment units, which may be worth $10,000 per unit or $250,000 per acre (after rezoning approval).

This equates to about $5.75 per square foot (43,560 square foot x $5.74 = $250,000 per acre).

Since the land was acquired for single family and changed to multifamily, the underlying use created an increased value of five times the original purchase.

sold by the square foot. It's really a convenience because it all reverts back to the dollar amount paid for the land, the ultimate sales price, and profit. This practice is convenient for both the buyer and seller. It's similar to the way we use inches as a measurement division of a foot. For example, rather than say it's one-quarter of a foot, we say say three inches, which is easily understood. Perhaps smaller measurement practices were used to influence a buyer's perception of the amount being paid for the product. It is like figuring out why gold is sold by the ounce and not by the pound. At the end of the day, it's perception.

Many other projects followed for me. I developed everything from business parks to large, master-planned communities. The lesson I learned through it all was to plan and divide the land, visualizing what a property could be and what it "wanted" to be. A residential community wants a compatible use like a grocery store, restaurant, pharmacy, or other convenience. That means forcing a property to a higher-return use doesn't make sense if it doesn't blend and fit into the surroundings. You've driven around your town and seen buildings that don't fit. The right products in the right places feel right and look right, and the neighbors know that. I saw how my friend, Joe Beer, went house-to-house to let the neighbors give input, to ask them questions, and most important, to listen as he petitioned for rezoning. This is a good practice particularly if you do this with forethought and patience and are willing to modify and compromise and be sensitive to the neighbors. You may actually find throughout the process that the land you bought by the acre may indeed be sold by the square foot.

Let me share a personal story. I was involved a few years back in the sale of a site for a post office. The buyer wanted an environmental report to ensure there were no hazardous substances on the site. This is very typical. But as my partners

> ### Three "Must Do's" to Buy by the Acre and Sell by the Foot:
>
> 1. Plan and divide the land thoughtfully.
> 2. Work with the neighbors in the community.
> 3. Always be willing to listen and compromise.

and I were working our way through the due diligence process with the buyer, an environmental problem came to our attention. Although the issue seemed to possess a very low chance of causing any real problem, the inspectors sent over a backhoe to test the area. During the test, a sample of soil showed a completely new problem: The sample contained oil. Impossible, we thought. So, they tested the same sample again with the same results. Perplexed and bracing ourselves for a costly soil remediation, which given the past use of the property seemed unfathomable, we decided to take a walk around the property. Thank goodness we did this. While we were walking by the backhoe, one of us noticed it had an oil leak. Upon further inspection, the oils matched up with the leaky equipment. Retested with a new backhoe, the soil turned up clean as originally expected. Walking the site can make all the difference. Hands on requires a physical look, not just reading a report.

TIP I have always enjoyed walking around the properties we are buying. For me, seeing is the difference between knowing and guessing.

WISDOM FROM THE FIELD

If you want to get involved in real estate (and not just when the economy is booming) then the following questions may come in handy:

HOW CAN I LEARN THE BASICS OF PROPERTY USES AND POTENTIAL CHANGES TO USE?

Each city and or municipality has its own ordinances and laws for permitted uses for property. Find a good zoning lawyer and inquire about current zoning and permitted changes. A planner or architect who has planned and designed other local projects is the best source for ideas. Real estate brokers are also an important part of determining potential tenants or other buyers and/or developers for parts or all of a properly thought-out land use plan.

Who Are the Key Members of My Team, and What Do They Do?

In addition to the zoning lawyer, the land planner or architect and the brokers (both leasing and sales) are critical. You'll need the following team members to help you along the way:

Feasibility Experts

This may include economists and often larger brokerage companies who gather and compile sector reports for vacancy, lease rates, absorption and other reports to help determine need for product type.

Accountant

This person can put together a financial pro forma to estimate sales, costs, and potential profits so you can determine your offer price and capital/debt/equity requirements. The broker should provide sales input projections.

Civil Engineers, Soil Experts, and Contractors

These experts will help you determine the improvement cost estimates you will need to fully evaluate the property's potential from topographical and physical maps to understanding wet and dry utilities.

When you consider the many disciplines required to make all this come together you see why many avoid this aspect of real estate. It sounds harder than it really is. Although patience and knowledge are required, after the first few deals the process becomes clear. It is much like an NBA point guard or a quarterback on a football field. Most of your time is spent knowing where your teammates are and who to get the ball to. Rarely do you shoot or run; passing the ball is essential. You learn by doing, and starting with a simple lot split for a couple of houses is an easy way to experience the process firsthand.

How Do I Find Property That Can Be Rezoned or Changed to Become a Profitable Venture?

This is the bottom line of the whole exercise. Knowing the market needs and economics of the specific product that will ultimately be built on the site takes study and some imagination. Ask questions and write them down. The more questions you have, the better. A few, but important questions you could ask are these:

What would improve the living quality and/or convenience for the people who live or work in the area?

How many people drive by this particular property each day?

How can I help people afford to live in the area or give them a better alternative for a retail shopping or dining experience?

What about better medical care closer to home or more convenient services in a certain area?

These questions stimulate the imagination and the possibilities. Most people ask too few questions. You can build a case for almost any business model if you ask enough of the right questions.

Bill Gates, founder of Microsoft, was interested in information at the speed of thought. Billionaire Warren Buffett considered simple businesses that are run well and provide capital to grow, as places to invest. These investment strategies have vaulted them to become two of the wealthiest men in the world. Mr. Buffett is the master of asking questions then boiling them down to the few most direct and succinct ones that become repeatable observations. True genius is when you can make the unnoticed concise. Ask and write down a few questions about land you have noticed regularly.

Why has this been skipped over by the path of development?

Who owns it?

What is the right use or fit for it?

How would the math look if it were used in a different way?

Who would buy or rent whatever I think should be built on this site?

After the experience of completing your first real estate process, you will have exercised your mind in a way that will help you look at land through new eyes. The fun for me is to drive by or walk into a project I have been a part of and know this was a piece of land few considered would ever be a place where people would want to live, work and play.

After thirty years of planning, negotiating, visualizing, building, and selling these ideas, I've learned that virtually anything is possible if you ask questions. Analyze and think through the answers, and take the steps to get your mind's ideas into pictures and then later into bricks. Remember, bricks are laid one upon another just like your thoughts. The hardest part is setting the first brick in place.

 **Mel Shultz** cofounded JDM Properties, Inc., in 1983 as a full-service real estate firm that develops and manages quality properties in Arizona and Colorado, including upscale residential and commercial space, and business parks. A principal of JDMD Investments, LLC, Mel and his partners are developing the largest master-planned community in the greater Phoenix area for more than three hundred thousand residents. Mel was a general partner of the Phoenix Suns basketball team until the team sold in 2005, and he was one of the original general partners of the 2001 World Championship Arizona Diamondbacks baseball team. Mel led the design and build team for the five-thousand-seat Dodge Theatre in downtown Phoenix. The company's Web site is www.jdmpartnersllc.com.

10

Curtis OAKES

It's All About Adding Value

I once accused Curtis of going "where white men fear to tread." He laughed out loud and said, "That's true." He went on to say, "I have basketball star Magic Johnson's philosophy of going into urban areas and bringing in development and businesses that lift the area up." Curtis then added, "Regardless of race, too many investors just suck the cash out of a neighborhood but never reinvest to improve it. I invest to reinvest and improve a neighborhood." This is why Curtis and his wife, Diana, are respected friends as well as fellow real estate investors.

Today, some of the most beautiful real estate is being boarded up as casualties of economic decline. It takes a special kind of investor to invest not only to make money, but to also bring an area in decline back up. I tried it once and did okay but not great. Truthfully, I was an outsider coming in, hoping to make a quick buck from a bad situation. Now personally wiser, I have a better appreciation for what Curtis does. It takes more than knowing about real estate. It takes knowing the people and the psychology of the neighborhood, and, most importantly, having a desire to be a part of the community. This is what I have learned about real estate from Curtis and Diana.

—Robert Kiyosaki

As a successful real estate agent, investor, and developer, I've shared a stage as a presenter with Robert Kiyosaki, who is a personal mentor to me. His ideas and guidance have been instrumental in much of my success. I have presented seminars with Donald Trump, as well as coauthored with him an audio CD entitled *Three Master Secrets of Real Estate Success*. At this writing, my wife and I are renovating a multimillion-dollar home in an exclusive San Francisco neighborhood. To boil it all down, I have achieved all of this by following a simple mantra, one that anyone can understand and apply to achieve similar real estate successes: Profit from problems. There are two foundational things that have been a constant for my wife, Diana, and I throughout our process: knowledge and faith.

"My people shall be destroyed because of a lack of knowledge," *Hosea 4:6*.

"Faith is the confidence that what we hope for will actually happen. It gives us assurance about things we cannot see," *Hebrews 11:1*.

TIP Your mantra should be this: Profit from problems.

A pristine property with affluent tenants sounds wonderful, doesn't it? No huge maintenance issues, little problem collecting rents, and so on. Yes, these types of properties are easy on the mind, *but they also have a significant cost and little chance to appreciate.*

A problem property, on the other hand, has an amazing, and fast, upside potential. For example, let's say that the going rate for a building in a certain area is $200,000. The problem property might be worth $140,000. Once the problems are fixed, however, its value will zoom to the going rate for similar properties: $200,000. Likewise, rents in a problem building might be low. After you improve the property, however, you can raise rents—increasing your amount of income.

This is the concept of "forced appreciation," which occurs when an investor purchases a property that's less than the going market value (usually due to inherent problems, such as high vacancy rates, severely deteriorated buildings, environmental problems, etc.), then fixes the problems that "force" substantial appreciation in value back up to the current market value. I also call this the value-added approach, where you take an asset, make various improvements, and have the asset increase in value. Forced appreciation provides you with a short-term paper profit, which you can then use to your advantage in a variety of ways. This value-added approach has helped many, many real estate investors build everything from small nest eggs to multibillion-dollar fortunes.

TIP I never focus on or count on appreciation when analyzing whether or not to purchase a property. To me, market appreciation is always a bonus: if it happens, great, but if the property doesn't go up in value based on the market, that's okay, too, because I know that I am making what I need to make on the property in terms of cash flow and depreciation. Likewise, when someone says that they have an investment that will provide capital gains, thank them, then turn and run in the other direction! Why? Capital gains are based on the speculation that something "might" happen in the future to drive up the value of that investment. The key word here is speculation; something might happen. By focusing on a value-added approach to real estate investing, you have much greater control over a property's ultimate value.

If you resolve to become a problem solver—someone who embraces rather than runs away from problems—your chances of achieving success in real estate investing will dramatically increase. The next step becomes finding appropriate problem properties.

MY STORY

I purchased my first home in Philadelphia, Pennsylvania, in 1979 for $27,800. I used the G.I. Bill, which meant I had 100 percent financing. I had an adjustable rate loan with an interest rate of 17.5 percent. That's obscene by today's standards, but at the time I didn't care. I was thrilled to be a new homeowner, period. This also was my introduction to leverage, which is using a small amount of money to purchase a large amount of something else (in this case, real estate). I began to buy properties as long as I didn't have to put much money down. I didn't care what the interest rate was; as long as I had a positive cash flow, I bought.

My life as a real estate entrepreneur took another big leap in 1982 when I resigned from my government job for the Naval Aviation Supply Office. From the beginning, I specialized in value-added properties. In Philadelphia, boarded-up houses were practically everywhere, and that's what I looked for. Buying and then turning was easy because I could buy a property for between $5,000 and $30,000 and then decide to either rent or sell.

I had an uncle who came to visit me from San Francisco, California. Every time he came to visit, he would go on and on about the San Francisco real estate market. In 1985 he finally convinced me to move to San Francisco to invest in value-added real estate. However, little did I know that my Philadelphia success in renting and flipping houses couldn't be duplicated in San Francisco. Why? Simply because property was so much more expensive. The average duplex at the time was $250,000. These prices sent my nervous system into shock and fear. While I had accumulated some funds to invest, I needed a lot more information about California real estate before I could begin.

TIP I've had my share of challenges and problems. But with patience and the right approach, value-added real estate investing can work for you, too.

In the meantime, the cost of living and real estate school was beginning to deplete my investment nest egg. What's more, this fear of potentially losing everything held me captive. I wouldn't do a deal if I saw one! I finally got my real estate license and immediately went to work in an area in San Francisco to duplicate my success in Philadelphia. However, in Philadelphia it was relatively easy to identify value-added real estate. Just find a boarded-up house at a cheap price, fix it up, and sell it. In San Francisco, however, there were no boarded-up houses. I had to figure out how to add value in other ways. I finally found the area and the niche. The area was called Bayview Hunter's Point, and the niche was called "in-law apartments." So I went to work buying single-family homes (which were selling, at the time, for $50,000 to $75,000) and adding in-law apartments in the rear of the garages for rental units. Once construction was completed, I could sell the house for between $175,000 and $199,000. I had a full-time construction crew, and we were rehabbing and flipping, and life was good. Now, there are potential pitfalls—I've had my share of challenges and problems. But with patience and the right approach, value-added real estate investing can work for you, too.

FINDING THE RIGHT PROPERTIES

Now we've come to the exciting part, right? Right! Finding the right properties to invest in is obviously at the heart of long-term and sustained success in real estate investing. It's the area that will tap all of your knowledge and creativity, and where over time you'll build experience and expertise. You'll come to rely on this time and time again. Finding the right properties is equal parts knowledge and your ability to creatively "see" a property's potential. In short, here's where we marry your brain with your intuition to achieve a complete solution (wholeness).

First, let's review property types and property classes.

PROPERTY TYPES

The three types of buildings I'd like to focus on in this chapter are as follows:

Residential. Users live in one to four units. Can be various types, such as single family, duplex (two units), triplex (three units), and fourplex (four units).

Commercial. Five or more business units, such as an office building or a strip mall.

Mixed Use. A single building with both residential (people live there) and commercial (businesses) options.

If you are just starting out investing in real estate, I suggest that you begin by purchasing a two-or four-unit property. This way, you can begin small, leverage your way into a property, learn all you can, and then move up to a larger property when you have experience and a positive cash flow.

PROPERTY CLASSES

There are four classes of properties:

Class A. A property less than ten years old, in excellent condition, and with desired amenities, such as a pool or workout center. Class A properties can ask for, and receive, high rents, generally have a better quality of tenants, usually have lower maintenance costs, and are easier to manage. These properties are usually held by (owned by) investor groups and have a lower rate of return. They are the most sensitive to any downturn in the local or national economy.

Class B. Buildings that are ten to twenty years old and in fairly good overall condition. Class B properties are considered the most stable of the different property classes, and are usually located in well-established, middle-income neighborhoods. They are new enough to offer amenities, yet still old enough to be affordable to the average investor and tenants.

Class C. Buildings between twenty and thirty years old with limited or nonexistent amenities. Both ongoing and long-term maintenance costs are higher because of aging and the general need for a cosmetic "facelift." They have a lower quality of tenants, including those on government assistance. Value can be added by updating the property.

Class D. Buildings more than thirty years old that need substantial capital improvements. Usually located in declining areas, Class D properties usually have substantial deferred maintenance issues, such as the need to replace the roof, the electrical system, the HVAC system, etc.

TIP For beginning investors, I suggest that you focus most of your attention on finding *undervalued Class C buildings*.

You can look for undervalued properties in any of the four classes. However, please note that for Class A properties, the velocity of your money—the amount flowing to you—will slow down simply because there is less upside potential. For beginning investors, I suggest that you focus most of your attention on finding *undervalued Class C buildings*.

STARTING YOUR SEARCH

Here are the steps I recommend to find undervalued properties.

STEP ONE: BECOME AN EXPERT IN A PARTICULAR AREA

This generally is the area in which you live. Attempting to become an expert in a city outside of the state in which you reside, for example, would be time consuming and costly. Do as much as you can to study the area. Read the real estate sections in the local newspapers, drive around, and attend open houses.

This area should be large enough to have diverse neighbors. For example your initial area might be San Francisco. Over time, once you feel that you've mastered this particular area, then move on to another area.

Here's an example:

1. Select San Francisco as your area
2. Explore it, study it, drive around, etc.
3. "Master" this area
4. Then select another area such as Oakland

STEP TWO: SEEK OUT THE LEAST EXPENSIVE SECTIONS WITHIN THAT AREA

Again, you want to find problem properties and then solve the problems. You'll find the juiciest problems—and thus the potential for the largest returns—in the least expensive sections of your focus area.

STEP THREE: LOOK FOR PROBLEM PROPERTIES

Once you've become an expert in a particular area and identified the least expensive section within that area, the next step is to begin hunting for problem properties in that least expensive section.

How do you identify problem properties? They're usually the eyesore on a street or block. Signs to look for include buildings with one or more of these attributes:

- vacant
- boarded up
- tall grass / weeds
- trash strewn about / overflowing trash cans
- broken windows
- peeling paint
- general poor appearance

You also should be alert to potential property changes, such as:

- building owner wanting to retire / leave
- foreclosures
- probate
- code violations
- zoning variances not renewed or up for re-hearing
- a big-box tenant just left a strip mall

Please note that searching for real estate investment opportunities can be extremely fun, but it also can be an extremely frustrating process.

Tips As You Begin Your Property Search:

• **Stay positive.** Searches take time and involve walking around neighborhoods. There will be missteps and false alarms. Stay positive and have fun, and you'll be in the right frame of mind when the right property appears.

• **Be present and focused.** As much as possible, shut out past failures, negative thoughts ("The market hasn't bottomed out yet"), fears of failure, fears of success, and all other factors that might prevent you from seeing—really seeing—an opportunity. Those who are present and open to opportunities are almost always the people who are able to grab a new opportunity when it comes along.

• **Put in the time.** There's a saying in the writing world: To write a book, apply the seat of your pants to the chair. The same is true when searching for real estate investment opportunities. You must get out and look for the opportunities. You have to study the newspapers, drive around town, and network with real estate agents and lenders.

• **Don't be put off by market conditions.** Rarely will you find "perfect" market conditions when making any investment. There are always problems and potential pitfalls. Know this and accept it. Don't let the media, friends, or anyone else discourage you from seeking opportunities.

This last point bears repeating—never be discouraged by fluctuating market conditions. Interest rates will always go up, unless they happen to be going down. Property values will continue to decline until they hit bottom, and then they will rebound. And so on.

TIP This should be your "Real Estate Opportunity Search" mantra: In *any* market, at *any* time, I can find a great deal.

TIP Here is your "Never Give Up" mantra: Diligence leads to destiny.

You should actively search out potential deals. As well, you should create networks of people, tools, and resources to send potential deals your way. Here are ways to create a flow of deals—or at least whispers about potential deals:

- www.loopnet.com
- other investors
- real estate agents and brokers
- real estate lenders
- attorneys
- CPAs
- property management companies

TABLE 10.1 Personal Reflections

Brainstorm and list who else might be a "deal source" for you:

PROPERTY CRITERIA AND ANALYSIS

Once you've identified a potential investment property, it's time to closely study the property for both short-term and long-term opportunities. You will want to put each prospective property through a rigorous review, using the following criteria:

1. Guiding Investment Principles
    a. Leverage
    b. Cash Flow
    c. Cash-on-Cash Return
    d. Capitalization Rate
    e. Gross Rent Multiplier
2. S.W.O.T. (Strengths, Weaknesses, Opportunities, Threats)
3. Trends
4. Demographics

Now, I could write an entire book about these four key areas of property analysis. Here, though, let me summarize each of these points quickly.

LEVERAGE

Leverage simply means that you want as little of your money as possible used to secure the biggest opportunity possible. The less money you have to invest in a property, in other words, the larger the opportunity for a big payoff. When analyzing a property, know exactly what you will initially need to invest.

POSITIVE CASH FLOW

A key to building my real estate fortune over the years has been cash flow. We call cash flow "king" because having cash is always our primary objective. Positive cash flow creates and maintains your investment's momentum. It also has significant financing and lending implications. For example, when purchasing an apartment building containing more than five units, the bank will base the amount it will lend you on the building's cash flow abilities. (Your credit score is secondary.) Cash flow also is a significant factor in the building's overall value. A building with poor cash flow will appraise much lower than another comparable building in the same area that has a stronger cash flow. Never forget that.

DOUBLE DIGIT CASH-ON-CASH RETURN

This is the velocity of your money. In other words, you want to know at the beginning of an investment how long it will take the money you invest (primarily the down payment) to come back to you. This is critical because you want to invest that down payment over and over again in other investment properties, so the quicker that you're able to receive back that initial payment, the quicker you can apply it to another opportunity.

TIP Cash-on-Cash Return defined: This is the amount of cash you receive from a property investment in a specified time period as a percentage of your initial investment in that property.

Here are several examples using the same down payment amount ($20,000) but different cash flow amounts per year.

TABLE 10.2

Down Payment	Yearly Cash Flow	Years to Pay Back Down Payment	Cash-on-Cash Return
$20,000	$20,000	1	100%
$20,000	$10,000	2	50%
$20,000	$6,000	3	33%

As you can see, this table shows how many years it takes for your down payment to come back to you. In the first scenario, it takes one year. In the second scenario, it takes two years, and in the third, three years. Your cash-on-cash return is 100 percent, 50 percent, and 33 percent, respectively.

Your goal as an investor should be a cash-on-cash return in the 10 percent to 20 percent range. Anything above 20 percent is considered an exceptional cash-on-cash return.

CAPITALIZATION RATE OF 7 PERCENT OR HIGHER

The cap rate measures a building's performance without considering the mortgage financing. If you paid all cash for the invest property, how much money would it potentially make? What's the return? A high cap rate usually means a higher risk investment and a low sales price. High cap rates are typically found in poor, low-income areas. A low cap rate usually indicates there's less risk and a high sales price. Low cap rates are generally found in middle-class to upper-income areas. If you know the net operating income (NOI) and the cap rate, you can calculate what the sales price should be using this formula:

$$NOI / Cap Rate = Sales Price$$

TIP The Cap Rate measures a building's performance without taking into consideration the mortgage financing. It is the Net Operating Income divided by the sale price.

GROSS RENT MULTIPLIER OF 9 OR LOWER

Gross Rent Multipliers (GRM) are used as a measure to compare income properties within a particular area or neighborhood. For example, for three properties within a similar area of town, you could calculate the gross rent multiplier for each, then compare the three. If all other factors were equal, you would select the property with the lowest GRM. In general, as the gross rent multiplier decreases, cash flow increases. And conversely, as the GRM increases, cash flow typically decreases.

TIP Gross Rent Multiplier is the ratio of the price of a real estate investment to its annual rental income. The lower the ratio, the better.

S.W.O.T.

S.W.O.T. stands for Strengths, Weaknesses, Opportunities, and Threats. A common business evaluation tool, S.W.O.T. also applies to investment real estate simply because each property will have its own unique strengths, weaknesses, opportunities, and threats. The savvy real estate investor—the one seeking guaranteed success—will put each property through a detailed S.W.O.T. analysis.

Please note that generally speaking, this is a subjective analysis. In other words, there are no "right" or "wrong" answers. Likewise, many factors are interconnected. For example, a property's weakness—such as needing a fresh coat of paint—might also be an opportunity—a fresh coat of paint can quickly increase the overall look of the property, and thus its value.

TRENDS

Part of your property-seeking work should be to pay close attention to trends, or similar new tendencies displayed by a large number of people. For example, in the past, many city dwellers moved out of the city into the suburbs. Over the last several years, however, the trend has become the opposite. Because of rising gasoline prices and other factors, people in cities are "cocooning"—they want to live within walking distance of work, stores, restaurants, and so on.

Learning about new trends through the media and other information outlets is important. An investor will have become exposed to even more opportunities if he "sees" a new or developing trend before it becomes known and published through the media.

How can you spot new trends as they begin to develop? It's a bit of an art, but generally speaking you can:

- **Observe what's going on around you.** Pay particular attention to what people are doing differently. For example, eight or ten years ago, SUVs were all the rage. It seemed like everyone had one. Over time, however—again, because of rising gasoline prices and other environmental issues—SUV purchases declined, and a new type of transportation emerged called hybrid cars.

- **Read, read, read.** Read as much as you can: newspapers, magazines, local real estate magazines, and so on. And vary the sources and subject matter. What do I mean by "varied"? Every so often, read something different, a newspaper or periodical that you normally wouldn't read. As well, do a little Web surfing. What are people discussing on blogs in your community? What new Web sites are popping up on housing, community life, and other related topics? The more that you can broaden the information you take in, the more you can begin to see emerging trends and other issues. This is known, generally, as "connecting the dots." Become a dot-connector.

- **Listen, listen, listen.** Get out in the world, and then listen to people. What are they doing differently? What are thinking about doing differently? What are they interested in? Excited about? Fed up with? Your friends, family, neighbors, and business colleagues are a fantastic wealth of information regarding what's going on in the world. Ask questions, then listen to them.

DEMOGRAPHICS

A final part of your property analysis should be demographics, or statistical data about a particular population, such as the people in the city in which you want to invest. Demographic research provides a snapshot of population, income, industries, biggest employers, and other economic details for a particular city or area.

Demographic information can be found at libraries, city and county government offices, and of course the Internet offers an abundance of demographic information. Suggested Web sites to locate demographic information include:

- www.freedemographics.com
- http://realestate.yahoo.com/Neighborhoods
- http://realestate.yahoo.com/Homevalues

- www.elook.org
- www.economy.com (fee site)
- www.city-data.com
- http://quickfacts.census.gove/qfd/

Demographics That Favor Investing

When reviewing demographic information and trends, watch for these characteristics that are generally favorable for investing in a particular property:

- More females than males (females tend to "nest")
- Higher percentage of singles vs. married (singles rent apartments)
- Higher percentage of younger and older people versus middle-age (middle-age people buy homes).
- Annual income at or lower than $40,000 (home prices push them to rent apartments)
- The stability and profitability of the area's largest employer

---

Key information you also want to review regarding the property's physical location include the following:

- How close is it to public transportation?
- What's the city's plan for that particular area?
- How close is it to a park?
- How close is it to a school?
- How close is it to shopping and restaurants?

Finally, you should ask yourself a simple question:
Do you want to invest in this area?

KEY SUCCESS PRINCIPLE: HAVE A GREAT TEAM

As my wife, Diana, and I began to acquire what become more than twenty cash-flowing properties in San Francisco, we eventually put together a team to begin tackling larger problems. Our most successful team consisted of attorney Elizabeth Erhardt, who specializes in evictions, and Sia Tahbazof, whose engineering and architectural brilliance could always see the intrinsic value that others often could not see on adding value to a property. Diana and I would buy buildings in San Francisco with brick foundations or with difficult tenants paying very low rents under rent control, and we would quickly pull the trigger and close the deal. Our goal was to add value by completely remodeling all the buildings we purchased. Liz would negotiate deals with the tenants, and Sia would get all our plans quickly through the planning process. On most of our projects we used a 1031 Exchange to acquire larger properties and others we rented. They all cash-flowed, but what was even better was that for most of the properties the value tripled and not because the market went up or down.

Here's an important point: The relationship we had with our team was far more important than all of the money we ever made. There will never be a deal that is more important than the relationships. Today, Liz Erhardt is one of San Francisco's top attorneys regarding tenant/landlord issues. We are still very good friends; she will take my call and we go on and on about our "war stories" from the trenches fifteen years ago. Sia Tahbazof is semi-retired and works only on his own projects these days, but we are still very good friends. To this day Diana and I work exclusively with Sia Consulting Engineering on our local projects.

TIP The relationship we had with our team was far more important than all of the money we ever made. There will never be a deal that is more important than the relationships.

I believe a large part of our success as a team was based on the saying, "Everyone stay in their lane." (I remember running anchor at the Penn State relays in middle school and the track coach always saying, "Stay in your lane!") Staying in your lane shortens the race. Curtis's lane was to be in charge of the demo and rough work, and Diana's was in charge of the finishes; Liz was in charge of tenants; and Sia was engineering, design, plans, and the city's approval.

Always be thinking about how you can build the best team possible to support both your short- and long-term efforts.

TIP I believe a large part of our success as a team was based on the saying "Everyone stay in their lane" because staying in your lane shortens the race.

PROBLEMS . . . OR OPPORTUNITIES

If you resolve to become a problem solver, your chances of success in real estate investing will dramatically increase. The key question then becomes: What is your tolerance for problems?

You see, opportunities are never easy. Problems, challenges, and setbacks almost always occur. Those who shy away from the hard work needed to embrace opportunities fail. Over the years I've had friends and acquaintances come to me wanting to partner with me on various real estate projects. Often they back out. Why? It's like a rope strung across the two sides of the Grand Canyon. They see a tightrope; I see a bridge.

What can we do to strengthen our faith so that we can embrace and overcome more problems? That answer is easy. Take more chances. Truly successful people pursue opportunities based on faith. They don't let fear get in their way. Successful people—the Donald Trumps of the world, for example—also are constantly strengthening their faith. They are admitting their fears but pursuing opportunities anyway. When we let fear rule our lives, we don't take chances. When we live by faith, we pursue opportunities and take controlled risks.

When I was younger, I left my government job, where I was earning $60,000 a year, to become a real estate agent and investor. I was excited. I had recently read Napoleon Hill's *Think and Grow Rich* and was ready to set the world on fire—and to do so immediately. But things didn't happen so quickly. In fact, for several months, no opportunities materialized. Zero, none, *nada*. My savings began to dwindle. And then do you know what happened? My mind, which had been positive and focused on possibilities, began to worry. My dreams turned—mentally—from delights to disasters.

Eventually I overcame this initial slow time, and my investing took off. Only those who have the courage and the tenacity to never give up *in the face of setbacks and other obstacles* will achieve success.

Success then isn't a straight line; it's a series of starts and stops, two steps forward, and then one step back. Here's what I thought success would look like:

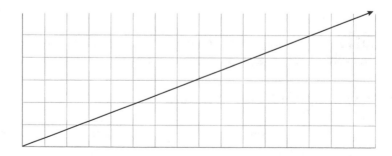

FIGURE 10.1 What I Thought Success Would Look Like

And here is what it actually did look like:

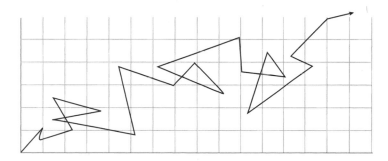

FIGURE 10.2 What the Path to Success *Really* Looks Like

TIP Only those who have the courage and the tenacity to never give up *in the face of setbacks and other obstacles* will achieve success.

If you have the patience to pursue and overcome problems, your chances for real estate successes will skyrocket. Remember your mantra:

Profit from Problems

You see, I believe that this concept of adding value to real estate can carry over into your life in many, many other ways. For example, too often I see and meet people who are focused on making less of other people or things. Instead, I want to encourage you to make more of every person you come in contact with. Avoid labels; there's no real right and wrong, just different points of view. Regardless of where you are in life right now, you can make the decision to reach up and out in your life and help others do the same.

 **Curtis Oakes** has been a top-performing realtor for Coldwell Banker in San Francisco for more than two decades, placing him in the top 3 percent of all Coldwell Banker agents nationwide. In 1994, Curtis and his wife formed the Oakes Group, specializing in San Francisco Bay Area real estate sales, investment, and development. His passion for helping others has permeated his real estate practice, and he's helped countless individuals realize their dream of home ownership and investment property acquisition. Through his proprietary Oakes Group Mentoring Program, he teaches wealth building through real estate.

11

Analyzing the Deal, or Adventures in Real Estate

I have known John for more than thirty years. He and I were both Marine Corps officers and played on the same rugby team in Hawai'i. He is known as the Burger King of Hawai'i because he brought the franchise to the islands. Although he no longer owns the franchise, having sold it a number of years ago for a stunning profit, he is still known as the Burger King of Hawai'i because the name fits. John is the king of using fast food franchises to acquire priceless real estate.

In my book Rich Dad Poor Dad I wrote about Ray Kroc, the person who made McDonald's famous and built it into a multibillion-dollar enterprise. In the book, Ray asks a group of students from the University of Texas, "What business am I in?" The response from the students was, "You're in the hamburger business." Ray shook his head and said, "No, I'm in the real estate business." Today, McDonald's owns the most expensive real estate in the world. Ray's formula was to use a McDonald's franchise to pay for the real estate.

John, the Burger King of Hawai'i, uses the same formula, the formula of using a business to buy property. I too use the same formula today. Today my apartment house business, fitness club business, and office rental business pay for my real estate. It is a formula used all over the world. The formula of your business buys your real estate.

—ROBERT KIYOSAKI

I have always been intrigued by the acquisition, ownership, and sale of real estate. For the majority of my professional life I've been advising people and making personal decisions about whether or not I should acquire real estate, how to acquire a particular piece of real estate, and finally whether to sell it, develop it, or simply hold it. That means as a practicing attorney and a private investor, I've reviewed hundreds of real estate transactions with a "stop or go" decision point. And the projects are varied. I have developed and sold office and residential condominiums (small and large); acquired and operated ranches and farms; developed and operated warehouse complexes; and financed, developed, and refinanced myriad other real estate–related business ventures.

However, my principal focus today and over the last forty years has been the consistent financing, development, and operation of quick-serve (fast-food) restaurants and convenience stores under franchise agreements with national franchise companies. It's fascinating work acquiring sites and handling the financing and development of those properties. It's also been fascinating to own, operate, and sell nearly one hundred of these quick-serve establishments over these past forty years. My efforts have taken me all over the western United States, Guam, Hawai'i, and Russia.

With this kind of background, analyzing deals has become second nature. And that's what this chapter is all about: "Analyzing the Deal" as it relates to the intelligent acquisition and operation of fast-food restaurants, convenience stores, and related franchise businesses. However, don't be mistaken that the principles set out here will apply only to quick-serve restaurants and convenience stores. That couldn't be further from the truth. The principles here are fundamental and will apply to entrepreneurial ventures of all kinds, particularly if they involve real estate.

Time and again, having a law background has helped when it comes to analyzing the deal at hand. But the true tempering of my deal-related judgment comes from my involvement in building and operating fast-food companies in Hawai'i, Guam, Nevada, Colorado, and Russia. The scope of my experience includes the location, financing, development, and operation of Burger King restaurants, Carl's Jr. restaurants, El Pollo Loco restaurants, Subway sandwich restaurants, Circle K convenience stores, and 76 gas stations, among others. This involvement in franchise deals has necessarily brought me in direct contact with major national brand franchisors with whom I have had extensive negotiations. Most of these franchise opportunities have proved successful, but there were a couple of spectacular exceptions, which I will get into later. In every case my experience in analyzing the deal at the outset proved to be a key to success or failure.

In this chapter, I will set out the principles that you can use in your own pursuit of workable, profitable real estate deals that meet your expectations. I am always suspect of people who talk only of their successes but not of their failures. The reality, as you and I know, is that no business endeavor is perfect. Heartache and despair happen from time to time. That's par for the course for someone who is truly driven by and committed to success. So don't expect all blue sky success stories; I will share with you some significant failures I have experienced as well. They were important learning opportunities for me, teaching me lasting lessons about this field. I know they will be important for you, too, because in most cases these costly mistakes resulted from my failure to analyze the deal correctly at the outset.

My goal is to provide you with a basic construct to direct your analysis of real estate and other deals, and to aid you in making intelligent stop-and-go decisions concerning these deals. It's critical to put some meat on these "bones of wisdom" so that you will be able to address any deal presented to you with practical and useful guidelines. These guidelines to intelligent deal analysis are particularly relevant in a tough economic climate, but they are also foundational and have stood and will continue to stand the test of time.

THE REAL WORLD OF ME

At the very outset of any deal consideration, one needs to engage in some serious introspection. Is this deal (job, purchase, career, etc.) what you really want or need? Does your self-image allow you to be passionate about the basic endeavor you are considering? Does the deal with its projected result produce the kind of monetary and emotional return you are looking for? Does "doing" the deal involve a sacrifice of time and/or require relocation, thereby effectively preventing you from pursuing more important life goals such as good and involved parenting, active and healthy lifestyle choices, team sports activity, church or civic leadership, continued or advanced formal education, personal relationships, or living in a safe and attractive home environment. In other words, if doing the deal, no matter how successful, will make your life or your family's life miserable, then keep moving. It's not for you.

TIP You don't need to do the first deal you see, nor do you need to pursue every deal that seems halfway good or reasonable. Wait for the deal to come down the track that is really for you.

My former partner, Robert Pulley, used to frequently say that deals are like streetcars since there's always another one coming down the track. Over time I have come to realize how true this postulate is. I used to pursue to thoughtful decision almost every deal that came across my desk regardless of what it was, where it was, or what it cost. By allowing my curiosity to take charge, I spent too much time spinning my wheels rather than focusing on realities. That curiosity and arrogance concerning my personal entrepreneurial capacity (I thought I could finance and manage anything) got me into some bad business spots, literally and figuratively. My experiences in Russia and in the nightclub and cemetery businesses (discussed later) represent painful memories that have stayed with me.

The fact is, you don't need to close on the first deal you see, nor do you need to pursue every deal that seems halfway good or reasonable. Wait for the deal to come down the track that is right for you. Your time is your most valuable asset, so spend it wisely. Let the obvious impracticalities of any deal you consider speak to you loudly. This is true no matter how apparently lucrative any deal may seem. Just because the latest and seemingly hottest franchise deal is available in your city doesn't mean that it's right for you. If flipping hamburgers in Detroit, selling cemetery plots in Guam, or polishing cars, creating signs and banners, or teaching math to preteens doesn't really fit you or create a passion within you to succeed, don't do it. Just fold up your cards and wait for a new hand to be dealt. Don't let your current circumstances, no matter how unsatisfying, chase you into a situation where you will work harder, go into debt, and actually lose money doing something you hate.

The Real World of Me

- Engage in serious introspection.
- Ask yourself, "Will doing the deal prevent me from achieving my personal life goals?"
- Deals are like streetcars since there's always another one coming down the track.
- If the deal doesn't fit, don't submit!

Spend some quality time on "the real world of me" before you invest your time chasing a deal that just doesn't suit you or takes you to places that will ultimately make you unhappy, even if you are successful.

WILL THE DOGS LIKE IT?

You've taken the time to be introspective; it's now time to look hard at the deal that's in front of you. You know, the one that looks, smells, and feels right for you.

A very astute Hawai'i-based Chinese businessman, whom I had the pleasure to work with in my early legal career, used to have a favorite saying to characterize any deal. He applied this saying to the many, many deals he considered. He would pause after reviewing the deal situation and ask, "But will the dogs like it?"

He meant that if a deal looks good, is workable, is affordable, and is in a good location, then the customers (tenants, purchasers, etc.) still have to show up to make it happen. He insisted at the outset that just because something may look right to you, it may not be quite so right to the man or woman on the street. You and your wife (partner, friend, banker, college business professor, etc.) might think you have the newest take on sliced bread; however, you must take off the rose-tinted glasses and look at the deal high and low. In other words, strive for total objectivity in your deal analysis.

TIP Just because something may look right to you, it may not be quite so right to the man or woman on the street.

A couple of deals from my past point out the usefulness of being truly objective. In 1977, my partner, Robert Pulley, and I opened the first Burger King restaurant in the state of Hawai'i, right across the street from a busy and well-located McDonald's restaurant. At that time in Hawai'i, McDonald's was pretty much the whole ballgame in terms of branded quick-serve hamburgers. After sampling Burger King's food and visiting existing Burger King restaurants on the mainland, we both agreed that the concept would work well in the Islands. And, even before we opened in Honolulu, we had customers banging on our restaurant doors to get in while we were still obviously under construction. We realized that we had a real winner on our hands. The "dogs" really liked our hamburgers. We set first day, first week, and first month sales records for gross sales for the entire Burger King chain. In fact, our drive-through service lane routinely filled up and cars backed up on the very busy Beretania Street for more than a mile. We had to hire off-duty policemen to control and direct traffic for seven months before we got things under control.

Our customers fell in love with Burger King. We had a very good product that was absolutely unique to Hawai'i at that time. There was a pent-up demand for fast-food hamburgers other than McDonald's hamburgers. To my partner's credit, we obtained a "bulletproof" location right across from a key competitor that we knew was very successful. And, we delivered good food fast. We had analyzed the deal objectively based on good information. In fact, as it turned out, we underestimated how much the dogs would like it.

On the other hand, I had the opposite experience with the introduction of the El Pollo Loco restaurant chain into Hawai'i some years later. I, along with my key employees, had eaten at El Pollo Loco in Southern California. The El Pollo Loco concept essentially involves charbroiling fresh and big fryer chickens to golden brown and serving the charbroiled chicken with tortillas, beans, and rice. The "dogs" really liked this product in Southern California where there is a strong Hispanic tradition. People there of all types are quite familiar with tacos, tamales, and tortillas, and fajitas. They viewed El Pollo Loco as a good Mexican food concept and made it very popular.

In addition to knowing the food was good and popular (in Southern California at least), we had the money and expertise to develop the chain in premier locations in Hawai'i. So we obtained the area franchise, and with the success of Burger King in Hawai'i encouraging us, we felt sure we could create another major quick-serve restaurant success. We opened two El Pollo Loco locations at about the same time. Imagine our disappointment when we found that the dogs didn't like the product in Hawai'i. Imagine our financial losses.

The El Pollo Loco concept depended on some customer familiarity with Mexican food preparation and service. What seemed routine in terms of Mexican food service to Southern Californians mystified many (if not most) of our good Hawaiian customers. The concept involved the simple act of pulling the chicken meat off the half-chicken serving and wrapping it in a warm tortilla with beans, rice, and salsa, thereby creating a world-class chicken fajita. In Hawai'i, the customers did not combine the ingredients (despite clever and instructive graphics on every table and menu); they typically ate the chicken serving, which was delicious, picked at the rice and beans, and threw the beautiful, warm flour tortillas away. We were stunned.

There was already *huli-huli* (flame-broiled) chicken all over the island of Oahu, which was a popular and long-standing fund-raising vehicle. Typically, community groups involved in fund-raising would set up huli-huli wagons in parking lots on weekends at several locations on the island. They would build charcoal fires in the huli-huli wagons and proceed to prepare and sell tasty flame-broiled chickens (whole and halves) to the public at relatively inexpensive prices. So in addition to our customer's failure to grasp the El Pollo Loco concept, we had a serious competitor that we never considered until it was too late.

Will the Dogs Like It?

- Is the product something that you would personally buy at the likely asking price?
- Is the product unique or better than the comparable products sold by competitors?
- Is the product too complicated or too much trouble for your customers?
- Take off your rose-tinted deal glasses and look at the relevant market objectively.

Without the customers' grasp of the chicken fajita preparation, the El Pollo Loco chicken was simply good chicken. It wasn't really very unique, and it was pretty expensive compared to huli-huli chicken. We actually didn't fail completely, but our losses forced us to sell out to Kentucky Fried Chicken. KFC wanted to get rid of El Pollo Loco on the Islands, and our modest success was hurting their business. So we took the easy way out with a lesson well learned.

GARBAGE IN, GARBAGE OUT

Projected financial results, as you can imagine, are the primary concern in analyzing any deal, and when it comes to the numbers it's garbage in, garbage out. Essentially, if your sales projections or your cost projections are bad going in, the resulting projected bottom line (profit and cash flow) numbers are not only unreliable but outright dangerous to your financial well-being.

Up until now, everything we have discussed has been preparatory to real deal focus. Now it's time to get to the heart of our task. As you've seen, the numbers aren't the only consideration, but they certainly are most critical to the stop-or-go deal decision. With my focus on the development of franchise deals, I often had access to very reliable historical sales data from other franchise operations in comparable demographic areas. Typical numbers relating to fast-food operations, convenience stores, gas stations, and other similar operations are often made available to the prospective franchisees in the mandatory disclosure document that each prospective franchisee must receive under the Uniform Franchise Act enacted in most states. These "pro forma" (projected) numbers are useful in analyzing the deal—and other deals involving the same or similar product delivery—in most franchise opportunities.

Of course, using pro forma numbers to analyze a potential deal amounts to, at best, intelligent guesswork. In every case, one has to massage these pro forma numbers to fit the situation at hand. The pricing construct has to be adjusted up or down to fit the intended location. Additionally, an equally important concern is to evaluate the relevant market (assuming the dogs like the product) to arrive at reasonable projected transaction counts and customer counts.

Counting "heads" is the first step in evaluating a fast-food location. I have spent many hours personally counting every vehicle passing by my target location. In tourist locations, I often count the people who walk by every hour in high- and low-traffic periods. Getting a good handle on real numbers of potential customers who have direct exposure to your location is really chapter one in the sales number guessing book. So don't skip actually doing a thorough, realistic head count or traffic count.

Of course, what your closest and most relevant competitor is actually achieving in gross sales is also absolutely key to your analysis of projected gross sales. And if you don't have a close competitor you are either really lucky or more often than not, in the wrong location altogether. I don't care how you get these competitor numbers, but you must get them. This sales data can often be discovered through a review of public tax filings (i.e., gross excise tax data) or by simply interviewing your competitor's former employees or managers. You might want to hire them anyway, so you certainly can interview them. In summary, you must get solid and realistic projected gross sales numbers to avoid creating garbage in, garbage out projections.

Projected sales are only half the story. Projected expenses are equally important when it comes to developing usable bottom-line projections. Projected expenses can almost always be estimated reasonably with hard work. We are fortunate in the United States to have the remarkably efficient distribution of goods and services at comparable and fair pricing (assuming you pay your bills on time). With the exception of utility costs and gas, which historically can make dramatic moves to the upside, your costs for food, paper, products, produce, and people tend to be relatively stable. In quick-serve restaurants, gas stations, and convenience stores, you can move your pricing daily if necessary so you can preserve your profit margins as costs move up. Of course, you are always limited by the competitive atmosphere, but given a product or products the dogs like, reasonable pricing, and a good location, you can come up with projected financial results that are sensible enough to make a deal decision.

If you have hit your mark in projecting future gross sales and have a good understanding of your expenses, you should be able to derive some fairly good and usable guesses at cash flow and profitability numbers. When I have really done my homework, I have been able to avoid the garbage in, garbage out syndrome that turns business projections into birdcage lining. When I didn't do the work of counting vehicles and heads, or failed to research the success or failure of my closest competitors, my deal analysis was faulty. If I failed to be diligent in projecting reliable expense numbers, I had garbage or unrealistic expense numbers to factor into my profitability formula. Sometimes I got lucky and things turned out better than I had hoped for. However, you can't rely on luck and the mistakes that are burned into my brain resulted from overly aggressive sales projections and garbage out at the projected bottom line.

TIP When I have really done my homework, I have been able to avoid the garbage in, garbage out syndrome that turns business projections into birdcage lining.

Years ago, I along with my partner, Robert Pulley, built a Burger King restaurant in the heart of Waikiki in Honolulu, Hawai'i. Although the site was on the ground floor in the front of the popular Kings Village shopping center, the actual walk-by traffic seemed a little thin for this very expensive location. However, one-half block away on Waikiki Beach were absolute throngs of tourists, mostly milling about at the popular corner of Liliuokalani and Kalakaua avenues. My personal tourist head count revealed several thousand potential customers passing through this adjacent and very popular intersection every hour.

The downside of this location was that the view from this key corner to my target restaurant site was largely blocked by a ticket and information booth. A bad deal! So if I was going to choose this site, I'd have to adjust my sales projections way down. After all, they were based on actual walk-by traffic at the time. The obstruction by the ticket booth meant there was nothing to draw customers our way from that busy corner. My partner and I fortunately engaged in some "what-if" analysis before passing on this potentially great site. Our conclusion was that if we could create unobstructed sight-line visibility from this major tourist corner to our site, the deal would work. So I made a last-minute potential "deal-breaker" demand to the landlord that the offending ticket booth be removed to clear up the sight line. Fortunately, the landlord agreed. They wanted us in the center. So we ended up with probably the most successful quick-serve restaurant I have ever built. The dogs liked us, now they could see us, and there were plenty of dogs! Our first-year sales were more than $2.7 million out of less than twenty-seven hundred square feet. These are hall of fame numbers for fast food.

On the other hand, I once developed a cemetery on a parcel of land that my then partner, Bernard Bays—also a contributor in this book—and I had acquired to develop high-end residential condominiums. How did a parcel of land go from high-end condos to burial plots? Simple answer: Hurricane Iniki and ancient but unmarked graves on the property. As you can well imagine, everyone I knew razzed me with the old joke, "Hey John, I hear people are dying to get into your new project." Yeah, wrong kind of dying. All joking aside, the gross sales potential on paper from any new cemetery is just phenomenal. Anytime you can convert, as an example, six acres into six thousand saleable grave plots in a major metro area, your potential ultimate sellout can be as high as $15 to $20 million! Since our land was already paid for, I had only to face cemetery approval and development costs, which I had a pretty good handle on. So I constructed some very elaborate and detailed sales and cash-flow projections that convinced Bays, myself, and several of our associates that we had a winner indeed, even if it wasn't via condo development. The cash flow-to-cost ratio was very favorable on what seemed to be ultimately reasonable sales projections. Our deal analysis looked really good, but it was very wrong.

Unfortunately, I grossly overestimated how quickly people would buy burial plots in the cemetery. We had originally built the cemetery with the thought of selling it to a major company involved in the funeral home/cemetery business. In fact, we had a basic agreement that this company would run the cemetery and ultimately buy the operation and property at a price yielding a substantial profit to our group. So, even though we really had no experience actually operating a cemetery, we proceeded to develop it anyway. We wrongly assumed that our deal to sell to the pros would go through before we actually had to operate the cemetery business. The projected cash flow made us confident of closing such a sale. Unfortunately, our prospective buyers went into bankruptcy a short time after completion of the cemetery. There I was a fast food impresario, taking over cemetery operations.

I was stuck with the job as head "cemeterian," which I knew little about and greatly disliked. I soldiered ahead because our projected numbers still looked terrific. We still had millions of dollars in unsold inventory already paid for and waiting to be sold. I just didn't figure that it might take my lifetime to sell this inventory. Talk about garbage in, garbage out. I would likely be buried in this cemetery, and there still would be more than half the plots left to sell!

Many years later after investing countless and thankless hours learning about and actually running the cemetery, I finally ended up selling it at a loss. My partners and I are now much older and wiser. My projections of cemetery plot sales were based on selling significant numbers of plots from the get-go. We did finally begin to see significant sales of plots every month. However, this sales tempo took years to achieve. What I did not factor into my projected plot sales was the essential attribute of "heritage," which every new cemetery must gain slowly if at all before significant plot sales can be achieved. This is particularly true in smaller cities with more limited population bases.

The simple truth is that it is hard to get families to bury their deceased loved ones in new places. If aunty and uncle are buried in the public cemetery, the rest of the family will also likely want to be interred there no matter how "seedy" the old town cemetery has become. People will come to a new cemetery, but it takes time. They are dying to get in but just not fast enough at a new cemetery. So my decision to proceed to build a cemetery was driven by sales projections that were honestly derived but simply too aggressive for this kind of business. This was particularly true since we lost our major cemetery consolidator/operator at the very outset. My deal analysis was faulty because of overly aggressive "garbage" sales projections.

Garbage In, Garbage Out

- Access and use sales numbers from the best sources available (franchisor standard disclosures and competitor numbers, for example)
- Count the "heads" and/or traffic personally
- Do your homework when you work up expense projections
- Ask the "what-if" question before passing on a deal
- If you build it to sell, you better have a "bulletproof" buyer

---

BUILD IT AND THEY WILL COME (OR NOT)

Now that I have discussed some practical concerns that will prepare you for getting into a deal and shared some stories and my opinion about the relevance of numbers to every deal, it's time to focus on the question of location. Although I have related most of my discussion to quick-serve restaurants, convenience stores, and related businesses, the location question is central to analyzing *any* real estate deal.

It is often said that the three most important aspects of any real estate deal are location, location, and location. This is true, true, and true in any fast-food-type deal, but it is also the compelling issue in most real estate deals. Certainly, it is the central issue in the real estate deals I am referring to in this chapter.

Choosing the right locations for fast-food, quick-serve, gas, and convenience store businesses becomes an art after you have done it time and again and enjoyed success and experienced failures. I discussed above in the numbers analysis section the importance of counting heads and checking competitors' sales. I also stressed that the visibility of any site is a key part of this location issue. And finally I emphasized being in an area where the demographics support your product, where it is both needed and wanted by the people. Remember, will the dogs like it? For as simple as those concepts seem, be assured that you cannot properly analyze any real estate deal involving commercial sales to the public without paying close attention to these basic principles of site selection. Take it from someone who has learned these lessons the hard way.

In most cases, the location you want and are sure of is easy to figure out but is unavailable because of zoning, expense, public ownership, size (too big to afford or too small to be workable), and/or access. The locations that are available often are available because no one wants them or can afford them. This is especially true in major metro areas. If the site is available, you'd better go slow because usually there is something wrong with it. Never assume your competitors are dumb or lazy. Proceed with caution or you will build the perfect store and nobody will come.

I can't tell you how many times I have fortunately passed on real estate deals that were just about right, meaning just about in a great location, but were slightly off for one reason or another. Maybe the site was just interior from the key dominant corner or was in a perfect corner location but on the second floor or down a half-flight of stairs. Or the site was blocked by a huge banyan tree, ticket booth, adjacent building, or some other obstruction so you couldn't see it from the "coming home" side of the road. I will assure you that you can't build or manage your way out of a poor location, no matter how hard you try or how much you spend. I refer here to my area of expertise involving quick-serve restaurants and convenience/gas facilities; however, I believe this location issue is at the heart of every deal that involves sales to the general public.

TIP You can't build or manage your way out of a poor location, no matter how hard you try or how much you spend.

Aside from location visibility, access for your customers is another important consideration. I have thankfully passed on a number of sites that seemed perfectly located but suffered from limited access because of traffic, traffic controls, or limited parking. If it's not convenient the "dogs" will pass on by to someplace that's easier to deal with. So, if you build on a location that your customers can't get to, they won't come.

My partner, Robert Pulley, and I had some fantastic successes by securing locations that were seemingly unavailable or unattainable for our quick-serve hamburger restaurants. I mentioned above the Waikiki location with the problematic ticket booth. Once we got rid of this visual impairment we had an absolute grade "A" location. We had many other successes that I like to think were enabled by creative thinking and action.

When I was looking for deals that would compete favorably with my number-one competitor, McDonald's, I had to be creative since this competitor had seemingly tied up all the available, really good locations. I always laughed when a real estate broker would tell me that I was ahead of McDonald's on any particular site or that I was being offered the site first. I assumed, usually with complete accuracy, that any site McDonald's wanted in my city would end up in their hands no matter who else was interested. They were definitely the "big kahuna" in my development area, and they usually got the first right of refusal on any newly available sites. I guess it's good to be the real boss.

So I, along with my partner, had to think creatively if we were going to grow and succeed. Our deal analysis on sites had to be not only accurate but innovative. This creative mind-set led us to open the first nationally branded fast-food outlet ever in a U.S. military installation at the Navy Exchange at Pearl Harbor, Hawai'i. (We lost this location some years later when we sold out to a Japanese company, but that is another story.) We opened, with great success, the first fast-food restaurant with a partner in the Honolulu International Airport, and we opened the first national fast-food franchise operation in a Hawai'i public park at Ala Moana park in downtown Honolulu. We actually retrofitted part of a YMCA building to create a Burger King restaurant next to the University of Hawai'i, which was another first.

We definitely had to be creative in our site selection to survive and grow our company. We actually built five or more of the most successful restaurants in terms of sales volume in the history of quick-serve restaurants. In every case, the successful location was equal or superior to our competitors' locations or was uniquely situated to avoid any competition. In every case, the location was the key to our success. Our deal analysis was spot-on in these unique locations.

However, I would be less than honest if I didn't tell you about a couple of bad experiences I've had because of poor site selection. By that I mean, I built it and they didn't come. The first example involved building a very fancy and expensive Burger King restaurant on the ground floor of a high-end residential condominium that my partner had developed in Waikiki. Honestly, my site (deal) analysis was skewed by the ready availability of this commercial site, which my partner had in his back pocket as the condominium developer. What I didn't see were some major problems with this "captive site," although it was located on a busy Waikiki corner. First, the dogs didn't like it. The homeowners were less than enamored by a fast-food hamburger restaurant at the entrance to their new, exclusive, and expensive condominium complex. To add further insult, a fellow high-end restaurant tenant sued to stop our restaurant's construction as a violation of his exclusivity clause. But the real oversight in our deal analysis was that our location was on the busy corner but one-half floor below street grade. The walk-by traffic didn't seem to find our location because it was below their sight line. A final straw was that, even though there were hundreds of cars passing by every hour, there was no parking.

Here's a lesson I learned that is for everyone: If you are in the convenience food/store business you had better be convenient and readily accessible. I have never had much success in this quick-serve/convenience area when I locate below or above street level. So in analyzing site locations, don't count on too much tenacity or insight on the part of your customers—they just don't care that much.

TIP In analyzing site locations don't count on too much tenacity or insight on the part of your customers—they just don't care that much.

My experience in developing, owning, and operating a nightclub was equally painful. In this instance, a close personal friend, Robert Mardian Jr., had given me some solid advice against building this club on the Big Island of Hawai'i. He was in the club business there, as well, and knew the ropes. Unfortunately, I ignored that good advice and proceeded with the nightclub development. My reason for going forward was simply that I had space in a warehouse complex that I owned, which had already been substantially built out as a nightclub at great expense. I recaptured the space after my tenant defaulted (that should have been my first clue), and I decided the best idea was to finish out the club and operate it. So I spent hundreds of thousands of dollars building a state-of-the-art nightclub that opened with considerable fanfare. Unfortunately, I soon found out that, even if the dogs liked the club, they wouldn't come if they couldn't find it.

TIP Another important and costly lesson I learned is that you can't turn a sow's ear into a silk purse.

I made two major mistakes here concerning location. I had failed to heed the clear and sound advice from a knowledgeable consultant who advised me that the club would fail because of location. Also, I should have known that no matter how much money you spend, you cannot build yourself out of a bad location. This just wasn't appropriate space for a nightclub because it was in the back of an industrial warehouse that was off the beaten track. People who actually wanted to come couldn't find it. I used to joke that people just needed to drive until they heard gunfire (this was a rough area late at night). I ended up disliking the nightclub business as much as the cemetery business.

By now I think you get it. Deals where the location is "bad, bad, and bad" won't work no matter what you do. We finally tore out the nightclub improvements and returned it to warehouse use. The entire complex has been full since. Another important and costly lesson I learned is that you can't turn a sow's ear into a silk purse.

Build It and They Will Come (or Not)

- Location, location, location is true, true, and true.
- Count heads, review access and visibility, and check out the competition.
- If the site is readily available there is probably something wrong with it.
- Think "outside the box" to get unique locations.
- If you are in the convenience business you'd better be convenient.
- Seek out and listen to the experts.
- Don't try to turn a sow's ear into a silk purse.

TROUBLE WITH TRAVEL

With any deal you are considering, you simply have to ask yourself, "Can I manage the deal effectively? If the deal is located more than one day's travel from your home, you'd better ask (and answer) some serious questions about your personal span of control. You can't manage the type of deals I have been discussing by staring at a computer. You need to be at the site at least weekly if you are the majority partner. Or you'd better have a good, capable, and trustworthy operator/partner.

And that leads to an important point. One of the most important considerations in analyzing whether to proceed with any real estate deal or development is the availability of good management. And usually the key to good management is your personal involvement in the development and operation. Having good partners can solve many of the concerns about good management; however, if your own money is at risk in any deal it will require your personal attention. The question then is whether realistically you will actually be able to devote sufficient time to a deal to make it successful.

TIP One of the most important considerations in analyzing whether to proceed with any real estate deal or development is the availability of good management. And, usually that means you, with direct personal involvement in the development and operation.

I have found if a deal or operation is located too far from my home base or is difficult to get to, I won't pay enough personal oversight and attention to the situation to ensure good management. I have also found that it is very rare to see any deal run on its own without major problems. If I have to get on an airplane or drive several hours to a location, you are not going to see me very often. It really amounts to the trouble with travel.

I once stretched the limit concerning my effective span of control by agreeing to be a founding member of a company formed to develop Subway sandwich restaurants in the old Soviet Union. Before we got the first restaurant built, the Soviet Union imploded, so we had to be satisfied with the nation of Russia with only 300 million people or so. My major point here is that you don't need to travel to the other side of the world to find trouble. You can usually find plenty of trouble right at home.

How I ever got involved in Soviet Subway restaurants is a story of seduction. I was intoxicated by the sheer potential magnitude of a deal that involved an entire nation, despite the fact that it happened to be Russia—a mere 12,500 miles from my home. The prevalent "kleptocracy" that seemed to be the dominant ideology in the early nineties in Russia should have raised a cautionary note in my Russia deal analysis. The fact that I would have very little to do with day-to-day management of the restaurants should also have raised my personal red flag. Despite these serious road blocks to good deal formation, I along with some other U.S. partners built the first Subway sandwich restaurant in Russia on Nevsky Prospect in St. Petersburg. It took some real creativity and out-of-the-box thinking to build a workable and visible restaurant in a two-hundred-year-old building.

The restaurant was a rousing success primarily because I sent one of my very best partners from Hawai'i, Steve Brown, along with his wife, Roberta, to build and run the Russian Subway operations. Of course, Steve was also enamored with the prospect of owning part of the hundred or more Subway Restaurants we intended to build throughout Russia, so I am not entirely to blame for disrupting his life. Shockingly, we were taking in wheelbarrow loads of rubles (literally) and lots of hard currency (dollars, marks, etc.) from the very start of operations in St. Petersburg. Under Steve's management with some help from me and the other three principals, we had one of the most successful Subway sandwich restaurants in the world—for about three months.

After weeks of hard work and success, Steve and Roberta finally took a short trip out of Russia to decompress, leaving one of our partners in charge as the managing director, which was required by Russian corporate law. Call it confusion about travel plans and return dates, but we had literally one day without a so-called managing director in charge of operations in St. Petersburg. Our Russian partner, whom we took on at the outset of our plans because of his apparent control over some key real estate and his political connections, chose that day to make his move. He had been sitting on the sidelines as we operated for ninety days without any active part in management. He expressed great frustration that we were banking all our net receipts to pay start-up bills before making any partner distributions. What we didn't realize at the time, was that our partner had some very bad characters who had control over him and were part of a major Russian mob.

Under mob instructions (we think), he was waiting for his chance to gain control over the restaurant as managing director. He seized that one day's opportunity. When Steve Brown returned from Russia a day later he found our Russian partner's security people (formerly our security people, ex-KGB apparently) in charge. They literally ran Steve out of the restaurant at gunpoint!

So we lost control of the restaurant and the backing we had lined up to build many more restaurants. And our Russian "partner" soon ran the existing restaurant into the ground. Talk about a mess!

> ## The Trouble With Travel
> - The trouble with travel is that it reduces your span of control.
> - Will you actually go there after you have built it?
> - Deals don't run on their own.
> - Foreign countries are especially dangerous turf.
> - You don't have to leave home to find trouble.

Despite the fact that our company finally got the restaurant back years later, we all lost most of our investment in this deal. Now we may ultimately get back some of our money as my old U.S. partners continue to build Subway sandwich restaurants through franchise agreements in Russia under the auspices of our former company. However, I have often reflected on my poor decision in getting involved in a deal so far from home and on hazardous turf we knew little about. I can't help but repeat that you don't need to travel halfway around the world to invest your way into trouble; there are plenty of landmines to step on right here at home.

DEALS ARE LIKE PARACHUTES

So far, we've covered many of the considerations involved in analyzing and negotiating good deals. Now let's discuss the importance of getting out of a bad or marginal deal. Think of deals as if they were parachutes. If you're freefalling or sinking fast, you need to be able to pull the rip cord to save yourself and get out of a deal that's simply not working. That means first and foremost, determine whether you can negotiate an "out" clause in your initial deal analysis. If you don't succeed in obtaining this concession from the landlord/seller you may want to pass on the deal.

When I first started building restaurants, my partner and I routinely signed personal guaranties on leases for long-term leasehold properties. We were reaching to obtain the best real estate available and believed, in many cases correctly, that we had no chance to obtain these superior sites without "kissing the paper," which is another way of saying signing personal guaranties. We ultimately stopped doing this since a personal guaranty on a long-term lease is like a life sentence. If the lease term is long enough you have to worry about whether the lease rent is being paid for the rest of your life. This is especially true if you have assigned this lease to someone else.

Although we ultimately got our names off most of these guaranties when we sold the restaurants and assigned these long-term leases, in some instances we could not get releases because the landlords were just too tough. And, our marker (guaranty) was called in a couple of times by landlords who we had no dealings with for years. So, if a personal guaranty is demanded, you must carefully consider whether you want to accept this liability for the term of the lease (or loan). This extra liability greatly burdens the benefit of any potential deal and should be factored into your deal decision making.

TIP If a personal guaranty is demanded, you must carefully consider whether you want to accept this liability for the term of the lease or loan— a potential life sentence.

After a couple of bad experiences, I not only stopped giving my personal guaranty on lease deals, but I began to insist on "rip cord" clauses to get out of leases that proved to be for marginal locations. In most instances, landlords met this demand for an "out" of a long-term real estate lease with stiff resistance or refusal. My resolve to leave a partially open door to get out of a bad deal was equally strong. My negotiating stance was to point out that I would be fronting significant improvement costs at the outset, which I would not walk away from without a really compelling reason. Sometimes I was able to negotiate only a qualified release from my personal guaranty, which was better than nothing. For example, my personal guaranty would go away after the rent had been paid for a short term of three to five years or on payment of a lump sum. But I was always prepared to walk away from deals that were just too tough in terms of personal guaranties or long-term lock-ins.

> ### Deals Are Like Parachutes
> - A long-term personal guaranty can amount to a "life-sentence."
> - Negotiate a "rip cord" clause in long-term leases if possible.
> - Be prepared to "walk" if terms are too tough.

MAKE MY DAY, MAKE MY LIFE

At some point in every viable real estate deal you have the opportunity, or at least the consideration, of whether or not to sell. In my experience, the decision to sell or not to sell is usually an easy or obvious one. If the price is right, everything is for sale. The analysis issue is which course of action—sale or retention—will optimize the return from your deal. I have personally made some great selling decisions and also some pretty bad decisions that irk me to this day.

Generally speaking, there are certain rules of thumb that are commonly used in the sale of operating businesses. Of course, these rules can be warped in a hundred different ways to accommodate the unique features of every different deal. Fast-food restaurants often sell based on a ratio of annual (trailing twelve-month) cash flow. Six times annual cash flow is generally considered at the high-end while four-and-a-half times cash flow is considered at the low-end of selling prices for such operating businesses. And, my reference to cash-flow really more correctly refers to earnings before interest, taxes, depreciation, and amortization, or EBITDA. There are other variations of this cash-flow acronym, but this is the one I use.

TIP There are certain rules of thumb that are commonly used in the sale of operating businesses. Of course, these rules can be warped in a hundred different ways to accommodate the unique features of every different deal.

Of course, operating businesses are sold for all kinds of reasons and all kinds of prices. I remember an old legend concerning the sale of a gas station/convenience store. Essentially, the owner of this business was a sharp operator who was trying to push the sales price beyond normal cash-flow rules of thumb. So every time a potential buyer was due to inspect the business, the owner would dump trash around the buildings, leave the restrooms in a mess, and generally present an untidy, dirty appearance about the business. Then when the buyer showed up, the owner would take him aside and point out the seemingly obvious fact that if someone would "just run the business properly" sales and profits would soar. It is also common for the owner/seller and spouse to add back to the cash flow their salaries (car allowance, expense account, etc.) to pump up the cash flow. This is true, even if the owner/seller and spouse are the very heart of the business management and operation. Owners play all kinds of games with the sale of operating businesses. More sophisticated buyers and sellers will rely on industry norms concerning cash flow and a real objective analysis of the numbers to arrive at a price.

Robert Pulley and I sold our Burger King restaurants in Hawai'i at a price that approached one times the gross sales, which probably doesn't happen very often. However, we had a business in the seemingly terrific state of Hawai'i, we had good management and good locations, and we had enthusiastic foreign buyers. The analysis of whether to sell or not in our case was an easy yes. I have sold restaurants at other times on the six-times cash flow multiple, but I personally have not seen another deal with a price approaching parity with gross sales.

Analyzing the deal in raw land sales, presuming one has staying power to hold on to the land, relates basically to the greed factor. How much gain is enough? There are no real rules of thumb concerning the sale of raw land or development land. You need to make the hard decision of whether holding the land or the further development of the land will justify holding costs. Of course, these decisions to sell raw land are often driven by the owner's inability to continue to pay carrying costs. In cases where you are going to lose the property otherwise, selling becomes an easy decision.

My most memorable mistakes in terms of selling prematurely involve selling houses in Hawai'i that practically doubled in value a year or two after my sale. We all have had or know of examples of seller's remorse in personal house sales. This was particularly true in many areas of the United States that were experiencing explosive increases in house prices. I, along with lots of other sellers, failed to judge the rapid upward move of the market.

Of course failure to sell during market peak can be an equally grievous error. We also have become familiar with holding strategies that lead to dramatic losses in rapidly declining residential and commercial real estate markets.

There are factors other than price that may impact the decision to sell or to buy. You might decide to sell if you no longer are able to manage a business or take care of a house. You may know of planned major infrastructure changes that will impact the relevant market negatively or positively. You might want to

---

Make My Day, Make My Life

- Utilize common "rules of thumb" to reach a realistic valuation decision.
- Cash flow rather than assets determine sales prices (usually).
- Unless you have a "crystal ball," you can get burned on market directions (up or down).
- If you can't afford the deal you need to sell it.
- Don't miss a once-in-a-lifetime opportunity to sell; i.e., the "make my day, make my life" decision.

sell to key employees to avoid losing them. In every case, the analysis of the deal, or the sale, requires every bit as much consideration as a deal to build or acquire.

WAYS TO LEARN MORE

Look for future writings by John Finney on the adventures on real estate.
   Rich Dad Poor Dad, by Robert Kiyosaki
   ABC's of Real Estate Investing, by Ken McElroy

John Finney is the current president of Industrial Income Properties, Inc., a company he formed to find, develop, own, and operate real estate, ranging from residential and office condominiums, cattle ranches, fast-food restaurants with adjunct convenience store and gas facilities, single family residences, farm properties, nightclubs, and other real estate ventures in Hawai'i, Guam, and the western United States. Prior to that, he and his partner Robert W. Pulley secured the Burger King franchise rights in Hawai'i and in ten years opened thirty-five stores and sold them in one of the biggest deals in Burger King history. And each has had many other real estate ventures in the United States. John is an attorney and a graduate of Stanford Law School and a former U.S. Marine.

12

Scott D. McPHERSON

Real Estate Due Diligence

I met Scott in 1999 at the Phoenix Open golf event. I knew of his reputation as one of the biggest mortgage bankers in Arizona, but I did not know that he knew me. Smiling as he walked up, he said, "I'm glad you're saying what you say about stocks and mutual funds. They're terrible investments."

At the time, I was under blistering attacks from financial planners and financial magazines that were supported by mutual fund company's advertising dollars. You may recall that in 1999, the stock market was red hot and people believed they were making billions in the new economy of the dot-com world. So to have a person of Scott's reputation back up my philosophy that stocks and mutual funds were risky investments was a welcome relief and validation. His pat on my back made watching the Phoenix Open even more enjoyable.

Today Scott is one of the three mortgage bankers I call when I need the straight story about real estate financing. It was Scott who, years ago, warned me of the real estate bubble being formed by the sub-prime mortgage fiasco. It was because of Scott that my wife, Kim, and I became more conservative in our real estate investments while others became real estate gamblers.

I'm an advocate for financial education because when you get smarter, you minimize risk. That's what this chapter is about. Scott has made me smarter, and

the knowledge he has shared with me minimizes my risk with every new invest-
ment I make. His wisdom in this chapter will do the same for you.

—ROBERT KIYOSAKI

When talking about the subject of real estate due diligence, you are really talking about nothing more than a team effort of discovery and verification. That's what due diligence is, and every real estate transaction you do, whether it is a single family home purchase or a very complex commercial real estate development, will require the buyer to take certain fundamental steps of underwriting. Only through that process can a buyer fully assess all aspects of the property he or she is purchasing. And if you are the buyer, you'll want to make sure you are diligent about due diligence.

TIP Benjamin Franklin once said, "Diligence is the mother of good luck."

When you as a real estate investor have identified a property that you want to purchase, you have come to the conclusion to buy it based on a series of somewhat superficial facts. You have usually seen the property, and generally have reviewed some of the financial information that the seller or broker has provided you. And based on this information and your belief that the property fits your business plan, you make an offer to purchase. Once the seller has accepted your offer, your work—or should I say your team's work—has just begun!

I am a real believer in putting together a very strong team when you approach a real estate acquisition. Many of the authors in this book have stated the exact same thing in their chapters. The fact is, most highly successful people or companies are built using a team approach to getting things done. No one can be an expert on every aspect of real estate, and frankly if you are investing on behalf of other people and are using their money, you should *always* seek competent third-party input.

In this chapter, I am going to walk you through a due diligence process and give you an overview of why the various members of your team are important. I am also going to include my Eight Tips and some real-life examples of why securing qualified and unbiased advice on your proposed acquisition is so critical.

To me, assembling a team to assist you with your due diligence is just like putting a puzzle together. Each of the team members have separate and specialized disciplines, but when they are brought together by you as the leader, the pieces come together, and all of a sudden the full picture comes to life. You can see what you are really buying!

I have separated the due diligence process into five main categories: physical review, legal, title, third party reports, and accounting tax. Let's start with the first one on this list.

> **Due Diligence Process Categories**
>
> • Physical Review
> • Legal Review
> • Title Review
> • Third Party Reports Review
> • Accounting and Tax Review

PHYSICAL REVIEW

During the physical review, you and your team inspect the property to see if it falls in line with your business plan and your expectations. Let me expand a bit on this. As an example, let's say that you are planning to buy an apartment building and then do some slight renovations to the units that will allow you to increase the rents over the next couple of years. So how does the process start?

Before you make your offer to purchase the property, you will want to interview and select a property management company to help you prepare your operating and renovation budgets for the property. The key word here is *before*! This is not something you want to do after you make the offer. The results of this work will help you decide whether the property is worth making an offer at all.

TIP If you are going to be a professional real estate investor, have your team lined up *before* you make the offer!

A successful and competent property management company can go over your operating and renovation budgets to make sure they are realistic and give you credible feedback on all the previous assumptions you may have made on the property—assumptions such as operating expense savings, new income opportunities, and even cash flow projections. They can look at your business plan and give it a thumbs up or a thumbs down and help you adjust it so it is attainable and realistic. Remember, you will rely on a property management company to make your business plan work, so you had better make sure you are both on the same page from the beginning.

The property management company will have its own sub checklists for its own due diligence process. The people in the company will walk through every apartment and check the condition of the property in a multifamily project, for example, and bring in the sub-trades such as roofing companies, landscape companies, etc., that can provide detailed reports on the condition of the property.

In addition to spearheading the physical inspection, the property management company will also review all the rent-rolls, the operating statements, and tenant profiles, all in an effort to gain an understanding of the true, current operating income of the property. Usually it will present you with a summary of the findings.

TIP The property management company is a critical member of your team. Find the best one you can and work closely with it.

I cannot tell you how many times during my career that this work and the report that it generates has helped buyers make the right decision about a property. Let me give you an example from two perspectives. I was involved in a twenty-unit apartment community that I was going to buy and convert to for-sale condominiums. When we did our walk-through, my property management company brought along several contractors who were going to do the work on the project once I closed.

To convert the apartments to condominiums, I planned to put about $20,000 of renovations—including adding a washer and dryer—into each unit. This was a non-negotiable expense since my market study indicated that other condo projects in the market all had washers and dryers. We needed to be competitive.

After the inspection, the owner of the property management company called me and said that everything checked out and there were no real surprises, except one. I asked, "What would that be?" He proceeded to tell me that his plumber and framer felt that because of the existing plumbing and stairwell configuration, putting in the washers and dryers would cost an additional five thousand dollars per unit. That added up to an *additional* $100,000. OUCH!

Well clearly, that unexpected expense was not in my budget, so I went back to the seller to renegotiate the terms of the deal. Specifically, I agreed to remove all contingencies after the completion of my due diligence, and in exchange I requested that the seller reduce the price by $100,000. He agreed. Having an expert in the room saved me $100,000! For as valuable as the property management company was in finding a potentially deal-breaking hidden cost, a property manager can also add strong value by reviewing the rent-roll and tenant profiles.

Here's my story: I was financing an acquisition of a large apartment building in Scottsdale, Arizona, that had been grossly undermanaged. My client was going to buy the asset and renovate the units and gradually raise rents. He thought the quoted street rents for this property were below market for the submarket and felt he could increase them once he renovated the exterior, improved the amenities, and did some minor interior work.

What the property management company reported after reviewing the rent-roll was both startling and exciting. They discovered that more than 25 percent of the existing tenants had not received a rental increase since they signed their original leases! Two tenants were actually paying the same rent they had paid when they moved into the property the day it opened . . . fifteen years prior! This news meant that the property's net operating income would indeed increase significantly simply by raising the old rents to the current market rates and once the additional rent kicked in, based on the planned property improvements. The property management company earned its keep that day.

LEGAL REVIEW

Hiring a lawyer that practices real estate law is a must. I am not advocating that you spend an incredible amount of money on legal fees, but with complex issues regarding title, contracts, entitlements, lender documents, and other items that you are certain to run into, you'd better have a good lawyer on your team. If you are an experienced real estate investor and you are buying a home or something without too many issues, maybe you can handle the transaction on your own. But regardless, the legal review phase is not the place to save money on professional fees.

In my experience, if you have a good lawyer who is a "deal maker" you should get him or her engaged on the issues he/she knows best. I have seen some problems arise when the lawyer becomes the negotiator for the transaction. Remember you are the team leader, and all of the members should be reporting to you. That's when a lawyer, as well as all your other team members, can really add value. There are many examples of how lawyers have added value in the numerous transactions in which I have been involved. Let me share a favorite.

I was financing both the debt and equity for a condo developer on a property in Portland, Oregon. My borrower hired a much-respected lawyer in Portland to review all title and entitlement documents regarding the property. He discovered during the title review that one of the owners had recorded a document requiring his approval before a property could be converted to condominiums. Without this owner's approval there was no way to get the state real estate approval to sell the units individually, and no way to deliver clear title to the buyers!

My borrower could not close the transaction without having this provision removed from the title. The only solution was to go back to this previous owner and get that person to remove the provision. Guess what? The previous owner was willing to comply, but for a price. My buyer was paying $48 million for a property that he was going to convert to condominiums and that he now discovered would not close until this provision was cleared up.

In this case, our seller and the previous seller agreed to a settlement, and we closed the transaction at no additional cost to my buyer. Thankfully, my client's lawyer had reviewed the documents thoroughly and was on top of this issue. This is the purpose of legal due diligence: finding the problems before they become insurmountable and providing you with the knowledge you need to make a go/no-go decision based on the findings and the proposed solutions. Just think if my buyer had closed on the property and *then* found out that he could not convert the property at all. Or worse yet, imagine the cost to remove the restriction post closing! My buyer would have been at the complete mercy of the previous owner.

TIP I do recommend strongly that if you are getting into larger and more complex transactions that require new debt or joint venture equity that you get legal representation at all times.

I am primarily a commercial mortgage broker. I provide debt and equity for commercial real estate transactions around the country. I can tell you that loan documents and joint venture agreements are extremely complex, and you do need someone who can thoroughly understand them and explain them to you.

TITLE REVIEW

Just as it's important to work with a lawyer you know and trust during the legal due diligence review, it's just as important to work with a title company you know and trust for this part of the process. In any deal I do, I try to control the title company choice in the purchase contract if at all possible. I find it best to go with a larger firm that has the capacity to provide a satisfactory level of insurance coverage for all parties.

TIP Using a title company that you know and one that is acceptable to your lenders and lawyer will save you a lot of time and effort.

I also like to use title companies to search comparable sales, foreclosures, or other owners in a particular area to help give you a feel of what is going on in the vicinity around the property. This is important intelligence you'll need as you formulate your marketing plans and your forecasts for a particular property.

Lawyers aren't the only ones who can save the day when it comes to due diligence. Let me give you an example of how a title company made me a quick profit on a house I was buying. The year was 1987, and the home was in Paradise Valley, Arizona. It was kind of a hidden jewel. I saw a sign on it one morning when I was jogging and decided to make a call. The house was small, but sat on two and a half acres surrounded by four other houses on five acres. I knew homes with that kind of acreage were not common, so I thought there might be value in this property.

When I got the broker on the line, he said his mother had passed away and they needed to sell the house quickly. They were asking $225,000 and would carry some amount for a quick close. I offered $185,000 that day, and they accepted my offer. That gave me thirty days to close and find the money!

Working with the title company, I asked them to pull up all the sales in the surrounding area so I could see who my neighbors were and how much they paid for their properties. What I discovered was that about five of the ten surrounding properties had changed hands in the last twelve months. Then I noticed something even more interesting about the sales. Each one was in a different name or entity, but they all had the same mailing address for the tax bills.

BINGO! The light went on that someone had been assembling these larger properties. I went to the address on the tax rolls and found out the entity was a land development company in town. Furthermore, I read in the paper that this land development company had just signed the Ritz Carlton and was going to announce a resort hotel development shortly!

Thanks to the information from my title company, I now knew that I was just about to close on a piece of property that the land development company needed to complete the assemblage for their planned resort development. After I closed on the house, I set up a meeting with the development company and subsequently sold them the property for $375,000. A whopping $150,000 more than I paid for it! On top of that windfall, I negotiated free rent to live in the house for one year. Remember what wise old Ben said: "Diligence is the mother of good luck."

THIRD PARTY REPORTS REVIEW

This is another crucial part of the due diligence process. The third party reports that I am talking about are primarily the Environmental, Property Conditions, Appraisal, and Market Study. You may or may not need them based on the type of property you are buying, but in most cases they are good to get and even may be required by your lender. Let's start at the top of the list.

ENVIRONMENTAL

I would highly recommend that you hire a company to provide you with an environmental study on the property. This report looks at soil composition, hazardous materials, and the like. Typically you contract for a Phase 1 report, which is affordable, approximately in the $2,000 to $3,000 range. This report is well worth the expense if the company turns something up like toxicity in the soil or some other hazardous materials.

TIP The downside risk is way too large not to spend the money on a Phase 1 environmental report. Do one, no matter what.

If you are using a conventional financing source, your lender will require a Phase 1 report. They often have an approved list of vendors, so I recommend that you check with your lender before you hire a provider to do this work. If you do not have a lender yet, you should hire a national company that has affiliates in your region, then ask them for a list of lenders they have done business with.

PROPERTY CONDITIONS REPORT

A property conditions report does just as the name states. It will call out issues with the property's condition that the inspections reveal. This would include structural issues, roofs, asphalt, sewer, and other building systems. The report also will give you an estimated useful life for those items. This is very important when you are capitalizing your budget.

TIP The property conditions report gives you a second opinion on the condition of the property and can either affirm/dispute the inspection findings that you and your property management firm did earlier. Or it can find something you both have overlooked. That's important to know.

When it comes to costs, property conditions reports can be all over the board, but this is no place to skimp. Not only do you want a firm that is experienced and knowledgeable, you want to hire a firm that has a national presence and is acceptable to your lender if you know who that is. As I mentioned earlier, if you have not yet chosen a lender, your inspection company may be able to help with a recommendation.

The other benefit of having a property conditions report is that it is a third party report and completely unbiased, in contrast to the report compiled by your property management company. If you go back to the seller with your property management report, asking the seller to pay for something that is wrong with the property, he or she may feel that the report is biased in your favor. That's hard to do when you are also holding a third party property condition report that reflects the exact same issue. This report gives you much more credibility and negotiating power.

APPRAISAL

Depending on how sophisticated a real estate investor you are, you may not think you need an appraisal. My advice is almost always to get one. If you are financing your project, you will need one anyway, and why not be sure that the property is valued where you believe it to be? It validates your own assessments, or in some cases refutes them. Either way, the knowledge is good to have.

As the borrower, it can get a little dicey if you hire the appraiser. Federally chartered banks have guidelines that they must adhere to. One of those guidelines is that the borrower cannot order the appraisal. Most banks and nonbank lenders are more comfortable making the decision on whom to hire. What I do in those instances is let the mortgage broker hire the appraiser or go to the lender with an appraiser in mind and let him hire that person. I generally want some say in the appraiser.

The mistake I see the most is when appraisers are hired and they are inexperienced in the type of property the buyer is purchasing. I run into this quite a bit with banks. They just send out a bid sheet to three appraisers and hire one not necessarily based on his expertise but on his time availability and price. A bad appraisal can bring the entire transaction to a standstill in a second.

To avoid this I always suggest having one or two appraisers that are good at what they do and qualified in your type of property that you can recommend to the bank. I also recommend that you take the time, or let your mortgage broker take the time, to share your vision of the property with the appraiser. If the appraiser does not see the value that you currently see or are going to create, you are toast. Finally, be proactive with him and provide him with as much information as you can.

TIP Remember an appraisal is an opinion of value. You may have, and are entitled to have, your own opinion, but you'd better be ready to back it up.

MARKET STUDY

Usually the appraisal will contain a good discussion of the market for your type of property. However if you are planning to do something a little more on the edge or something that is complex like a condo conversion, hotel, golf course, or some kind of unique single family project, for example, you may need an additional market study not only for your own knowledge but to help move your ideas forward with the people around you.

There are companies, both regional and national, that can do market studies geared directly toward your kind of project and just about any other kind of project including ones I mentioned in the previous paragraph. Consider engaging them to do the report and show it to everyone who you think needs to see it. What I mean by that is show your market study to clarify and support your vision and to defend your position.

TIP Show your market study to clarify and support your vision and to defend your position.

Warning—these market reports can be expensive. It is common to see them run in the $10,000 to $30,000 range. But at times, they are worth their weight in gold. I have successfully used these types of reports to argue the assumptions used in an appraisal that came in low. Again, it is much easier to argue your points on absorption, price points, rents, etc., when you have a credible third-party report supporting you.

ACCOUNTING AND TAX REVIEW

This is the last review on our list, and it is the one that can make you very happy at tax time. Having an excellent real estate and tax accountant on your side is critical. You are going to have to make decisions prior to closing the transaction and post closing, and the advice you need can come only from people who make their living understanding and staying on top of complex tax code. Prior to closing, they can work with your lawyer to develop the best ownership structure for you and/or your partners. Is it an LLC? A corporation? And how should it be structured? It matters because as you learned in the chapter on entity structures in this book, these decisions have tax implications. Post closing, your tax accountant can file the K-1 forms (the form used to report each owner's share of income and certain expense items) and perform audits if necessary.

TIP If you do not have a good real estate and tax accountant, get one.

One of the great benefits of being in the mortgage brokerage business is that I get to see amazing real estate projects and have the privilege of helping very creative entrepreneurs put those real estate projects together. I have learned much more from their good practices and bad decisions than I ever did in school or in my own real estate investment career.

Real estate is a magical way to use leverage to your advantage and develop sustainable wealth. With that as a premise, it also requires you have a professional focus that not only sees the big picture or vision but also forces you to pay attention to the details.

All real estate involves taking risks. The difference between the professional investor and the amateur is that the real professional tries to manage this risk by surrounding himself or herself with an incredible team that adds value at every turn. Property due diligence is one of those turns and it is too critical to just roll the dice!

 **Scott McPherson** is a principal and cofounder of a highly specialized real estate finance company called Capital Advisory Group, LC. Established in 2001, the firm has successfully closed around $3.5 billion of structured debt and equity in the United States. Scott has financed everything from raw land to high-rise condominium towers from Portland, Oregon, to Tampa, Florida, and has successfully sourced and closed multiple projects in excess of $100 million in cost. For more information, visit www.capitaladvisory group.us.

13

Creating Value from the Inside Out

I often refer to Kim Dalton as the chameleon. She is the interior designer my wife, Kim, and I hired to be a member of our design team—a team of professionals that included our architect, general contractor, landscape architect, and interior designer. I describe Kim Dalton as a chameleon because there were days I did not recognize her. She would show up at the job site completely transformed with a totally different look and a totally different energy. She would change as the nature of the project changed. She was that flexible, and design flexibility is essential for an interior designer.

Today, when people walk into our home or our business offices, they often say "ooooh" and "aaaah" because the impact of Kim's work is powerful, yet subtle. Kim's input to our projects is priceless. Not only does she increase the immediate sales value of our projects, her work gives our home and business environment warmth. Her work increases our desire to stay at home and also to be at work.

As a professional real estate investor, I think there is nothing worse than a multimillion dollar project that goes cheap on interior design. I have been in homes, condos, and commercial projects where the developer went cheap or went boring, leaving the interior design up to him or his wife. Rather than inspire a sale, cheap and tacky interior design can drive buyers away. You'd be surprised how inexpensive coats of paint in different or unique shades can make a $100,000 project look *like a million dollar project. That is why Kim Dalton's professional design touch is essential to our success in real estate.*

—ROBERT KIYOSAKI

Perhaps I'm biased, but I consider interior design to be an essential part of real estate investing. Whether you are planning a spec home, preparing an existing home for resale, rehabilitating a multifamily complex, or renovating a commercial property, appropriate interior design can always help to increase the value of a property. It can also dramatically shorten your sales cycle. Thoughtful interior design will carefully organize space while integrating color, light, pattern, and finish in order to supplement function, flow, and performance.

Don't be confused. Interior design is not home staging, which was developed years ago to help homeowners sell residential properties. Staging specialists are trained to maximize the perception of space and light using principles that appeal to a broader audience of potential buyers rather than family, friends, and guests. Interior designers do all that plus include the elements of aesthetics, temperature, sound, smell, balance, and harmony. All of these are value-added elements that will help your property sell quickly and easily. They are certainly worth your consideration as an investor and could very well be the difference between selling a property and getting top dollar for a property.

ASSEMBLING YOUR TEAM

Although you may see putting together a team of professionals for your real estate project as a costly and unnecessary expense, in reality it can be the smartest investment you make beyond the investment in the property itself. Strongly consider any or all of the following professionals to help you make the most of your investment project. I am and have been very careful with my team selection. I started my business by aligning myself with a great architect and that relationship has lasted for more than twenty years. I know that the way my team collaborates is instrumental in the outcome of any project I undertake. Your team should include an architect, interior designer, general contractor, landscape architect, engineers, and appropriate subcontractors. Your architect and general contractor will usually recommend engineers and subcontractors with whom they work, but it never hurts to have a few in your back pocket.

How to Select Your Team

1. **Interview.** Ask the tough design questions, but also try to get to know the person to understand how he or she works.
2. **Conversations with references.** Ask about the outcome of the project, but also listen for clues about work habits and service philosophy. Always ask the question: "Would you hire this person again?"
3. **Site visits to similar projects.** Visit and view the end result to assess if the final product lives up to the words.
4. **Willingness.** How willing is this person to work holistically to achieve a common goal, that is, a profitable product that sells quickly and easily? If a potential team member balks at the collaborative approach, it may be best to move on.

Assemble your team right at the start because early involvement will benefit both the process and the outcome. Delivering value is key, so the sooner the team is assembled, the sooner everyone can begin contributing. The earlier in the process those ideas surface, the more likely it will be that they can be implemented.

Real Life Story: Having a Team You Can Count On Really Counts

We have a wonderful client who has several homes. Some time ago, we were awarded an elaborate remodel of their vacation home in Santa Fe. Because we were based in Scottsdale, Arizona, we thought it might be more cost effective to hire a local contractor to handle the details for phase one of the project. We learned the value of a cohesive team the hard way.

Although we made several trips to check on the project and oversee the construction, we hit a few roadblocks. The contractor had challenges he could not handle with the team he had assembled, and communication was difficult from the get-go. When we embarked upon phase two of the project, we decided to use our Arizona-based team to handle the project. Instantly, our communication improved and we were able to solve problems much more quickly than before. Moreover, because our tradespeople had worked together so often in the past, they were able to effectively collaborate and avoid potential pitfalls even when they were on site without us.

Teams make great things happen. One day several years ago, Robert Kiyosaki stopped by to visit me in my office. He wanted to discuss a new project he had for me. My excited staff gathered around to hear all about it. Robert humbly mentioned that while he was not a very knowledgeable man (highly debatable by many), he did consider himself to be excellent at assembling a team of experts in their respective fields. He considers that to be of utmost importance when embarking on a project of any type. He has come to call that team his "trusted advisors," many of whom appear in this book.

Now let's get to the people you'll want on your team.

TEAM MEMBER NO. 1: THE ARCHITECT

The right architect can be invaluable in providing not only a set of drawings for construction but also insight into current trends in construction, engineering, lighting, and environmentally friendly design. I don't do anything today without an eye toward green sustainable design. Depending on the size and scope of your project, you can look to an architect to help guide the planning, design, documentation, and construction administration of your project.

The architect on any project is usually considered the team leader. Not only will he or she be able to provide a wealth of recommendations for other team members, the architect will also be instrumental in keeping the project on track, both from a budget standpoint as well as in terms of scheduling. Additionally, because of the nature of their work, architects must be up to the minute on current building codes and requirements. Building code violations can severely impede the construction process by the assessment of fines and a significant disruption in schedule. A good architect can also be an invaluable asset when applying for building permits.

You'll want to select an architect who will assume the role of team leader, while allowing his or her team to flourish under his guidance. Again, collaboration is the key here. While an architect is valuable for many parts of the project, he or she must rely on team members for their respective talents. Of course, basic chemistry is always a good barometer. Trust your intuition. Is this someone whom I could trust with my project? Remember, the whole idea of assembling a team is to allow you to achieve something you do not have the experience or expertise to accomplish yourself.

When it comes to money, architectural fees vary with the project scope and needs. Most architects will prefer to work on a fixed-fee basis with a defined scope of work, or on an hourly basis with a "not to exceed" fee limit.

TEAM MEMBER NO. 2: THE INTERIOR DESIGNER

The right interior designer is the one who not only shares your vision but enhances it. He or she is the next necessary addition to your team. An interior designer differs from an architect in many ways. While an architect is concerned with the structure of your space, the interior designer helps you create spaces that work and that flow in a logical and functional way.

Because an architect's role encompasses several aspects of the design and construction process, the interior designer can focus on realizing the overall vision of the project. Several years ago, I was hired to design a home on the coast of Oregon for a longtime client. Luckily, I was brought on early in the project to work with the client and the architect before they had completed the plans. We traveled to Oregon, walked the site, and talked for hours about what the house was to be. From those many discussions, we developed a set of rules for the house. This would allow both the architect and me to adhere to those rules and keep the design intent consistent. It becomes the designer's job to ensure the interior of the space will function as the team intends. Finishes, lighting, and furniture are all integral parts of a successful project. The interior designer can assist in any or all of these areas as well as in accessorizing and art placement.

The same rules for selecting an architect apply to selecting a designer. Fortunately your architect can often recommend a designer or two from his own team who would be ideal for your project. That's how I began working with Robert and Kim. Several years ago, they bought a very tired, but charming home with the intent of lovingly restoring and adding on to it to make it their own. They hired an architect who referred a general contractor. They also hired an interior designer referred by a friend to complete their team. While Kim and Robert are very easy to work with, the process did not go smoothly. A second designer was hired with similar results. She simply did not share the vision the team had. This is in no way a reflection on those designers or their capabilities. It is simply a reinforcement of the importance of the team as a whole. Nevertheless, the contractor arranged a meeting between the team and me, and the rest is history. The team certainly faced its challenges along the way, but we all shared the same vision, had a common goal, and were determined to produce the best project possible.

TEAM MEMBER NO. 3: THE LANDSCAPE ARCHITECT

The landscape architect is in charge of site design, and this is the one person, more than any other, who will set the property's first impression. When you think landscape architect, think curb appeal, and if you've bought or sold a home, you know the importance of that. Look to a landscape architect for regional neighborhood context design, site planning and furnishings, and high-impact features with low maintenance. You want a design that enhances the overall quality of the building or development and mixes well with the environment. Here's what I mean.

I recently completed a facelift for a twenty-year-old office building. The owner wanted to sell and felt a fresh look to the building would speed up the process. Without a huge budget, we knew we had to rely on color and landscape to do the trick. We selected exterior paint colors to work with the existing natural stone and brought in a landscape architect to accentuate the building's best attributes. He suggested we clean up the entry by reducing the number of overgrown plants, replacing them with smaller, easily maintained varieties. This gave the building a cleaner aesthetic as well as an enticement to potential buyers who were looking for less exterior maintenance. He also worked to accentuate the main entries of the building, leading tenants and visitors to the entrances with ease.

TEAM MEMBER NO. 4: THE GENERAL CONTRACTOR

Very often, team members will recommend a general contractor with whom they have successfully collaborated. If not, please refer to your local state agencies to assist with the selection of a qualified contractor. When choosing a general contractor, I look for a company or a person with whom I would enjoy socializing. I know that sounds strange, but remember, this will be the team member you will see most often. Of course, this person must meet all the other criteria as well, but you really must have a good relationship with your contractor. After all, he will be responsible for spending your money. Whenever Robert and Kim embark on another project, we all look forward to the reunion of our team, knowing the general contractor will ensure we get the project done with minimal problems.

Many investors opt to handle the oversight of a project on their own. While this can work well, it more often than not goes badly, particularly if the person is inexperienced. My advice to clients is to always consider the scope and complexity of the job before making that decision. Think about it. Do you have another career that will keep you away from the jobsite? What is your time worth compared to a contractor's fee? Are you familiar with the local building codes, construction methods, backup trades if necessary? Do you have strengths in scheduling, budgeting, and managing people?

The value of an experienced contractor to manage the project and trades-people is often a smart investment. On the other hand, if your remodel includes little more than paint and carpet, you may be fine managing the project. A brief consultation with an interior designer can help you select materials and provide recommendations for appropriate trades. Bear in mind, however, sometimes small projects lead to bigger ones. I've witnessed the discovery of problems that are bigger than any owner can handle.

Eventually, the more you work with your team of experts, the more they will become your trusted advisors, and you'll consult them for projects big or small. The more longevity you have with your team members and the more your rapport and working relationship with them grows, the better your outcomes will be. I've found that projects become easier, move quicker, and deliver better results the longer I work with my team. Robert understands this, and that is one of the benefits of this book. His trusted advisors—his team—can now be your team through the pages of this book.

As a real estate investor, you will want to maximize your return. And just as good property management plays a huge role in a property's value, so does the design of that property. But how do you know what design will bring in the bucks and what will just be another expense that lowers your bottom line return? Here are the guidelines I use for different types of real estate endeavors.

EXISTING HOME STRATEGIES THAT SELL

The trend of purchasing an existing home, remodeling, and selling it has made the need for staging unavoidable. Everyone wants to buy a home that looks like a builder's model. This concept was first developed by Barb Schwartz in 1972 and has grown over the years to become a widely used selling tool. It's all about merchandising the rooms to make them look like much more than just four walls.

TIP The goal of interior design for a residence is to personalize the space according to the tastes and preferences of the homeowner. Staging is the opposite. The professional stager's job is to depersonalize the space and allow potential buyers to imagine themselves living there.

As I mentioned before, professional staging is often confused with interior design and actually, the two couldn't be more different. Let's talk about staging for a moment because it is crucial to selling an existing home. When you decide to sell, agree that you will live there in a much different way. In fact, you'll want to get packing early because all the personal effects in your home must go. Precious collections, photos, mementos, all the things that are "you" will say to prospective buyers that this is your home, not theirs. So if you hire a stager or do it yourself, get serious and get rid of the clutter. It's all about vision.

As an interior designer of both residential and commercial spaces for more than twenty years, the last thing I thought I needed when preparing to list my home for sale was a stager. My realtor tactfully suggested that I meet with her stager, "It can't hurt," she said. I grudgingly agreed. I will warn you, this is a humbling experience. It's unsettling to have someone tell you that your collection of exquisite Chinese foo dogs may be best placed in a box in the garage. My advice is to listen and obey. I had spent seven years working to create a cozy space out of a large, open tract house. She told me I had succeeded. That, however, is not what the typical homebuyer is looking for. Light, bright, and airy still seems to be the best rule of thumb when preparing to sell a home. Also, clean, uncluttered rooms provide the most appeal.

In tough real estate markets when nothing is selling, the staged house will nine times out of ten be the one that sells first. So, as much as you won't like them, here are the five C's of successful staging:

1. **Clean.** Everything should be immaculate. That means carpets, floors, walls, counters, and bathrooms should look model-home perfect.
2. **Clutter Free.** Make counters, tables, and shelves ready for the buyer's favorite things, not yours. Remove everything, and then some more.
3. **Color.** You may have loved it wild and crazy to match your purple sofa, but buyers want to picture their own furniture and colors. Hot pink walls make that difficult.
4. **Creativity.** Give buyers something to talk about and remember. They'll be looking at a lot of homes that eventually all blend together. Make yours unforgettable.
5. **Compromise.** Stagers will tell you to do it all, and you may find that you'll only go so far. No problem. Compromise and do those things that matter most.

Did you know that most buyers make their buying decisions within the first fifteen seconds of seeing a property? That's a prevailing rule in real estate that I believe to be absolutely true. What does that tell us? First impressions are everything. It's worth spending extra time and money on curb appeal or the wow factor of the house.

Sell That House in Fifteen Seconds or Less

First impressions are everything and buying decisions are made in the first fifteen seconds. Here are the top five areas to spruce up:

1. The front yard, including lawn, trees, walkway—clean, sweep, and plant flowers with lots of color.

2. The front door and entryway—Give your door some color, or at least remove the cobwebs, and then be sure the first few steps inside the home are memorable.

3. Exterior and interior paint—nothing freshens a home more than new paint.

4. Flooring, including carpets, tile, etc.—no stains, no worn carpet, no dirt allowed.

5. Healthy green plants—emphasis on healthy, shiny plants without dead or dry leaves, dust, messy pots or water stains. Placing plants and trees near windows will blur the gap between inside and out, thus making the space feel larger and more connected to nature.

Staging will make your property look so good that, if it is your own home, you'll wonder why you lived in it the way you did for all those years. I advise everyone, particularly after my own experience, to hire a stager to help you weed out the clutter. It takes brutal honesty, and stagers are known for it. Stagers will rearrange furniture to maximize the appearance of space as well as downplay less desirable features. If you want to take things to the next level—and in tight markets you may have little choice—hire a professional stager and allow him or her to use their existing inventory of accoutrements to enhance your home.

If you are selling a home that is unoccupied, don't listen to people who say an empty home sells better than one that is furnished. If that were true, no builder would ever furnish a model home, and most all of them do. Stage the home as best you can within your budget. If you can't rent furniture from a stager for the main rooms, set up small vignettes within the home. This can be as simple as adding a few wall hangings, live plants, towels in the master bath, and soft music. You'll be surprised at the results.

The tangible aspects of a home are important, but there are intangibles as well that you must consider. Have you ever walked into a space and immediately felt uncomfortable, but had no idea why? That's energy flow, and all spaces have it. That discomfort usually comes from stale or bad energy in a space. There are consultants who specialize in clearing spaces of this negative energy. The ancient art of feng shui incorporates these principles and has done so for

---

Real Life Story: It's All About Experience

Recently my real estate agent, Joanne Callaway, related a staging success story to me. She had been trying for months to sell a seemingly marketable home. The only problem area was the dining room. It had one red wall to match the homeowners' linens. I was surprised that this was the problem area as I often paint dining rooms red. Nevertheless, Joanne called upon the services of her favorite stager who immediately had the wall painted, changed the linens, added cushions to the dining chairs, and the house sold in one week!

---

more than three thousand years. Listed at the end of this chapter are Web sites that will help you understand energy flow and how to improve it in your home.

Believe it or not, your own energy will either add to or detract from your home. A positive attitude will create better energy in the space. Instead of worrying about how long it will take you to sell the house, imagine how great those precious foo dogs will look in your *new* home.

I know this all sounds like a lot of effort, but consider the statistics—having homes properly staged significantly shortens the selling cycle as well as brings a higher selling price.

There are lots of helpful resources to learn more about staging, such as home stagingresource.com and stagedhomes.com. Perhaps the best book on staging is by the creator of staging itself, Barb Schwarz. Her book, *Home Staging: The Winning Way to Sell Your House for More Money* is the bible on the subject. And she's right about staging paying dividends. Homestaging.com. sites a recent HomeGain Survey that shows home staging delivered as much as a 169 percent return on investment. That's a significant figure, making staging well worth the time and effort.

MAKE YOUR MULTIFAMILY HOUSING PROJECT A WINNER

Just as selling your own home is less about you and is all about the buyer, when investing in multifamily housing, it's all about the target resident. Ask yourself, "Who is that person, and what will he or she want or expect from this property?" Then, how can you take those expectations one step further to truly wow them? Whether you developed the project from the ground up or are rehabilitating an existing property, spend your money on the things that will count in the eyes of the target resident. Of course, you'll want to contain your ambitions to a reasonable amount in proportion to the potential rent you can collect, but you will need to focus on those things that will leave a lasting impression. If a property isn't special in some way, it will not be easy to rent. Ask yourself, "Why would someone rent this property instead of the one down the street?" Consider these factors when preparing a multifamily project:

1. **Curb appeal.** Clean up the trees, bushes, add a fresh coat of paint, dress up the windows with awnings or shutters, repair steps and walkways, re-sod the lawns, and plant flowers, lots of flowers.

2. **Accessibility.** Make sure you purchase properties with ample parking for residents and guests. Inadequate parking is next to impossible to change. The property should be ADA (Americans with Disabilities Act) compliant, or you may have to make it that way, which can be costly.

3. **Location.** This is real estate, after all, and location is everything.

4. **Security and safety.** Walls, security gates, security alarms, and security cameras all add up to making residents feel safer, and can also justify higher rents for very little up-front investment.

5. **Durable finishes.** If you are rehabbing the property, use the best finishes you can afford and still maintain your profitability projections. Check your competition in the area. If they have tile counters, you may need to have tile counters.

6. **Neutral finishes.** This is so important in multifamily projects. Choose colors that work for everyone, which usually means light, light, light.

7. **Common area aesthetic.** Is there a pool? Is there a clubhouse? Is there a courtyard or garden? If so, it should look picturesque, clean, and be a true amenity, not an eyesore. Make it a point of difference.

8. **Views.** People buy views, and views can be big wow factors. Even if your project doesn't look out to rocky mountain majesty, be sure it doesn't look out on the dumpster or an unkempt parking lot. If you are building, plan for internal views to gardens or pool areas.

Showing a rental property is no different than showing a home. Here we go again! Yes, you'll want to furnish a model if you can. Rental spaces are usually small and look even smaller without furniture. Once furniture is in place, however, spaces look bigger, and people can visualize living in them. They can see that the space isn't small after all. It is cozy, livable, and oftentimes just right.

Senior living properties are another type of multi-unit housing. As the baby boomers age, the concept of the traditional nursing home is changing rapidly and drastically. Independent living facilities are being built all over the country, and there are new requirements for them, not all of which are coming from government regulations. I'm talking about buyers' requirements. This aging population demands a much higher level of design than the generation preceding it and they are willing to pay accordingly.

I am currently working with a developer on a number of senior living communities. Think twenty-first century; they in no way resemble the nursing homes of the past! These independent living communities are based on the desire for an active lifestyle with minimal constraints from the residents' pasts, i.e., home maintenance, yards, housekeeping, etc. These communities focus on the active lifestyles of this population with the utmost attention placed on comfort, autonomy, and quality of life. Obviously, we are working to respect and deliver on the changing needs of this population as it ages, but research has proven that it can be done with good design and thoughtful planning. One project will be set on the side of a mountain, and the hilly terrain obviously presents potential obstacles for an aging population. The architects and landscape architects have worked on a site plan that will take advantage of the scenic views and the wonderful climate by means of a series of covered breezeways and no stairs. This is just one example of how we can maximize accessibility without calling attention to potential limitations.

COMMERCIAL SPACES THAT STAND THE TEST OF TIME

As you venture into the world of commercial real estate, many of the principles we already talked about still apply. But first and foremost, you still need to take the target tenant into account first and create a fantastic first impression. After all, people want to be proud of where they work, and they want that space to be functional and comfortable. That charge isn't always easy because commercial properties can often be quite large, quite complex, and rather impersonal. The key is creating personal, more intimate spaces inside or outside a large building to add that personal touch and provide respite from a busy day. It doesn't take much. A shady tree, a fountain, or a comfortable bench away from the hustle and bustle can achieve this important goal. Alcoves within a lobby space with nice art and comfortable furniture can work, too, while they welcome visitors and provide a gathering place for tenants.

If your project is new construction, get an architect and an interior designer on board right from the start. An architect's primary role is creating the structure itself. An interior designer's role is to design the interior spaces. Unless you do this for a living, creating the design by yourself will not work. I've seen the aftermath of do-it-yourself commercial projects, and many of them are beyond hope or beyond the pocketbooks or the profit potential of most buyers to rehabilitate.

Lifecycle costs (meaning how long do you want these materials to last, will a new tenant mean new finishes?) and total budget are great places to begin your discussion with these professionals. They'll want to know who your target market is because they will design differently for a medical building than they would for a day care center, for instance. You've probably heard this phrase before: "form follows function." Well, this is what they mean by it.

While form and function are absolutely critical to good commercial space, so is using the natural environment as a guide to design. In fact, it has and, I would go so far to say, always will be a failsafe guide for many interior designers and architects in their quest for interiors and structures that stand the test of time. That's why certain styles of design and architecture are common to certain areas of the country and, indeed, the world. Suitable architecture and design respond to the environment rather than fight it. By using the natural environment as a guide, interior designers and architects establish rules to help guide the design process. And it's best to stick with them.

Unfortunately, rules get broken, and not always in a good ways. One building comes to mind in Phoenix—a desert city with desert mountains surrounding it and very bright sun most days of the year. Smack in the midst of mostly stucco buildings is a dark, wooden, modern for its circa-1970 construction structure that looks like it should be in the middle of the Rockies in Colorado. Interestingly, when I look at this building in Phoenix, it seems terribly out of date and out of place, but if I picture it among the pines and aspens in Colorado it would be spectacular. That's what I mean. The architect and designer of this project did not look to the environment and, therefore, the building design did not last.

So when I hear the common question when starting a new project, "Will it be outdated in five years?" I always have the answer: "Not if we build in harmony with the environment." The best way to avoid the problem of short-lived trends is to use materials and color palettes derived from the surrounding environment. The natural environment will not change drastically, and that means a timeless aesthetic to your building.

The only time this doesn't work is if the design is for a high impact space that needs an extreme reaction to attract tenants or visitors. These projects tend to be controversial and often get early press attention because one group or another loves or hates the design. But once completed they often become well-known and admired landmarks. Projects that fall into this category could include an art museum or a high-end jewelry store.

TIP The best way to avoid the problem of short-lived trends is to use materials and color palettes derived from the surrounding environment. The natural environment will not change drastically and that means a timeless aesthetic to your building.

Renovating a property requires a different tack because there are subtle trends in design that when followed will improve your chances of success. For instance, color preferences change from decade to decade, and you absolutely want to be up to date, not a throwback from the last century, unless your property is historic and then you'll want to go two centuries back. But kidding aside, color is critical. We've all seen buildings or been in offices with outdated colors of walls, cabinetries, floors, and carpets. They don't look like places with companies poised for future growth; they look like places where companies go to stagnate and die. It's amazing how interiors drive our impressions, but right or wrong, they always do.

To find out what colors are trending up, take a walk through some of the newest retail centers—the highest-end ones you can find—and you will see many examples of colors and materials. Locations that come to mind are Kierland Commons in Phoenix or La Encantada in Tucson—both Westcor properties. The Power & Light District in Kansas City, The Palazzo in Las Vegas. There are many others.

Of course, you will have a plan for the revitalization of your commercial building, and it will be based on projected net operating income and cash flow. But some designers don't relate to the numbers side of the business and can develop designs that spiral costs out of control. Choose a designer that understands the business fundamentals of an investment property and be critical when evaluating a proposed plan to update a building. Believe it or not, simple things like paint, landscape, and signage can go a long way when sprucing up an existing property.

As with the other types of properties, commercial buildings require balance and harmony, too. Office buildings are meant to house large numbers of varying businesses in the same overall space. When you utilize the principles of balance, harmony, light, and accessibility, it can only enhance the workplace experience.

Commercial Building Must Have's

1. Accessibility. ADA compliance is a must, as is ample parking and easement access.

2. Ease of circulation, both internal and external. Well thought-out placement of elevators, doors, lobbies, signage, etc., go a long way.

3. Intuitive way finding. Buildings and office spaces built like mazes are not fun. They leave guests lost and sometimes even embarrassed. In emergencies they can be dangerous.

4. Customization. What is the unique wow factor for this building? There should always be one.

5. Familiarity. Way finding is a method people use to intuitively navigate a space. Using landmarks like the big painting or the blue floor or the potted plant to remember the way lessens any anxiety about being in an unfamiliar place.

6. Smell. Some people are going so far as to run scent through their ventilation. Scent matters because our sense of smell affects our mood and is closely tied to memory centers in the brain (UPI, October 17, 2008).

7. Sound. If you can hear the quiet, break the silence with soft music that fills the room. Match the music to the mood you are trying to convey and you'll have a winner.

8. Location, location, location. When it is all said and done, location is the key.

SUSTAINABLE DESIGN

In recent years we have seen an enormous push toward sustainable or green design. Sustainable design means using our resources efficiently while creating healthier buildings. A green building is one that is designed, built, renovated, operated, or reused in an ecological and resource-efficient manner. You may think that green building design is more expensive than conventional building practices, yet while some up-front costs may be higher, the long-term benefits, both financially and environmentally, generally outweigh the initial costs. Proper design can significantly reduce operating costs over the life of the building while helping to preserve natural resources and minimize waste.

The first stop for anyone interested in green design, and today that should be everyone, is the Green Building Council and its Green Building Rating System called LEED, Leadership in Energy and Environmental Design. This rating system is the nationally accepted benchmark for the design, construction, and operation of high-performance green buildings. LEED process certification provides building owners and operators with the tools they need to have an immediate and measurable impact on their building's performance. LEED principles have now been adapted to a variety of residential and commercial building types.

The city of Scottsdale, Arizona, was one of the first in the country to adopt a voluntary Green Building Designation Program. Those homeowners, developers, and builders wishing to participate must complete a detailed checklist based on a point system. Points are given for meeting or exceeding environmentally considerate building materials and practices. Applicants must meet the point total necessary for certification. These categories range from recycled building materials to the use of indigenous materials, which cuts fuel consumption, to energy use.

Green Building Check List

Use this checklist when developing your green design plan.

1. Sustainable site. Opt for an existing site rather than undeveloped land.

2. Water efficiency. Think about adding on-site infiltration systems and storm water management.

3. Energy and atmosphere. Consider the location of the building as it relates to natural light, and explore the use of solar power.

4. Materials and resources. Always research the possibility of using reclaimed construction materials.

5. Indoor environmental air quality. Reducing off-gassing from furniture and finishes can lead to improved overall indoor air quality.

6. Research. Do your homework to ensure you have carefully considered all viable options to help ensure the completion of a sustainable project.

Once you get your green designation from the city or town, you'll be in a position to take advantage of it. Here are just a few of the benefits of green building:

1. Social and economic revitalization of depressed or disadvantaged neighborhoods and renewed sense of community pride
2. Greater market demand for the project
3. Water conservation and lower costs
4. Reduction of air and water pollution

5. Great energy and power reliability and reduced dependence on the local power grid

6. Reduced waste clogging up our landfills and conservation of new resources

7. Improved health of construction workers and building occupants

8. Superior indoor air quality

All these add up to a better, more responsible working environment that people can be truly proud of, enjoy working in, and feel better about. That signals more productivity.

Of course anyone doing any new building, remodeling, or revitalization knows that the quicker you can get through the city planning and zoning review process the better. Plan reviews can often take up to several months, and you know what they say: "Time is money." But some municipalities are providing incentives. For example, builders who participate in the Scottsdale Green Building Program projects receive "fast track" plan review service. This means green building projects receive building permits in half the time as regular projects, depending on the degree of complexity.

On the other hand, site inspections tend to be more thorough, scrutinizing environmentally sensitive aspects of the building to make sure they measure up to the standard. The city also provides Green Building site signage, which tells the world that this owner is willing to invest in the protection of the environment. Anyway you slice it, that adds up to good public relations as well as responsible development.

Government agencies in Arizona have become involved in enticing companies to "go green" by offering sales tax exemption for the purchase of solar energy devices. Also, local power companies offer rebates to those companies willing to invest in solar power. I fully expect to see tax concessions on the use of environmentally supportive or recycled materials in the coming years.

THE FINAL WORD

Design, whether it be green or any other color in the rainbow has the power to add value to your property. From residential to commercial, every property can benefit from good interior design, and it can save you from making costly mistakes that, once made, are hard to correct. The key is maximizing the space and the light, and working in harmony with the environment. Hire the right professional to pull all this together and you'll have a timeless building that you'll enjoy or will generate income for you for years to come.

WAYS TO LEARN MORE

www.epa.gov/brownfields
www.epa.gov/owow
www.energycodes.gov
www.ashrae.org
www.asgbc.org/resources
www.spiritualclearing.com

 **Kim Dalton** is an award-winning interior designer with more than twenty years of innovative interior design experience. She has the unique ability to transform clinical and institutional spaces into supportive, healing environments that are cohesive, economical, and timeless. Since founding Dalton Interiors in 1990, Kim has designed significant real estate projects, including Phoenix Children's Hospital, Del E. Webb Memorial Hospital, Christ Church of the Valley, and suite renovations at Chase Field in Phoenix.

14

Financing for Real Estate Investors

*S*cott McPherson is the mortgage broker I go to when I want to know the straight story about what's going on in real estate financing. He's more than just a mortgage broker; he is an investor, and, again, like all the others in this book, he lives what he teaches.

I can count on Scott to be a part of teaching the classes I hold on finance. He donates his time, just like he did to contribute to this book, to teach others how to be smarter with their money and with their investments. He has years of wisdom, is smart and experienced, and is an excellent resource particularly during times of economic chaos.

I met Scott in an unlikely place at the Phoenix Open Golf Tournament in 1999. His reputation preceded him; I knew him, but I did not think he knew me. When I discovered he agreed with my position on stocks and mutual funds, I felt relief and affirmation. Few agreed with me at the time, and I was under attack. Now people are learning otherwise, and they are seeing their stock and 401(k) portfolios slashed. The critics aren't so loud anymore.

From that day forward, Scott has been a great friend and a trusted advisor to Kim and me. He has the ability to see what's on the horizon. He has saved Kim and me a lot of money and saved us from a few investments that would have been *mistakes. I cannot emphasize the importance of having trusted advisors around you. If you can find a mortgage broker like Scott, you're very lucky.*

—ROBERT KIYOSAKI

I have always believed from early on, that there is no substitution for actual experience, no matter what you take on in your life. I can tell you that I am not a professional writer, but I am very active in the real estate finance business.

The principles of real estate finance are basically the same whether you are buying a single family home to rent or you are converting three hundred rental apartments to for-sale condominiums in Scottsdale, Arizona. The key to understanding real estate financing is really not a secret; it is just how to ask yourself some basic questions and follow some very simple steps along the way.

What I want to do in this chapter is walk you through the fundamentals of real estate finance and give you the pathway to apply them to your particular situation or requirements.

BEING BORN WITH A SILVER PAINT BRUSH IN HAND!

When I was studying real estate and finance at Arizona State University, I thought I had the world by the tail and could hardly wait to get out and carve my niche in the real estate business. I was living in an upscale apartment near campus, driving a nice car, and was doing well in my classes. I became the president of the Real Estate Club on campus, and at that point no one knew more about real estate (at least in my mind) than me.

That all changed when my father, Douglas McPherson, who was a successful real estate investor and owner of a prominent commercial real estate brokerage firm, sat me down and said, "Look, you think you know a lot about real estate, but it has only been from textbooks with no practical experience. If you really want to get in the business, you need to step up and buy something!"

I was planning on going to work after school for my father's company, but I did not know that it was predicated on me actually going out and buying some property. That twenty-minute discussion with my father was probably the best advice I have *ever* received in my career, and here is why.

I went to work trying to find a single-family home to buy, live in, fix up, and rent in order to get into the game. I got the newspaper out and suddenly realized

I did not know where to even begin. After a couple of weeks looking at homes in locations that I wanted to live in, I quickly realized I was way out of my affordability range and unsure what to do next.

It was very hard for me to accept that I was about to get a degree in real estate and finance from a major university, and I was not prepared to buy a house!

I asked my father for help, so he spent two weekends with me, driving neighborhoods and reading want ads in the newspaper. We finally found something that sounded interesting. It was a small ad by an attorney who represented a widow that wanted to sell two houses for $15,000. AS IS. We went and looked at them, and I was completely not interested. They were in an older neighborhood in Phoenix and needed lots of clean-up work.

My father and I went to lunch, and he proceeded to tell me what a great deal this was. He pointed out that the properties were below replacement costs, and were in good rental neighborhoods. My problem was I could see these homes only as places for me to live and not as a real estate investment!

The other benefit of this deal was that the seller would carry her own paper or mortgage back because of the property's condition. I had no idea what this meant at that time, but I quickly learned that it was the key to becoming a real estate investor. I bought the property for $15,000 with $1,000 down, and the seller carried the mortgage of $14,000. I was on my way!

My father made me put together a budget for the property acquisition and renovation along with a stabilized pro forma once rented. I cannot stress enough how I struggled trying to figure out if this was a good deal or not. My father put up half of the down payment; $500 for half of the profits and turned me loose.

I really struggled at first, but I realized I had to make this work because my whole career was on the line. I spent a year fixing up the properties and leasing the homes and eventually sold the properties for $25,000 in eighteen months. During that time, I learned about basic property renovation, negative cash flows, property management, partner issues, tenant lease issues, and how to develop an exit strategy for my investment.

I learned more about real estate from owning two fix-up homes in a rough area of Phoenix than I did my entire time in college.

TIP I went on to purchase twelve houses over the next two years and I found one common thread in all my purchases: Understanding the financing was critical.

I was now addicted to real estate investing! I went on to purchase twelve houses over the next two years and I found one common thread in all my purchases: Understanding the financing was critical. Just like the first two homes that I purchased, I almost always had sellers carry the mortgages for me. This did two things: One, it allowed me to get much better leverage and financing terms than a conventional lender would or would not give me; and, two, it allowed me to close very quickly without appraisals. When an owner wants out, he or she wants out fast.

I quickly realized that having a good knowledge of how to finance these homes was paramount in my business plan. I actually enjoyed trying to come up with some pretty creative ways to get someone else to put up 80 to 100 percent of the capital to make my business plan a reality.

THREE BASIC STEPS TO UNDERSTANDING AND OBTAINING FINANCING

HAVE A BUSINESS PLAN!

In my business, it is a pleasure to come to work and see very creative real estate transactions and hear the sponsor's or developer's vision. I can tell in the first fifteen minutes of our discussions if this person is really someone we can finance and is truly a real estate investor. I have a policy that we promote internally in my office that if we (being the mortgage broker) are steering or making too many of the decisions for the borrowers, it is time to rethink their abilities.

Business plans can be very simple or complex based on the amount of moving parts, issues, or challenges your particular real estate transaction might have. All of this has significant impact on the type of financing that you should pursue.

I would encourage you to ask yourself the following questions:

Why am I buying this real estate?

Shelter. You need a place to live? If that is your motivation, then how much can you afford on your own, or should you bring in someone to help you with the down payment, or be a tenant?

Investment. What kind of investment? Short-term trade? Long-term hold? Buying for income? This can be very complex because everyone has different reasons for investing. The reason this is so important is that you need to match the appropriate financing with your correct business plan.

Real Life Story: Two Properties . . . The Financing Was Not Created Equal

Let me give you an example of how different the financing can be for the same type of real estate with two different buyers who had two different business plans.

When my son was born, I purchased a two-bedroom condominium in a complex that I had placed the financing on for a developer client of mine. **I purchased the condominium for the sole purpose of having someone else fund my son's college education through rent!** I set up the financing such that it was amortized more than twenty years and coupled it with enough down payment that a tenant's rent would cover the mortgage payment and the HOA dues.

I then leased the unit and let another person just gradually pay the loan down monthly though his rent. I was not concerned if the property appreciated one dollar. I just wanted the property to be free and clear when my son was ready to go to college.

Another friend of mine purchased another unit in the same complex and wanted to hold it for six months and sell it. He borrowed as much as he could and paid a higher interest rate than I, but he was able to pay the loan off in six months when he sold the property for a profit, without any prepayment penalties. He used leverage to his benefit.

Both of these loan structures were appropriate for the investors; however, they were very different in structure and actually had two different types of lenders.

How much risk am I willing to take?

You need to ask yourself how much risk you are willing to take. Ask some tough questions of your personal finances and lifestyle. If you are a financially capable, sophisticated real estate investor then leverage and debt can be your best friend. If you are not in that category, be honest with yourself and borrow less or spread your equity risk by bringing in a partner.

TIP One of the strongest traits that I see in my business is that successful real estate investors know their risk tolerance levels.

A good example of this was when another customer of mine wanted to build 400,000 square feet of speculative industrial space in the Phoenix metro area.

This would be the first development for this client in the Phoenix market. He has done similar projects throughout the other southwestern states.

He hired me to find an equity joint venture partner and a construction loan. We spent quite a bit of time talking about how to finance the development, and he decided that he wanted a low-leverage construction loan and a large institutional partner that could weather any bumps in the road.

I brought him a pension fund that put in all of the equity and had a very long-term investment strategy. My client was very happy to get his first Phoenix project started with minimal equity requirement from him. This client could have easily done the project all on his own but decided to reduce some risk. This is probably why he has been in business forty years!

DEVELOP MULTIPLE EXIT STRATEGIES

For your piece of mind, your investors, and the lender's, please know how you are going to get your money back, along with everyone else's!

When I look at any real estate investment, I always start by asking how am I going to get out of the deal. You may have the greatest idea in the world for buying, building, or converting something, but with no clear way to get your capital along with a lender's capital back, you will never attract anyone to the deal!

TIP When I look at any real estate investment, I always start by asking how am I going to get out of the deal.

BUILD A CREDIBLE TEAM

It does not matter how talented you think you are, you need to surround yourself with a very good team! As I pointed out earlier, my father really jumped in and became my team when it came down to actually buying something.

Try to sit down and put together a list of people to hire to help you execute your business plan. Here's the short list:

Real Estate Broker
Appraiser
Property Manager
Mortgage Broker

Your Exit Strategy Options

Exit strategies can be very easy, depending on the type of real estate project you are doing. Here are the options:

No Exit. If you are buying a home or duplex to live in, your exit is you! Very simple. However, just be sure you and your lender understand that.

Refinance. Maybe your plan is to renovate one hundred apartments that have been neglected and raise rents. If so, put together a forward-looking proforma with your team (more on this in step two) and show your investors or lenders how a refinance will get their capital back.

Sale. If the plan is to buy and then re-sell the property, then you must show how, when, and why that will occur. If your plan simply is to buy and let the market make you money, you are going to have a tough time just relying on that unless you made one incredible buy.

Accountant
Real Estate Attorney
Contractor
Property Conditions Reports
Environmental Consultants

Let me give you an example of how and when I would use these team members. For this example, I am going to use a twenty-unit condo conversion project that I purchased in Scottsdale, Arizona. The property was a tired twenty-year-old property in a transitional neighborhood and needed major renovations before we could convert it to for-sale condominiums. Prior to closing:

- I interviewed (more on that process later) residential real estate brokers who gave me the condo market resale analysis and pricing matrix for the individual units once I had them completely renovated. I also asked them to provide me with a timeline for getting them sold. *Remember the exit strategy!*

- I hired a well-known appraiser to value the individual units as if they were fully renovated.

- I interviewed and hired a property manager to audit the existing operational statements and to create HOA budgets and run the HOA when it was turned over to the homeowners.

- The mortgage company interviewed and hired me! The reality would have been to interview a mortgage broker who has successfully financed condo conversions and could help me structure my debt and equity requirements. I did hire a residential mortgage broker to provide take-out loans for the buyers. *Remember the exit strategy!*
- I used my accountant to minimize our tax liability.
- I hired a very experienced attorney to set up our ownership, HOA, and condominium subdivision documentation.
- Since this property required about $35,000 per unit in renovations, I wanted to be sure my contractor did not miss anything. I matched his scope of work with my property conditions report along with the required finish levels that my residential real estate broker developed. *Remember the exit strategy!*
- I also engaged a property conditions report to backstop my contractor and to make sure I had a sound building. I coupled that with an environmental report to point out any environmental issues I needed to deal with.

When I assimilated all of this information and hired all of my team, I looked like the best condo converter that walked the planet! My goal was to fully understand what I was getting into before I went to a lender or investors to get the capital needed to do this conversion prior to closing on the property.

By hiring the best team you can, you have demonstrated to yourself, your lender, and your investors that you recognize areas that you need some support with. You also will potentially eliminate the "oops!" factor down the road that can become extremely costly in terms of profits and credibility.

How to Hire Your Team Members

How do you hire team members? My answer is very simple, once you locate them through referral or other means. Please go meet with them and ask these tough but basic questions:

- Have you done this type of work before?
- How many of these have you done?
- Would you mind if I spoke to one of your clients about your abilities?

If they stumble on any of these questions walk away. You have too much at risk not to get the "A" team because they are out there for you.

SHOW ME THE MONEY!

You now have found a property, created a business plan, and assembled your team. Now where do I get the money?

Most people when asked where they will go to get money for a real estate transaction will say "to the bank, of course." Clearly the local, regional, and national banks are a source for capital, but by no means are they the only place you should look. Have you considered any of the sources at the right?

All of these lenders will not fit all types of financing requirements. That will depend on size, risk, or property type, but you should be aware that there are many ways to find the debt and the equity to do your transaction.

I have done many multimillion dollar financing deals with a borrower that had marginal financial strength. What he did not have in financial net worth he made up for in a very strong business plan and an incredible team.

> ### Capital Sources Other Than Banks
>
> Credit Companies
> Life Insurance Companies
> Real Estate Finance Companies
> Mortgage Funds
> REIT's Thrifts / Industrial Banks
> Investment Banks
> Hedge Funds
> Pension Funds
> Credit Unions
> Private Debt / Equity
> Opportunity Funds
> Mezzanine Debt Funds
> Offshore Investment Funds
> Friends and Family
> Angels
> High Net Worth Investors

Remember this, lenders want to make you a loan or provide you with equity. They make money only when they loan money out. It turns from a liability to an asset on their books.

They also want to do business with people they have confidence in and who can repay the loan at some point in the future. *Remember the exit strategy!*

HOW DO I OBTAIN ACCESS TO THESE LENDERS?

If you are an experienced real estate investor, you may have some access to these types of lenders already. Unfortunately, if you are not on top of these lenders on a daily basis they may be out of the market when you need them.

If you're starting out and want to do this financing on your own you can talk to *successful* real estate brokers for the particular product type and ask for a referral. You can search the Internet and real estate finance publications. You can also go directly to some of your local banks to see what they can do.

I suggest you hire a competent mortgage broker. It may sound a little self serving, but here is why.

First, when you go to hire a mortgage broker you need to be sure you are really hiring someone who knows how to help you and adds value. If you are buying a single-family home, you should go to a good residential mortgage broker that can help guide you through the various programs that she or he can deliver. If he works for a bank and can deliver only limited programs offered by that bank, you move on because you are not being exposed to all the financing products you may need.

On the commercial side of the business, it is also very important to interview several commercial mortgage brokerage firms and ask the tough, but basic questions we talked about before:

- How long have you been in the business?
- How many financings like this have you done?
- Could I see one of your loan submission packages?
- I would like to talk to someone you have done similar business with.

A credible and competent mortgage broker should not have any hesitation in answering these questions.

Financing for real estate investors is really a blending of using good common sense and surrounding yourself with the best talent possible. I started with one

Hire a Good Mortgage Broker First

I recommend hiring a good mortgage broker before you go looking for properties for these reasons:

- He can give you a realistic view of the capital markets for your type of transaction. This is extremely important to you as you are preparing an offer to purchase the property.
- He can provide another set of qualified eyes as to your underwriting assumptions and financial modeling of the property and the market.
- He can suggest credible team members to join you such as contractors or lawyers.
- He can package you and your property properly, so it will be presented in the best light to potential lenders.
- And, finally, he should be able to present your property to a wide variety of lenders that never would have access to, hopefully giving you multiple options to choose from.

team member—my father—and have developed additional members over the years as needed.

I encourage you to find the opportunities that are out there in the real estate market today. Go after them, knowing that there is a way to secure the appropriate capital for the transaction regardless of current market conditions.

WAYS TO LEARN MORE

The best way to learn more is from the professionals you surround yourself with. Seek them out. Ask them questions. Be an active learner.

 **Scott McPherson** is a principal and cofounder of a highly specialized real estate finance company called Capital Advisory Group, LC. Established in 2001, the firm has successfully closed around $3.5 billion of structured debt and equity in the United States. Scott has financed everything from raw land to high-rise condominium towers from Portland, Oregon, to Tampa, Florida, and has successfully sourced and closed multiple projects in excess of $100 million in cost. For more information, visit www.capitaladvisory group.us.

15

Craig COPPOLA, CCIM, CRE, SIOR

Lease It and Keep It Leased

Craig is the most well-organized person I know. Not only is he one of the most highly regarded commercial real estate brokers, but he is also an investor in his own right, and together, he, Kim, and I have done several deals together. I say that Craig is organized, but I really mean he is very goal oriented. He has accomplished more in his life than many of us could achieve in several lifetimes. He attributes this to goal setting and prioritizing what he really wants from life. Craig is one of those rare people who chooses what he wants carefully, then goes after getting it with a vengeance.

He has his days planned to the minute and is constantly self improving. He studies and invests in his personal development on a regular basis. Yet, his family takes the highest priority, and he is very involved in his children's lives. Again, what I learn from Craig beyond just about everything I know about commercial real estate is priorities.

Craig has a lot of designations after his name, but I don't need them to know that he knows what he's talking about when it comes to commercial real estate investing, leasing, and brokering. His track record and his guidance speak loud enough. He has shown us that commercial real estate takes a different set of eyes than the ones we have as investors in multifamily residential properties. Whenever Kim and I see a commercial building that we think looks interesting, we call Craig.

It usually only takes a few answers to a few questions that Craig asks us before he tells us whether the property is worth any more of our time or if we should keep driving the deal. He's that good.

He takes the time to teach with every deal, and he actively teaches and mentors others in his profession. Like the other contributors in this book, Craig practices what he preaches. He lives the real estate life he talks about.

—Robert Kiyosaki

If you build it, they will come. And if you own it, they will lease it from you. No they won't! On both counts. As much as you may like to think that everyone will be as excited about your real estate investment as you are, this simply is not the case. In most markets, there are several buildings for rent and lots of choices for business owners regardless of whether they are looking for a Class A high-rise for their $500 per hour law firm partners, or a master carpenter looking for multiuse workshop space to create custom furnishings, and everything in between. Choices abound, as they say.

So what does it take to lease your building and keep it leased? It takes attracting good tenants. It takes professional management that makes the experience of being in your building an exceptional one. And it takes understanding the difference between a leasing company and a management company. There is a big difference.

I see so many first-time commercial property owners, and even those who should know better, think they can lease their properties themselves. While many of them know they don't want to *manage* the properties themselves, after all the thought of the Friday 5 p.m. toilet clog is enough to tame that crazy notion, I'm always surprised when people say they want to do their own leasing. My only conclusion is that they don't realize what is involved. I know from experience if they are not set up for leasing—and most building owners are not—it is nearly impossible to successfully lease a building. Building owners may also rationalize by asking why should they pay a commission to an agent when they can do the leasing themselves.

In my book, right up there with being able to analyze a deal and performing good due diligence is leasing your property. Why is this so important? Because leasing drives your cash flow. And cash flow is a significant definer of property value.

The Types of Leases Available

You may have heard terms like "triple net" or "full service" when it comes to buildings. This is the language of leasing, and there are four kinds of leases in all. The type of leases that you have for your tenants will dictate the amount of involvement that you and your property managers will have maintaining and paying for upkeep to your properties.

The decision to go with one lease or another depends on the market and what tenants are accustomed to paying in that market. In Chicago or New York, for example, it's called triple net for office space, whereas on the West Coast it's called "gross." Even within a single building there can be different tenants signed to different types of leases.

Here are the types of leases that are out there. Get to know them. They will become your language as you continue along your path as a real estate professional.

- **Gross.** Gross means full service. You as property owner would pay for all utilities, upkeep, and maintenance. The tenant pays for everything in one check to the owner.

- **Net.** This can mean a number of things, but generally it means the tenant pays for one or more aspects of the property's utilities, upkeep, and maintenance. For example, "net utilities" means the tenant will pay for utilities. "Net janitorial" means the tenant will pay for janitorial.

- **Triple Net**. In this type of lease, the owner is responsible for structure, roof, parking, etc., or maintaining capital elements to the building. But the tenant covers all other expenses it takes to operate the building, including utilities, taxes, utility repair, and maintenance. Companies like Walgreens and Jack in the Box, for example, typically sign triple net leases. Triple net is designated NNN in the industry, and you'll see it often on sales literature.

- **Absolute Triple Net.** Here, the tenant pays everything—real estate taxes, janitorial, and all capital improvements, including if the roof caves in. This is the least amount of work for you, but you'll find these leases are typically in single-tenant buildings where the tenant almost owns the building. They are typically long-term leases, and sometimes they are known as "sale lease back" deals in which a tenant owner sells their own building to an investor then leases it back for a long-term agreement.

LEASING IS MARKETING

The reality is that in most cases investors can't lease the building themselves because it takes leasing and communications knowledge most investors don't have. Leasing is actually marketing, and unless you know this specialty, investors' efforts are trial and mostly error. I am an investor, but I am also a leasing agent/advisor and have been for more than two decades. I know through my own successes and failures how to effectively lease a building. And I know that leasing a building starts with a good marketing plan. You may think that all there is to leasing a building is putting a sign out front and praying, but there's a lot more to it. In fact, when I am working with a client, we develop an entire marketing plan that is designed to generate awareness of the building and interest in its features and benefits.

Our basic approach is two-pronged. First we go business-to-consumer, meaning we market directly to those persons or companies that may be in a position to lease. And second, we go business-to-business within our trade, so that every other leasing agent/advisor is aware of the property, its particulars, and its availabilities. A good leasing agent/advisor knows how to work his or her industry and knows how to create buzz about a property. He or she knows how to position your property as more lucrative than others to these fellow leasing agents and advisors. They know how to steer them toward you and away from your competition.

The truth about leasing is that the space always follows the business. By that I mean that business owners look for space that reflects what the business does and how it operates and how it succeeds. A creative advertising business, for example, would not seek out a plain-Jane, white-walled shell with a sea of built-in cubicles. No, a creative business like that would look for space that is interestingly designed with unexpected hallway angles, unique finishes, and moody lighting. How many of those spaces exist? Not many. That is why so much of leasing is looking at a space for what it can become, not what it is at the moment. It takes a very skilled leasing agent and advisor to have this vision and then be able to communicate it to the client. If the company doesn't see itself in the space, then that's it. No deal.

TIP The truth about leasing is that the space always follows the business.

A funny thing about this business is that every building owner thinks his own space is not only wonderful, but that everyone will want it. Owners tend to think that it will lease or sublet very easily because it's so perfect. They are always surprised when no one shares their enthusiasm. But they shouldn't be. The building and the space is a fit for the owner or the existing tenant, but not necessarily a fit for anyone else. It happens all the time, so be prepared to either have a lot of vision or hire someone who does, and then knows how to market the sizzle along with the space.

LEASING IS SELLING

Leasing is marketing, but leasing is selling, too. And that's the part that surprises many property owners. I'm not exactly sure why. When I am working with a property owner, the sales and negotiation process is time consuming and takes experience and expert knowledge of selling and the market. It takes professionals years to discover what works when it comes to positioning the benefits of a product, minimizing the shortcomings, and overcoming objections.

It's also taken me years to get that gut instinct about a prospective tenant. And as much as I wish I could teach you that in this chapter, I can't. I can tell you a horror story, however, about a project in my market and an owner who decided to go it alone and lease the rest of his building after the first two floors were leased by a broker. He had found and placed in those spaces excellent businesses that were growing and successful—upstanding, too. The top floor of the building was being saved for one big tenant that had the type of business that would value the exceptional views the nearly floor-to-ceiling windows afforded, and who could handle the pricier rent.

Well, the building owner got a little impatient and got a little greedy, thinking he could do this himself. After all, leasing doesn't seem that hard. Why should he pay a leasing agent/advisor for something he could do himself? He fired his broker. Within no time, the building owner had a tenant. The problem was, the tenant wanted only a portion of the top-floor space, so the building owner figured what the heck and leased it. That was a bad decision. Another bad decision was that the tenant was a medical practice for transgender surgery. Everyone is entitled to his own life choices, but let me to tell you what happened to the building.

Within a year, the quality business tenants in the lower floors had moved out, and on the top floor near the medical practice a hair club for men moved in. It was all downhill from there. In less than a year, a solid class-A property with a quality tenant mix became an undesirable property to all but a few fringe businesses. Quite a shame. Professional leasing agents/advisors know what can happen if you lease to the wrong kinds of tenants. Little did this guy know we turned down the businesses that he naïvely signed. You get what you pay for.

In my experience, the best leasing folks are the ones who know how to provide the vision that the client wants to hear. But they don't do this out of thin air or try to stuff ten pounds of potatoes into a five-pound bag. They do it by knowing the client and understanding the needs and the business. They have a feel for the kind of space that will really excite. The best leasing people know how to create a match between client and space, and then they have the ability to sell the vision, even if it is not completely obvious.

TIP The best leasing people know how to create a match between client and space, and then they have the ability to sell the vision, even if it is not completely obvious.

But the vision is more than just how the space looks—or can look—on the inside. There are many more variables, which we will get to shortly. And many of them are just as important, if not more so, than the interior space itself. No building is perfect, but it is the job of the leasing agent/advisor to assemble the top picks, inspire, and close the deal.

LEASING IS DETAIL WORK

Leasing a building is seldom easy; actually it is quite the opposite. That's becoming obvious. It's generally very labor intensive. When we're doing a marketing plan for a building, we begin by looking at the property and effectively positioning it in the market. That requires us to do an intense market study of all competing properties—both the ones that are already there and the ones expected to be completed in the coming months or year. By understanding the market, we can find the gaps that will make the property we're representing far more desirable and therefore more leasable.

But our work doesn't stop there. We look at all the comparables and analyze each deal to understand the specifics and find the clues we need for our own success. We even look at the transaction activity rate within the vicinity of the property we are representing to see any trends up, down, or sideways. We don't stop until we have a full picture of the market. From these details we formulate the true value of a building or a space, and that enables us to set the rental prices and all the terms that accompany a lease. This includes operating expenses, tenant improvements, free rent, other concessions, parking terms, security deposits—I could go on and on. It's pretty extensive.

Often, I see people who are doing their own leasing and end up pricing a space out of the market. The first reason they do it is that, as you recall, their space is perfect and everyone will want it, right? We know that argument doesn't hold any credence. The other reason is that they have not done their homework or they have done it poorly. Often they are comparing their building or space to space of a higher quality or class. The final reason they overprice is that they are setting the price based on how much they paid for the building itself. How much you pay for a building has nothing to do with how much you can charge tenants for rent.

TIP An important lesson of leasing: The market sets the rental prices, not you.

As with any good sales function, eventually prospecting begins. From lists and sources that we have developed over time and others that we would develop specifically for the project at hand, we send our literature and make cold calls to gauge interest. We work inside and outside the target location, and we even do out-of-state prospecting, targeting companies that are coming into town. We give a lot of presentations to tenants in other properties that are in our target size and business range.

As I mentioned earlier, we'll also work within our industry and communicate regularly with the other agents/advisors in the community. We identify which ones specialize in buildings like the one we are representing. We do our presentations to their offices and their staff. We use e-mail, direct mail, and host parties to keep others informed about the properties we represent.

And, of course, we use the sophistication of the Internet to help us target those business prospects who are using the Web to troll for new office space. Our sophisticated Web sites are searchable and detailed. We are connected directly to listing services, and our user interface is the result of more than ten years of improvements. Clearly, you're beginning to see that a lot goes into finding the right tenants and getting a lease signed sooner rather than later.

Once we understand how we're going to market the property and to which companies, we create a development strategy that will outline our plans to fill the building. This is a complete plan that includes rent rates, leasing terms, expense stops (the maximum expenses per square foot for the building), tenant improvement limits, other concessions, even commissions.

The sign in front of the building may be the most visible part, but it is the smallest part of the marketing efforts for a building. If only it were as easy as hammering a sign into the ground and answering the phone. The truth is, experience is everything in the process. There are literally an unlimited number of pits that the novice can fall into. Over our careers, we have fallen into them all. That's another reason leasing agents/advisors are so valuable; they've already taken the falls for you.

THE DEAL MAKERS AND DEAL BREAKERS IN LEASING

Earlier in this chapter, I mentioned that it takes more than the vision of great space—space that matches the business—to actually get the business. There are more variables that come into play. I believe there are numerous variables that every client will consider before signing on the dotted line. Here's my top-twenty list:

1. **Rates.** Of course every client is going to be concerned with the rent and the cost per square foot because most every client has a budget. He knows how much his business can allocate to this expense-line item. I work to stay within my clients' budgets, not trying to oversell them. It is in everyone's best interest to have a client who pays on time every month. Rental rate is one of the most important considerations on the list.

2. **Term.** The length of the lease agreement is another important factor. Sometimes my user clients are looking for a short-term fix, and sometimes they want the lease agreement to run longer in exchange for some other consideration. This can be a highly negotiable variable, and the match is made when the term connects with the client's objectives.

3. **Free Rent.** Many building owners offer free rent for some length of time as part of the negotiated agreement. What's negotiated is the number of months and what is included. Is it just the rent, or does it cover common area maintenance fees, parking fees, etc.?

4. **Tenant Improvements.** Many lease agreements have negotiated into them some allowance money for tenant improvements, or "TIs" as they are called. This can be a lot of money or a little money. A good leasing agent/advisor will know the current market and know what is a realistic, yet generous, amount to request. A rookie can really mess up an otherwise good deal by demanding too much, or cause a client to overpay by not asking for enough.

5. **Layout.** This refers to the interior floor plan and the shape and size of the space. Sometimes square or rectangular spaces are a plus, and at other times oddly shaped space is what a client is looking for. It all depends on the client

and the business. Again, when I know a client's objectives, I know what space configurations will work and which ones won't.

6. **Quality of Building.** The building exterior on a commercial property is like the curb appeal on a residential property. It says a lot about your business, just as a home says a lot about you. A prestigious building with excellent upkeep and landscaping says to the world that this company is a player. That it is reputable and can handle my business. A shoddy-looking building tells the world that a company might be fly-by-night, not very progressive, or just plain cheap. If "the clothes make the man" as the saying goes, the building exterior makes the business.

7. **Parking Type and Ratio.** I've walked away from buildings as an investor and as a leasing advisor because the property is under parked; in other words, the number of parking spaces for the size of the building is light. I know my client's customers will not be happy if every time they visit, they have to allot an extra ten minutes to search for a place to park. Nothing is worse than a building that doesn't have enough parking, and in most cases there is little that can be done about it.

8. **Parking Location.** As bad as it is to not have enough parking spaces, clients also don't like having to park far away from a building. The reasons are obvious with safety concerns being one of the biggest. No one likes the idea of walking a great distance through a dark parking lot or alleyway to get to the car. And it's no fun to walk a distance—briefcase, workout bag, coffee cup, and cell phone in hand—to get into the building in the morning. We won't even talk about rain, snow, and ice. Parking should be easy and safe.

9. **Efficiency.** Clients look for generally efficient buildings, meaning that they are easy to find, get into, walk through, locate the businesses in, and find the restrooms, etc. Some buildings—and you probably can think of a few yourself—are just poorly designed. It's hard to find the entry, it's hard to find the elevator, it's hard to find the office numbers, it's hard to get to the restrooms, and the list goes on.

10. **Access.** Here's a big one. Accessibility means how easy it is to get into and out of the building site. Some buildings have excellent access, and others do not. I just moved one company because the business owner hated making an unprotected lefthand turn across a very busy street every time he turned into the building. While we were looking for his new space, he would joke that he was going to hold me personally responsible if he got into a wreck while he impatiently waited! We found him space with better access, and he is much happier.

11. **Signage.** Some businesses need very visible signage, and others do not. This is one of the negotiation points that is critical for businesses that rely on either walk-in business or that want to use their building signage as awareness advertising.

12. **Amenities On Site.** Some buildings have shopping, banking, places to eat, dry cleaners, and more perks right on site in lobbies or in underground retail centers. To some of our clients, these conveniences matter. I know one person who leases in a building on a small municipal airport runway that has hangar space for corporate jets. That's a big amenity for some business owners.

13. **Amenities Off Site.** Then there are some buildings that seem to be on an island all their own. There's no place to go for lunch, there's no grocery store nearby, there's little to nothing around. Sometimes this is the nature of new development—retail and restaurants have not moved in yet—but sometimes it's just the way it is.

14. **Property Management.** Good property management is like a gourmet meal that has great presentation, tastes amazing, and completely satisfies you. And best of all you never have to be concerned with any of the details. It's just there for you to enjoy. Bad property management lets you know it's there at every turn. To go back to our gourmet meal, you have to ask for the salt, your silverware isn't clean, the food looks overcooked, and, in general, the whole experience is unpleasant. All you see are the details—the missed details.

15. **Ownership.** The ownership matters as much as the property management. Some owners can be terrific landlords, and others have baggage. One friend of mine leases space in a building advised by our company. The building owner is a very successful entrepreneur who makes his rounds every so often to his tenant businesses just to see how things are going and to catch up. He's a good guy, a welcome visitor, and a friend to those who lease from him. There's another building owner down the street who jets off for Cabo every other week and is incredibly unresponsive.

16. **Americans with Disabilities Act Compliance**. To many businesses, this is a very important consideration. It is critical that those who use wheelchairs have easy and safe access to all areas of the building and grounds.

17. **Location, Location, Location.** Some space has views of beautiful vistas, and other space has no view at all. Some space is visible right off the elevator, and other space is tucked back in some insignificant hallway corner. The location within the building matters. It says a lot about a business.

18. **Location of the Building Itself**. This is most critical requirement, and that's why it is not just number 18 on our list, but 19 and 20, too. The right location is one of the absolute musts.

What to Look for in a Leasing Agent/Advisor

My hope is with the stories and the work load described in this chapter so far that I've convinced you to at least consider the value of having a leasing agent/advisor working on your side. If that's the case, then I should also point out that not all leasing agent/advisors are created equal. There are leasing agents out there who don't do their homework and say "yes" to shaky businesses all the time. There are leasing agents who don't know the market, leasing agents who are terrible negotiators, and leasing agents who simply can't sell. If you're going to hire a leasing agent, and I suggest you do, hire a good one, a true advisor. Aside from the obvious qualities like experience, motivation, organization, intelligence, expertise, and integrity, here's what else to look for:

Relationship vs. Transaction

Although real estate seems like a huge industry, it really is a small local industry. Each city or town has a small, tightly knit, and very intertwined real estate community. It is critical to find a leasing broker/advisor who sees his or her job as one of relationship building, not just completing transactions. I have spent the last twenty years doing deals and in the process building excellent relationships with the real estate professionals where I live and work. And this effort pays off for me and my clients every day.

The reality is that most transactions happen through other leasing agent/advisors. The opportunities come in through them, and we market our owners' opportunities outbound through them. How eager would they be to bring to me top-quality tenants, or even be interested in looking at space I pitch to them, if I had a reputation for win-lose arrangements where I win and they lose? Not very.

As a rule, I put a great deal of time and energy into providing lots of information to prospects and clients. Even if there is no agreement for representation, I generally am eager to help because I know that's how to build a relationship. And experience has proven to me that relationships eventually pay off. One story I recall was when a large healthcare insurance provider was moving into town. A high-powered agent came in from New York and called our office and said she was coming in to look at space. I asked if she needed local representation, and she said no. Regardless, I told her I'd get her a list of available buildings by the next day.

We met, and during that meeting I helped her in any way that I could. When she returned to New York, she told her boss she met an agent who could really help and who she wanted to work with. He said no, but she insisted. Long story short, she got her way, and I ended up doing not one but nearly fifty transactions with that company. Had I not been willing to freely give of my time and knowledge, I would not have been on the receiving end of that lucrative piece of business.

RAPPORT WITH YOU

This whole leasing effort has to be a partnership. There has to be a good rapport. A good leasing agent/advisor understands your objectives, and then works to match the right space and the right tenants. Plus, a good leasing agent/advisor willingly takes on even small businesses or buildings and educates clients as they grow into bigger businesses. I found space for one software company many years ago. It was their first space when they were just three people strong. I think the office was all of twelve hundred square feet. At the time, I was doing much bigger deals, but to me that didn't matter. We developed rapport and within a few years, I handled the transactions surrounding their 137,000 square foot corporate office and their more than forty-four offices worldwide. It happens.

LOCATION KNOWLEDGE

Any leasing agent/advisor you work with must have not only a versed knowledge of the metro area, but also intimate knowledge of the submarket area where your building is located. This comes back to the fact that real estate is really a small, localized industry. The best leasing agents/advisors are hands down the most knowledgeable people around, not about the whole city or town, but about one square mile. Find this person, and you'll be in good shape. It's not hard; just drive around and look at whose name appears on the leasing signs most frequently.

DEAL MAKER VS. PROCESSOR

There are leasing agents out there who are not advisors. They are the people who do little more than play middleman and parrot messages back and forth between prospect and building owner. That's not the type of representation you want. You want an agent/advisor who will add value by working for you and negotiating on your behalf. Anyone who has some training can relay information and process paper; that's not what you are paying for. You want to find a true advisor who can weed out the ridiculous and the no-chance-in-you-know-where offers and deal points to get to the end game quickly and efficiently.

REPUTATION

Finally, and this probably goes without saying, you want a leasing agent/advisor with a solid reputation in the community. How can you be sure? You ask around. You talk to other building owners and talk to other business owners who have worked with the person you are considering. It's worth the extra time and the effort to do this and can be the first step to developing a leasing agent/advisor partner for life.

These are the qualities I have developed in myself over the years, and they are the same qualities that I work to foster in young people who are entering this profession. Not all can cut it. The requirements are demanding. And if they can't cut it, they either get out of the business altogether or move over to my competition. Either is okay with me.

Choosing your leasing agent/advisor partner is one of the most important decisions you will ever make. It can mean the difference between a property that generates positive cash flow and one that doesn't. It can mean the difference between owning an asset or a liability. A good leasing agent/advisor can actually enhance the reputation and standing of your business within the community and bring you more business along with more profitability.

The Last Word: Coppola's Five Rules of Leasing

I will not need every deal.

I will discuss challenges with the client immediately.

I will not allow a commission to drive any transaction.

I will consider long-term relationships more important than any fee.

I will develop a professional profile that provides me access to all decision makers.

WAYS TO LEARN MORE

SIOR (Society of Industrial and Office Realtors)
CRE (Councilors of Real Estate)

 One of the premier commercial real estate brokers in the United States, **Craig Coppola** has been awarded the Arizona Office Broker of the Year six times in the past thirteen years by the National Association of Industrial and Office Properties. He has completed more than twenty-five hundred lease and sale transactions over the past twenty-three years, totaling a value in excess of $2.5 billion. As founding principal of Lee & Associates Arizona, Craig has earned the top three designations in the real estate industry: CCIM, CRE, and SIOR. Only thirty-five people worldwide hold all three designations. He is a Rich Dad Advisor and author of the forthcoming book *The ABC's of Commercial Real Estate: Your Guide to Finding, Evaluating, and Purchasing Your First Commercial Property in 9 Weeks or Less*.

16

● Ken McELROY

The Perils of Careless Property Management

O*ne of the great pleasures in my life is having best friends as business partners. In my life, Ken McElroy is one of those rare persons. On top of that, Ken has made me a millionaire many times over.*

There have been many valuable lessons I learned from my rich dad. One lesson is "Out of every bad deal comes a good person." This lesson has been priceless because it makes me less hesitant about having business deals go bad. Explaining further, I will often go into a deal, even if I do not trust the people. I go in because I know that I will probably meet a good person along the way, even if the deal goes bad.

I met Ken in a deal that went bad. In fact it was a horrible deal. The person who put the deal together—a young man I will call George—eventually went to jail. The Securities and Exchange Commission (SEC) eventually shut his operation down. Unfortunately, George was married with three kids.

Ken and I smelled a rat early on and did not participate in George's investment scheme. We almost invested, but we passed on his bogus opportunity. The good news is I met Ken, just as my rich dad's lesson taught me.

Today, Ken is a Rich Dad Advisor, writing on real estate. His books, The ABC's of Real Estate Investing, The Advanced Guide to Real Estate Investing, *and* The ABC's of Property Management *are must reads for anyone who is interested in real estate investing. He also has a priceless product entitled,* How to Increase the Income from Your Real Estate Investments. *It includes a due diligence checklist, which is an essential checklist that every investor should go through before buying a property.*

The thing I like most about Ken is that he is extremely generous with his knowledge. He and I have traveled to many parts of the world to speak about our favorite subject: investing in real estate.

He and his wife, Laura, are two of Kim's and my favorite friends. We have a great time together, teaching, sharing knowledge, and supporting each other's families in becoming richer and more financially secure in a financially volatile world.

—Robert Kiyosaki

O f all the subjects in this book, property management might be the most misunderstood. The reason for this is simply the fact that in order to be a successful real estate investor, you don't necessarily have to be a successful property manager.

That statement might seem a little odd to you at first, but if you think about it for a second, you'll know it's true. You can have tremendous instincts and ability to find, analyze, and even take down phenomenal real estate deals. You might have an extensive network of equity sources and solid and trusted investors waiting for your next deal. You can have a solid team of lawyers, mortgage brokers, and general contractors. All of these things will enable you to be successful at finding and investing in real estate. But they are all transactional. By that I mean they are needed to *invest* well in real estate. This is often the focus of many real estate investment books. None of these things, however, will make your investment successful once you actually *own* it.

One of the things I appreciate about Robert Kiyosaki and the Rich Dad team is that they understand that being a successful real estate investor goes beyond just finding and acquiring quality deals. They know you have to manage those deals effectively to realize their full wealth-making potential. That is why I'm so glad that Robert contacted me to write this chapter. Mark my words, you can have the most incredible real estate holdings in the entire world, but if they are mismanaged they could quickly become worthless. Why is this? Because in order to be a successful real estate investor, the first rule you have to remember is that real estate values are typically based on performance, *not* on the asset itself.

And in order for your real estate portfolio to run at its maximum potential you need to manage your property professionally.

TIP **The first rule you have to remember is that real estate values are typically based on performance, *not* on the asset itself.**

In this chapter I'll show you why property management is so vital to the health of your investments. The topic of how to manage a property effectively, while an important thing to know as a real estate investor, is much too large a topic for the space I've been given here. Rather than try and give you a crash course on how to manage properties effectively, my efforts here will focus on:

1. Why professional property management is essential for success
2. What successful property management entails
3. How to find an exceptional property manager for your assets

I guarantee that a fuller understanding of the importance of property management will make you a more successful real estate investor. In fact, I would venture to say that it's essential.

AN OUTSIDER'S PERSPECTIVE

Just like you, I didn't begin my career as a successful real estate investor. I have people like Robert and the Rich Dad team to thank for opening my eyes more fully to the immense wealth-building potential that real estate investing affords. Well before I began investing in real estate, I made my living by managing other people's assets. In the process, I've built some of the largest and most well-known property management companies in the southwestern United States.

In the course of managing more than 20,000 apartment units, I saw firsthand how poor property management can cause untold damage to a property's value and to the net worth of an investor.

I still remember the day when John called me at my office. John was part of a group of investors in Colorado who had purchased a multifamily property in Phoenix, Arizona, and he was in a bit of a panic.

"What can I do for you, John?" I said over the phone.

"I think we have a bit of a problem with one of our properties," was his response. "I was wondering if you could help us out with our operations."

As it turned out, John had more than a just a *little* problem. His company's property was literally in shambles. What brought them to this point was a series of mistakes that, in the course of my career as a property manager, I've seen over and over again.

John's first problem was that his group purchased a large multifamily building with very little research, which is commonly called due diligence, and they had little knowledge of the local real estate market since they were based in Colorado.

John and his partner's second problem was that they decided to be cheap. In an effort to save some money (or to make money off the property), they gave the task of managing their property to someone in their office, who was located in Denver, and who had no experience in property management. This person flew down about once a month, if that, to see how things were going. Why an investment group of very smart individuals would trust a multimillion-dollar asset to someone with no experience is a mystery to me.

I knew things had to be bad because John was basically firing himself for poor performance, and things are usually in pretty bad shape for this to happen. In fact, things had gotten so bad that they were having trouble making their mortgage payment.

I reluctantly told John I was willing to help him. After hanging up the phone, I shook my head. I knew the property he was talking about, and while it was in a good location and in a great neighborhood, the property itself was known for having high turnover of residents and high crime. Drug activity was prevalent at this property, and members of local drug cartels were actually living in some of the units. In the first week that we took over, one of these problems came to a boiling point when one resident, a local drug dealer, was shot down in cold blood inside his unit right in front of his girlfriend. It was well known that this was a gang-related incident because the man's hands were tied behind his back, and he had been shot point blank in the head, execution style. His girlfriend was unharmed and is now in the witness protection program. So, as you can see, this was definitely not a *little* problem.

You're probably asking yourself: What kind of property was this? What a terrible neighborhood! I can tell you that this property was in an upscale area near major employers, a school, and an upscale regional mall. This kind of thing can happen anywhere.

When my team surveyed the 250-unit property, we were shocked at its condition. We already knew its reputation, and we were expecting it to be bad. What we didn't expect was just how poorly the asset itself had been maintained—the physical condition of the property was astonishingly bad. The landscaping was completely shot, decks were rotting through and posed potential safety risks, and more than 20 percent of the interiors of many units were so rundown that they were not rentable. The result was that while comparable nearby properties were enjoying occupancy levels in the mid-90 percent range, this property was collecting less than 70 percent of the potential income. This, of course, is because many units were vacant, and many of the current tenants were not paying their rent.

Beyond that, people were leaving the property in droves because they were worried about their own safety and disgusted at the condition of the property.

So, the owner's problem was twofold: They couldn't rent to new residents because they did not have the money to fix up the property and the existing vacant units; and many of the current residents were moving out, citing health and safety reasons. As a result, the financial performance of the property was very poor.

We quickly realized we had a lot of work on our hands. Thankfully, my company has tremendous experience in turning around poorly performing properties, and we were eventually able to get this property in good condition. But it took a lot of time and a lot of money. In the end, the poor decision to "save money" cost John and his partners millions of dollars. But the damage to their partnership was irreparable. The tensions boiled over, and their partnership came unglued. Harsh words were spoken, friendships were destroyed, and John's reputation was severely damaged.

I had little pity for John and his partners. While it is unfortunate that they lost so much money, those losses could have easily been avoided if they had retained a quality property manager to partner with them in both the due diligence process when purchasing their property and to help them manage it effectively after they acquired it.

KNOWLEDGE: THE KEY TO SUCCESS

You may be thinking that this is just a severe, isolated case of stupidity. I assure you it is not. Every day, smart investors become idiots because they lack knowledge of the importance of property management and underestimate the work involved in managing a property well. I now make my living by capitalizing on situations just like John's. Because of my years of experience in property management, I buy deals just like John's at a significant discount from their market value and turn them around and reap huge returns for my partners.

Here's the good news. If you take the time to understand the importance of property management and to attain a thorough knowledge of how successful property management is achieved, you too can find the key to success as a real estate investor.

So this begs the question: What does successful property management look like?

THE TRIPLE THREAT

In my experience, successful property managers know how to improve the value of a property in three general areas—what I like to call the "triple threat" of property management: **income**, **expenses**, and **systems.**

TIP Property managers know how to improve the value of a property in three general areas, which is what I call the "triple threat" of property management: income, expenses, and systems.

INCOME

As I stated earlier in this section, the value of a property is not based on the asset itself, but rather on its financial performance. The number one misconception that can turn a good real estate investment into a bad one is by not understanding that real estate is a business, not just an investment. As such, the most important aspect of your investment is not how it looks, where it's at, or even how much it costs. While those things are important, they pale in comparison to the importance of the bottom line. In order to be a successful real estate investor you must understand that the value of your property, just as with any business, is based on how much *net operating income* it produces, that is, income after expenses.

Income - Expense = Net Operating Income (NOI)

And when it comes to maximizing your property's NOI, nothing is more important and easier to control than the actual *total income* your property produces.

In investment real estate, total income is determined by a number of factors. They are:

- rent
- occupancy
- other revenue opportunities

RENTS

One clear indication that a property could be mismanaged is when its rents are obviously substantially less than what the rest of the market is charging. I come across this frequently when I'm looking at a potential acquisition, and it excites me. As an investor, buying a property with low rents is a substantial opportunity.

In order to understand the importance of getting your rents right, you need to understand a little bit about how an investment property is valued.

TIP The value of a property is not based on the asset itself, but rather on its financial performance.

The most common way to value a property is by using a capitalization (cap) rate. In any given market, cap rates will vary. You don't have to worry about how to figure out what a market's cap rate is; you can get that number from a knowledgeable broker. For our purposes, you do have to understand how cap rates are used to estimate the current value of a property. The equation looks like this:

$$\text{Net Operating Income} \div \text{Market Cap Rate} = \text{Value}$$

What Does This Look Like?

For simplicity sake, let's assume we are looking to buy a two-hundred-unit property that makes $500,000 in annual NOI. And let's assume the market capitalization rate is 7 percent. That would mean the estimated value of your asset in that market would be $7,142,857.

$$\$500,000 \div 7 \text{ percent} = \$7,142,857$$

Now, let's look at why keeping a close eye on your rents and making sure that they are in line with comparable properties is so important and, quite frankly, the easiest way to add value to your property.

How NOI Affects a Property's Value

Let's assume our property has an average rent of $800. During our due diligence, we find out that the average market rents for comparable properties is $900.

CONTINUED

That would mean that the current ownership, with absentee management, is realizing a rent loss of $20,000 per month (two hundred units times $100), which equals out to $240,000 per year in lost potential income. That would mean that instead of an annual NOI of $500,000, our property should be making $740,000 per year. Let's see how that affects the value of our property:

$$\$740,000 \div 7 \text{ percent} = \$10,571,428$$

Amazing, isn't it? While it takes time to increase everyone's rents by $100 per month, it is worth it because by doing so, as shown in this example, we have created an additional $3,428,571 in value. The best thing about this is that I am creating value through good property management of the existing property and with the existing residents, so my business plan is not just based on relying on market appreciation, but I usually get that, too!

That's the power of effectively managing your property's income and the reason why keeping a close eye on not only your rents but the market rents is so vital to your property's financial health.

OCCUPANCY

Another great way to add value is to increase the occupancy. Remember, the Net Operating Income determines your value, so any and all income is very important. One very basic method to create better occupancy is have a good base of residents who take good care of your property and who do not move often. This is done by properly screening every occupant.

It is typical for many property managers to not run credit and criminal background checks for every occupant—a practice that every professional property management company does. It doesn't take a rocket scientist to explain the potential problems of renting to someone who cannot pay the rent or who creates problems in your property, but in a rush to fill vacant units, this basic function is often overlooked.

Problem residents can, and do, create vacancy and decrease your occupancy and can cause damage to the property itself. They can drive out good paying residents, which lowers occupancy, and many times they end up on a delinquent list, creating more work for the owner, eventually to be evicted, which also lowers your occupancy. Higher vacancy creates higher expenses with increases in maintenance, advertising, payroll, and supplies.

There are countless other ways that a good property manager can increase your occupancy; get him on your investment team and you will see the results.

OTHER REVENUE OPPORTUNITIES

In addition to rents, a property can realize substantial income if you look for numerous other revenue opportunities. These would be things like utility sub-metering, adding washers and dryers, charging pet rent and large pet deposits, charging rent premiums for prime locations . . . there are literally dozens of ways to increase your property's income like this. The problem is that most people don't know that these opportunities even exist, let alone charge for them.

A Real Life Story: How 288 Washers and Dryers Netted $1.9 Million

My partner, Ross, and I recently purchased a 288-unit building in Tulsa, Oklahoma. One of the strategies for our investment was to add a washer and dryer in every unit. This property already had small laundry rooms with all the electrical and plumbing in every unit. All we had to do was purchase the machines and install them. Before we did this we checked the local market to determine what additional rent we could get for a washer and dryer. As it turned out, many of the residents were already renting them, in many cases, for $40 to $50 per month.

We decided to buy 288 sets of washers and dryers and install them in the first year of operation. We budgeted a $40 increase to be realized over a two-year period. Let's look at the value we created for our investment.

288 units x $40 per month = $11,520 per month

$11,520 x 12 months = $138,240 in potential annual NOI

$138,240 NOI ÷ 7 percent cap rate = $1,974,857 added value

There are many revenue opportunities that may be great ideas to you but are considered ordinary for a professional property management company.

EXPENSES

When it comes to property management, expenses are generally the factor you have the least control over. The reason for this is that they are most often dictated to you. Typical expenses are for advertising and marketing, repairs and maintenance, management fees, payroll, utilities, property taxes, and insurance.

Property taxes, insurance, and utilities will be the biggest expenses a property will face. To a large extent, these are costs you simply can't control.

However, there are a few things you can do. For instance, a professional management company might have better purchasing power when it comes to insurance premiums and can get a better rate than the average person because of the size of its account, and you can also negotiate the property limits and the deductibles. A good property manager will utilize a tax consultant to analyze whether he might be able to challenge the property tax for the property.

Remember talking about running credit and criminal background checks? Well, let's examine the expense side of this. The actual credit check itself is paid for by the potential renter, so the cost, which is usually less than $50, is not paid by you. If you have ever bought or refinanced a house, you know that you pay for your own credit check.

TIP The cost of *not* running a credit report and a criminal background check is very high. Eventually, you will get burned.

The cost of *not* running a credit and criminal background check is very high. Eventually, you will get burned. Here is a typical scenario. You spend your hard-earned money getting a unit rent ready from the last move out, let's say $500 for cleaning, painting, making minor repairs, and cleaning the carpets. A bad resident moves in. You now have a renter who does not pay you. You are losing revenue because you cannot re-rent this until they move or are evicted. The cost to serve notices and to evict varies by state, so let's say it costs about $500. Eventually they move out, owing you rent plus legal costs, plus damages. You now must get the unit ready to rent, again which costs you another $500.

Don't get caught up in the estimated amounts; the point in this scenario is that you learn a lesson to run background checks. So far, you would have spent $1,000 to get the unit rent-ready two times. Legal fees were $500. Unpaid rent, late charges, etc., are estimated at $800. All in all, this mistake cost you $2,300. There was $1,500 in actual expenses, plus your time and lost rent until you could rent the newly vacant unit.

I think you realize that this story concerns just one unit. Imagine if this were happening on a two-hundred-unit property. These additional expenses resulting from high turnover due to poor management can and will lead to a lower overall property value.

SYSTEMS

In our discussion here about systems, I want you to think back to the story about John and his investors. While they were facing management issues surrounding both income and expenses, they were also facing serious issues regarding their property's systems. They didn't have any. What I mean by this is that due to poor management, they allowed a horrible resident base to move into the property, and the property itself was in serious disrepair due to deferred maintenance issues. All of these things added up to major losses for John and his partners.

Had they had solid management systems in place, that management would have used strict occupancy standards for potential residents. They would have performed extensive background checks, verifying the potential resident's income, job history, and rental history. They would have trained staff that would handle the daily reports to the management company and perform daily maintenance. The property would have been following an approved operating budget with monthly goals. The vacant units would have been "rent ready" within three days of the prior move-out. The lack of all of these systems or policies and procedures equaled lost income.

DO YOU FEEL LUCKY?

I've only scratched the surface of how property management, whether good or bad, can affect the value of your investment. Needless to say, there are hundreds of other factors that go into effectively managing a property. And the margin of error is very small. One seemingly minor oversight can end up costing you hundreds of thousands, if not millions of dollars. It should go without saying that managing a property is a full-time job, requiring an inordinate amount of time and expertise.

So the question you have to ask yourself is "Do I feel lucky?" Well, do you? Do you feel confident that you have the expertise and the time to effectively manage your hard-earned investments? If so, then this chapter should be a reminder and a catalyst for you to further increase your property management knowledge and to go back and reevaluate how effectively you are managing your properties. A timely review of your practices, and a little time spent furthering your property management knowledge could net you even more income than you are already realizing.

If you don't feel confident in managing your own properties, or don't feel that you have the time available to do it effectively, then by all means, find a good, professional property manager and hire him as soon as possible. It will be one of the best business moves you will ever make.

Finding a good property manager is not as simple as picking up the yellow pages and calling the company that sounds the

> ## Ken's Top-Five Words of Wisdom
> 1. Use your team
> 2. Trust, but verify
> 3. Find the right fit
> 4. You get what you pay for
> 5. Money matters

most professional. Given the information we've covered already, it stands to reason that choosing your property manager will be one of the most important decisions you'll make in regards to your investment. Here are some helpful to-do's for finding the right fit for your property. This is by no means a comprehensive list, but it will get you thinking in the right frame of mind. For a more comprehensive discussion on this topic see my book, *The ABC's of Property Management*.

1. **Use your team.** As Robert Kiyosaki says, "Business and investing are a team sport." If you don't know of a reputable property manager that you can trust fully with your investment, then ask the members of your team. Chances are they will be able to refer you to an excellent company. But don't take their word for it. As I always say, "Trust, but verify."

2. **Trust, but verify.** If you were smart, you conducted a thorough due diligence on your property before you purchased it. You probably dug into every financial, scrutinized every lease, and walked every unit. You need to perform the same level of due diligence when looking to hire a property manager. Get a full client list, and interview the existing clients of the management company in question. Do they like the service they receive? Have there been any obvious mistakes or blunders you should be concerned about? Ask how the property management company has increased the value of the owner's property. Also, interview the employees of the company and the potential on-property manager for your property. Make sure they are upbeat, knowledgeable, and a good fit for your personality. You will have to interact with these people on a continual basis.

3. **Find the right fit.** There are tons of different types of management companies out there, each with their own specialization. Some companies will specialize in commercial property management, while others will specialize in

apartments. Some companies will be better suited for large properties; others will be a perfect fit for smaller properties. The point is that, even if you do find a good management company, they might not be good for you and your needs. You wouldn't want to hire a large property management company that specializes in large apartment buildings to manage your duplex. They might be awesome at what they do, but your property would get lost in the fold—it would be too small for them to give it full attention. On the other hand, a smaller, local property management company would jump at the chance to manage your asset, and they would give you personalized service and attention.

4. **You get what you pay for.** Too often, people want to save money, and they balk at the fees a management company charges. Don't. Management fees vary by market and property type and size. But I will say that if a fee looks too good to be true, it probably is. Every investment in the world, if it is managed, costs you money. The beauty of property management is that you at least know what the fee is. Often, with investments like mutual funds and stocks, the fees are hidden (and substantial) so you don't feel them. You know what they say, "Ignorance is bliss." But with property management, the fees should be clearly explained and spelled out up front. I guarantee that if you find a good company, it will be worth its fees. In just a few simple (and common) examples, I've shown you how much income an effectively managed property can pull down.

5. **Money matters.** Make sure that any company you retain has a very good accounting department. When it comes to managing your investment, proper accounting is a must. You want the company that you use not only to understand what is going on with your property's operations, but also what's going on with your property's finances. Also, make sure that your property's money will be held in a separate account.

In Conclusion

Nothing is more important to the success of your investment than good, knowledgeable property management. Oftentimes it is the difference between meeting your investment goals and losing untold amounts of money. Whether you manage your property yourself, or have someone else do it for you, don't try to "save money." That always leads to disaster and loss.

The good news is that now you know. And if your investments aren't being properly managed, the solution is easy, and the ability to increase the value of your assets almost instantly is right in your hand. So, take the plunge. I promise you won't be disappointed.

WAYS TO LEARN MORE

Knowledge is the key to success. So, here are some of my suggestions on how to find property managers and how to increase your property management knowledge.

www.irem.org

www.naahq.org

www.kenmcelroy.com

The ABC's of Real Estate Investing, by Ken McElroy

The Advanced Guide to Real Estate Investing, by Ken McElroy

The ABC's of Property Management, by Ken McElroy

How to Increase the Income from your Real Estate Investments (audio book), by Robert Kiyosaki and Ken McElroy

How to Find and Keep Good Tenants (audio book), by Robert Kiyosaki and Ken McElroy

The Property Management Tool Kit, by Mike Beirne

As copartner of MC Companies, www.mccompanies.com, **Ken McElroy** has more than twenty years of partner-level experience representing more than 20,000 units of multifamily asset/property management, development, project/construction management, investment analysis, acquisitions, and dispositions. As host of WS Radio's weekly *Entrepreneur Magazine's Real Estate Radio* program, Ken interviews experts in the real estate, finance, and legal arenas. He is a popular speaker at industry events, and his accomplishments as an author include *The ABC's of Real Estate Investing*, *Rich Dad's Advisors: The Advanced Guide to Real Estate Investing*, and *The ABC's of Property Management*.

PART 3

Creative Ways to Make Money in Real Estate

Gary GORMAN

17

Getting from A to B
Without Paying Taxes

T axes are our greatest expense. Today the average person is paying more than 50 percent on income taxes and hidden taxes. One of the beauties of real estate investing, when compared with investing in stocks and mutual funds, is the ability to pay nothing in taxes, legally. As far as I know, this real estate loophole is the biggest and best legal tax loophole remaining, and that is why Gary Gorman is my friend and advisor. Gary has both saved and made Kim and me a lot of money.

While this tax loophole has saved a lot of people money, it has also caused people to lose a lot of money. Many people lose money because they sell a piece of property, deferring their tax bill, but fail to plan their next real estate purchase. This failure to carefully plan their sell and their next buy causes them to either pay the capital gains tax anyway, or purchase a bad piece of property just to avoid the tax. Often, rushing to buy a bad piece of real estate is worse than paying the capital gains tax.

Today before I sell or buy a property, I call Gary Gorman's company for strategic advice. I call Gary before I call a real estate broker.

—ROBERT KIYOSAKI

One of the last great tax shelters left in the United States deals with the ownership of real estate, and more importantly, with how it's taxed when you sell it. There are essentially four different classes of real estate: property you own for development, property you own for a short time (less than one year), your personal residence, and investment property you own for an extended period of time (at least a year). Each is taxed a little differently. Here's a quick overview.

First, property you own for development is subject to ordinary income taxes, as well as self-employment tax (the self-employed equivalent of FICA). Short-term property, by contrast, is subject to short-term capital gains tax, which is typically taxed at the same rate as your salary and other ordinary income. There's no self employment tax. Your personal residence is treated differently, too. It qualifies for a gain exclusion of different amounts, depending upon whether you're single or married. That leaves us with *investment property that you've owned for at least one year*, and this is where real tax shelter advantages kick in.

Four Property Types and How They Are Taxed

1. Property owned for development—is taxed as ordinary income.
2. Short-term property—is taxed as short-term capital gains.
3. Personal residence—qualifies for a gain exclusion based on marital status.
4. Investment property—is the place where real tax shelter advantages kick in!

The government actually wants you to invest in long-term, investment-type real estate. So to encourage you to make this type of investment, it offers you a couple of tax benefits: The first is that you are allowed to write off the cost of the property, over a predetermined period of time, through annual *depreciation deductions*. The benefit of this depreciation deduction could be used to offset other income that you've earned.

For those of you who want to sell your property, you'll pay long-term capital gains tax, which is at a much lower rate than ordinary tax rates. Another author in this book, Tom Wheelwright, does a great job of discussing these benefits in Chapter 21 of this book. My chapter, however, is about my favorite tax benefit, which is available only with long-term investment property, and that is your ability to roll the gain from your old investment property over to your new property. This is called a 1031 Exchange because Section 1031 is the Internal

Revenue Code section that allows you this benefit. The 1031 Exchange is a beautiful thing.

All sophisticated investors include 1031 Exchanges as a critical technique in their bag of investment tools, and if you're not using this tool, you need to learn how powerful it can be to the creation of your personal real estate wealth. Start by understanding how an exchange works: When you sell your old investment property and buy a new investment property, you can roll the gain from the old property to the new one without paying the tax until some time way in the future. Investors who are experienced with this tax code section often can actually pick the amount of tax they want to pay, and when in the future they want to pay it. The obvious benefit of doing this is that you don't have to write a check to the government every time you sell a property. An even bigger benefit is that it allows you to buy a bigger property, which will result in more cash for you somewhere down the road.

To illustrate this, let's say Fred and Sue are selling their rental property, and the tax on their gain would be $100,000. Fred and Sue decide to do an exchange instead so that they'll be able to plow this money back into their new property. Because they are getting a 75 percent loan on their new property (which means that their lender will loan them three dollars for every one that they put into the deal, or $300,000 to their $100,000), Fred and Sue are able to buy $400,000 *more* property than they would have if they had paid the tax and not done an exchange.

$$\$100,000 + \$300,000 = \$400,000$$

Let's say a few years go by and their new property doubles in value, and they sell it. The *additional* $400,000 of property they bought with the 1031 money is now worth $800,000. After paying off the $300,000 loan they used to buy this additional property, they have the balance of $500,000. In other words, by doing an exchange, Fred and Sue were able to leverage the $100,000 tax check they would have written to the government into a half-million dollars' worth of cash in their pocket (before taxes of course)!

TIP 1031 Exchanges are a great way to build wealth!

So, what must you do to have a successful exchange? Well, there are six basic rules to an exchange (which is another way of saying that there are six things that the IRS will look at if it audits your exchange). Speaking of the IRS, and before I start, let me clarify that because Section 1031 is an IRS code section,

> ## Real Life Story: How $5,000 Grew to $200,000
>
> About ten years ago, I bought a small, two-bedroom condo for $55,000 by putting $5,000 down and borrowing the rest. I rented the bedrooms to my son and daughter while he was going to college and she was finishing law school. After they were out of school, I sold the condo at a profit and exchanged into a very nice condo unit at the top of a building in downtown Denver that had beautiful views of snowcapped mountains. I have great monthly cash flow off this unit, I've gotten my original investment back many times over through cash flow, and my $5,000 equity has grown to about $200,000—just because of the exchange I did. There are two lessons to this story: The first is that you don't have to be Robert Kiyosaki or Donald Trump to do an exchange. Exchanges hold equal power for everyone. The second lesson is that exchanges are a great vehicle to pyramid wealth and build cash flow.

the IRS must allow you to do an exchange. However, Section 1031 is a *form-driven* code section. That means that you really do have to dot the i's and cross the t's, and the tiniest misstep could get your exchange disallowed. Keep that in mind as you read the six rules.

> ## The Six Rules of 1031 Exchanges
> 1. Hold property for investment
> 2. Adhere to the forty-five-day identification period
> 3. Replace the property within 180 days
> 4. Use a qualified intermediary
> 5. Follow the title holding requirement
> 6. Buy equal or up, and reinvest all the cash

RULE NO. 1: HOLD FOR INVESTMENT

Section 1031 applies only to property held for investment, but if you meet this rule you can sell any type of investment property and buy any other type of investment property. In other words you can sell a rental house and buy a duplex;

you could also buy an office building, an apartment building, a warehouse, or bare land. We have clients who sell bare land, which is not income producing, and then buy rental properties, such as apartment buildings, which do produce income. In other words, they use an exchange to create cash flow. We also have clients who sell one income-producing property and buy another in order to increase their cash flow, and we have some who sell income-producing properties, generally apartment buildings, and buy bare land in order to get out of the hassles of managing their property; they use an exchange to simplify their lives.

TIP 1031 Exchanges are a great tool to help you accomplish your investment strategy.

A common misconception that people have about 1031 exchanges is that if you sell a purple duplex, you have to buy a purple duplex, and this is not the case; simply put, both your old property and your new property have to be *held for investment*.

One of the ongoing debates is whether vacation homes (or second homes), qualify for 1031 Exchanges; many of you own these type of properties. The debate is whether or not vacation homes are investment properties (which *do* qualify for exchanges) or personal-use properties (which *don't* qualify for exchanges), and since vacation homes by their nature fall somewhere in-between, the debate has raged for years. We do a lot of counseling with our vacation home clients to make sure that they are doing everything they can to protect their rights to exchange their property, and if this is the kind of property you have, I suggest that you work with a good intermediary (which I'll define in a moment) to make sure that you follow current law. Current law, by the way, allows you to exchange vacation homes if you follow very strict guidelines.

One of the things that Section 1031 does not allow is the exchanging of property held for resale. The IRS, however, does *not* define the terms *held for investment* and *held for resale*. Guidelines for these terms have arisen from a series of court cases that give us a pretty good understanding of what an investment property is versus a property held for resale. I expect that as time goes on, the court will continue to refine these definitions, but for now a property is held for investment if you hold it as such for at least one year and one day before you try to sell it. Property that you try to sell within the year after you bought it is generally considered to be held for resale. While a defined holding period is not mentioned in the code section, most exchange professionals are comfortable with a holding period of more than one year because one year is the required holding period to get long-term capital gain treatment if you sold the property and did not do an exchange.

A classic example that defines the term "properties held for resale" is the "fix-and-flip." A fix-and-flip is where you buy a "fixer-upper," clean it up, and then put it back on the market. Because your intent is to sell the property right away, the property does not qualify for an exchange, even if you have trouble finding a buyer. Does this mean that you can't buy a property with the intent to fix it up? No, you just have to hold the property for investment. How do you do that? The best way is to hold the property for at least one year and one day before you put it back on the market.

TIP Hold your investment properties at least one year before you try to sell them.

In the past, I've bought fixer-type properties, but I always make sure that I hold them for at least one year before I try to sell them. I might fix the properties up, rent them for at least one year, and then sell them, or sometimes I will rent them for at least one year and then fix them up before I sell them. Regardless of the process, the important lesson here is that I always make sure that I hold them as an investment for at least one year before I sell them.

One last thing before I go to rule number two is that, obviously, if your old property is real estate, you have to buy real estate as your replacement property, and anything that is land, or attached to it, or part of it, qualifies as real estate. Timber rights, water rights, and mineral rights are all examples of real estate. I sold a property several years ago, did a 1031 Exchange into another property, but had about $100,000 of cash left over after the purchase (which I did not want to pay tax on). I took the cash and bought some oil and gas interests to complete my exchange. The oil and gas interests provide a nice, consistent, monthly cash flow without my having to manage the investment.

RULE NO. 2: FORTY-FIVE-DAY IDENTIFICATION PERIOD

Starting the day you close the sale of your old property, you have exactly forty-five calendar days to come up with a list of properties you might want to buy.

On this list you may place up to three properties with no limitation. For example, if you sold your old property for $100,000, you could list three properties for $10 million each, for a total of $30 million. While this may seem like a strange example, I actually had a client with this exact scenario several years ago. He was in the market to buy a shopping center and was actually looking at three different properties. Before he could complete his purchase, he got a call from a tenant who wanted to buy a small condo that he owned. Since my client was going to buy one of the shopping centers anyway, he threw the sale of the condo into the mix and did a 1031 Exchange so he wouldn't have to pay tax on it. It was just lucky timing for him, and he was able to sell the condo without a tax liability, even though it was insignificant to the overall transaction.

You may put more than three properties on your list, but if your list has more than three properties the IRS will subject you to an additional set of rules that says, in effect, that the combined purchase price of everything on your list may not exceed twice the selling price of your old property. This is called the 200 percent rule. Going back to my example above (where you sold your old property for $100,000), if you had put four or more properties on your list, the combined purchase price of everything on your list would be limited to twice ($200,000 in my example) the selling price of the old property. In other words, you could list three properties for $30 million or more, but once your list exceeded three properties your whole list is limited to $200,000 (twice the selling price). My advice: Keep your list to three properties or less.

TIP Keep it simple—keep your forty-five-day list to three properties or less.

As I said, the forty-five days are *calendar* days, starting the day you close the sale. This means that if the forty-fifth day is a Saturday, a Sunday, or a holiday, that is the date that your list must be completed, and you don't get until the following business day to complete your list. And no, you cannot get an extension of this time limit.

When you make your list, you have to identify the properties clearly enough that if you get audited the IRS agent could look at your list and go directly to the property. In other words you have to state: "123 Main Street, Phoenix, Arizona." You *cannot* say "a three-bedroom, two-bath house on Main Street in Phoenix."

You then give your list to a person called a qualified intermediary, which I'll discuss in rule number four.

RULE NO. 3: 180-DAY REPLACEMENT PERIOD

Again, starting on the day of closing of the sale, you have exactly 180 calendar days in which to purchase your replacement property, but whatever you buy has to be on your forty-five-day list. You can buy one of the properties, two of them, or all three if you wish, but whatever you end up buying has to be on your forty-five-day list, and it has to be closed by the 180th day.

As with the forty-five-day requirement, these are calendar days, which mean that if the day falls on a Saturday, Sunday, or holiday, that's the day, and barring an emergency declaration by the president, there are no possible extensions. Note that your timeframes are forty-five and 180 days—not six weeks and six months. Both the forty-five and the 180-day requirements are cast in concrete. You either meet them, or your exchange is toast.

TIP The time limits are very critical. Obey them.

RULE NO. 4: QUALIFIED INTERMEDIARY REQUIREMENT

You are not allowed to touch the money from the sale of your old property during the time between that sale and the purchase of your new property. The law requires that you use the services of an independent third party, called a *qualified intermediary*, to hold these proceeds and to prepare the documents the law requires to document your exchange.

Despite the implication that by being *qualified* the intermediary has been somehow approved by the IRS, qualified intermediaries are essentially ungoverned. They're not required to pass any tests of their knowledge and abilities, and for the most part, they may do as they wish with your money while they hold it. In most states, anybody with enough money to print business cards can hold themselves out as an intermediary.

There has been a pattern in the exchange industry of periodic losses of exchange proceeds by intermediaries who have used the funds for their own purposes or have made bad investments with the funds. Some of these bad intermediaries have been attorneys, some have been successful business people with successful track records, and some have been title companies. These losses have ranged from the comparatively small to the spectacularly large, but they all stem from the practice by the intermediary of *commingling* (or *pooling*) the funds of their clients. In other words, they put all clients' funds into one pool or account.

Intermediaries hold their clients' monies in one of two ways: Either they commingle all the funds into one account, or they set up a separate bank account for each client. Every problem that has arisen from intermediary theft stems from commingled accounts. Despite this fact, approximately 95 percent (from my informal poll) of the intermediaries commingle funds.

California, Nevada, and Idaho are the only states that at this point have adopted statutes designed to regulate intermediaries and protect consumers. A number of other states have proposed legislation to protect their citizens, but not surprisingly, the intermediary industry has strongly resisted any type of regulation. So, the bottom line is that you are on your own to protect your money.

Since you are required to use an intermediary to handle your exchange, what should you look for when you pick one? First, make sure that your money is not commingled, but placed in a separate account with your name and tax identification number associated with it. Call the bank frequently to make sure that the funds are still in the account. One of the intermediaries that failed had led their clients to believe that they had separate accounts, when in fact, the monies were commingled. So when you call the bank, keep a record of when you called and whom you talked to.

TIP Make sure your money is placed in, and stays in, a separate account for you.

Second, make sure that they know what they are doing. Many intermediaries have little or no background in tax law, real estate law, or 1031 law, yet they are all too happy to handle your exchange and hold your money (these intermediaries are easy to spot by the low fees they charge). Ask them how many exchanges they've done? How big is their staff? Will they give you a list of referrals? Have they ever had a complaint filed against them? Don't get hung up on who they are or what their degrees are—it's your job to protect your money because no one is looking out for you.

When you watch the news at night and some reporter is interviewing a fraud victim, the victim never says, "It doesn't surprise me that he ripped me off. I never trusted him; he just seemed like a crook." No, they never say that. Instead they always say, "I can't believe that he ripped me off. He was the nicest, most trustworthy person. My kids go to school with his kids; we go to the same church; his wife is so sweet; I just can't believe he could do this to me." So, if you can't trust the people you *can't* trust, and you can't trust the people you *do* trust, who do you trust? Nobody but yourself! You are the only one who is responsible to safeguard your money.

TIP When it comes to your exchange funds, if you can't trust the people you *can't* trust, and you can't trust the people you *do* trust, who do you trust? Only yourself!

RULE NO. 5: TITLE HOLDING REQUIREMENT

Section 1031 deals with the *taxpayer* who owns the old property, sells it, and does an exchange. That same taxpayer is the one who has to do the exchange, report it in their tax return, and buy the new property. A lot of our clients want to change the title to the property midstream, which as a general rule you can't do.

TIP You have to complete the exchange using the same taxpayer that sold the old property.

Let's say that Fred and Sue Jones are selling their purple rental house, which they own in their names, and want to have Jones Investments, Inc., the corporation they own, take title to their new property. Since the corporation has a different tax identification number, this would not be a valid exchange.

Since that won't work, what if Fred and Sue transferred the ownership of the rental house to their corporation right before the sale closed (that way the seller of the old property and the buyer of the new would be the same entity)? This won't work either because, if you remember from rule number one, you have to hold the property for at least one year and one day for it to be investment property. If Fred and Sue transferred ownership right before the sale, the IRS will argue that the corporation owned the property for resale rather than investment because it sold it right after it got title to it.

TIP The best time to structure the sale of your property to minimize the tax is when you first buy it.

The main reason that our clients want to transfer ownership to another entity in the middle of the exchange is that they want to own their new property in an entity that limits their liability. I fully agree with what they are trying to do, but doing it in the middle of the exchange is the wrong time to do it. There are ways to accomplish what Fred and Sue are trying to do—ways that are beyond the scope of this chapter. Call us and we'll walk you through your options to accomplish this, but the best advice I can give you here is that the best time to structure the sale of your property to qualify for a 1031 Exchange is when you first buy it.

Rule No. 6: You Must Buy Equal or Up, and You Must Reinvest All of the Cash

In order to pay *no* tax on your exchange, you have to do two things: you have to buy equal or up, and you have to reinvest all of the cash.

Let's go back to Fred and Sue selling their purple duplex. Let's say that they sell it for $100,000, there is an unpaid mortgage, and closing costs associated with the sale total $40,000. This means that if I was their qualified intermediary I'd receive the balance of the proceeds of $60,000. If Fred and Sue then buy their replacement property for $90,000, they'd pay tax on the *buy-down* of $10,000 (they sold for $100,000 but bought for only $90,000, hence the $10,000 buy-down). Note that the buy-down does not toast their exchange; they simply pay tax on it. And note also that the whole buy-down is taxable—they can't offset any of their tax basis against the buy-down gain.

Let's change the example—Fred and Sue still sell the purple duplex for $100,000, but instead they buy the new property for $150,000, so in this case they bought up from $100,000 to $150,000. To pay for this purchase they plan to get a mortgage of $100,000, which means that they need only $50,000 of the $60,000 in funds that I'm holding to close the sale. So what happens to the unspent funds of $10,000? They are taxable; and again, the entire $10,000 is taxable.

TIP In order to pay *zero* tax on your exchange, you have to buy equal or up, and you have to reinvest all of the cash.

To recap this last rule, in order to pay no tax on your exchange, you have to buy equal or up, *and* you have to reinvest all of the cash. In these two examples, my implication is that Fred and Sue inadvertently ended up in taxable situations. Some of our clients actually want to buy down and are willing to pay the tax, or more typically they want some cash from the sale to buy a car or pay off a credit card.

If you are one of those people who want some cash from your exchange, there are a couple of ways to approach this: If you don't want to pay tax, you can wait and borrow from the new property after the closing. Let's go back to my second example above, where they're selling for $100,000 and buying for $150,000—by getting a loan for $100,000 they end up not spending all their cash. Remember, they have $10,000 left over. That's the taxable amount.

But what if they want the $10,000 in proceeds? Is there a way they can get that money without paying tax? Yes, if they buy the property for the $150,000 using all of the proceeds I'm holding (meaning their loan is only $90,000), they've completed their exchange and they can then refinance and pull proceeds from the refinance without paying tax. How long do they have to wait after the purchase to refinance tax free? One *nanosecond*! Yes, it's true! They can refinance the new property immediately. I say refinance, but a good intermediary can show you how to set up the loan on the purchase of the new property so that you can walk away from the closing with cash without having to get two loans. There is one caveat, however: The refinance has to be on the new property—if you try to do it on the old property before you sell it, the IRS could argue that you've violated rule number four and touched the money.

Refinancing tax free works great if you are buying equal or up, but what if you are buying down? When do you get the proceeds from the buy-down? Go back to my first example; Fred and Sue sell for $100,000 but are buying for $90,000. When do they get the cash from the buy down? There are actually two places that they can get the $10,000. The first place is at the closing table when they sell the purple duplex, and the second place is after the 180 days when their exchange has ended. If you know that you want cash from the sale of the old property, you have to convey that to the intermediary before the closing takes place so that the intermediary can prepare the exchange documents to allow this. Otherwise your money will be tied up until the end of the exchange period. Once the transaction closes and the intermediary has your proceeds, you cannot touch them until the exchange period has expired.

One last thing before I finish this chapter: I did *not* say that you have to have debt on your new property at least equal to the debt on your old property. This simply is not the case, even though a lot of intermediaries and most CPAs and attorneys seem to think so. If Fred and Sue sell the purple duplex for $100,000, netting $60,000 in proceeds, and then buy their replacement property, also for $100,000 by using the $60,000 that I'm holding, the balance of the purchase funds can come from any source: a savings account, a loan on the property, or some combination of the two. For example, they could use the $60,000 I'm holding, take $20,000 from their savings account, and get a loan for the balance of $20,000.

Now that you've finished this chapter, sit back for a moment and see the big picture: 1031 Exchanges are a great way to get from A to B without paying taxes. The place to start is with this question: "What are you going to do with the money when you sell your investment property?" If one of your possibilities, even with part of the money, is to buy another investment property, then you want to take advantage of this great code section.

Gary Gorman is a well-known educator and published author on the subject of 1031 Exchanges. He has written *Six Basic Things You Need to Know about 1031 Exchanges* and *Exchanging Up!* With more than thirty-six years of real estate tax experience, Gary is recognized as an expert witness in the federal courts on 1031 tax issues. Revolutionary exchange systems such as 1031Connexions.com, 1031 TaxPak, and 1031Access have all been developed by Gary to benefit the industry.

18

● Carleton H. SHEETS

No Down Payment®
Using Other People's Money

*C*arleton is a legend in the world of real estate. He has single-handedly taught more people about real estate than anyone else I know.

Years ago, when I was just starting out, I was watching Carleton's television infomercial on real estate. I bought his program, and it is one of the smartest investments I have made.

Carleton and my Rich Dad are cut from the same bolt of cloth. They come from the same philosophy. They believe in cash flow and see value that most people overlook. They are not afraid of investing in distressed areas. They understand the need for a roof over a person's head, regardless of how much money the person makes.

Today, Carleton and I work together with the Professional Education Institute. PEI supports Carleton's work through his real estate coaching program, and supports me through all of my Rich Dad coaching programs. Regardless of which coaching program you select, PEI does a fabulous job for anyone who is serious about their financial future.

—ROBERT KIYOSAKI

In my many years of teaching people how to build wealth by investing in real estate, probably the most common objection I hear is this: "But I don't have any money to get started." That one common misconception has kept so many people sitting on the sidelines rather than pursuing their dreams.

TIP **Lack of ambition (not lack of money) will lead to failure.**

I could have been one of those people, but something happened that changed my life forever. After graduating from college, I started working in the private sector, working for one company eight years and then another for eighteen months.

I was pretty aggressive in trying to climb the corporate ladder, and as I look back I honestly think that I exceeded my capabilities. I was fired from the second company. I toyed with the idea of going into business myself, but I suddenly had a revelation. I realized that I had moved four different times with those two companies, and that each time I bought and sold a home I had made $5,000 to $8,000. That was a world of money back then! So I thought, why not go into real estate? However, I had very little money and no credit.

The "no credit" mind-set was a carry-over from my conservative midwest upbringing where my parents had instilled in me this philosophy: Never borrow money except to buy a home; otherwise pay cash. And since all of the money I had made from selling my previous homes had been reinvested in larger and more expensive homes, I needed to find something to support my family and enable me to make mortgage payments and to pay for all of the other expenses of everyday living.

So, I decided to become a real estate investor. I went back to school and attended seminars. I read books and studied courses. I sought out other investors and brokers who could advise me. The good news is that I quickly learned that you don't need a lot of money or perfect credit to successfully invest in real estate. What you *do* need are the time-tested and proven creative techniques to invest in real estate the smart way—by using other people's money.

When you think about it, this concept is used in business all the time—but with different terminology. When a large corporation changes hands, it is often the result of a "leveraged buyout." In essence, this simply means that the buyers used leverage instead of their own cash to accomplish the transaction. In other words, they used other people's money. But can this method work for you? The answer is "Yes!" The only major difference between the leveraged buyout of a huge corporate enterprise and purchasing a single-family home using other people's money is the number of dollars.

TIP The basic concept is this: Use other people's money.

You might ask, "What people, and where can I get this money?" These are legitimate questions, and I'll share a number of answers with you. It all depends on which creative techniques will work in a given situation. For example, some techniques involve the seller, some use partners, and still other techniques bring in additional investors.

The techniques that I am going to share with you are timeless; they work in any market: markets with high interest rates or low interest rates, boom markets such as in 2003–2005, and down markets as in 2008–2009. But they're not one-size-fits-all. Each investor has his or her own unique goals and circumstances and skills, and each property he or she analyzes will have a different set of circumstances. That's the beauty of these creative methods! You can pick and choose whichever techniques are best suited for each situation. As you learn the details of each strategy, you will recognize certain elements that will not work for you, while other elements will be a perfect fit. Control of the situation is in your hands, and once you've learned the ropes you will know precisely what to do when opportunity knocks.

THE SELLER CAN HELP YOU FINANCE YOUR PURCHASE!

One of the most obvious sources for funding to consider when purchasing a property is the owner. After all, who has a more vested interest in seeing that a sale occurs? The seller is the person who will answer either yes or no when you ask, "Are you open to financing arrangements?" or "Are you willing to take a promissory note?"

TIP Always remember that the seller has the most invested in making sure the deal happens.

Depending on how motivated the seller is, he or she may have a very attentive ear when you offer to pay the asking price—in return for working cooperatively with you to make the sale happen.

One of the key words to consider here is "motivated." Motivated sellers are those who don't just want but need to sell the property and may not have the time or patience to sell it the "traditional" way—that is, listing the property for sale, waiting for a qualified buyer, negotiating price, then finally selling the property months after they listed it. Sellers may be motivated for any number of reasons, including divorce, foreclosure, job relocation, or even a death in the family. These sellers are not "down and out"; they are just in a position where they are anxious to move on.

When you use creative financing, you can make the situation a win-win for both buyer and seller.

Ways to Use the Seller as a Source of Financing

There are many ways you can utilize the seller as a source for financing. You can:

- Ask if the seller will hold a second mortgage, in lieu of a down payment. For example, obtain a 70 percent loan from a lending institution or through partners, and ask the seller to hold a second mortgage note for 30 percent.
- Ask if the seller would give you credits at closing for repairs. For example, negotiate a $5,000 credit at closing for roof repairs and new carpet allowance. The credit will appear on the closing statement, and you may even get money back at closing.
- Ask if the seller would consider a lease option or a land contract. (I'll talk more about these techniques later.)
- Ask if the seller would trade services for a discount on the property. The key is: Don't be shy!

You may feel uncomfortable asking someone to help you finance the sale of his own property, but this will get easier for you in time and when you know the facts. You will feel more confident in your offer and be able to explain the win-win scenario to the seller. These suggestions are only the beginning. You are limited only by your lack of creativity when problem solving.

Using these tools will also help you educate buyers when you become the seller!

THE PROPERTY ITSELF CAN HELP FINANCE YOUR PURCHASE

Every property has worth. The value lies not only in the actual value of the house and land itself, but in other areas as well. Trees and mineral rights may have cash value. A vacant lot next door or furniture left on the property may also provide a source for cash.

TIP Online valuation services, and even some comparable market analyses from a real estate professional, usually don't include the value of trees or mineral rights. Check with a realtor or city or county office before you purchase a property. Educate yourself as to what local code enforcement or zoning will allow. Don't be afraid to ask questions, and always do your due diligence.

A property's value is often calculated by the sales of similar properties in the same neighborhood. You can research this information yourself or have a realtor help you. For a ballpark valuation, you can look online at a number of Web sites, including www.zillow.com, www.realestate.yahoo.com/homevalues, and my favorite, www.netronline.com. Visit www.CarletonSheetsRealBook.com for up-to-date links and resources.

Real-Life Story: Carleton's Success Story No. 1

Some time ago, I bought a forty-eight-unit apartment building creatively with very little money down. I then converted the apartments into condominiums and sold them in blocks of four and five to individual investors at nearly twice what I had originally paid on a per-unit basis. While the use of the building did not change, the legal framework did and, by doing this, I was able to make a huge profit.

INVESTORS ARE ALWAYS INTERESTED IN REAL ESTATE

People seem to have no problem putting money into the stock market. However, it can be risky and difficult to figure out exactly what to invest in. For example, when you buy a piece of rental property, you can reasonably anticipate what the future rents and expenses will be. But if you buy a stock, the value of the stock could drop in half almost overnight, and its dividend could be totally eliminated! Real estate, by contrast, is a much safer investment. Moreover, you will find that investing in real estate becomes easier and easier as you acquire more properties. In fact, once your friends and acquaintances see how you're amassing properties, they'll often ask if they can "get in on your next deal." When investors don't have the time, but do have the cash, they will frequently loan money to you at a good rate of return, or perhaps even agree to share in a portion of the profit upon resale of the property.

Where can you find investors? Check your local newspaper for "money lenders," or do an online search. It may even be as simple as a friend who isn't happy with his or her return in the stock market and is willing to lend you a large sum to purchase the property, while they hold the mortgage, and make a good return on their investment through your monthly payments. And if you have an investor willing to loan you only a portion of the purchase price, be sure to find out what your lender's requirements are before you structure a deal.

Real-Life Story: Student Success Story No. 1

Lupe began building her reputation by purchasing and rehabbing condos, one by one, in a run-down complex in her town. Her reputation spread by word of mouth, and, before long, investors were approaching her to get a better return than their 401(k)s were paying. These investors didn't have the time or knowledge of investing in real estate, but they did have some money they were willing to invest.

PARTNERS WILL PUT MORE SKIN IN THE GAME

Partners may sound like just a synonym for investors, but actually there is a distinct difference. Partners are people who will actually be purchasing property with you, not simply financing a loan for you.

TIP Partnerships are a great way to get started. A partner can help expand your portfolio and borrowing power, while sharing the work load. There are many types of partnerships, and I suggest you investigate each type and tailor yours to fit your individual needs. Seek professional help if you are unsure.

Where will you find your partners? For starters, ask family members who have the foresight to realize the relative safety and potential of investing in real estate. Over a period of time, you may have a dozen or more partnerships comprised of family members, friends, and business associates. Each partner will have put up cash (or services) in return for an equity position (ownership) in the property.

Real-Life Story: Carleton's Success Story No. 2

When I first started in this business as a real estate agent, my first listing was an apartment building. I kept wondering why it had not sold. It seemed like such a good investing opportunity. One of the seminars I had attended had focused on the benefits of partnership investing: accomplishing with others what you cannot do by yourself. I had learned some very effective techniques from the instructor who had a solid background in forming syndicates or partner groups, so I decided to acquire the building. I put together a partnership that consisted of two investors who contributed 100 percent of the required cash down payment, with the seller financing an 80 percent first mortgage. I contributed my "expertise," and we were off to a profitable start and, I might add—the beginning of a career that has spanned more than four decades.

But be aware: Partnerships can be a double-edged sword. Partners might see their responsibilities, duties, and partnership goals differently, which could lead to conflicts that can destroy the partnership. Make sure that all partnership agreements are in writing. Go to www.CarletonSheetsRealBook.com to find out more about my program that is devoted entirely to partnerships. As always, consult an expert for legal advice when necessary.

BORROW THE BROKER'S COMMISSION, SERIOUSLY!

Sometimes when a property listed is by a broker, it requires just 10 percent down. The reality is that the seller just wants to receive enough cash at closing to cover the broker's commission and closing costs.

The typical broker's commission ranges from 5 to 7 percent. In a real estate transaction, there are usually two brokers—the "listing" broker who listed the property on the MLS and represents the seller's interests, and the "buyer's broker" who represents the buyers and sells them the property. If one broker both lists the property and sells it, he or she gets all of the commission (subject to state law and the commission-splitting arrangement that the broker may have with the brokerage company he or she works for); if one broker lists the property and another broker sells it, the two brokers split the commission.

TIP What is the MLS? MLS stands for Multiple Listing Service. It is a regional or local (depending on where you live), fee-based service whereby members of the Board of Realtors exchange their listings.

For a real estate investor, the best opportunity to "borrow" the commission to use as the down payment is to negotiate with the listing broker, because he or she is in a position to receive up to 100 percent of the commission.

TIP It is helpful if you work with a real estate broker or realtor who is also an investor. They understand creative financing and using other people's money, and they may be more apt to loan their commission in the form of a note against the property.

Building rapport and credibility with brokers is crucial. Brokers may be reluctant to consider delaying receipt of their commission, but that reluctance can be tempered by an offer in which you give the broker a note for an amount higher than the commission, for example, $3,500 for a $3,000 commission. The premium price is offered for the broker's cooperation in accepting a note in lieu of full payment at closing.

YOUR OWN SERVICES, SKILLS, AND RESOURCES

Here's a technique that most people never even think of, and yet it's a great way to buy property without putting a lot of money into it. Many properties won't interest conventional buyers and investors because of needed maintenance or repairs. Sanding, painting, replacing—all of these "needs" have a dollar value. However, without having to put up actual dollars, you or a partner may be able to convert services or skills to dollars by identifying and meeting these needs. And you could negotiate a credit to be paid to you at closing to reimburse you for the cost of performing these repairs. The credit will appear on the closing statement and will decrease the amount of cash you need for closing (or will increase the amount of cash you receive back at closing).

TIP Negotiating repair credits at closing can be enough to cover the down payment.

Do you have something of value, say, a boat, jewelry, a 401(k), or an insurance policy that you can borrow against? Tapping into the equity of these assets by using a line of credit can be a great way to leverage a piece of property. Caution is advised, though. You will have to pay back a line of credit, usually through monthly installments, and you may not be able to deduct your interest expense. Again, consult an accountant to understand the specifics in your situation. Make sure that you can afford to make these payments. Alternatively, you could arrange a private loan from an investor using one of these assets as collateral.

Real-Life Story: Student Success Story No. 2

Some investors use the actual asset itself as a down payment. Scott is one of my students who sold sixteen of his properties as a package. His buyer purchased them by trading a condo and a lot the buyer owned "free and clear," as his down payment. A bank financed the balance of the $1.6 million transaction. So at closing, Scott received a mortgage-free lot and condo, and he also gained a monetary profit from the sale.

THE MOST TIMELESS TECHNIQUE OF ALL: THE LEASE OPTION

I'm often asked which is my favorite technique for buying or selling real estate. Well, my program is filled with dozens of great techniques I have enjoyed using successfully over the years. One that has performed particularly well for both buyers and sellers, especially since the real estate "meltdown" that began in mid-2006, has been the lease option.

TIP A lease option works in any market!

In simple terms, a lease option is a contract between a buyer and a seller that gives the buyer tenancy in a property, as well as the legal right to purchase the property at a predetermined price, or formula for price, on or before a specified future date. When you enter into a lease option with a seller, you promise to lease the property for a certain period of time and to make specified monthly payments. In return, the seller is obligated to sell the property to you under terms specified in the lease option agreement if you choose to exercise your option.

At first glance, it appears that a lease option benefits only the buyer. After all, the buyer is not obligated to buy the property. But if he or she does choose to buy the property, the seller is required to sell. If the lease option is carefully structured, however, it can be good for both the buyer and the seller.

When a buyer enters into a lease option with a seller, he or she is betting that the value of the property on a specified future date will be greater than the

TABLE 18.1

Benefits for the Buyer (Optionee)	Benefits for the Seller (Optionor)
The risk is low, and the financial leverage can be high.	The agreed-upon price of the property is frequently at the top of its current market value range.
The buyer receives control and possession of the property.	The option money that the seller receives is tax-deferred until exercised or expired.
Very little, or no, initial closing costs.	The option is forfeited if rent is not paid on time.
The buyer can walk away from the contract if the value of the property on the specified future date does not justify its purchase at the agreed-upon price, or the buyer can attempt to renegotiate the price or terms of the purchase.	The seller receives all the equity buildup (amortization) on the mortgage during the option period.
	The tenant has pride of ownership and, therefore, an incentive to take good care of the property.
	The rent, including the amount, if any, that is applicable to the option purchase price, is at the top of or above the fair market rental range.
	The ability to regain possession and control of the property in the event of the optionee's default in meeting the terms of the agreement.

agreed-upon purchase price. Even if this doesn't happen, considerable equity may still be achieved as a result of the credits of some or all of the monthly payments from the purchase price. As a result, there is a high chance that by purchasing the property at the specified date and price, he or she will gain instant equity. If, however, the value of the property on the specified future date is less than the specified purchase price, the buyer can walk away from the contract or attempt to renegotiate the price.

The seller is free to keep any option consideration (something of value, usually money, given as an inducement to enter a contract) that may have been paid and realize the gain from a monthly rental income. And if the buyer walks away, the seller is also free to start the process over—to either sell or rent or lease option the property.

TIP Over time, the real estate market is bound to change. The lease option technique allows both buyer and seller to take advantage of any market change and "bridge the gap," so to speak, with minimal risk.

Lease option contracts can be written to include several options—for both buyer and seller. These can include the following:

- Lease optioning a property with the intent to sublease to another person with a purchase option (sandwich lease).
- Lease optioning, then selling or assigning your position to a third party.
- Lease optioning a property requiring a modest rehab to sell to an end user or keep as a rental.

The lease option can be used on commercial investment properties as well as residential or investment properties.

Real-Life Story:
Student Success Story No. 3

This lease option was negotiated a number of years ago. The numbers may seem low, but the principles and the economics of the transaction are very much applicable in any market. The buyer (my student) owned a house worth roughly $100,000. There were a fair number of rental homes in the area; most of them rented in the $500 to $700 range.

Seeking to find a substantially nicer home, the buyer sought out a nearby upscale town where the home values exceeded $200,000. Rentals in this upscale area were fairly scarce. The buyer found a home for sale for $220,000, and it appeared to be reasonably priced. The seller was very anxious to sell since he had already moved out of state, and the home had been on the market for several months. The buyer proposed a lease option, and they ended up agreeing to a four-year option at the asking price of $220,000. The monthly rent was $900 (low for this particular house, but high in comparison to almost all other rentals in the surrounding areas), and the buyer received a 50 percent rent credit ($450 per month) toward the eventual purchase. The seller was to pay taxes and insurance during the option period, and the buyer agreed to pay for all of the maintenance (an inspection revealed that the house was in very good shape). The buyer put down $3,600 as a nonrefundable deposit for the option consideration, which was equivalent to less than 2 percent of the option purchase price!

The buyer was amazed when he figured out the "effective" interest rate that he was paying. He realized that, of the $900 a month he was paying, only $450 was the true "cost" of owning the house. From that, he subtracted the cost of taxes and insurance (which were $340 per month—an amount he would have had to pay had he owned the property) to yield a net "cost" of $110 a month. This worked out to an incredible effective interest rate of 0.6 percent ($110 times twelve months equals $1,320, divided by $220,000, which equals 0.6 percent). *That's less than 1 percent*!

After three years, the buyer was certain that he was going to exercise his option at the end of the four-year period (because, among other reasons, property values had been increasing very nicely in this area—at about 7 percent per year), but he figured it was worth the effort to see if the seller would be willing to extend the option in exchange for some additional consideration. The buyer and seller ended up agreeing to extend the option for one additional year in return for the buyer paying $10,000 of additional option consideration (which meant that it would be fully applied to the purchase price, but it would be forfeited if the buyer did not buy the house). Was this a good move? I sure think so. Even if it cost the buyer 10 percent interest to borrow the $10,000 for a year (which is $1,000), it was a small price to pay for another year of ownership at the effective interest rate of less than 1 percent.

After the five-year period, the buyer exercised the option and obtained the necessary funds by simply securing an owner-occupied loan (loan programs specifically designed for owner-occupants) for $179,400, which was the total amount due to the seller ($220,000 less the deposit of $3,600, less the additional consideration of $10,000 paid in year four, and less the rent credit of $27,000, which is equal to $450 for sixty months or five years). The property appreciated, and it appraised for $290,000; thus, the new loan was for only 62 percent of the property's fair market value. (By the way, the buyer eventually sold this house about a year later for $320,000 and, you guessed it, has since moved on to an even nicer home!)

The buyer's "profit" on his initial investment of $3,600 was $90,000—based on the property appreciation of $70,000, and the $20,400 savings of not paying taxes and insurance while living in the house. Under a lease option like this, the buyer (and seller, in this case) benefited in that the real estate taxes remained fairly steady throughout the five-year period because there had not been a reported sale of the property.

The action that the buyer took at the end of year three (asking for and getting the seller to agree to an additional year's extension) is an excellent example of the power of creative thinking. This would have been a great investment even if that had not occurred, but by thinking creatively and being willing to ask questions, the buyer turned what was already a great investment into one that was even better!

Let's take a look at how the buyer and the seller fared over this five-year deal.

TABLE 18.2 Benefits for the Buyer and the Seller

Benefits to the Buyer	Benefits to the Seller
Flexibility of option to purchase any time within a four-year term (this option was additionally extended for one more year).	The seller received full asking price.
Out of the total monthly rental payment of $900, $450 is credited toward the purchase, which makes the cost of occupancy $450 a month.	The seller is relieved of all maintenance responsibility and cost associated with the property.
Initial down payment of $3,600 and subsequent option extension of $10,000 are credited directly against the purchase price.	The seller receives sufficient income to cover the property taxes, insurance, and the principal and interest payment on the existing mortgage, plus a monthly profit.
The buyer had the advantage of time to put himself in the position to buy a home that he may not otherwise have been able to afford.	The seller receives a nonrefundable deposit up front.
Based on appreciation of approximately 7% per year, the buyer will enjoy instant equity of $110,600 ($290,000 fair market value minus $179,400 option purchase price balance).	The seller retains the $54,000 in rent payments ($900 per month) and the $13,600 total option deposit if the buyer fails to exercise the option. If he exercises the option, the seller credits back these amounts against the purchase price.
The buyer will have a much easier time obtaining favorable loan terms with $110,600 in equity in the property and therefore needs a mere 62% LTV (loan-to-value) to pay off the balance of the option purchase price.	The seller enjoys the reduction of the loan principal, which increases the amount the seller will cash out at closing or the equity the seller will have in the property if the buyer does not complete the transaction.
	The seller enjoys the deferment of taxes on the portion of money applied to the option purchase price (including the $3,600 and the $10,000 consideration) until the option is exercised or abandoned.
	The seller has the peace of mind of knowing that the property is under contract and is being maintained by someone motivated to take good care of it because, hopefully, he will soon own it.

This story is a perfect example of how a lease option can be very powerful for the buyer, and yet still represent an attractive proposition for the seller.

To learn more about lease options, and many other creative techniques to purchase property, go to www.CarletonSheetsRealBook.com to view my free online programs.

PUTTING IT ALL INTO ACTION

These are powerful techniques, but there is still one additional step that you need to take: learning to negotiate and structure offers. The best creative financing in the world won't gain you anything if you don't use it as part of a well-planned strategy with terms that are favorable to you. It's not really as difficult as it may seem. You might even discover that you are a better negotiator than you thought you were.

For me, it all begins with trust and credibility. For starters, keep in mind that people are naturally suspicious when it comes to conducting business with strangers. Yet in more cases than not, we find ourselves (as either buyers or sellers) negotiating with people whom we are meeting for the very first time. The number-one question on both parties' minds, therefore, is "Who do I trust?"

TIP Use the seller's name in conversation.

I once read a book that made the case that people are successful in life only to the degree that they are able to make people like and trust them. This is certainly true in negotiating. When talking to a seller, take a few minutes to establish a rapport. This builds a trusting relationship that is so essential to negotiating. If sellers feel comfortable with you, they often will be more forthcoming with important information, such as their true needs.

So how do you convince a seller that you're on the up and up? How do you establish that magical relationship based on rapport? One of the simplest techniques is a very basic one. When you get the person's name, remember it! Write it down, and be sure to get the right spelling. Then, when engaging him or her in conversation, be sure to use it. It isn't, "I'll tell you what," it's "I'll tell you what, Joe." That's a quick and easy way to begin building a rapport with the seller.

TIP Avoid being overly critical. You'll seldom, if ever, force the seller into lowering the price or terms by harsh criticism.

Another important element of rapport and trust building is being a good listener. As you talk to the seller, remember to always be an empathetic listener. Imagine yourself in his or her situation and try to experience, emotionally, what the seller is experiencing. By doing so, you might gain a new perspective on the negotiation and be able to make an offer that the seller is more likely to accept. People like to know that they're being listened to.

USING NONESSENTIAL CONTINGENCIES

Establishing a good rapport with someone is not in and of itself a negotiating strategy. It is merely one component of your overall approach. Compromise is what negotiations are all about. If you enter negotiations with an open mind, the seller is more likely to have an open mind, too. This mind-set allows both of you to create a win-win situation.

During negotiations, both parties must give something to get something; therefore, good negotiators always use nonessential, but purposeful, contingencies as negotiating tools. In other words, when you use a nonessential contingency—such as requesting that the seller include some, or all, of the furniture—you ask for concessions that you do not necessarily need or even want (concessions you are willing to "negotiate away"). In return, the seller concedes on a point that is important to you.

By using nonessential contingencies, you will arm yourself with effective negotiating tactics. You might only want the seller to pay all of the closing costs, for example, but by adding the other nonessential contingencies, you have some extra items that you can "give up" to get the one that you truly want.

MAKING MULTIPLE OFFERS SIMULTANEOUSLY

The "traditional" way that people make offers on real estate is to make one offer, wait for the seller to counteroffer, go back and forth once or twice on terms or price, and then come to an agreement. By making more than one offer simultaneously, you will be able to pinpoint what the seller's needs are, and how your offer can meet his or her needs.

You may want to consider using a letter of intent when making multiple offers (or, for that matter,

Multiple Offer Options:

A cash offer at a deeply discounted price.
An offer that incorporates seller-financing.
A lease option.
Make sure all amounts are clearly stated.

with any type of offer you are making). A letter of intent is a letter stating a buyer's intent to make an offer to acquire a certain property. It is not a binding contract, but it shows a good-faith desire to own the property, and it can be a real time saver compared with filling out a formal contract offer to purchase. If a seller responds in a positive way, it could be the basis for further negotiations. If you are proposing a creative way to purchase the property, it may be helpful because you can show exactly how the transaction will benefit the seller by using a letter of intent.

In your letter of intent, you can bullet point two or three different scenarios that would work for you in purchasing the property. Make sure the seller understands that he or she cannot combine the offers. If you are filling out a formal offer to purchase, you will have to fill out one per offer with the creative details in the addendum.

To view a sample letter of intent, as well as many other forms, log on to www.CarletonSheetsRealBook.com.

TIP If you are working through a real estate agent, request to be present when your offer is presented to the seller. You will be able to explain any questions that the seller may have, as well as establish a sense of professionalism and build rapport.

It should also be noted that these negotiating skills work equally well when you are either the buyer *or* the seller. As real estate investors, we tend to always think of ourselves as the buyer, but this is not necessarily true. In fact, in many instances, one of the best ways for you to turn a profit is by knowing when to sell one of your properties. This is especially true when you have bought a fixer-upper with the intention of flipping it for a significantly higher amount of money. Knowing how to use other people's money in creative ways can make it much easier for you to find buyers. And the negotiating tactics we've been discussing will come in handy for you when you are the buyer as well.

SOME GOOD ADVICE—BASIC DO'S AND DON'TS

I'm often asked for advice from my students, such as, "Should I do this deal?" But mostly it's, "How do I get started?" Well, it's difficult to answer everyone's questions, personally. But I've adhered to some guidelines over the years that have helped me—and may help you get started.

TABLE 18.3 Carleton's Do's and Don'ts

DO	Keep an open mind	New ideas always seem strange at first. Imagine what it must have been like for the Wright brothers when they told people that they could fly! But new ideas can lead to a wonderful new way of life. And when it comes to real estate investments, the person with an open mind, who is always willing to entertain new ideas, is the kind of person who is most likely to succeed.
DO	Write down your goals	It's amazing what a difference a piece of paper can make. Once your goals are committed to paper, you are much less likely to veer from your plans or to be distracted. Writing down your goals will also make you better organized and help you to maintain your focus. Having dreams and aspirations is a good thing. In fact, I strongly encourage it. That doesn't mean, of course, that you should keep your head in the clouds. Be a down-to-earth, practical and realistic dreamer. Set achievable goals for yourself, and then enjoy the ride as you achieve them one by one.
DO	Commit yourself 100%	Making goals is not enough. You must commit to achieving those goals. Set aside a reasonable amount of time and energy per day or per week to pursue your real-estate-related activities. Stick to your schedule, and don't be distracted. Small steps add up and you will be surprised how much you have learned and how far you have progressed in a short amount of time.
DON'T	Listen to naysayers	As we all know, there are positive people in our lives and negative people, some who want to see us succeed and others who would be jealous of our success. Negative people will always find reasons to tear you down and criticize what you're trying to do to improve your life. Do not listen to these people or let them influence you. They are not being your friends and will only hurt your chances for success.
DON'T	Be afraid to fail	The most successful people in the world have had more than their share of failures. They know all about the concept of trial and error. Don't be afraid of making mistakes. Instead, allow every failure to teach you a valuable lesson. However, always make sure that your "worst-case scenarios" are something you can afford to live with. If not, then the risk is too great and you should move on to the next opportunity.
DON'T	Get emotional about a property	I realize that homes are often more than just buildings; they have emotional and sentimental value for the people who live in them. However, as an investor, you need to always keep in mind that this is a business—your business—and everyone involved in buying or selling real estate has a right to profit from each transaction, as long as it is conducted in an honest and ethical manner.

THE WAVE OF THE FUTURE

I've been involved with real estate investing for many years, and one thing I can say for sure is that the market is always changing and evolving. What might be true today may not be true tomorrow. As you know, there are buyer's markets and there are seller's markets (compare 2005 to 2009!). That's why success takes more than just learning a set-in-stone collection of rules. You have to be flexible and take into account the cyclical, ever-changing nature of the real estate market.

All of the sources and techniques I've outlined in this chapter will work for both buying and selling properties. You have to determine which techniques will work best for you in a given situation and market.

The United States recently experienced a sharp increase in the number of homes in foreclosure. This is a tragic situation for many homeowners. It happens for a variety of reasons; in short, people get into financial difficulties and can no longer afford the mortgage on their homes. For the investor, however, this means a large pool of highly motivated sellers. One of the most popular techniques involving foreclosures is known as a short sale. A short sale takes place when the lender agrees—with the homeowner's approval—to accept less than the amount owed on a piece of real estate.

A short sale could happen for a few different reasons, but the most common is the value of the property has declined below the value of the loan. This could be due to the property being in distress, or it could simply be that values in the area have significantly declined since the property was purchased.

Although foreclosures seem to be the "buzzword" between the years 2008 to 2009, don't overlook estate sales, tax liens, or tax deeds (depending on your state) or "for sale by owner" properties for leads to motivated sellers. That's one of the many things I love about real estate—you can find your own niche that best fits your goals and your level of risk.

TIP To learn more about how to invest in foreclosures, visit www.CarletonSheetsRealBook.com for my complete foreclosures program, which is absolutely free.

Another definite trend of the future—if you're not already using it—is using the power of the Internet. More than ever before, people have information at their fingertips. And they can demand answers at the touch of a "send" button. Almost any resource an investor would need is available almost instantaneously by searching the Internet. Using the Internet, you can:

- Search for local investment clubs for networking opportunities. For example, take a look at www.reiclub.com, or www.creonline.com.
- Market your properties through online advertising, or build your own customized Web site. Check out www.fsbo.com, or www.forsalebyowner.com

for "by owner" opportunities. To build a specific Web site inexpensively, try www.yahoo.com, or www.networksolutions.com. However, if you are looking for a pre-built Web site designed specifically for real estate investors, consider www.investorpro.com.

- Pinpoint properties that fit your investing profile through a variety of online service providers, including www.realtytrac.com, www.realtor.com, and www.fsbo.com.
- Search the public records online to find past sales prices and owner information (or even to find out how much neighbors, friends, or family paid for their homes). I recommend www.netronline.com for links to local county records .
- Find lenders. Try www.lendingtree.com, or search "money lenders" on your favorite search engine.

Go to www.CarletonSheets RealBook.com to access any site I have mentioned. The possibilities are endless, and this is by no means a comprehensive list. But my point is that it has never been as easy to find information—and all from the comfort of your own home.

YOU CAN MAKE MONEY IN ANY MARKET

No matter what the market dictates, one fact remains constant: people still need a place to live. Whether they are renting or owning, there will always be situations where a growing family needs to upsize, or a retiree needs to downsize. The real estate market is never totally stagnant. And any market can be a good market to invest in—as long as you know how and when to apply the techniques I've given you.

TIP You can tailor your real estate investing techniques to mirror market conditions. When the market is good, consider flipping properties. When the market is slow, consider buy-and-hold strategies—it's all up to you!

The changes that have taken place in recent years, within both the real estate market and the banking industry, are actually very good changes for the savvy investor. And using my creative financing methods is likely to become even more necessary to succeed in real estate in the future. Banks now have lending requirements that are stricter than in the past—which potentially impact both buyers and sellers. When participants on both sides of the transaction have an even greater incentive to do things in a more innovative way, they will consider creative options that they may not have even thought of before. Ultimately, that sort of creativity is good for the market and can keep it a dynamic, ever-changing arena where good ideas and strong visions are handsomely rewarded.

WAYS TO LEARN MORE

Visit Carleton Sheets on the Web at www.CarletonSheetsRealBook.com. This site is your source for all things real estate. You'll find many of Carleton's best-selling real estate programs online for free, as well as links to Web resources, current trends and real estate news, blogs, products and services, and a forum for networking with other investors nationwide.

 **Carleton Sheets** is recognized as the best-selling author of the *No Down Payment*® home study course as well as other successful real estate books, video, and audio programs. He has sold more than three million copies of his programs in the United States alone. In 1984, Carleton partnered with the Professional Education Institute to distribute his message nationally about creative real estate investing. His *No Down Payment* television program is now accredited as being the longest-running program of its kind, spanning twenty-five years. After thirty years of successfully selling his programs, Carleton began sharing his real estate programs online at no charge. His wish is to reach as many people as possible to help them achieve their dreams—as he has achieved his—with real estate. Today, on his own or with partners, Carleton has bought and sold more than $50 million of commercial and residential income-producing real estate.

19

Dean GRAZIOSI

Marketing: Your Ticket to Finding and Profiting from Foreclosures

I first saw Dean on television, with his "Motor Millions" television infomercial. I was very impressed with his communication skills. He was clear and to the point, and his sincerity came through the screen.

A few years later, I saw his new infomercial, this time on real estate. While I do not know much about cars, I do know a little about real estate, and I could tell that Dean did, too. His wisdom on real estate came through the television screen as well.

A friend of mine, Joe Polish, called one day and asked if I would like to meet Dean. When the two of them walked into my office, it was like looking at a pair of bookends. I have known Joe for years, and he is what I call a "natural entrepreneur." So is Dean. Listening to the two of them talk about their businesses, I realized both young men were born entrepreneurs. I had to learn to be one. For several hours I listened to both guys educate me on subjects I thought I was pretty good at. Both Joe and Dean are natural teachers.

Dean has the gift of being good at business and being good at real estate investing. It is a perfect combination of skills for anyone who wants to live their life doing something they love, while they become rich and financially free. That is why I invited him to be a part of this book.

—ROBERT KIYOSAKI

326

I've never met a person who couldn't become wealthy investing in real estate. It doesn't matter who you are or where you come from. I didn't come from a family that had money. I had no mentors and never went to college. I was not even smart enough to read a book like this one to gain wisdom from people who were smarter than me when it came to investing in real estate. Learning from other people's trial and error, and success and failure is by far the fastest way to success. I know this now and have been fortunate to write a few *New York Times* best-selling books myself. But it took a while for it all to sink in. So you have more going for you than I did when I first started, and I congratulate you for taking action and being ready to learn.

Although I didn't have money, a degree, or a mentor, I was fortunate enough to have a strong desire to get the things I wanted out of life and a mind that was open to possibilities. I didn't like the fact that my single mom worked two jobs to make about $90 a week when I was growing up. I hated that we lived in a trailer park for part of my childhood and that money was always an issue in our home. The pain caused a major drive inside of me. What is *your* motivation for getting the life you deserve? Find it, and don't let anything knock you off course.

TIP What is *your* motivation for getting the life you deserve? Find it, and don't let anything knock you off course.

When Robert asked me to write a chapter in his book, I was happy to say "Yes" and share some capabilities, strategies, and wisdom that could shorten your learning curve for acquiring foreclosure property—so your downside risk will be minimal and your upside gain will be huge.

In this chapter I am going to share with you one of my most guarded secrets on how to make killer foreclosure deals actually come to you, automatically, rather than spending a ton of time, effort, and money going out and looking for them. In fact, my students who have bought my *Be a Real Estate Millionaire* book love this technique the most.

So, to make sure I do my best to *wow* you, I'll be sharing my marketing strategy with you right here. But first let me tell you the story of one of my first real estate investments. This deal took place in the late 1990s and I have been making money from real estate ever since. As I am writing this, I currently have thirty-something deals in the works. So I don't just *write* about how to profit from real estate, I *live* it every day. Here we go.

My First Deal

In my late teens, I was flat broke and constantly looking for some opportunity to make money. There was an apartment house in town that had once been a decent place, but the owners had let the wrong tenants in, and the place began to deteriorate. This apartment house was for sale, but its horrible appearance meant that no bank was going to give anyone a loan to buy it. I started talking with the sellers, asking them questions, and bringing up the things that needed repair on the building. I told them, "I'd like forty-five days to clean that place up, but then you have to sell it to me. . . . To keep you from selling it to anybody else, I'm going to give you a tiny down payment. But in forty-five days, I will start pursuing a bank loan. Then I want sixty days to close on a bank loan." The seller agreed.

Looking back, what I did next is pretty scary, and I would not suggest this to anyone else. Once the seller and I had a deal, I immediately went to work on the place before I even knew whether I could get a bank loan. I thought if the bank happened to look at this place before I made it look pretty, I would never get the loan.

So I blindly put my heart, soul, and sweat equity into cleaning up the place. First, I got rid of the junk in the front yard by calling a junk dealer who took everything away for free so he could sell it for scrap. Then I got together with some friends and hired the cheapest laborers I could find. Together we fixed all the broken windows, the front door, and the porch. My contract with the owners allowed me to evict some of the worst tenants, so I got rid of the ones who were unwilling to be part of the massive cleanup.

We planted flowers across the front, mowed the lawn, trimmed the hedges, and painted the front of the building. Then we went inside and painted the hallway and cleaned up a couple of the apartments where some of the evicted people had lived. They were nice apartments; they just needed to be cleaned.

In forty-five days, the building looked gorgeous. I then went to the bank and was fortunate enough to get a loan. In fact, I got a loan for 100 percent of the money I needed because the property appraised for much more money than I was buying it for. I kept that apartment house for many years, and each month I enjoyed great positive cash flow from it. Then I sold it during a peak cycle and made a wonderful profit.

Looking back, that property was a foundation for many amazing future properties.

What a great learning experience, and what a great sense of accomplishment. To this day, I can remember standing on the front lawn, looking at the building after I purchased it, and feeling the sense of accomplishment that came from knowing I did everything I said I was going to do.

I was so aggressive because I knew what I wanted, and I wasn't going to let anything stand in my way. There was no "what if" option—only "when."

I don't know if I've gotten smarter or just more cautious, but I don't invest like that anymore. One reason my first real estate deal worked was because I never thought that it wasn't going to work. My youth and inexperience kept me focused on winning and nothing else. If I had been older and had overanalyzed the situation, I may never have done it. That's an important lesson to remember. I don't know a successful person alive who didn't also fail a lot at the beginning. The fear of failure is always lurking in the background of the mind, waiting to sabotage one's success. If you pretend it's not there, you can't deal with it. Acknowledge it. Then move forward and do your best. If something you try fails, learn from it. Don't let life's failures talk you out of future accomplishments. The past is the past. Use it as research and development, and then start fresh—looking forward to what's next.

TIP I don't know a successful person alive who didn't also fail a lot at the beginning. The fear of failure is always lurking in the background of the mind, waiting to sabotage one's success. If you pretend it's not there, you can't deal with it. Acknowledge it. Then move forward and do your best.

In the twenty years that I've been investing in real estate, a great amount of my time and effort also has been spent studying direct marketing. Smart marketing makes a huge difference in your level of success as an investor. There are a host of classic marketing ideas that will help you stand out in the crowd of investors who are competing for the same properties, as well as some nifty little tricks on how to mail letters of interest to homeowners that get opened and read.

Just like other investors, I've used many of the strategies and time-tested techniques borrowed from direct marketing. They are great for helping to find potential deals, and they make the process easier.

The more I continued to study and use direct marketing, the more I realized that I could come up with new ways to target specific types of investments with smart marketing. I threw out all my conventional "investor" thinking and took a strict marketing approach. In other words, if I was trying to market a product to a certain group of people, I asked myself, "How would I do it?"

Well, one of the things I would want to do is avoid competing for the same investments. I would not want to advertise in the same places my competitors would advertise. I also would want to automate as much of it as I could.

You may have seen or heard of the technique of using free recorded messages. Movie theaters have used recorded messages for years to deliver the schedule of shows and show times. Marketers use these to offer everything from free information to educating prospects and generating leads. Real estate agents use recorded messages to deliver automated information on homes they list, and investors do the same. It's a tremendous time-saver and a smart way to automate the task of providing duplicate information to many individuals.

TIP Avoid competing for the same investments. Don't advertise in the same places your competitors advertise.

I'm going to teach you a method of using recorded messages targeted to homeowners with direct response marketing[1] that allows me to attract deals that no other investor may be able to find out about, and then funnel the deals in such a way so that I'm left with only the deals I am interested in. It has revolutionized the way investors can find and profit from investments. It completely reverses what 99 percent of other investors are doing. The difference is this: Instead of me making a "cold" contact with a person, I use some very specific, marketing strategies, sit back, and let them automatically contact me!

This method will work regardless of the type of property I want to find, but I'm going to explain how I use it to invest in pre-foreclosures.

AUTOMATED MARKETING FOR FORECLOSURE AND PRE-FORECLOSURE INVESTING

As you may know, *foreclosure* is the legal process in which a lender sells or seizes a person's property to recover and repay the debt attached to that property. Foreclosure occurs when someone borrows money to buy real estate but cannot pay the agreed-upon monthly payments.

I hope that you will agree with me that none of us wish hard times on anyone else, but when a foreclosure does occur, it creates an investment opportunity. Someone is eventually going to take advantage of it, so my philosophy is to be first in line. The great thing about foreclosures is that you can make money

---

1. Direct response marketing is a form of marketing designed to solicit a direct response that is specific and quantifiable.

TIP *Foreclosure* is the legal process in which a lender sells or seizes a person's property to recover and repay the debt attached to that property. Foreclosure can be prevented by bringing payments current. But most often, homeowners can't catch up, and they lose everything. My strategy is to come in prior to foreclosure, buy the property, allow the homeowner to pay off the loan, and save their credit rating.

with them in any market cycle, but *down* and *bottom* markets are the best to find and make money with foreclosures. This marketing strategy literally makes people in pre-foreclosure and other stages of foreclosure contact you!

Again, when homeowners are facing foreclosure, they have the opportunity to stop it by bringing their payments and any other associated fees current. But most often they can't catch up, and they lose everything! My strategy is to come in before that happens, when the owners can sell their property to a third party (me) during what is called the pre-foreclosure period.

Now this may *sound* like a horrible position for me to be in as the buyer— approaching a person who is losing his home, and I'm looking to buy it and make a profit. But look at it realistically. The person is going to lose that property because he can't make or catch up on his payments. A sale of the property means the owner can pay off the loan and avoid having a foreclosure on his credit history. Then he can go out and find another, more affordable home, without the black mark of a foreclosure on his record.

Getting to the owner *before* he goes into foreclosure gives me a jump on other investors who rely on methods that depend on the entry of foreclosures into public records or paid listing services. It also eliminates all the grunt work associated with locating properties using those methods!

Here's how it works.

STEP 1: FINDER STRATEGIES

I use direct response marketing methods to create "finder strategies" that *find* and *drive* qualified prospects to me. Let's start with what I'll call *finder ads* for now. I create finder ads for a number of different applications. I use classifieds, business cards, flyers, mailers, yard signs, and even ad words on Google.

These finder ads must all follow the rules of good direct response advertising:

1. They all have a compelling, targeted headline.
2. They make a big promise to create interest.
3. They ignite a desire to find out more.
4. They tell the prospect what action to take.

The key to these finder strategies is that they have to promise helpful information to people, or they won't work. Anyone facing a potential foreclosure is going to experience a wide range of emotions. He can be angry, afraid, depressed, and even ashamed.

A foreclosure can occur for a lot of reasons: a job loss, an illness, an unexpected death in the family, even a change in the interest rates. Any of these events can get in the way of people being able to continue making their mortgage payments. If a homeowner can't keep up with the payments, the lender puts the property in foreclosure.

The first step toward foreclosure usually happens when the lending institution notifies the owners in writing that they are in default of payment. In most cases, the lender will bring in an attorney to start the foreclosure process after three consecutive payments are missed.

The attorney will send a letter informing the owners that if they do not pay what is owed, the lender will be forced to begin a foreclosure proceeding. The lender can also request a trustee sale or judicial foreclosure, where the property is sold at public auction.

The homeowners can still avoid foreclosure at this time by making the loan payments current and paying all overdue amounts after the notice of the default has been recorded. This is called the *right of reinstatement*. The last date possible for the money owed to be brought up to date and paid is called the *cure date*. It is usually no later than a few days before the property's impending sale.

If the homeowner cannot make these overdue payments, the foreclosed properties often get sold at a real estate auction or trustee sale, where it is sold to the highest bidder.

If the property is worth less than the total amount owed to the lender (which can occur if property values have dipped since the homeowner took out the original loan), the lender can seek a *deficiency judgment*, and the homeowner would not only lose the home, but also be saddled with the additional debt, which would be the difference between what the home sold for at auction and the balance of the loan.

Sometimes people simply give up and walk away from their property, letting the foreclosure occur. Most people are looking for ways to stop the foreclosure and save their house, or at least prevent a foreclosure by trying to sell it. So they want answers and solutions to their problem, and they want them fast. The finder ad must be structured to address not only their concerns, but their emotions.

STEP 2: POSITION YOURSELF AS AN ADVOCATE

Although the *finder ad* is designed to attract people long before they show up on any foreclosure lists, some of the people who respond will have had some kind of encounter with another investor. That investor may have left an impression of being interested only in taking the property for profit. The person facing foreclosure, however, is interested only in ending his own pain, not in helping an investor make a profit. So in my finder strategies and recorded message, I achieve the end result of positioning myself as an advocate, not an "opportunistic" investor.

"Quick List" Important Elements of the Recorded Message

The recorded message explains the real options to stop a foreclosure.

It gives them a true understanding of the reality of their situation.

It helps gain the owner's trust.

It screens out the deals that would not work, or deals that I don't want.

I end up with the best of the best to choose from and pursue.

I do that by providing the person with a number of potential, step-by-step solutions to stop his foreclosure, and only mention the possibility of *maybe* being able to buy his home. By doing that, I am 99 percent more likely to be perceived as an advocate. Truth be told, if I shared with someone a way for him to save his home and I didn't get a chance to buy it—that would be wonderful to me. I truly want to be an advocate for people in trouble, not pretend to be. If the real-life suggestions and tips I provide do not work for them, and their situation is irreversible, then I get to be the investor.

STEP 3: REMOVE EMOTIONAL BARRIERS

All the finder strategies will direct people to a twenty-four-hour *free, recorded* information line. As I mentioned earlier, this is a well-known technique that smart marketers have used for years to automate their marketing. I take it to the next level by using the message to sift, sort, and screen out the bad deals. That way I spend time on only the incredible deals.

The finder ads clearly state that they are calling a recorded information line. This makes calling a very nonthreatening action for people to take. They know they don't have to talk to anyone when they call. They don't have to be afraid of being "pressured" into anything. It's risk free, so anyone who is even slightly interested is more likely to call, and it "saves face" (remember, anyone who is ever faced with losing his home has varying degrees of negative feelings about the situation). Compared to calling and talking to a live person, the recording can help alleviate any sense of shame or fear a person might feel.

The message the caller hears is strategically written. To help me create my message, I hired a professional copywriter (even though I have written best-selling books, and I feel very confident in my ability to write and communicate). I provided him with the important facts I wanted to communicate, and he wove them into verbiage that is empathetic to the person's situation, and gives callers seven options they can take to stop their foreclosure. It reveals to them the specific actions to take, depending where they are in the process.

Attract Homeowners to You

Here is part of a message I use to attract owners who are skeptical of being scammed:

My name is Dean, and I want to thank you for calling my Foreclosure Scam Warning Line. In just a moment I'm going to reveal to you some scams to watch out for, and then I'll provide you with tips and facts that most lenders and banks don't want you to know. Tips that can prevent the foreclosure process from ever starting, and even stop it once it has started.

By the time you're done listening to this message, you'll know exactly what your options are, and you will be able to make an intelligent, informed decision about the correct course of action to take.

You may want to have something handy to take notes, as I'm going to be going through this material rather quickly. However, at the end of this recording I'll provide you with my contact information if you missed anything or have further questions.

Let's get started with the things to watch out for.

If you are facing the threat of losing your home to a foreclosure, beware of certain individuals and companies offering to "help" you out of your difficult financial situation because some of them are scams.

These scams specifically target homeowners who are in financial distress. Scam operators advertise just like legitimate businesses. You may find their ads on the Internet and in local publications. They often copy legitimate businesses by plastering flyers on telephone poles and at bus stops. They drop flyers off on people's front doors

> *or contact people whose homes are listed in public foreclosure notices. Sometimes they direct their appeals to specific religious or ethnic groups.*
>
> *The typical scenario is where the scammer offers to "buy" your property by paying off your overdue amount on the loan. Then the scam artist convinces you to move out and deed the property over to him or a third party. Signing over a deed in no way releases you from your mortgage responsibilities!*
>
> *These scammers even have been known to give you the option of renting the property with the option to buy it back later. Neither of these promises is ever delivered on. They never pay off the overdue amounts, and if you are naïve enough to pay them rent, you later wind up faced with eviction from the home, still owing the original loan amount.*

The message continues, and after it gives all the options for preventing a foreclosure to callers, it offers them one more: If none of the solutions I have already suggested work, that "I may be able to buy their property" and prevent a foreclosure. Then, it qualifies them for me. The message asks the questions I need answered before I can consider their property for purchase.

Questions like this:

What is the amount owed on their mortgage? And how many payments have they missed?

What's the location of the home, the home's age, square feet, and the number of bedrooms?

What's the condition of the home?

Do they have an appraisal of the home?

Has a "Notice for a Sheriff's Sale" been sent?

Has the bank sent a list of additional expenses owed to them for the foreclosure process?

PUTTING IT ALL TOGETHER

So what does this all look like? A sample finder strategy used in a classified ad might look like this:

Free Foreclosure Help

Learn What to Do If You Are at Risk

FREE RECORDED MESSAGE
Call anytime twenty-four hours a day
xxx-xxx-xxxx

Here is another example:

7 Ways to Stop Your Foreclosure
Don't let the bank steal your home and ruin your credit! You do have options.
In the next 5 minutes you can find out
exactly what to do and it's provided FREE!
Call this 24-hour recorded consumer message now and learn how to
stop this nightmare!
Call xxx-xxx-xxxx

Again, the ad drives people to my recorded message. The recorded message educates them, screens them, and provides a means for them to request contact, or to contact me. The people that I ultimately do contact are highly qualified. I can get as specific as I want with my message to sift deals down to the tiniest details. The beauty of it is, this method will sift, sort, and screen the best possible deals for me, every day, twenty-four hours a day, seven days a week.

Investors use the classified section all the time to find folks in foreclosure, but when people see my ads, they want to know what the secret is, so they call. I also use the same strategy on business cards, larger ads, even postcards.

DON'T FORGET THE INTERNET

I also direct people to a Web site that contains all the same information as the recorded message. However, from the Web site I can capture their e-mail address and put them on an auto-responder series that drips out professionally written e-mails that repeat the helpful information and also remind them that I am there to help if possible.

This method saves so many wasted hours that in itself would be enough for any investors to stay excited about it. But the fact that it drives deals to my door before others investors can even get wind of them makes it unique and highly profitable.

When people see one of these "finder" ads, it will grab their attention. It speaks to their emotions in a very compelling way—*and* it's nonthreatening. I am able to attract far more deals using this system than I could by old-fashioned, labor-intensive methods.

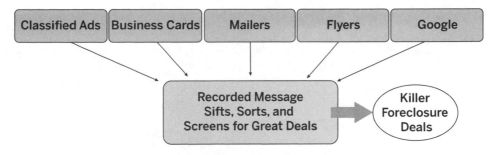

FIGURE 19.1 Marketing Strategy

It helps me create more win-win situations than anything else I could possibly do. Even people who aren't in foreclosure see my notices and they often tell a friend or acquaintance who is in foreclosure.

Real Life Story: Marketing Works!

One of my students is named Jackie and she lived in Indiana. Jackie *told everyone she knew that* she was starting a real estate investing career and was looking for property. By simply doing this, one of her friends responded and told her about a couple who were losing their home.

They were in pre-foreclosure status and the couple owed only $10,000 on it. This was a great buy because homes in the area were selling for $20,000 to $30,000 more than what was owed on this home. This was Jackie's first experience in buying a pre-foreclosure home, and it fit her investing budget. She was nervous about approaching the owners—almost as much as the owners were nervous about getting bank tellers.

She asked the right questions and found out that they would be happy if they could just walk away from the home and not owe anybody anything. Jackie found out the exact amount owed to the bank and then asked the bank whether they could help with some of the penalty costs because she was going to pay off the debt. The bank agreed and took a flat $10,000 for the home!

Jackie had just enough in savings to purchase the home, and afterwards, because she owned it free and clear, she had the options of refinancing and pulling out cash to remodel the property or do a quick fix-up and resell it. There are many other ways Jackie could have done this. She could have borrowed the money from a hard money lender. She could have gotten a new loan to purchase the home, as it was appraised for much more than her cost, so you don't have to have cash reserves to make it work.

I use this concept to find and choose the best deals and purchase them myself, but it can also be used to find deals to offer other investors, and make your money in the middle.

My students do this all the time; here's one of their true stories.

Real Life Story: Find the Deal and Win

Brett was a twenty-two-year-old college student who wanted to get involved in real estate but did not have enough money for a down payment. That didn't stop him. He found one property owner who was in foreclosure and owed around $450,000 for the house and was three weeks away from foreclosure. After doing a little work to find comparable houses in the neighborhood, Brett knew that the house was worth between $500,000 and $525,000, so the deal had a good amount of equity. Brett immediately called an investor he knew in the San Diego area and explained the situation, asking for a 2.5 percent finder's fee from the investor.

Brett sent over a spreadsheet showing the asking price as well as the comps for other houses in the area. The investor called Brett and agreed to his terms. Brett put the owner and the investor in contact, and they closed the deal in two weeks. The owner was able to walk away with a few thousand dollars and his credit intact. The investor was able to get a great deal on a house and had to pay only 2.5 percent instead of the traditional 3 percent or 6 percent that a realtor charges. Brett profited more than $11,000 without using any of his money and very little of his time. It was a win-win-win situation for everyone.

It really isn't rocket science! Sure, deals like this aren't on every corner, but they are out there, and with a little bit of effort and the right marketing actions, finding them isn't as difficult as one might think.

When investing in foreclosures there are a few do's and don'ts to pay attention to.

You can be successful. We all have obstacles that we face every day, some minor some horrific. But with the right strategy, you can turn your life around in a second and change your destiny.

You've heard the old adage "knowledge is power," right? Well, I disagree. Knowledge is only as powerful as the extent to which it is applied. I say "Knowledge + ACTION = Results." Knowledge with no action is just *trivia*.

Foreclosure Do's and Don'ts

Do predetermine what you will do with any property you purchase. Will you sell the property right after it's purchased, commonly called "flipping" or keep the property and rent it out for positive cash flow?

Do set a goal of creating win-win situations for everyone involved in the deal.

Do enough research on areas where you are considering properties, and learn to identify your local market condition.[2] For example, if you plan to reinstate and rent, you'll look at the deal very differently than if you plan to flip the property wholesale to another investor.

Do learn how to structure your deals carefully; mistakes can be costly.

Don't become emotionally attached to a property. There may not be enough equity to make it worth your time.

Don't get greedy or arrogant. Both can make you careless, and neither of those traits are conducive to making good decisions.

Don't fleece folks by trying to squeeze every last cent of profit possible out of a deal. I promise you this: At the end of the day it feels better to take a little less money on a deal, where I helped a person avoid foreclosure and still let him walk away with some start-over capital, than to be the only one walking away fat and happy from a deal.

---

2. National and local market conditions can differ greatly. Assessing them is essential to making good investment choices. See chapters 4 to 6 of *Be a Real Estate Millionaire* for an in-depth explanation (New York: Vanguard Press, 2007).

I hope I have provided you with some new knowledge and have provoked you to take action and make a change, to create a better life—with confidence.

Knowledge + ACTION = Results–That's Power!

WAYS TO LEARN MORE

Check out the *free* online community of other investors at http://www.dean graziosi.com.

You'll find it is an amazing resource for "everything real estate investing" from *free* real estate investing forms and calculators, to free forums.

Want the complete system Dean detailed in this chapter? You can get it. To see the "plug and play" Automated Foreclosure Finder he created at his students' requests, visit www.automatedforeclosurefinder.com.

Listen in on Dean's monthly teleconference training calls on current real estate topics for *free* by visiting www.askdeang.com.

Dean Graziosi is an entrepreneur, successful investor, author, speaker, and teacher. His Think a Little Different Real Estate program and his book, *Be a Real Estate Millionaire*, have touched the lives of hundreds of thousands of people and have transformed countless lives from debt and worry to prosperity. Dean is a thriving and successful real estate investor with real estate holdings valued in the multimillions. His books, *Totally Fulfilled* and *Be a Real Estate Millionaire: Secret Strategies for Lifetime Wealth Today* are both *New York Times* best sellers.

• W. Scott SCHIRMER

20

Entitlements
The Sleeping Giant of Real Estate Profitability

S cott is my neighbor. He lives directly across the street from Kim and me. Every year, our neighborhood has a number of parties, and at every party I look forward to seeing Scott and asking him for his views on the world of money, real estate, and investing. Not only is he a neighbor, but he is a great friend, and someone I look to when I need more sophisticated information on the subject of real estate.

One aspect of real estate is politics. Being a developer, Scott needs to be tuned in to the local politics of the areas he is developing. Being a developer means he must be looking years into the future, years before he breaks ground. As some of you know, many times a worthy project—a project that will lift the value of the area—will be shot down by local neighborhood organizations that are resistant to change. This is where politics comes in.

I do not care where you live, politics and real estate go hand in hand. Local politics and politicians can improve or destroy the value of the real estate in an area. For example, at our last Christmas party, I was asking Scott about a local Arizona politician and that person's relationship to the police department. It was Scott's point of view that this politician and the police did not see eye to eye. That is why the crime in this one area was increasing and values of the property were going down. I did not invest in the area based on Scott's view of the future of this area of town. Today, many people who did invest in that once-friendly neighborhood are *losing financially as crime infects the area. This means, when I talk to Scott, I am often talking politics, but really I am discussing real estate.*

If you are to become a professional real estate investor, you must, and I do mean must, have a person like Scott who you can talk to about local politics and then talk about real estate.

—ROBERT KIYOSAKI

TIP *The current financial crisis in the United States is likely to be judged in retrospect as the most wrenching since the end of the Second World War.* —ALAN GREENSPAN, FORMER U.S. FEDERAL RESERVE CHAIR, MARCH 17, 2008

Missing from Mr. Greenspan's assessment is the other side of the coin: Those getting into a critical aspect of real estate now, who prepare for the eventual upturn, will be among the most successful in gaining wealth and security. How can that happen? This chapter will show you how to add value to real estate today—often without even owning or developing it—to capitalize on large returns tomorrow.

Whether you want to work in the area of entitlements or not, it is important that you understand this critical area of real estate. The knowledge can make you money, and it can make your life easier. Ask yourself a question: When you drive around your state or across the country, do you ever wonder who owns those acres and miles of raw land? The answer is that someone possesses every square inch of it, and it is owned by the federal government, the state, the county, the city, the Indian Nation, or a private party such as a company or an individual. Most people believe that private parties are the biggest property owners of our country. But this is not necessarily true. In Arizona, for example, only 15 percent of the land is privately owned.

Another illusion when it comes to real estate is if you own land as a private property owner, then you can do what you want with it. You own your property, you pay taxes, you buy insurance for it, and you maintain it. You own the right to do all that. But what you *do not own* is the right to do anything you want with the property. Surprised?

This is where the term *entitlement* enters the equation, and it is not a complicated concept. It simply means what you are entitled (or *"allowed"*) to do with your property as defined by the city, county, or state in which the land is located with regard to development. Those decisions are controlled by entitlements granted by the federal, state, county, or local government agencies. These agencies tell you whether your land is useable for agricultural, commercial, residential, or industrial uses. They tell you how much you can build on your property; whether you can remove vegetation; how to mitigate wildlife disturbances that exist on your property; whether you have rights to access streets, water, or sewer; and whether a septic system is permitted, along with many other governmental controls.

TIP Here is an old adage that will serve you well today and tomorrow: In reality, *owning* an asset is not as important as *controlling* an asset. And those who *entitle* an asset have the potential to obtain great profits from their endeavors.

LOVE THY NEIGHBOR?

Today, one of the most unquantifiable controlling factors that involves the use of your property is your neighbor—a factor that has historically caused owners and developers much grief. Neighbors have always held that they should have a say about what is done with the vacant lot they view over or visit, now and forever. Today more than ever, neighbors believe they have an inherent right to use a parcel of land as *they* see fit: parking, playing, cycling, jogging, walking, dumping, and controlling it, even if that vacant lot now happens to be *your* property.

Neighbors feel that when it comes to your property, whether vacant or with existing structures on it, you, the property owner, should abide by their rules and wishes. Because I've heard these complaints so often, I've given them their own name and formalized the list into: "The Top-Twenty Neighborly Complaints for Nondevelopment." Are these complaints fictitious? Believe me, I could never make this stuff up. Each one is based on a real-life situation I have experienced, and I marvel at the list every time I read it.

All developments, whether residential, commercial, or industrial, have many of the same neighborhood concerns. Commercial development adds the apprehension that you may be bringing people from other areas of the community into their neighborhood. Industrial development embodies fears about pollution and the potential hazards of large vehicles in the area. These neighbor issues have always been present but to a lesser degree than what they are today. There are two reasons for this increase in neighborly concern:

1. There has been a shift of political thought in the country from an attitude of self-reliance to an attitude of rights and entitlements. Your project might be

The Top-Twenty Neighborly Complaints for Nondevelopment

Do not change the height of the existing building, for it will hurt our privacy.

We have always walked across the land and must continue to do so.

You will disturb the habitat of existing animals, and this you must not do.

We will not be able to see over or across the land, for you will block our view.

You will create traffic, and that is unacceptable to us.

Development will overburden the number of children in the schools.

You must not change the character and compatibility of the neighborhood.

The old building that is on your property is historic; do not touch it.

There are rare biological plants that must be nurtured forever.

The apartment complex you want to develop will bring in undesirable people.

Your development will import crime into the neighborhood.

Whatever you do will not be environmentally friendly, so you may not do it.

The developer is out of state, and we are wary and suspicious.

The developer is greedy, and we are not. End of discussion.

If we let the owner develop, it should be with less density.

The owner should take less money for the property.

Any development will increase noise, and that is not good.

The lights from the development will destroy the night sky.

The city is too crowded, and we do not want anyone else in our neighborhood.

If we refuse to let you to build the roads, people will not come, and that is good.

the proper development for the site, but the neighborly feeling is, "Not in My Back Yard." (Such people are commonly referred to as NIMBYs.)

2. There has been an increase in the ability for a small group of NIMBYs or activists to organize a vocal minority of people through the Internet. The Internet has changed the political landscape. What has not changed is the axiom that a squeaky wheel does get the oil, and on the Internet a little squeaking goes a long way in creating an adverse situation between neighbors and owners.

Our society has evolved in a way that is less social in nature and more segregated geographically in political thoughts and beliefs. As someone who grew up in the Midwest, I knew all of our neighbors. We watched out for each other. I had a feeling of self-reliance, but I knew my neighbors were there for me if I needed help. And I was there for them. It was a close reflection of the Ozzie and Harriet Nelson society.

Moving to the West, I find our communities are developing in a way that segregates people. Neighbors are transient. They don't know each other. There is little feeling of community and of looking out for each other. It has forced people to push what they perceive as their "rights" onto others. The Nelsons have given way to *The Simpsons* and *Married . . . with Children*.

Assembling this disenfranchised group is easy through the Internet because it provides empowerment, and it offers pervasive access to large numbers of people almost instantaneously. This, in turn, creates a purpose for social gathering, often led by a vocal resident who feels validated to carry the cause: the self-appointed squeaky wheel.

Why have I spent time talking about this? Because whether you realize it or not, it is not your desires but the vote of the politicians to whom you present your product for approval that determines the use of your property. And it is the NIMBYs who elect and therefore influence those politicians who hold the cards.

TIP "All politics is local." —REP. TIP O'NEILL, LATE SPEAKER OF THE HOUSE

THE WORLD OF LOCAL POLITICS

Is it just me, or have politicians changed over the years? "To better serve your community" is no longer a motivation to run for office; it has become a campaign slogan void of reality. It seems that a large number of elected officials are in political office for their own personal gain. They want the office as a career; indeed, they feel as entitled to it as the neighbors who embrace a personal ownership of the property *you* own. Once such politicians have tasted the power, control and benefits of their positions, they will do whatever is necessary to keep their positions. Therefore, a small group of vocal voters do make a huge difference in the outcome of your project.

Real Life Story: The Politician Who Wasn't

As young people starting out in real estate development, my colleagues and I assembled one hundred adjoining parcels in a rundown area of Phoenix and presented a master plan for redevelopment to the Phoenix City Council for approval.

CONTINUED

CONTINUED

Two hundred people showed up to rally against the redevelopment. I remember Mayor Margaret Hance standing up in front of the angry crowd and wagging her finger, telling the crowd how good this was for the city. The project passed over neighborhood opposition. Mayor Hance was a leader, not because she voted for a project I was involved in but because she took a stand in support of a project that may have been against her own personal political interest, but that was nonetheless good for the city. She was a popular mayor in Phoenix, in part because she was recognized for her caring about the city. She was also an exceptional politician because she didn't act like one. Most of the time, you will not be dealing with that kind of leadership. You'll be dealing with quite the opposite.

Real Life Story: The Politician Who Was

Recently, I made an application for a mixed-use residential development in the city of Phoenix for my firm, M3 Companies. There was NIMBY opposition from a group that elected a councilman from the district in which this parcel was located. Before city council heard the application, this councilman announced he was against the development. He said he needed to take an early stand; that he was showing leadership. In this case, he was afraid to do what was best for the city. He wanted to appease the vocal NIMBYs for his own political gain. I'd like to say this is a rare occurrence, but it is not. You will find this behavior to be very common in today's political landscape.

ENTITLEMENTS = PROFITS

Are entitlements difficult to secure? The answer is yes. Then why not purchase property that has already been entitled? You can, and most developers do. But you can make a lot of money by entitling property for yourself or for others without the financing or capital risk that other areas of real estate require. Entitlement can be a profitable area of real estate just by relying on your learned skills. Your profits have nothing to do with how much money you have to buy real estate.

There are three secrets to entitlements that lead to success and great profitability. You will hear them from me more than once in this chapter. Please remember:

1. Knowledge
2. Knowledge
3. Knowledge

How do you obtain this knowledge? To quote from J. R. R. Tolkien (with apologies to *The Lord of the Rings*), "The tale grew in the telling." The way I gained my knowledge was by starting slowly and deliberately, and from there I worked my way to a comfort level where I could begin to take action. You can start and grow this way, too. Only I'm going to make it easier for you with my reality-based Detailed Entitlement Process. Each area is based on what I've learned, and these guidelines continue to serve me well. The remainder of this chapter is about the *Process* and it contains everything I do to profit from entitlements.

You'll find this Process to be a huge advantage as you learn. But, it will be only as valuable as your willingness to put in the time and rely on self-motivation and determination. There are no shortcuts to building a knowledge base, but there are long-term gains to be made. Give yourself at least six months to acquire the foundation necessary to succeed.

Scott's Detailed Entitlement Process

Know Your City or County Plans, Ordinances, and Ways of Doing Business

Become knowledgeable with your city's or county's goals and planning. This will help you understand what the city or town is doing or plans to do and why. You also need to understand how business is conducted to avoid rookie mistakes. Trust me, I have made them.

Your mission:

- Study the general plan for your city or town.
- Read the zoning code and ordinances.
- Learn how the "game" is played.
- Think in terms of how you can benefit the politicians, not the other way around.

Be on Top of City and Town Politics

Learn the political structure. Every city or town is governed by elected and staff individuals. (I will get to them in a minute.) Developing relationships is important. And believe it or not, mayors and council members are approachable.

Why? Because they are always looking for new people to help secure their positions and advance their self-interests. This is not cynicism; it is the way of the world. A lifelong friend of mine, Dr. Mark Horowitz, is both a businessman and

---

Real Life Story: When a Hole Is Not the Whole

I acquired a twenty-acre piece of property that was in a great location but was a massive hole. It was an eyesore to the community and was preventing a major road from being built in the area. This property would require six hundred thousand cubic yards of compacted, clean dirt to fill the hole. For reference, a large dump truck carries about eighteen cubic yards of dirt, so when I say it was a big hole, I mean it. It would take about thirty-three thousand dump truck loads to fill it!

I wanted to develop a commercial shopping center on the property, which would require that I change the zoning from residential to commercial. The city was enthusiastic and said it would support my application. I deeded the right-of-way the city needed to allow for the development of the road. That was my first major mistake. Then I made the application to rezone the property. The process would take six months. Immediately after applying for rezoning, a contractor approached me with a request to dispose of dirt from a nearby canal project he had been awarded. He would fill the hole in my property with clean, compacted dirt at no cost to me. Naturally, I thought I had hit a homerun since I would not have to pay to fill the hole.

It took the contractor three months of night-and-day hauling of dirt to fill the property. The property looked great when it was completed! That was my second mistake. Timing is everything, and as fate would have it, my rezoning request was heard before the city council a month *after* I had filled the unsightly hole. I was thrilled! I had held up my end of the bargain. As fate would also have it, at the city council hearing a number of NIMBY residents turned out to protest my application. They didn't want commercial zoning in their neighborhood.

Astonishingly, the politician who promised me his support (pre-right-of-way and pre-hole) suddenly had a change of heart and led the charge *against* my rezoning request. It turned out that with the roadway and hole problems solved in his district, he was now worried only about votes. Thanks to my fine work, he had the right-of-way for the city road, *and* he had the "eyesore" problem solved. His job was done. He had the whole enchilada!

Lesson Learned: Make sure that you receive what is promised to you *before* you perform your end of an obligation with a politician.

a scholar of early Tudor England who has spent much of his life researching and understanding the relationships between those in power and those who benefit from the powerful. In a special issue of the journal *Historical Research* commemorating the five hundredth anniversary of the death of the first Tudor king (1509–2009), Mark defines *politics* as "the pursuit of self-interest and self-preservation through the use of power." Henry VII is a model for all leaders and for those seeking benefits from them when it comes to cultivating relationships for "political" ends. Half the battle is simply showing up.

The same is true for you. For example, on Tuesday go to the planning committee meetings, and on Thursday the council meetings. In between, hold meetings with staff members and make appointments with developers. Go to their functions, help them, learn about them, and become known to them. Position yourself positively. When it comes time for you to make an application, they will all know you, which will go miles in helping you get your project approved.

TIP Remember: Those in power are motivated by self-interest and self-preservation, and they are looking for new faces and new ideas to help them with both!

These are the critical players in any city or town that you will want to get to know and that you will want to know you.

THE STAFF

The staff in the planning departments are a constant. They are government employees until they retire. Politicians, on the other hand, are elected every two or four years. Politicians and elected officials come and go. The staff in the planning department stay year after year. They play a very important role in the political support for your project.

Your mission:

- Meet the planning staff. Get to know them personally. Take them out to lunch, a cup of coffee, or play golf with them.
- Ask for their help. Make your project their idea. (Self-interests, remember?) Understand how they think.

APPOINTED BOARDS OR NEIGHBORHOOD GROUPS

Even though these groups may be informal and volunteer-based, they are powerful and should not be underestimated.

Your mission:

- Go to every neighborhood meeting.
- Get on neighborhood boards.
- Determine the leadership structure and who the decision makers are.

PLANNING COMMISSION

This usually consists of a board whose members are appointed by the elected members of the city council. Their decisions are usually advisory only, but they serve an important role as political cover to members of the city council.

Your mission:

- Go to every planning commission hearing and meet every planning commission member.
- Get to know them and learn their backgrounds.
- Make friends with them.
- Understand how they vote and determine which of them are business-friendly and which are neighborhood-friendly.
- Understand the alliances they form and why.
- Determine whose vote you need to pass your project through.
- Support their ambitions and causes.

CITY COUNCIL

This is the ultimate voting body. It will make or break your project, and it has the power to hold it up indefinitely.

Your mission:

- Go to every city council hearing.
- Meet the mayor and every city council member.
- Support them politically.
- Become their friends.
- Get to know all members and what their hot buttons are, and try pushing a few.
- Become known and trusted by them.
- Understand how they vote, and know which ones are business-friendly and which are neighborhood-friendly.
- Understand the alliances they form and why.
- Determine whose vote you need to pass your project through.

- Work on political campaigns and attend political functions.
- Go to events where they are present and make yourself visible.
- Find out the local election dates and when different members of the city council are up for re-election.

TIP When it comes to politics, you do not want to bring a controversial case before the city council within twelve months of the election of any member of the city council whose vote you will need. The politician's desire to be re-elected will work against you every time.

Does all this homework, knowledge-building, and cultivation of relationships guarantee success? The answer is yes and no. Yes, it will lead to great successes for you, because you are way ahead of the curve and therefore ahead of your competitors who do not make the time or the effort. But no, like all of life, there will be some setbacks. It is therefore important to know when to cut your losses, and I am the first to admit that despite all my success in the realm of real estate and entitlements, some things are beyond my control.

Real Life Story: Crack the Code to Corner Your Market

Some time ago, I was trying to purchase a corner that was zoned properly for the commercial retail center I wanted to develop. I had a major grocery chain interested in leasing part of the property, but the grocery store representative wanted to have a meeting with the head of the city planning department before moving forward.

At that meeting, the head of the city planning department asked the grocery store to locate to another property that was miles from my site, stating that he believed the trade area my site was located in was already adequately served, and the property he was offering had a trade area that was underserved. This is city "code" for saying that the city can generate more income from sales tax revenue by locating a business in one area over another. The city views each piece of property based on varying degrees of revenue-producing potential. Luckily in this case, the sales pitch didn't work, and the grocer ultimately located on my site due to the stability of the trade area.

Lesson Learned: Altruism usually isn't. Crack the code, and you'll understand the real motives.

STAY AHEAD OF NEIGHBORHOOD OPPOSITION

No matter what project you propose for a neighborhood, there will be neighborhood opposition. Indeed, I began this chapter giving you the Top-Twenty Neighborly Complaints. Expect these opposing views and build them into your plan. Again, knowledge is power. But as you are planning, be proactive.

Your mission:

- Study the leaders of the neighborhood opposition.
- Is it the same person or group of people who show up for every entitlement case? What are their backgrounds?
- Are they NIMBYs responding only to issues next to their neighborhood or are they full-fledged activists on zoning issues with the community at large?
- Talk to them. Listen to their issues. Become their friend.
- Do they use the Internet to communicate with one another? See if you can get on their e-mail list.
- Try to get hold of the database to be able to communicate with all of the neighbors. Then when it comes time to present your project, your message will be heard directly from you, without filtering.
- Go to every neighborhood meeting. Get on neighborhood boards.
- Set up your own Internet Web site as a proactive approach to groups or individuals both for and against your project.
- Use your Web site to educate the public about your project. Include testimonials and quotes from supporters of your project, especially neighbors. This will be a counterweight to NIMBY Web sites and help you control your message.

Most important, do not view NIMBYs as your mortal enemies, although they clearly can have an impact on your aspirations and your billfold! I approach them as citizens who want to be heard for some reason, and not necessarily the reason they may be voicing. Sometimes it can be a gripe or grievance that can be addressed without any harm to your project. Treat them with respect, and some can even be turned around to your point of view.

HAVE A TIMETABLE AND PATIENCE

Depending on the jurisdiction in which you are working, entitlements can take anywhere from six months to many years. Here is the short and the long of it:

- **Short timetable:** This comes into play only if you have the full support of all parties; it is just the actual process itself that takes time.
- **Long timetable:** If you encounter opposition to a project and/or if you have

> ## Real Life Story: Turning a Mountain into a Mole Hill
>
> One project I developed early in my career involved a residential community. The owner of the property adjoining mine believed that my property would stay vacant forever. (See Complaint No. 2 in the Top-Twenty List.) Now that I had arrived, he feared that my development would impede his view of a mountain. We talked about his concerns at length and after some homework I came back to show him how I could reorient the houses to maintain his view. (See Complaint No. 4 in the Top-Twenty List.) In effect, I converted an adversary into an advocate and the project went through.
>
> **Lesson Learned:** Compromise can turn NIMBYs into allies.

developmental issues (e.g., water rights, environmental, access, etc.), your timetable will be extended.

Realistic timetables are critical to your success for several reasons:

- You don't want your case to be heard in an election cycle.
- If you are working with a landowner and you are purchasing the property subject to receiving entitlements by a fixed date, you don't want to run out of time with your seller and be unentitled: You will have invested too much time, effort, and money to get to this point.
- The market cycle in real estate may pass you by.
- The capital markets change. The supply of money, interest rates, and underwriting criteria may change.

GET TO KNOW THE DEVELOPERS AND BUILDERS

Just as you have met every staffer and every committee and council member at city hall, meet every developer and builder that makes an application. Call them on the phone and make an appointment to learn about their projects. Meet them at all hearings. They will be enthusiastic to tell you about their projects because they will want your support.

Your mission:

When you speak with the developers and builders, seek to answer the following questions:

- What are the opposition's issues, and how are you, the developer or builder, overcoming those objections?

- What third-party vendors are you using? These may include the following: land planner, architect, civil and structural engineer, zoning attorney, traffic engineer, contractor, and their subcontractors.
- Who does your soils report, and who performs your environmental studies?
- What title company and escrow officer do you use?
- What real estate broker are you using?

After attending a number of meetings, you'll have a good idea of the vendors who do quality work and can perform on time. These vendors will become invaluable to you when the time comes to put your own team together. Think of the education you will be getting from actual practitioners. And it's free!

UNDERSTAND WHAT DEVELOPERS AND BUILDERS WANT

To repeat: *Knowledge* is your most important asset. I made getting it a point early on in my career and continue it to this day. When it comes to developers and builders, I try to find out everything I can from each type. I want to know as much as I can about single-family, multifamily, retail, office, industrial, or mixed-use development. These developers and builders are putting their knowledge, reputation, and capital on the line. Why not learn as much as you can from them? All of these resources are coming to the city seeking approvals. It's a "knowledge vein" that is yours for the mining and is much better than school-based education. This is the real world, and that is where money is made. Your only impediment to success is your own lack of effort in mining this knowledge.

TIP Builders want to acquire *entitled* property! Hence, you are of great value to them, and they will pay for that value.

Entitlements involve all types of real estate: apartment buildings, residential, commercial, medical, mixed use. The key is to be aware of the specific requirements of each and understand the differences. Then, learn as much as you can about similar projects and how they have been entitled.

Here are the questions that I have asked of developers and builders. This will get you started and will help expand your knowledge base for planning your first project.

Your mission:

Ask residential builders these questions:

- What size lots do you want to develop. Why that size?
- What are the setback distances from the front, back, and side yards?

A Few Truths About Buyers and Builders

- A new home buyer is sold on a home before he or she walks in the front door.
- The streetscape of the subdivision, landscaping, and the elevation of the home are most important for the sale.
- School districts matter. Locate your residential developments in the best ones.
- Cities with the best images may be more expensive but create the most security for your investment.
- See if the builder will share his infrastructure costs with you. Find out:
  - On average, how much is the cost to engineer the subdivision to a recorded plat? This is called "paper lots."
  - How much does it cost on a per lot basis to construct the streets, sewer, water, common area amenities, and landscaping?
- It's good to know how much it will cost a homebuilder to improve a single family lot. Builders will pay 20 to 25 percent of the sales price of the home for an improved lot.

- What are the sizes of the homes you are building?
- How many phases do you plan for? How many lots per phase?
- How many lots do you need in order for you to develop a model home complex? Where do you like to locate your models within the subdivision? Why?

Beyond just asking questions, visit their subdivisions. Go through their model homes. Talk to the salespeople. Find out what are the most sought-after home features buyers ask for, and why. By knowing the kind of product they build, you'll be in a better position to provide them the entitled land they are looking for down the road.

Your mission:

Ask apartment builders these questions (the same as above, plus these additional):

- What density do you like to build? Usually it is fourteen to twenty-one units per acre, depending on the city and projected rental rate of the project.
- How many units does it take to make a project operationally feasible?
- What do you pay per unit (referred to as per door) for a piece of property that is entitled?
- What unit mix—one-, two- or three-bedroom units—are best for the market?
- What size—one-, two-, or three-bedroom units—do residents want most? What is the best mix?

- What rental rates does the market accept?
- What amenities are being offered and why?
- How many parking spaces per unit does the city require versus the market demand?
- What is the land size necessary for the density needed to operate and park properly?
- Are there any specific lighting, trash locations, and noise abatement issues?
- What kind of vehicle and pedestrian integration into the adjoining neighborhoods is needed?
- What about schools and crime?

YOUR FIRST PROJECT AND JUMP-START GAME PLAN

After six months of hard work, you now possess the three secrets to entitlements that can lead to great success, and you should be able to rapid-fire repeat them by now:

1. Knowledge
2. Knowledge
3. Knowledge

Gaining these assets has brought you to this point, and no one can take your knowledge from you. You can succeed or fail using other types of "capital," but your best chance of success in entitlements is directly proportional to your knowledge "capital."

TIP Principal Rule: Use your knowledge base as capital to create value.

Your mission:

Put into action my Jump-Start Game Plan to get your first project off the ground.

SCOTT'S JUMP-START GAME PLAN

1. From the knowledge you have gained, you can put together the best team of third-party vendors, such as surveyors, land planners, environmental companies, etc. Quality and reliability are key.
2. You know which areas of the community are sought after the most. Ask your real estate broker to map out vacant land or redevelopment opportunities in this area. Try to locate in a popular school district.

3. Compare your prospective sites to the city's general plan.

4. From your learned knowledge, work with your land planner in developing a plan which will be marketable to a buyer upon receiving entitlements.

5. Because you learned from the builders what they are willing to pay for entitled property, apply that number to the value of the property.

6. From that price, subtract the following:

   –The cost of the land.

   –Unusual or extra costs of construction required for the property you are considering. This might include rocky or expansive soil conditions, bringing in utilities to the property, undergrounding power lines or irrigation ditches.

   –The cost of your team's work to entitle the property.

   –Your cost of resale, brokerage fees, and title work.

7. If you are successful in entitling the property, this total will be the profit you earn for your knowledge and hard work. Determine if that bottom line is acceptable to you for your time and effort and cost of planning.

8. Meet with the people you are now familiar with in the city's planning department. Ask what use and density they would recommend for each property you have potentially selected. See if it matches your estimate.

9. Narrow the scope of your search to the most profitable properties if they were entitled for what you want and what the city staff would recommend.

10. Work with the landowner of the property you want to purchase. The landowner already has his capital in the land. Find out the motivation behind the landowner's desire to sell. If you can meet the seller's need, you might be able to get enough time to purchase the property subject to getting it entitled. Again, your profit is the value you create through entitlements.

Real Life Story

Be prepared for unusual requirements or actions that often defy logic. You will be exposed to every imaginable roadblock for your project, from underground mice to crashing airplanes! Do not be discouraged. I have encountered the most outrageous hurdles. Approach them with tenacity, and later you'll have great stories that will keep everyone laughing.

Hurdle No. 1, or the Mouse That Roared We were working on a master-planned development in Colorado. The fish and game department was concerned that an endangered animal known as a Preble's mouse might exist on the property.

CONTINUED

CONTINUED

Unfortunately, the only way to prove that supposition was to catch mice, kill them, and check their DNA for a match, thus potentially endangering the endangered species in the process. The department decided that we needed to set aside property within the development to provide habitat, just in case the mouse existed. Moreover, they told us that we had to impose a ban on the ownership of cats by residents since they might hunt and kill the mouse, should it exist. (This is no joke!) Through negotiations, we were able to change the department's requirement from forbidding cats entirely to making it a requirement in the Convenants, Conditions and Restrictions (CC&Rs) of the community that any cats residing in our community would have to remain indoors. We complied, fully realizing that this was the political solution to a problem. Commissioners, developer, residents, and mice were all happy campers.

Hurdle No. 2, or Sinking the Boat to See If It Floats We wanted to subdivide 620 acres in Santa Barbara County, California. It was an area where water was scarce and permits were rationed for homes. However, we had three wells on the property, and the hydrology reports concluded that there was more than enough water for the development. The county determined the reports to be insufficient and decided that, despite the scarcity of water in the area, they would need to measure the water in the wells by letting the water run into ditches . . . for an entire year! At the end of the year, and at great cost and enormous loss of water, it was determined that in fact there would be sufficient water for the development.

Hurdle No. 3, or Playing It Straight For a seemingly simple single-family residential subdivision with improved lots, we proposed a layout that was a little out of the ordinary. It involved adding curves to roads rather than creating a straight grid plan where houses lined up like barracks. The staff for this city said the plan was unacceptable. "Why?" we asked. It was then that the city informed us that elderly people who might not be able to make the subtle turns could be driving the streets. They could run off the road. (We call this protecting every issue that isn't an issue.) We countered by saying that elderly people can make a subtle turn, and that if they cannot they shouldn't be driving. Moreover, like the mouse in Colorado, no one knew if in fact there was a problem to begin with, in this case regarding the street design. The staff would not compromise, and the streets were built perfectly straight. In fairness, we believe no elderly people have run off any of the roads to date.

Hurdle No. 4, or It's a Bird! It's a Plane! It's You're Kidding, Right? A vacant piece of land was already developed on three sides. The fourth side fronted on a major road. We designed a small residential subdivision with one access point. The city didn't like this plan because they wanted two access points, which in fact was physically impossible to accomplish. Why two access points? One city staff member offered this explanation: "What if an airplane crashed in the entryway of the project? How will the fire department get in and save the people?" My response was plain and truthful: "They wouldn't get in, and everyone would die." Of course, it is an absurdity to think that you can plan or respond to every event that more than likely will never happen. Moreover, even with two access points, the fire department, under these circumstances, wouldn't be able to save anyone anyway. The result: We took the staff's objection and went to the city council, which overruled the staff and approved the subdivision. Indeed, they saw the logic to our plan. I am happy to report that after thirty years, maybe a few birds, but no airplane has crashed into the subdivision. No meteorites have, either.

Lesson Learned: Prepare to get very good at jumping hurdles ... calmly.

KNOW THE POWER OF CONTROL VS. OWNERSHIP

Remember, control of a piece of property is as effective as owning it, with the additional benefit of minimizing your risk. If you purchase a piece of property before it is entitled, you will need to think about the following factors that could impact your investment:

- Capital. You'll need either your own or your investors to purchase the property.
- Risk. You risk the capital invested if your entitlements are unsuccessful.
- Unprofitability. Your cost of capital and interest may eliminate any potential future profits.
- Marketability. You now have an unentitled property that you may not be able to sell.

You may be wondering why would a seller give you the time to go through the entitlement process without risking any money. There are some very valuable reasons. First, you can offer the seller more money than his property is presently worth, which is obviously appealing. You can do this because, remember, if you purchased the property outright, you would be paying interest on the capital used to purchase the property so you might as well give that to the seller in the form of an increase in price.

Another reason a seller would allow you the time needed to gain the entitlements relates to taxes. If the seller sold the property, most likely he or she would pay capital gains tax on the sale (currently 15 percent federal tax, plus state tax). Then, when that money is reinvested and earning interest, that interest would be taxed as ordinary income (up to 38 percent under current law for federal income tax plus state and local taxes). If you offered the seller more money for their property to "buy" the time to get the entitlements and close the deal thereafter, the seller will be paying tax at the much lower capital gains rates instead of the higher ordinary tax rates.

Another incentive is offering to give the seller the survey, environmental report, soils report, traffic study, utility study, land plan, and title work you are doing as compensation for the time if you are not successful with entitlements and do not purchase the property. The seller will need those studies anyway with another buyer, and that information will decrease the time and up-front money needed by a new buyer. This information is worthless to you if you are not successful.

You can even find out if the seller will pay for the reports mentioned above. You can offer the seller an increased price for the land and a percentage of the increased value you are creating from your knowledge and entitlement work. Since you don't have to pay for the reports, now you don't have any capital at risk and only upside potential with the increased value you will be creating through entitlements. This is the best real estate position to be in.

Time can also be a blessing when a seller wants to find an exchange property before closing the sale of the current property, so there is no exposure to the strict time constraints for a 1031 Exchange. By giving you time to get the entitlements, the seller gets more time to search for another property investment. Exchanges must be executed within a specified period, and this allows the luxury of time most sellers would love to have.

Finally, a seller may want to be a part of the development on his property. The property may have been in the family for generations. There may be family pride regarding what is developed on the land. The motivation of a seller will either be monetary or family legacy.

AN AGREEABLE AGREEMENT—FOR YOU

Have your real estate attorney draft a standard Letter of Intent (LOI) for you to use with each seller. An LOI outlines the terms and conditions of a sale, is usually a nonbinding agreement but is used as a "gentlemen's handshake."

Once you have an executed LOI, ask your attorney to draft a purchase agreement for execution using the signed LOI as your guide. Make sure you have the right within the agreement to rezone the subject property for your intended use. Once the purchase agreement is signed, you have the property under your control. I repeat: It is not what you own that leads to wealth generation, it is what you control.

Once the purchase agreement is signed by all parties, open escrow with the title company and escrow officer you have learned to be the most reliable. Have the title company give you a title report with all recorded easements and liens and the requirements for an extended or lender's title policy.

Your mission:

- Have your real estate attorney draft an LOI.
- Execute the LOI with the seller.
- Have your real estate attorney draft a purchase agreement with the appropriate provisions from the LOI, particularly the right to rezone the property.
- Get the agreement signed. You now control the property.
- Open escrow and get the title report.

SOME DILIGENCE IS DUE

It is important to continue growing your knowledge base to protect your investment and avoid unwanted surprises. Consider these steps:

Your mission:

- Review your title report with the help of your title company. Make sure there are no recorded Covenants, Conditions or Restrictions (CC&Rs) recorded against the property that would affect your intended use.
- Check for deed restrictions that would affect ownership or use of the property.
- Read the recorded easements and understand who has the right of access. Make sure you have legal access to your property.
- See if there are any assessments recorded against your property that you will become responsible for.
- Study who has the rights to the minerals on the property.
- Give the title report and all recorded documents to your civil engineer to create an ALTA Builders/Lenders Survey.
- Once you have control of the property, have your team's real estate agent contact potential buyers for the property subject to your acquiring the entitlements. Don't think of a good real estate broker as a cost. Rather, he or she

is a valuable member of the team. A good broker has developed creditability over many years with builders and buyers. This will help ensure your success. If the deal can't afford the real estate fee, don't do the deal.

- Work with that builder/buyer in the planning process. Do not plan your property around one buyer unless that person has paid you a sizeable, non-refundable deposit if you are successful in entitling your property and he does not perform. If planned around one buyer, you might ultimately receive the entitlement but no one else can use the plan.

Real Life Story: Removing Rocks from Your Soil May Be Mining

Recently, M3 Companies were involved in moving 6 million cubic yards of dirt on one of our two-thousand-acre master-planned communities. We were not selling the dirt or rock during the grading process but simply sifting the dirt to eliminate rocks for the golf course. We also crushed the larger rocks on site to a more manageable size.

By chance, a representative of the Bureau of Land Management (BLM)—a federal governmental agency—was driving by the site and noticed what we were doing. When he returned to his office he wrote us a letter saying we owed the BLM a royalty right for mining the minerals on the property since it owned these rights from the original governmental patent.

Almost every development crushes rocks on site and moves earth materials and screens soil. We explained that we weren't moving any material off-site or selling it, and therefore we did not believe we were mining minerals on the property. They replied to our argument that if we picked the rocks out of the soil by hand, instead of using machines, they don't consider it mining. The rocks were far too big for that.

Never before had they imposed this requirement on any other development of this scope. We ultimately negotiated a settlement with them to avoid the costly delays in construction and litigation.

Lesson Learned: Expect the unexpected, and bone up on your negotiation skills.

SURVEYS AND REPORTS

The next step is securing a lender's survey, which shows all of the recorded title report issues such as easements, property lines, and net/gross acreage/square footage. It also outlines unrecorded roads and encroachments, legal descriptions, etc. It is used as the basis for all other planning on the property.

Your land planner will use the survey's information for computing acreage and for laying out everything that you do. It is your foundation. Below is a guide you can use during this important phase.

Your mission:

- Review your survey to see if there are any encroachments such as fences, structures, etc., that your neighbors have on your property or you have on theirs.
- See if anyone is using unrecorded access points on your property or unrecorded paths and roads across your property that may be a claim for adverse possession by the using party. This may restrict financing and ability to develop.
- Determine if there are any power and gas line easements and how that may affect the usability and marketability of your property.
- Make sure your engineer includes floodplain information on the survey.
- Give the survey to your land planner to help you develop a land plan and layout.

I never rely on my land planner's input only. I've found my learned knowledge and research is just as important to the final product. There is a belief, with some merit, that you design for a plan with a greater intensity and density than you really need so you can cut back at a later date. Why? So that the NIMBYs and politicians can feel they have pushed the developer back and got their way. You are catering to today's political correctness.

Your learned knowledge will tell you whether you should bring in a representative of the NIMBY group to be part of the land planning process. It is always better to have the NIMBYs as part of the planning process.

- Be prepared to cover your third-party vendors with liability insurance when they go upon the land of your seller to do their work. I would recommend that you provide at least $1 million of coverage. This insurance is relatively inexpensive.
- In addition, get these reports done up front. There's no point in waiting.

A SOILS REPORT

A soils report determines if there are any soil conditions that will increase the cost to build on the property and therefore lessen the price someone can pay for the property. Some sites have expansive soil that would increase the cost of construction. Some sites have hard rock and may need to be blasted. That would increase cost, too. If you were going to use septic tanks instead of city sewers, your soil condition might not meet the peculation requirements. Some sites even have underground fissures that are not readily determined. How important is a soils report? I have a true story.

> ## Real Life Story: Low-Cost Property Can Be Very Costly
>
> During the frenzy of the recent soaring real estate cycle, a buyer purchased nine hundred acres of land at a low price with the intent to "flip" it for a profit. The buyer came to me to help him after he had bought the property. The buyer did not order a soils report during the due diligence period prior to him buying the property. If he had, he would have realized that the soil was very expansive. That particular soil condition would make the foundation work for each house so cost-prohibitive that the homes would have been priced out of the market. Sadly, although the land was acquired at good price, the actual cost of the property was very high due to the increased development costs to mitigate the poor soil conditions. There wasn't much I could do. The buyer could have avoided all this by doing homework . . . and getting a soils report!
>
> **Lesson Learned:** Soil matters. Never skimp on things that cost little and can save you a bundle.

A PHASE I ENVIRONMENT REPORT

This report will show you if your property is located within a Superfund site area, or if there are any environmental issues recorded on adjoining properties that may affect your property. It would include such things as a previous gas station on the adjoining property that had a fuel tank leak, which is now flowing under your property.

If any issues are discovered, you'll receive a recommendation to do a Phase II. This is more expensive and extensive. Laboratory testing will determine if contamination exists and what remediation methods need to be used. The remediation of environmental issues is often next to impossible to quantify. If your Phase I report comes back with a recommendation for Phase II, back away from the property . . . do not look back, and most of all *do not* move forward on any property with environmental issues at this stage of your career. And one more thing. If your proposed property is in a rocky, granite area, you should have your environmental engineer do a radon gas study to see if there is a need for mitigation.

A CONSTRAINTS REPORT

Besides doing the survey, have your civil engineer prepare a constraints report on the property. This will be a study of all the utilities to service the property. It will include water, sewers, telephone, gas, electric, cable, fiber optics, and storm sewers.

This study will show the location, capacity, water pressure, service providers, and methods of access to these services. It will also ascertain whether you are going to incur extra development costs by resizing existing utilities to serve your development or extending utility lines to provide these services to your property.

Have your engineer provide any Utility Development Fees and Utility Recovery Charges/Agreements in their report.

A DRAINAGE REPORT

This report will determine if you have any 404 issues. These are federal regulations by the Army Corp of Engineers on all navigable waterways. Don't think you need a stream on your property to come under this jurisdiction. It may be only an irrigation ditch. You also want to determine if there are any excess costs for retention, detention, or runoff of water from your property.

ARCHEOLOGICAL STUDY

If you are in an area that has artifacts or where artifacts are believed to exist, you should do an archeological study. Just because you are far away from a colonial settlement or an ancient Native American village does not mean that "something" may not be buried on your property.

Real Life Story: Unfortunately the Builder Didn't Strike Gold

A home builder was well into the development of his project when he discovered artifacts while digging water and sewer lines. The project was immediately put on hold—for eighteen months—while archaeologists, tiny picks and brushes in hand, meticulously uncovered and retrieved the artifacts. It almost bankrupted the builder because his capital costs, debt payments, contracts with vendors, and other cash outlays were dependent on his completion of the project on time. An archeological study in advance of development may have prevented this calamity.

Lesson Learned: If it *can* happen, it just might. Don't tempt fate.

FAA (FEDERAL AVIATION ADMINISTRATION) REVIEW

Make sure the FAA has not imposed any restrictions on your property. Is it located out of the noise zone and flight paths? It's a good idea to be sure.

WELLS

Check to see if there are any water wells on the property and if they have been properly recorded with the State Department of Water Resources. Also check to see if there are any historical records on the depth of the well, pumping capacity, and draw down of the water table. Make sure all abandoned wells are closed properly.

THE APPLICATION

We're getting close now. You can begin to see the light at the end of the tunnel, assuming that all your reports came back positive and you didn't have to "back away from the environmental hazards" or anything else. It's time to make an application for the entitlement you are requesting. Every jurisdiction has different requirements. Some may require a traffic study, drainage study, landscape design, or letter from the school district on the impact of your proposed development on schools. Spend money only on the reports as are necessary.

Your mission:

- Take your plan door to door and give every neighbor within six hundred feet of your project a personal presentation of your plan. Bring with you:
    - A full-color site plan and renderings of your development.
    - Traffic information generated by your development.
    - Letter of support from the school district.
    - Your business card and contact information.
    - A petition for the neighbor to sign in support of your project.
    - Printed cards giving the location, times, and dates of hearings, and the names, phone numbers, and e-mail addresses of the mayor and city council members.
- Start your presentation with the neighbors farthest from your project. They may be the least interested. You will have a better chance to get their signature on a petition of support.
- Use those signed petitions of support when asking the next neighbor for his support. Keep building those support petitions for your presentation to the neighbors that are closest to the project and to show to members of the city council. Give only those supportive neighbors your printed cards with the times and dates of the hearings.

How to Talk with the Neighbors

It's easy to make mistakes when talking with neighbors. Follow these guidelines and you should come out without incident:

Things You Should Do

• Dress neatly and be enthusiastic about your project.

• Always be polite.

• Present facts and be honest.

• Be prepared to answer objections.

• Listen. Don't debate.

• Make friends and develop relationships.

• If you do not know an answer to a question, return to personally give an answer. It gives you another chance to develop a relationship.

• Be proud of what you are doing.

• Ask for support and get contact information.

• Communicate with your neighbors.

• Ask supportive neighbors to invite their friends to a small meeting so you can explain your project.

• Get petitions of support signed. Ask supportive neighbors to be at the hearings. Have dates, times, and locations of meetings ready as a handout that you can distribute.

• Ask for them to e-mail and call city council members expressing their support. Have that information available to give to them as a handout.

• Get the support of the Chamber of Commerce, Homebuilders Association, and Board of Realtors.

Things You Should Not Do

• Do not leave any project information behind except for your business card and hearing information, and give it only to supportive neighbors. You may need to change your site plan while you are going through the process. If you leave your initial site plan behind, you will be accused of being deceitful by your neighbors if it changes in process.

• Do not exaggerate your project.

• Do not have group meetings initially. Group psychology is more difficult to cope with than handling individual concerns.

• Do not allow your differences with neighbors to become a matter of principle.

• Do not threaten neighbors with alternate uses, but point out to them the range of possibilities for which the land could be developed.

AT THE SAME TIME . . .

Continue to call upon all of the people you have met over the previous six months, including your friends on the city planning staff, on the community boards, the planning commission, and the city council. Try to get the leaders within each group to support your project. Use that support and visit with every member of each group. This is very important.

Politicians you have developed relationships with want to help you, but you need to give them the political reasons to support you, including narrowing the objections of the NIMBYs. Let the politicians know if there is neighborhood opposition, what objections they have and what you are doing to resolve their issues.

A politician always needs to understand why it is in his or her political interest to support you in the face of opposition: self-interest and self-preservation! Being prepared for this through your previous six months' worth of studying how the politician has reacted to other cases before you made your application, you will have insight into the right answer almost instinctively.

Remember, the vote that counts is the vote of the city council. Know that you have the votes that are required for approval before you allow your application to be heard for a final vote. Postpone the hearing until you have the votes committed.

THE END GAME

What are the best-case scenarios for all your hard work?

- Your acquired knowledge and relationship-building will help you obtain the right to purchase property you will entitle.
- You will get your property entitled, creating value.
- You will have a builder buy the property, with you profiting from the difference between the negotiated price from the landowner and your markup for entitling it.
- You will have succeeded by applying your knowledge, and not your capital.

TIP Remember: *You don't have to own a piece of property; you just have to control it.*

KNOWLEDGE, KNOWLEDGE, KNOWLEDGE

Starting small is the way to learn. But what you'll soon discover is that the size of the project is meaningless. You will go through all of the same steps for a small project as you would for a large project. That means the bigger projects have the potential to net you more money with the same amount of effort. It's just a matter of building confidence.

The M3 Companies have taken this direction, using our expertise in the planning, entitlement, and execution of master-planned communities from our learned knowledge over four decades of work. From developing a 610-acre American Ranch community in Prescott, an 1,100-acre Prescott Lakes community, and the 2,100-acre Wickenburg Ranch community (all in Arizona), to the 2,000-acre American Ranch Sandstone community outside Denver and our 6,000-acre community in Eagle, Idaho, we have taken advantage of our entitlement knowledge to succeed.

But make no mistake—you will make a lot of mistakes. Everyone does. Cut your losses short and let your gains run. Your own drive is the only limit to your success.

THE FUTURE

What is the future for someone who specializes in entitling real estate? We can count on governmental bodies to continue to impede property rights with each new law, regulation, ordinance, and environmental mandate. It becomes harder and harder each year to navigate through this minefield, and there are fewer people willing to make the attempt. Yet the demand from development companies and builders for entitled property increases each year: In adversity there is advantage and opportunity for those willing to pursue entitlements.

And what is the key? Knowledge. It is the knowledge you will gain that will make you one of the most sought after "properties" in the real estate industry. You can work for yourself, consult for others, or be in an executive position with a development company. Entitlements are the future of real estate. This chapter has given you the tools to create that future for yourself.

Knowledge is your capital when it comes to entitlements. But unlike other forms of capital such as cash, equity, or debt, *your capital* can never be taken away. And it can only grow and help you succeed.

Most important: Your capital is most valuable when the economy is in a recession. Sellers of properties are more receptive to giving you the time to entitle their property. Lenders who have taken properties back need someone with the knowledge to prepare their properties for resale. Why? Because you can *add value* to property that is losing value in the marketplace. That makes you indispensable, sought after, and in a very profitable position for yourself.

It takes many months to entitle a piece of property for development or for resale. Use the downtime of a recession to entitle a property. When the recession ends, as it always does, you will be ready immediately to take advantage of the recovery because your property is ready for development. It is called *great timing*.

Friends in High Places During Low Times

During a recession, you can process your application more quickly because the city staff has very few applications to process. Furthermore, it is more difficult for political leaders to turn your project down in the face of growing municipal deficits. Don't forget, landowners are willing to give you the time to work on entitlements. They need you!

My last words of wisdom are these: Be a contrarian. In a recession, people focus on their jobs, the economy, and the stock market. They rarely see an opportunity to take advantage of what only appears to be a dismal situation. When no one is investing money, when no one can borrow money, and when equity is disappearing on properties, keep this in mind: You have the most valuable capital during this period—your knowledge.

Let others spend their time looking backward and protecting their current declining assets. You will be using your time pursuing the Sleeping Giant of real estate profitability: entitlements. It's time to get going.

W. Scott Schirmer is a managing partner for M3 Companies. M3 Companies' core competency is developing master-planned communities that honor and advance the timeless heritage of the West. Schirmer is president of Schirmer Ball Company and CEO of SMDI Company. Since he began working in Arizona real estate in the late 1960s, he has entitled, acquired, syndicated, financed, developed, managed, and brokered real estate in Arizona, California, Idaho, Illinois, Oklahoma, and Utah. Schirmer and the M3 Companies charities are children-based, giving support to Childhelp, The Boys and Girls Club of Scottsdale, SARC, ANOZIRA Foundation, and The Solid Rock Foundation.

21

The Tax Lien
Investment Strategy

Tom Wheelwright is one of those people who is not just an expert in a very important aspect of investing, he is an investor himself who practices what he preaches. I like to surround myself with people like Tom because they don't just talk about what others should do; they actually do what they say. Tom is a CPA—a tax strategist who knows that the government rewards people who know the tax code and play by its rules—and he is also a real estate investor.

Tom has spent more than twenty-five years working with sophisticated investors to help them develop innovative tax, business, and wealth strategies. Tom is a teacher at heart, and even in his early days when he worked for a Big 4 accounting firm, he managed the training for thousands of CPAs. He makes the complicated simple, and that is no easy feat because, in order to do this, it takes a complete understanding of your subject and an ability to boil down the details to the ones that matter. Tom's skill comes from his years as a trainer and from his firm grasp of taxation and tax strategies.

But Tom has influenced my life in a much more profound way than just through his knowledge of wealth strategies. If you read my introduction to Chapter 1, Tom's first chapter, then you know I mentioned his Mormon faith. Through Tom and others like him, I have learned much about the beliefs of this faith. His religion has many important lessons to share with a world that is in financial turmoil.

One lesson that comes from the Mormon faith and that seemed odd before, now doesn't seem quite so odd. That lesson is the Mormon practice of storing enough food, water, and money to survive for at least one year. Many of my Mormon friends do this, and so do my wife, Kim, and I. We put these necessities away in case of economic disaster, or worse, financial collapse. How close did we come in 2008?

We are all used to a world of plenty and don't think twice about what we would do for food and other necessities in an emergency. As many of us know, our supermarkets only have enough food to last three days. And if you have ever lived in an area that is hurricane prone, and the forecast is predicting a storm on the way, you know how quickly the most critical supplies are snatched up. Water, bread, canned goods, batteries, and other vital supplies vanish from the store shelves in a matter of hours.

In 2008 the world came very close to becoming a world of collapsed credit cards. Think about this for a while: What would happen if the world stopped accepting credit cards? What could you buy with only the cash you have on hand, the money in your wallet, the change in that jar? Not much. I believe the world would shut down.

Of course I don't wish for financial disaster, but Tom has taught me about preparation. And being prepared allows me to keep my mind free of worry, to think clearly, even as we enter a period of economic chaos, and to seize the opportunities. These are the times when fortunes are made.

Tom has been an influence to me on many levels, and I honor his integrity. This chapter and the knowledge he shares is a must read for anyone seizing investment opportunities now and in the future. I greatly value him personally and professionally. He is a true friend.

—ROBERT KIYOSAKI

If you have even taken a quick glance at the chapter titles in this book, or considered its sheer size, then you are probably realizing there are as many ways to invest in real estate as there are models of homes. The key, of course, is to invest in the type of real estate that best suits you and your personal investing preferences. Your investment preferences may include risk level, tax advantages, and simplicity, among others.

For example, some people prefer investing in single-family homes because they like the simplicity, and there isn't a lot of management involved. Others prefer commercial real estate so they have to manage only a few properties and can deal with business owners as tenants instead of dealing with families. Still others prefer to invest in apartment buildings where the loss of a single tenant doesn't make a major impact on the overall cash flow from the investment. And then there are those who prefer to invest in raw land where there are no tenants at all.

So before you begin investing in real estate, take some time to figure out which type of real estate is best for you based on your personal investing preferences. You are likely to be more successful by doing something you enjoy. And, of course, it makes life a lot more fun!

The question I get most often from investors just starting out in real estate is how to decide which type of real estate investing is right for them. Again, remember to focus on your personal investment preferences. For a complete list of the personal investment preferences we review with our clients, go to our ProVision School of Wealth Strategy at www.ProVisionWealth.com/products.

Once you have figured out your personal investment preferences, it's time to figure out which type of real estate investing most closely matches these preferences. This book is a great place to do some initial analysis of the different types of real estate investing.

One of the least known and most lucrative real estate investments is known as tax lien investing. Some of the best bargains in real estate are found through these tax liens. At ProVision, we have several clients who have made millions of dollars investing in tax liens. Let me start by giving you a brief explanation of how tax liens work. Then, we can discuss whether tax lien investing is right for you and if it is, which tax lien investment strategy might work best.

WHAT'S TAX LIEN INVESTING?

Tax liens are investments made possible by state law. Governments love to use tax money, but they really don't like being in the tax collection business. And they especially don't like to be bankers. Governments want their money now, so they can balance their budgets. So they have a serious challenge when a taxpayer, for whatever reason, decides not to pay his property taxes on a particular parcel of real estate. In fact, sometimes it takes years to collect the taxes from the owner of the property, and sometimes the owner never pays the taxes owed. As much as governments hate being the bank, they hate being property owners even more. What they really want is the cash, and they want it now.

So instead of becoming a creditor of the property owner and waiting for the money until the taxpayer ponies up, many local governments (usually counties) have figured out how to get their money immediately. It's called a tax lien. In the simplest terms, here's what happens:

1. The government assesses taxes on a piece of property, which is called a parcel. In most cases, the owner will simply pay the taxes that are due.
2. But what if the owner of the land decides not to pay the taxes on time? Then what happens?
3. The government puts a lien on the parcel for back taxes.
4. Then the government sells the lien to an investor, such as you or me. The lien is sold at a public auction with an opening bid made up of the amount of back taxes and other costs.
5. If the lien is sold at auction, multiple investors bid on the lien. Although variation exists among tax lien states, there are some general similarities. First, all primary sales must be held in a public auction and ordinary citizens like you and me may take part in the sale. Some states use a process in which the price of the lien is bid up (i.e., increased) based on competition for the lien. In this situation, the price paid for the lien may be bid higher, but the interest rate earned on the tax lien remains fixed and does not fluctuate due to the bidding. Other states use a bid down system. In this situation, the interest rate earned on a tax lien is bid down by the bidders. The standard interest rate on tax liens varies among states but can be as high as 18 percent.
6. The lien earns simple interest based on the standard rate or auction final bid rate.
7. The interest "accrues" (accumulates) until either the taxpayer or another lienholder (such as a bank holding a mortgage) ultimately pays the interest and the back taxes to the investor in order to have the lien on his property removed.
8. After a certain period of time if the lien is not paid, the investor can foreclose against the property and can end up owning the property outright for only the price of the back taxes and foreclosure/legal fees.

TABLE 21.1 Summary of a Tax Lien

Step 1	Property owner does not pay taxes due on the property (parcel)
Step 2	The government places a lien on the parcel for back taxes
Step 3	The lien is offered for sale at a fixed interest rate or at auction
Step 4	If lien is sold at auction, multiple investors bid on the interest rate of the lien
Step 5	The lien earns simple interest based on the standard or auction rate
Step 6	The interest accrues until the property owner or another lienholder pays the back taxes
Step 7	If the lien is not paid, the investor can foreclose against the property and own the property for the price of the back taxes

The great thing about foreclosing on a tax lien is that a tax lien supersedes nearly all other liens. So if you are able to foreclose on a tax lien, you get the property for the cost of the unpaid taxes, and in the majority of situations, any other liens are wiped out. Pretty cool, huh? Well, at least it *can be* in the right circumstance, but more about that later. In any case, there are several important steps to investing in a tax lien, and we are going to take them one at a time.

STEP NO. 1: YOUR TAX LIEN STRATEGY

So there are two possible outcomes of investing in a tax lien. First, and most likely, is the outcome that you will earn interest at a stated rate that can be as high as 18 percent. The other possible outcome is that the lien is never paid off (redeemed) and you get the property. These two outcomes are the basis for the two different tax lien investing strategies.

TABLE 21.2 Possible Outcomes

A	You earn interest at a stated rate, or
B	The lien never gets paid and you get the property

While it may seem to be the luck of the draw whether a tax lien is redeemed or not, in fact there are several factors that can give a strong indication of which outcome is likely to occur. Because of this, anyone investing in tax liens should first decide how tax lien investing fits into his investment strategy. Do you want the interest, or is your goal the underlying property?

TABLE 21.3 Investment Strategy

Strategy A	Strategy B
☐ I want interest paid	☐ I want the property

You really must decide what you hope to get out of your tax lien investment up front because this decision will affect everything else you do pertaining to tax lien investing. Why? Primarily because the type of property for which you are willing to buy the lien is going to differ based on the interest rate investment strategy versus the property acquisition investment strategy. The type of property owner will also be a factor, since some property owners are more likely to pay their liens than others. So let's look at why you would choose one strategy over the other.

THE INTEREST RATE INVESTMENT STRATEGY

In actuality, interest rate investing and property acquisition investing are almost completely opposite investment strategies. The interest rate investment strategy is a fairly short-term, cash-flow strategy with little or no possibility for long-term growth. This may be a good place to park some cash at high interest rates while you are waiting to make another investment. Or you may have accumulated a lot of assets and you just want the pure cash flow as "mailbox money" (money you get in the mail with no effort other than the initial investment and a little monitoring). This can also be a good investment strategy for money you have accumulated in a retirement plan, such as a pension plan, 401(k), or IRA (superannuations or RRSPs for you Australians and Canadians). The interest will be tax deferred, and there won't be any real tax or leverage benefits to holding an interest rate tax lien outside of a retirement plan.

TABLE 21.4 Interest Rate Investment Strategy

Considerations
☐ Short/mid-term investment
☐ Desire cash flow (mailbox money)
☐ Little or no possibility for long-term growth
☐ Good use of extra cash while waiting to make another investment
☐ You have retirement money to invest

PROPERTY ACQUISITION INVESTMENT STRATEGY

A property acquisition investment strategy is completely different from the interest rate investment strategy. Rather than looking for quick cash flow, you are hoping for the opportunity to foreclose and own the underlying property for a long-term investment. This could be part of a long-term land hold strategy or a development strategy for property that you expect to be in a redevelopment zone.

While it is possible to do property acquisition investing in a retirement plan, in most countries there are real tax benefits to holding property outside of a retirement plan. It could be, as it is in the United States, that the gain on the sale of the property would be taxed at preferential capital gains rates. Or you may be able to do a like-kind exchange and not pay taxes at all.

Furthermore, if the underlying property is improved, you could receive depreciation benefits from holding the property. Or you may find yourself with significant equity in the property, and you may want to refinance to take advantage of the leverage opportunities of real estate. These opportunities typically are substantially restricted inside a retirement plan. These and other reasons point to holding this investment outside of your retirement plan in the eventuality that you end up owning the property.

TABLE 21.5 **Property Acquisition Investing Strategy**

Considerations
☐ Long-term investment
☐ Desire to foreclose and own the property
☐ Property could be in a redevelopment zone with good appreciation potential
☐ Like-kind exchange into more desirable investment property is possible
☐ Depreciation or leverage opportunities

STEP NO. 2: YOUR TAX LIEN INVESTMENT CRITERIA

Once you have your strategy in place, you can begin creating your criteria for the tax liens you want to acquire. Let's look at the interest rate investment and property acquisition investment strategies separately.

INTEREST RATE INVESTMENT STRATEGY CRITERIA

When you think about investing criteria, think about what's essential for a specific investment to meet your standards. What rate of return do you want? What level of risk are you willing to assume? In the case of tax liens, how much are you willing to risk that you will end up with the property? How long are you willing to hold the lien until it is eventually redeemed?

TABLE 21.6

Interest Rate Investing Criteria	Your Standards
Rate of Return	
Level of Risk	
Amount willing to risk to take hold of the property	
Length of time to hold property	

As with any investing strategy, the clearer your criteria, the easier the investment process. With clear criteria, you can easily eliminate most of the available tax liens and concentrate solely on those that meet your specific needs. A little later on in this chapter, we will look at how to determine whether a particular tax lien meets your criteria.

PROPERTY ACQUISITION INVESTMENT STRATEGY CRITERIA

When your goal is to acquire the underlying property, you start looking at your criteria much differently. Here are some of the questions you need to ask yourself:

- How likely are you to be able to foreclose on the property?
- What is the likelihood that the owner or another lienholder will pay off the lien before you can foreclose?
- How many years will you have to wait to foreclose?
- What are the property taxes that you will have to pay in the future (before your foreclosure waiting period is up)?

TABLE 21.7

Property Acquisition Investing Criteria	Your Standards
Likelihood of foreclosure on the property	
Likelihood the owner or other lienholder will pay off lien	
Years you prefer to wait until foreclosure	
Property taxes you may have to pay in the future	

And then you have to look at all of the criteria you have for your property investments, including the following:

- Does your investment strategy call for investing in raw land or improved property?
- Are you going to develop the underlying property?
- If improved, what type of improved property is within your focused investment strategy?
- Is it industrial property, commercial office buildings, multifamily housing, or single-family homes?

To be a focused real estate investor, you must be able to focus on a single type of real estate. This is the only way you can become an expert in a particular type of property investing. Once you have this focused strategy in place, you can look at the specific criteria for your tax lien investing.

TABLE 21.8

Criteria for Property Investments	
☐ Raw Land	
☐ Develop the underlying property	
☐ Improved property	Type:
☐ Industrial	
☐ Commercial	
☐ Office Building	
☐ Multifamily Housing	
☐ Single-family Homes	

- What is your criterion for rate of return?
- Do you want the property to cash flow?
- And if so, how much cash flow is required?
- Do you have a particular location of concentration?
- What about the expected appreciation of the property?
- What is your maximum holding period for the property?
- What tax benefits are you expecting from the property?

TABLE 21.9 Real Estate Criteria

TYPE OF REAL ESTATE CHOSEN:

Specific Criteria for Tax Lien Investing	Your Standard
Rate of return	
Cash flow (if so, how much)	
Geographic location	
Expected appreciation	
Maximum hold period	
Tax benefits expected	

STEP No. 3: EVALUATING THE TAX LIEN INVESTMENT

With your criteria in place, you can now begin looking at tax liens and evaluating whether they fit within your criteria. Between two weeks and one month before the tax lien auction, the county will release the information on the properties with tax liens that will be available for purchase. Begin your evaluation by determining which of the available tax liens will fit within your investment strategy.

INTEREST RATE INVESTMENT STRATEGY EVALUATION

Interest rate investors should look for properties that are less likely to be abandoned by the owner. Properties less likely to be abandoned include:

- improved property
- owner-occupied property
- property with other liens, such as a mortgage
- property that has a lien because the tax bill was sent to the wrong address

PROPERTY ACQUISITION INVESTMENT STRATEGY CRITERIA

Property acquisition investors should look for liens on properties that are more likely to be allowed to go to foreclosure, including:

- properties that have been abandoned by the owner
- properties where the owner has died, so the property is in probate or has passed to an estate or trust
- property where ownership of the property is free and clear of other liens
- property that has several years of unpaid back taxes
- property owned by someone living out of state

Once you have narrowed down your investment possibilities to those that fit within your strategy of interest rate investment or property acquisition investment, you need to further focus on which liens you should go after in the bid process.

If you are an interest rate investor, you'll want to understand exactly how the interest rate is applied in the state where you are investing. Once you determine this, find liens that are less likely to have multiple bidders or that are located in a state where the interest rate remains fixed at the auction. In a state where the interest rate is "bid down" at auction, look for properties that are likely to have the tax lien redeemed, but they have some attributes that might scare away other investors. These liens will retain the highest interest rate because they will have the least amount of interest in the bidding process. Look for tax liens with the following attributes:

- The property is located in a remote area of the state
- The property is small or an odd shape
- The property has other undesirable features

If you are a property acquisition investor, you'll want to find liens on properties that you want to own. Begin narrowing down the properties by researching only those properties that meet your criteria. For example, suppose you want to invest in raw land, which, by the way, is the most likely property to be available for foreclosure. Suppose also that you want land that is likely to be developed in the near future. In this case, you would want to find liens on property that

- is near other developed property
- is in a redevelopment area
- is in an area that will likely be developed in the next few years due to the growth patterns of the county
- does not have restrictions that could hinder development

A ProVision client purchased a tax lien on a 1.5-acre parcel a few years ago in a bad part of town. Across the street from the property was a lot of industrial junk. But the area was on the verge of being redeveloped. There were ten years of taxes owed on the property, so the liens were not likely to be redeemed. And the client noticed that the owner of the property was an estate. This client purchased the tax lien for the current year and then went back to the other tax lienholders and redeemed all of the other tax liens. The total cost of ten years of tax liens was $7,000.

The client then went to the owner of the property and asked if he wanted the property. The estate was willing to deed over the property just to get rid of

TABLE 21.10 Summary of Evaluation for Tax Lien Investments

Interest Rate Investment	Property Acquisition Investment
PROPERTIES LESS LIKELY TO BE ABANDONED	**PROPERTIES MORE LIKELY TO FORECLOSE**
☐ Improved property	☐ Abandoned properties
☐ Owner-occupied property	☐ Death of property owner
☐ Property with other liens	☐ Property is clear of other liens
☐ Liens due to tax bill sent to wrong address	☐ Property has several years of back taxes
	☐ Out of state owner
Bid Process	
LESS LIKELY TO HAVE MULTIPLE BIDDERS	**PROPERTIES YOU WANT TO OWN**
☐ Property is in remote area of state	☐ Property near other developed property
☐ Property is small or odd shaped	☐ Property is in a redeveloped area
☐ Property has undesirable features	☐ In an area that will likely be developed

it and not have the headache of the tax liens or the cost of a foreclosure. Six months after purchasing the tax liens, a developer approached the client about buying the property.

The developer wanted to consolidate several parcels of land in the area to do a large commercial development. But he didn't want to deal with the legwork of the tax lien process. So, once the liens were all cleared, he approached our client and made an offer of $197,000 for the property. The result? Our client made a profit of $190,000, after owning the property for just six months.

STEP NO. 4: DUE DILIGENCE

Once you have decided which properties fit within your strategy and your criteria, it's time to do the due diligence on the properties. Due diligence is the process of assessing the risks of both the tax lien and the underlying property. At this point, you should have already assessed the risk of the lien being redeemed. But there are other risks to the lien that you will need to consider. And let's not forget about the underlying property. You need to assess the risks of that as well.

LIEN RISKS

Tax lien risks can be separated into two categories: property owner risks and tax lien process risks. Let's go over each one.

PROPERTY OWNER RISKS

The biggest risk with respect to the property owner is a property owner's bankruptcy. If the property owner files bankruptcy, you will not be able to foreclose on the lien until after the bankruptcy is resolved. Of course, bankruptcy courts normally respect property tax liens and give them a high priority when the bankruptcy is resolved. However, in a Chapter 7 bankruptcy, the bankruptcy trustee could have the tax lien subordinated to administrative expenses. In this case, the tax lienholder could become an unsecured creditor and wind up with little or nothing. Luckily, there are steps you can take to guard against this.

A very small percentage of properties may have mortgages held by a bank now administered by the Federal Deposit Insurance Corporation (FDIC). When a bank fails due to insolvency (i.e., not enough money), any loans owed to the bank are administered by the FDIC. If a loan administered by the FDIC is attached to a property on your list, it could mean delays during the foreclosure. The good news is that it is easy to check for FDIC-held loans. With a few simple steps, the risk of a delayed foreclosure due to an FDIC-administered lien is quite remote and easily avoidable.

Another risk is that the owner is in the military. It's very difficult to foreclose on an active member of the military. Another difficult owner to deal with is an owner who lives in a foreign country. In this case, the difficulty lies with finding the owner and serving him or her with the foreclosure papers. Yet another risk is that a minor or a mentally disabled person owns the property. This could cause delays in the foreclosure process and additional litigation costs.

Finally, there is the off chance that the lien is on government-owned property. Since the government is normally exempt from property tax, once the lien is corrected, the investor will likely receive his/her investment back but may not receive any interest. Good research will prevent this and other owner problems because you can easily determine the owner of the property and avoid buying the lien. Researching the owner is not as difficult as it may sound. The owner of the property is public information that is typically available at the county assessor's office. You can then go to the county recorder, county treasurer, and bankruptcy court to find out additional information about the owner, including other liens he may have outstanding and whether he has filed bankruptcy. A quick search on the Internet about the owner may also turn up helpful information.

TABLE 21.11 Lien Risks – Property Owner Risk

Risk 1	Property owner files bankruptcy
Risk 2	Property owned by an active member of the military
Risk 3	Property owned by someone who lives out of the country
Risk 4	Property owned by a minor
Risk 5	Property owned by a mentally disabled person
Risk 6	Property owned by the government

Real Life Story: Research Paid Off

While owning property can be a risk, it can also be a great opportunity. My client, Ellen, acquired a tax lien a few years ago that was owned by a hotel chain. In her research, Ellen discovered that the hotel chain had changed its strategy and no longer was interested in the community where this property was located. So she purchased that tax lien for $7,000. Less than three years later, Ellen sold the property for $360,000. In this case, the property owner's intentions almost assured Ellen of a great investment so her research about the property owner really paid off.

TAX LIEN PROCESS RISKS

Several risks can arise due to the lien itself. These are risks that typically involve litigation costs or delays in the foreclosure process that increase the cost of ownership. They can arise because of disputes over property ownership, disposition of other liens, and getting clear title to the property after foreclosure. In addition, there is the risk of too much success. How is that? What if you successfully acquire a property that needs a lot of fixing up? Are you prepared to invest the additional money required to get the work done? And will it be in

TABLE 21.12 Lien Risks – Tax Lien Process Risk

Risk 1	Litigation costs
Risk 2	Disputes of ownership
Risk 3	Disposition of other liens

your best interest? The key to minimizing these risks is evaluating the potential of the property, quantifying the potential additional costs of litigation or improvements, and determining whether the tax lien meets your criteria, including the possible additional costs to complete the foreclosure process.

Real Life Story: More Due Diligence Was Due

Andy purchased tax liens against all of the condominium units of an apartment building. During his due diligence research, Andy had learned that the out-of-state owner was no longer interested in the property. Andy foreclosed on the property, only to find out that it needed $300,000 of repairs to a building that was worth only $200,000. More due diligence would have saved Andy from this disaster.

PROPERTY RISKS

Once you have evaluated the tax lien risks and have concluded that there are a number of liens that meet your criteria, you can then evaluate the underlying property. Some of the risks to evaluate are as follows:

ENVIRONMENTAL RISKS

Perhaps the biggest risk in any property investment is that there is an environmental hazard that will be expensive to clean up. Reviewing the history of the property and contacting the EPA and state department of environmental quality about possible environmental problems is essential in any property investment, but particularly in a tax lien investment. An environmental problem could be the very reason that the owner has not paid the taxes.

VALUE OF THE PROPERTY

The most obvious risk, of course, is that the property will not be worth the cost to buy the lien (and other tax liens, both previous and subsequent to your lien). Include in your analysis the administrative costs of foreclosing on the property and getting clear title to the property.

STEP NO. 5: FORMING YOUR TEAM—THE REAL KEY TO REAL ESTATE INVESTING

At this point, you may be thinking that all of this is just too much work. As I was writing this, I had the same initial reaction. But remember that you don't have to do all of the work yourself. In fact, we like to say at ProVision that the three most expensive words in the English language are, "Do It Yourself."

While some of you will enjoy the research and the details, others will be content with a little lower return and a lot less work. The answer to this is to build a Tax Lien Team. You can reap the rewards of tax lien investing without doing all of the legwork yourself. Rather, hire others to do the work for you.

You already have determined the criteria for your tax lien investing. And you know the risks associated with tax liens that you are going to have to consider with every tax lien investment. You just don't want to spend all of the time and effort on the details of going through the various liens and the properties all by yourself.

Remember that there are lots of people who are looking for employment and are very competent at research and details. I know this; I hire these people myself, both for my accounting firm and for my real estate investing.

If you have clear criteria and create good procedures to follow for doing the due diligence, you can turn it over to someone else to do. I suggest you pay these people primarily based on results, but you can also pay them a small hourly wage. I like to give my team members large bonuses for success. Let's take, for example, the tax lien that my friend Jim acquired several years ago.

Jim found a property with twelve years of taxes owed. The property consisted of eighty acres of raw land located in a floodplain near a power plant. Most people would pass this property by, but Jim noticed that the property was not far from developed property and was zoned for industrial use. (Industrial zoning usually means that just about any buyer could use the property. It's normally fairly easy to rezone industrial property to a more conservative use of the property, such as commercial or residential.)

After doing all of his due diligence, Jim acquired the current year tax lien and then went to each of the prior lienholders and acquired their liens as well. Because he now owned all of the old tax liens, he could foreclose immediately. The total of the tax liens was $40,000. That's $500 per acre for property that was close to developed property.

A few years after buying the property, a solar energy company came to Jim and asked to purchase the property. Jim negotiated a price of $9,500 per acre for a total sales price of $760,000—a profit of $720,000!

The due diligence and research into this tax lien took Jim a lot of time and effort, which he was happy to do. But suppose he didn't want to do the work himself. What if he had hired someone to do the research for him? He might have paid this person $10 to $12 per hour plus a bonus when the property sold. Suppose he offered a 10 percent bonus on the increase in value from the total cost of investment. The researcher would have received a bonus of $72,000. Knowing that this type of bonus was possible, you can bet that the researcher would have been very diligent in his or her research and would have made sure to find only the best properties.

Some of you are thinking, "Wow! What a high price to pay for research." But think how many properties you could find if you had multiple researchers doing the work for you. And it really costs you very little. You have a small out-of-pocket cost for the initial wages, but you have no risk for more than that. Yes, you give up 10 percent of the profit, but that's a small price to pay for 90 percent of the profit that you didn't have to work for!

Now let me tell you the rest of the story of this property. When Jim sold it, he did a tax-free exchange for a sale/leaseback on a fast food restaurant location. This property came with a twenty-year lease with options for an additional twenty years. It is paying Jim $4,300 per month of lease income. In addition,

TABLE 21.13 Example of Tax Lien Team Members

1	Someone to research the available tax liens
2	Someone to identify the tax liens that fall within your tax lien strategy
3	Someone to evaluate the tax liens that fall within your tax lien strategy
4	Someone to complete the due diligence (risks) on the tax liens that fall within your tax lien strategy

Jim had $80,000 left over from the sale that he put into another piece of land—all because he found the right tax lien on the right piece of property.

Just think, if Jim had not had to do all of the work himself, how many more tax liens he could have found and how much more property he could have acquired.

What other team members do you need? Here is a list of possible positions:

1. Real estate appraiser to determine the value of the underlying real estate
2. Real estate banker/mortgage broker so you can refinance the real estate once you acquire it
3. Real estate attorney to assist with foreclosure proceedings and other legal matters throughout the lien process
4. Tax lien auction bidder. If you don't want to handle the auctions yourself, in most instances you can outsource so long as you provide proper guidance to the bidder.
5. Bookkeeper. You will need to keep good track of the properties you acquire and the costs to acquire each property for tax and investment analysis purposes.
6. Property manager if you plan to acquire improved property
7. Real estate broker to handle the sale of your acquired real estate
8. Banker to handle financial transactions
9. CPA to assist with the tax aspects of tax lien investing and property transactions, including like-kind exchanges of acquired property for desired property
10. Foreclosure assistant to follow through on all of the details of foreclosing on tax liens and obtaining clear title
11. Wealth coach and mentor to help you create your tax lien investment strategy and to keep your investing moving

STEP NO. 6: SETTING UP TAX LIEN INVESTMENT SYSTEMS

Like any good investment strategy, tax lien investing should be set up as a business. This includes setting up your team in Step No. 5 and determining a good strategy. It also includes setting up the systems to make your investing efficient and effective. In order to maximize your investing while minimizing your time and your risk, consider setting up the following systems:

DUE DILIGENCE SYSTEM

This will include a due diligence checklist, a list of your investment criteria and reports from your due diligence team members to let you know their progress so they can ask you questions.

INVESTMENT REPORTING SYSTEM

This will include reports monitoring the progress of the tax lien investing as well as reports indicating the returns on your investments. There are some good software packages available to track and monitor your tax lien investments, including rate of return and deadlines.

AUCTION SYSTEM

This includes policies and procedures for your auction bidder to follow when attending tax lien auctions.

FORECLOSURE PROCEDURES

Make a complete list of the steps for your foreclosure assistant to follow in beginning, handling, and completing the foreclosure process and obtaining clear title to the property.

SALES PROCEDURES FOR REAL ESTATE

Make a complete list of steps for your real estate broker to take in order to market and sell or exchange your properties.

Now you know about tax lien investing, which is a lucrative way to participate in real estate. And you have the strategies, steps, and checklists you need to begin exploring it if you so choose. As I mentioned in the beginning of this chapter, whichever real estate investing opportunity you choose, it should be

TABLE 21.14 Steps for Tax Lien Strategy

Step 1	Determine Your Tax Lien Strategy
STRATEGY A INTEREST RATE INVESTMENT	
STRATEGY B PROPERTY ACQUISITION INVESTMENT	
Step 2	Identify Your Tax Lien Investment Criteria
Step 3	Evaluate the Tax Lien Investment
Step 4	Complete Your Due Diligence
Step 5	Form Your Tax Lien Team
Step 6	Set Up Your Tax Lien Investment System

one that meets your objectives and one you really enjoy. That one factor alone will increase your chances for success considerably.

AUTHOR'S NOTE

I would like to thank Mark Manoil, Esq., for his assistance with this chapter. Mark is the foremost authority in Arizona for tax lien investing and his book, *Arizona Property Tax Liens*, was the source of much of the technical information included in this chapter. Mark was also gracious enough to spend some of his valuable time giving me his personal insights into tax lien investing.

I would also like to thank Darius Barazandeh, Esq., for his assistance with the state variations and subtle nuances of tax lien investing. Darius is an expert in the field of tax lien investing and his training, *Attorney Secrets to Investing in Tax Liens*, covers the subtle yet vital variations among states for those wanting to use a multistate investing strategy.

WAYS TO LEARN MORE

Please go to www.ProVisionWealth.com/products for more information regarding the wealth strategy information contained in this chapter.

For more than twenty-five years, **Tom Wheelwright** has strategically developed innovative tax, business, and wealth strategies for sophisticated investors and business owners across the United States and around the world, resulting in millions of dollars in profits. His goal is to teach people how to create a strategic and proactive approach to wealth that creates lasting success. As the founder of ProVision, Tom is the innovator of proactive consulting services for ProVision's premium clientele, who on average, pay a lot less in taxes and earn much more on their investments. He coaches select clients on their wealth, business, and tax strategies; lectures on wealth and tax strategies around the world; and is an adjunct professor at Arizona State University.

22

Wayne PALMER

Horse Trading
The Original Way to Wealth on the Great American Frontier

S ome of the happiest days of my life have been spent sitting with Wayne Palmer in real estate exchange meetings. In the span of just two or three days, a group of real estate exchangers share information on several hundred investments, and exchanges get made. These meetings are perfect opportunities for Wayne to use his innate sense of creativity and his ability to see the opportunities that most people miss. That's what makes him a master of this forum. Wayne's ability to confidently navigate the waters of a real estate exchange meeting is nothing short of genius. For me, exchange meetings are as close to poetry in motion as you can get as an investor.

Wayne introduced me to real estate exchange meetings, and they make me feel like I'm a starving man at a Chinese buffet. It's a rush being invited into these groups where the sheer power of deal making creativity flows hour after hour. As a person who is sick and tired of hearing ordinary people say, "I can't afford it" or "I don't have any money," sitting in these exchange meetings is a breath of fresh air. They are an escape from the self-imposed financially and creatively handi-capped. Here people are making deals happen with little or no money, and they are doing it all day long. Sitting in a real estate exchange meeting with Wayne is *far more exciting than playing cards or rolling the dice in Las Vegas. It's the thrill of the hunt, the challenge of creativity, and the drive of winning all rolled up into one.*

Whenever I am at a dead end, brain dead, and in need of a shot of creativity, Wayne is the first person I call. I can count on him to help me see a deal or a situation in a completely different way. And he doesn't just tell me what I want to hear. When I call Wayne, I know I will always get honest feedback. He'll tell me if the deal I'm looking at stinks, and he'll show me ways to creatively—while legally, ethically, and morally—make a good deal into a great one.

Wayne is a great friend and teacher to me. In this chapter, Wayne will teach you some of what he has taught me. This chapter about exchanges will open your eyes.

—Robert Kiyosaki

When I was a small boy, my father had a metal sign planted on the side of the road at the edge of our farmyard that read:

Dad's story is a classic tale of the American entrepreneur. He grew up on my grandpa's farm during the Great Depression. When he was a young man, the farm wasn't profitable enough to support more than one family, so he was obliged to leave the farm to find work. This bothered Dad because he loved the farm, and he especially loved livestock. His dream was to have a place of his own, where he could make a living working with his animals, without having to sell his time to someone else for money.

**Hay / Horses
Sell or Trade
Val Palmer
254-4768**

FIGURE 22.1 Farmyard sign

When I was a baby, Dad moved our family to California so that he could search for work. He got a job driving a building materials delivery truck for Chambers Hardware in Orange County. At that time, the economy was much better in California than it was in Utah. In the space of two or three years, Dad was able to pay off all of his own debts as well as the remaining debt on Grandpa's farm. Being debt free was his ticket out of California and back to the rural environment of his youth.

Back in Utah, Dad took a job driving a garbage truck for Salt Lake County. He despised working for someone else. He was independent by nature and wanted to be his own man. However, he had a plan and realized that he couldn't work for himself without a grubstake to get started. While on the garbage truck, Dad and his crew worked extra hard to complete their route by two o'clock in the afternoon. In Dad's book, that left the other half of the day available to pursue his own business.

To eliminate rent or mortgage payments, he moved a home from a neighboring town onto the corner of Grandpa's farm. From the day we moved into that house, it was paid for. Without any debt of any kind, Dad started using his excess income to purchase assets, just as Rich Dad teaches. In my dad's world, animals were assets because he could buy them for one price and sell or trade them for a higher price. Farm commodities such as hay and grain were also assets. They generated cash flow.

He bought hay from local farmers at bulk prices and sold it to horse enthusiasts, priced by the bale. He delivered it using his 1956 Ford pickup truck that had a flat wagon hitched behind. He would buy horses from individuals, clean them up, work with them to make them better behaved, and then re-sell them at a premium to those who could afford the classier animals. While doing all of this, he also rented land next to our home on the neighboring farm and planted potatoes. He had a harvest one year of spuds so spectacular that the entire crop was contracted by the Country Club Potato Chip factory. In each of these transactions, Dad made a modest profit and added it to his business capital. Each small deal brought him closer to getting out of the rat race.

After three years of driving the garbage truck and running his own business part time, Dad quit his job at the county and bought his own red Ford semirig with a thirty-two-foot flatbed trailer. He finally had his own full-time trucking business that would be big enough to support his family. He moved from the E quadrant to the S quadrant within the Rich Dad CASHFLOW Quadrants.

It took me years to understand the power of what Dad had done. If someone had cash to buy hay or horses, he would accept their cash. However, it eventually became clear to me that Dad understood something that perhaps most businessmen today don't, which is if entrepreneurs are willing to accept items other than cash for their stock in trade, they can often dramatically increase the volume and profitability of the business they do.

My dad was a gifted horse trader. Dad traded hay for horses and cattle for hay. He traded his trucking services for animals, and he even traded livestock with old-school grocers and shop owners for food and clothing. When we remodeled the house, Dad traded hay and livestock for materials, labor, cabinets, and the skills of various tradesmen. Why didn't I see it sooner? After all, barter was the way business was conducted before modern money was introduced. It had always worked, and come to think of it, I suppose it always will.

I probably didn't see it because I was in the real estate business, not the agricultural business. As the economy faltered in the early 1980s, interest rates soared and the cash purchase of real estate slowed to a crawl, I started hearing about a little-known sector of the 1031 Exchange industry known as "exchanging," or "equity marketing." Either term may be used to describe this industry niche. While the technical aspects of exchanging under the rules of Internal Revenue Code Section 1031 are adeptly covered elsewhere in this book by Gary Gorman (see Chapter 17), what I include here will open up an entirely new world of wealth-building possibilities for anyone who taps into this information and qualifies himself or herself to play in this arena. Here's how to do it.

Equity marketing is an alternative way of practicing real estate investment that rejects the idea that cash is necessary to complete a real estate transaction. Instead, the focus is placed on the *equity value* of each party's property and on exchanging those equities to achieve greater benefits for all. In a traditional buy/sell transaction, the emphasis is on how much cash the seller can receive and how little the buyer can pay. This puts buyer and seller at odds with each other, "competing" for the same dollars. If Dad had waited for every farmer to sell a horse before the farmer could pay for hay to feed his cows, you can begin to see it would have taken my father much longer to win his independence. Trading the hay for the horse accelerated the process.

Real estate professionals who practice equity marketing are called "equity marketers" or "exchangors." In the exchange industry and throughout this chapter, those terms are used interchangeably. Exchangors hold regular meetings where they gather together to explore ways that they and their properties can be matched with other owners and properties in profitable exchanges. These meetings are hotbeds of opportunity. They constitute one of the most vibrant and effective marketing forums in the real estate industry.

TIP Perhaps most importantly, because equity marketing doesn't rely on cash, it continues to thrive, even during downturns in the real estate industry at large.

Exchangors are often able to continue building wealth while those in other factions of the industry stagnate during tough times. How important is that advantage over a lifetime of investing? Exchanging can make a world of difference in one's net worth over a period of years and protect an investor from the losses that often take place during a down cycle.

In October of 2005, Robert Kiyosaki was invited to be the keynote speaker at an equity marketing meeting sponsored by the National Council of Exchangors (NCE), which was held at the historic Brown Palace Hotel in Denver, Colorado. After a few minutes in the room, and seeing a flurry of offers made on properties that were presented for exchange, Robert turned to me with boyish enthusiasm and said, "This is my CASHFLOW game in real life!" Wow, I had never thought of it that way, and to my surprise and delight, I realized he was right. I could instantly see the correlation:

- The venues where the meetings are held might be compared to CASHFLOW game boards.
- The bylaws of the organization and its codes of conduct are the rules by which the game is played.
- The book of opportunities that is published for each exchange meeting is full of one-page property data sheets that contain essentially the same information found on CASHFLOW game cards. Some are small deal cards, and some are large deal cards. There are properties, lease rights, water rights, timber, and even an occasional business opportunity. Some are high-risk deals, and some are relatively low-risk deals.
- Just as the CASHFLOW game sets the context for teaching the Rich Dad education system, the equity marketing arena provides a context that allows people to learn and play the exchange game with others, for real. And like the Rich Dad Company, NCE and other national exchange groups, such as the Society of Exchange Counselors (SEC), foster a commitment to lifelong learning for their members.

TIP Exchange organizations teach real people, in real life, how to get out of the rat race, using real estate as the primary vehicle.

As a boy, I went to livestock auctions with my dad where we sold some of our animals from time to time. Now I go to exchange meetings to trade properties. For the average person, equity marketing may be the most powerful tool there is for building wealth in real estate in any economy.

Robert quickly sized up equity marketing as an important addition to the Rich Dad real estate system. In subsequent meetings, he expressed his deep desire that his students not only learn about money, but also be made aware of avenues for putting their knowledge to work in acquiring real wealth. His vision is not only to provide quality financial education, but to point the students to real-world tracks they can run on to become wealthy. Robert and I have since teamed up around that vision to share the concept of equity marketing with the Rich Dad community.

The results have been rewarding. Kiyosaki students, already armed with the Rich Dad philosophy, have used equity marketing tools and formulas to reposition their assets, increase their cash flow, grow their net worth, streamline management commitments, and reduce their taxes, to name but a few of the benefits they have realized.

TWELVE-YEAR-OLD JOHN PAUL

One example of successful equity marketing involved a boy from Texas. Robert asked me if I would consider mentoring then twelve-year-old John Paul Pigéon. John Paul started reading the Rich Dad books at the age of seven and had devoured the entire Rich Dad library before his twelfth birthday. Following the Rich Dad/CASHFLOW pattern, he had started two businesses, had written a book, and had produced a music CD, prior to our meeting. He had a goal to own his first property before he turned thirteen.

I flew to Dallas/Fort Worth to meet John Paul and his family. The love and respect shared in the Pigéon home is impressive beyond words. The emphasis they place on education and the way they work together as a family to secure their financial future is inspiring. I noted John Paul's single-minded desire to learn only what actually works in the real world. Even at age twelve, he displayed little patience for empty theory. I was also astonished that the mind of a mere boy could so quickly grasp concepts and retain vocabulary that certain adults sometimes struggle to understand. He had already attained an aptitude and a passion for learning—two life skills for anyone who wants to excel financially. It was clear to me that exceptional parenting had produced an extraordinary young man who could indeed be coached in business, even as a preteen.

I had dinner with the Pigéon family, along with my friend and partner, John Spinola, a former president of the NCE. As you might guess, John Paul took to our wealth-building and exchange formulas like a duck takes to water. His mother was newly licensed in real estate, so we introduced Mrs. Pigéon to equity marketing. *Within a year, thirteen-year-old John Paul had realized his goal, acquiring a minority interest for his family in an RV park valued at nearly $1 million,* using only his mother's commissions as a down payment. He had taken his first step toward real estate wealth, thanks to the combined power of the Rich Dad system, the equity marketing forum, and remarkable parents.

> ## Cooperation Replaces Competition
>
> In an equity marketing transaction, the buyer and seller "cooperatively" seek to exchange more than the deed to a property. They exchange a package of benefits that results in a much more profitable transaction for all parties. For example, the added benefits of an equity marketing exchange may include enhanced tax treatment, reduced management duties, lesser or greater leverage (debt), a better location for both parties, a more favorable property type, or a bigger opportunity for profit based on the particular talents of each investor. Equity marketing identifies what unique needs and capabilities each party has and engineers ways of matching them to amplify the benefits of the exchange all around. It is synergy at its finest, a true win/win.

TURNING LEMONS INTO LEMONADE

One of the most powerful forms of leverage I have accessed through equity marketing is the ability to exchange as a way of solving problems in my portfolio. For example, as a lender I made a loan against a four-acre horse property. The borrower went into default, and I eventually had to file foreclosure. My loan was junior to the first mortgage, which was also in foreclosure. That meant that I had to assume the first mortgage to protect my position in the property. I wrote a check to the first mortgage holder to satisfy their demands and foreclosed on the borrower. I became the new owner of the property through foreclosure. Following foreclosure, I discovered that the borrowers had left the home in poor condition. It was going to require significant work and expense on my part if I hoped to get the full value upon sale. I was holding what for me was a bitter lemon.

Before undertaking the rehab, I presented the home for exchange, priced at $225,000 and in "as-is" condition, at a local equity marketing meeting. That was a price I wasn't confident I could soon command in the buy/sell market, even after fix up. A gentleman in attendance at the meeting said that he thought his daughter and son-in-law might be interested in the property. He offered to trade me two lots as a down payment on the home.

The first parcel was a luxury view lot located fifty miles north of my home in an older, but stable subdivision of good values. The problem was, it was so steep that we referred to it as the "billy goat" lot, since nothing but mountain goats could climb the embankment to the street. It required some special engineering to make the lot useable. Having had experience in construction, I wasn't nervous about the geology of the parcel, but the seller was. I was more nervous about an empty horse property on which I was servicing a $150,000 mortgage. My vacancy didn't bother him because his daughter was willing to occupy the property.

The second lot was zoned for a duplex and was close to home, but the subdivision in which it was located was nonconforming. That means that the county of jurisdiction had never fully approved the subdivision, so no building permit could be issued for any structure on the lot. Consequently, unless the county's regulations could be satisfied, the lot was of little commercial value. It seemed to me that the problem was resolvable, given the investment of some time and perhaps some engineering work, which was necessary to prove to the county that the boundaries, placement of utilities, and drainage were all conforming to county standards. I also felt more comfortable with the duplex lot than with the empty house.

We structured a transaction wherein he traded the two lots to me for a combined value of $75,000, and his son-in-law secured a new mortgage for $150,000, meeting my asking price of $225,000 on the foreclosed home. The exchange became the sugar that turned my lemon into lemonade.

Not long after we closed, I was approached by a young couple about buying the duplex lot. The husband worked in the county planning and zoning department and had an inside track to secure the needed variances. After the lot was approved for a building permit, the couple paid me $50,000 cash for it. I eventually sold the billy goat lot for $70,000. Consequently, by using an exchange I was able to get $120,000 for the equity in the foreclosed home that probably wasn't immediately worth $75,000 in a cash sale. More sugar, more sweet tasting lemonade!

BENEFITS ARE MORE IMPORTANT THAN PRICE

It is not uncommon to realize more than the cash asking price in an exchange because equity marketing focuses on more than price. Remember, it focuses on structuring benefits for both parties. Under the equity marketing system, an owner's equity, rather than cash, becomes her stock in trade. An exchangor tallies how much equity an owner has and lists the benefits a new owner could derive from that equity position. Then potential transactions are explored that might allow the owner to increase her equity while improving the benefits she receives from it. The benefits become so valuable that there is little motivation on anyone's part to haggle over price.

In the previous example, the other party's lots provided me with the benefit of an immediate upside potential in value if I could overcome certain conditions, namely, the topography of one lot and the zoning status of the other. Although these conditions were a detriment to the existing owner, they were a benefit to me because I had the experience to solve the problems.

My property provided added benefits to the other gentleman, as well. He found a home for his daughter, and he consolidated equity in lots he no longer wanted into a single property that could provide shelter for his grandkids while the property appreciated through upkeep and market forces.

Neither one of us had to go through the hassle of marketing the properties in the traditional fashion. Rather, we were able to close quickly and move on. The benefits we both received were over and above the mere asking prices of our respective properties. True synergy was created in the transaction because we both solved immediate problems and set ourselves up for greater gains in the future. I made at least an extra $45,000 by concentrating on the benefits rather than a cash price.

By working this combination of equity and benefits within the framework of the equity marketing arena, you can amplify multiple forms of leverage for all parties. Notice in the foregoing example how I was able to leverage my experience in construction and the process of getting zoning entitlements to increase the value of the lots. The other owner leveraged his daughter's need for a home and his son-in-law's credit to consolidate his equity in one property that they could fix up and make more valuable. For both parties to the exchange, the equity became fluid, or liquid, without first converting it to cash. This is a very important distinction! Equity marketing allows us to spend our equity to acquire a new property without first changing it to cash. The equity in each property is liquefied through the power of thought, ideas, talents, knowledge, agreements, networking, and formulas that when knitted together, create a synergistic (bigger than before) win/win for all parties.

TIP Equity marketing allows us to spend our equity to acquire a new property, without first changing it to cash.

In other words, when we exchange equities, as opposed to engaging in a mere cash sale, my equity and the new benefits that my property offers you, plus your equity and the new benefits that your property offers me, equal much more for both of us than the stand-alone equities ever could. And it is all accomplished without first having to find the cash to do the deal! Imagine the advantage this gives you during times of tight credit or rising interest rates that undermine traditional financing.

EQUITY MARKETING = THE FAST TRACK

If we again liken equity marketing to the CASHFLOW game, you'll find it can be your path to the so-called fast track, which is exactly what I believe Robert saw in his first exchange meeting. In the exchange forum, just like on the fast track in the CASHFLOW game, you are able to move forward faster, earn more, and experience a synergistic multiplying effect. Everything suddenly becomes more fluid.

Consider the benefits to the two parties in the following story of another exchange transaction:

My friend Magi Bird, who is nationally revered as an exceptional instructor on equity marketing techniques, had some clients who had outgrown their home. Mom, dad, three kids, a dog, and a cat had overrun both the house and the small yard. They needed something bigger but didn't feel they could afford a larger house payment. They also owned a piece of recreational land in a distant community that they hadn't seen in seventeen years. Magi suggested they consider trading their existing house and the land for a bigger home.

They found a large, two-story home on three acres that was perfect for the family. The owner of the home was an elderly widower who had recently undergone hip surgery. He could no longer tolerate stairs, and being alone, he didn't need the extra space. The big yard was a burden on him as well. He desperately needed a smaller, single-story dwelling.

Magi and her clients made an offer to the old gentleman to trade the family's modest one-story house, plus the recreational lot in a straight-across exchange for the larger home. He accepted their offer. The price of his home equaled that of the smaller home and the lot combined. Each party moved into a home that was better suited for their current needs at essentially the same payment they had each been paying. The exchange was made solely on the basis of the nonmonetary benefits. The family got a roomier home and a bigger yard without going deeper into debt. They also activated the equity in a lot that had cost them money for years in property taxes. The elderly man moved into the smaller, more comfortable home that was safer for him and much easier to manage. He also received an extra lot in the process that required no upkeep, unlike the big yard he left behind. The extra lot gave him an option to either sell it to augment his income or keep it and leave it to his heirs at his passing.

TIP Benefits! It's the benefits in an exchange that are often more important than the price of the property.

Jim Keller, a fifty-year veteran of the exchange business—one of my personal mentors and a man for whom I have profound respect—tells the following story about completing an exchange for one of his clients, strictly based on benefits.

A couple owned a large home in Incline Village at Lake Tahoe. The couple divorced and both moved down the mountain to Reno, Nevada. The home was empty, and the ex-husband was writing checks totaling $8,000 a month in mortgage payments, taxes, upkeep, and management fees. As his broker, Jim Keller brought the man an offer to trade his equity in the home for fifty-two time-shares in Padre Island, Texas. Jim's client replied, "I don't want that."

Jim quickly responded by saying, "Yes, you do, and let me explain why." Putting his problem into monetary terms, Jim pointed out the reality of a $96,000 per year negative cash flow on the home at Incline. The maintenance fees on the time-shares by contrast were only $14,000 a year. The client immediately saw the benefit of reducing his overhead by $82,000 a year on a home he didn't need or want. The exchange closed. The subsequent owner tore down the house to build a new home on the prime Tahoe lot. Jim's client was almost $7,000 a month better off. What was more important to the client: the price of the vacant home, or the benefit of saving $7,000 a month?

TWO-WAY, THREE-WAY, OR MULTILEG EXCHANGES

All of the examples used so far are of two-way exchanges. That is to say that one party traded their property straight across for another property. While this is the simplest of exchanges, it presents the added challenge of having to find someone who wants your property and also has what you want. As you may imagine, that kind of match made in heaven does not always come easily. Included in the format of exchange meetings are one or more methods for discovering who wants what and how those pairs can be connected to form three-way or multileg exchanges.

Here is an illustration of an actual transaction that closed recently between the members of the Salt Lake City, Utah, exchange group.

Mr. Blomquist was seventy-three years old and lived in a multistory house. He had a degenerative spinal condition that made it increasingly more difficult for him to walk, climb stairs, and maintain normal mobility. Not long ago, he lost his balance and tumbled from the top of a flight of stairs to the bottom. Thankfully, he incurred no serious injury but was shaken by the experience. He realized some changes had to be made. He and Mrs. Blomquist purchased a ranch-style home around the corner. They then had two homes and two house payments. They moved into the new home and put the other home on the market, without results. Mr. Blomquist came to the local exchange meeting and offered the multistory home for trade.

Mrs. Rusche was attending the meeting and offered to trade two condos and $20,000 in barter credits for the home. Mr. Blomquist didn't want her condos, so no two-way exchange was possible.

At the same meeting, partners Mr. Covey and Mr. Welch, presented a parcel of commercial land for trade, located in a rural area and approved for the construction of storage units. Mr. Blomquist was interested in the land, but Covey and Welch did not want Mr. Blomquist's home.

However, Covey and Welch were interested in trading their land for Mrs. Rusche's condos and barter credits. Finally, everyone found something they wanted and someone who wanted what they offered. Here is how the three-way exchange was structured:

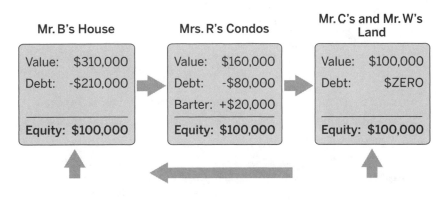

FIGURE 22.2

Mr. Blomquist took the commercial land, Covey and Welch took the condos with the barter credits, and Mrs. Rusche got Mr. Blomquist's house.

Remember, we said exchanging focuses on equity, not on price or cash. Notice that the equities were all traded in balance at $100,000 each. Also notice that Mrs. Rusche had only $80,000 equity in her condos, so she had to add something of value to balance. She could have added cash, or she might have added a promissory note payable to Covey and Welch to make up the difference. However, she offered barter credits, which can be spent within the barter company system for various goods and services from other merchants who accept those credits. The $20,000 in credits together with the $80,000 in equity gave Mrs. Rusche the $100,000 she needed to balance her part of the exchange.

Now let's consider the benefits each received over and above the $100,000 in equity.

Mr. Blomquist got rid of the extra house he no longer needed. He reduced his debt by $210,000 and his monthly outgo by approximately $1,650. He moved his equity in the house that wasn't likely to appreciate much over the next year or so into a development property that he could improve to rapidly increase his equity. He had no capital gains tax due on the transaction because the home he traded was his primary residence for at least two of the prior five years.

Mrs. Rusche got rid of her condos that were far away from her home in exchange for a larger, nicer property closer to home. While she took on more debt, she had someone to lease the home with an option to purchase within two years. She got ease of management, less travel, a larger basis that increased her tax shelter, and the possibility of a sale in two years that will liquefy her equity once again, allowing her to move forward and make another profit. She paid no capital gains tax on the sale because the transaction qualified as an exchange under IRS Code Section 1031.

Covey and Welch disposed of the land they had been sitting on. They no longer have the negative cash flow associated with paying the property taxes. They have two condos that are rented for a positive cash flow. They also have an increase in basis of $80,000 that they can begin to depreciate, thereby providing them with tax shelter that they didn't have on the land. They also paid no capital gains tax on the sale because the transaction qualified as an exchange under IRS Code Section 1031.

Are you beginning to see that the benefits of the exchange are often more important than price and cash? As Rich Dad often says, "Cash is trash!" While we all like some cash on hand, holding it as the primary motivation when building a real estate portfolio can be much too costly. It is more lucrative to exchange for a valuable package of benefits. Exchanging benefits grows wealth faster than accumulating cash ever could in the same transactions. You see, trading causes the same acceleration in real estate as it did for my dad when he swapped livestock and commodities rather than the slower method of waiting for the cash to come along. That is one of the valuable lessons I eventually learned from life on the farm.

OTHER ADVANTAGES OF EXCHANGE GROUPS

RELATIONSHIPS

As is the case in so many other arenas in life, it is, in my opinion, the people I have met at the exchange groups who make up the most valuable element of exchanging. I consider it a privilege to associate with a group of several hundred people from all across America who, on the whole, live by a code of conduct that is refreshing in a financial world that is frequently rocked by greed and corruption. I can say with some authority that my experience of exchangors has been that they are smart, honest, reliable, and dedicated to the respectable practice of their trade. I have found a few exceptions to that rule, but that is to be expected I suppose, inasmuch as we are still dealing with human beings.

Tapping into such a network of reliable professionals is one of the unspoken advantages of affiliation with organizations such as NCE and SEC. It drastically increases my potential field of operations. I am comfortable investing outside of my own area, as long as I have exchange friends there. Their presence allows me to contain the risk that would normally be incurred by venturing too far from home. I can call someone in every state in the Union, in almost any community of any size, and get up-to-the-minute information on what is happening in that area. Such a network allows me to become mobile with my equity. I can enter almost any economy with the confidence that I am making sound decisions based on local experience and involvement, and they can do the same in my town.

More and more, regional markets behave independent of each other, based on employment trends, government policies, local economics, energy, and even weather. Instead of having to wait out a downturn in my own market until things improve, effectively sitting on the sidelines of the game until an upturn, I can exchange my equity from town to town, state to state, and take advantage of opportunities in micro-markets. I can invest in oil states when energy is hot, agricultural areas when farming is good, and housing when there is localized demand. My network of exchangor friends empowers me to capitalize on employment trends and to anticipate growth in multiple markets with the steely confidence that comes from having reliable allies with "boots on the ground" in the area.

As I said, the people I have grown to love and respect and with whom I now do business through various exchange organizations comprise the biggest benefit of being an exchangor. I am honored to number such marvelous people as my friends and associates. I am a wealthy man, if only by virtue of those associations. Because exchanging is what originally brought me into relationship with Robert and Kim Kiyosaki, I include the entire Rich Dad family when I count my blessings of these priceless friendships.

THE BRILLIANT BRAIN TRUST

In all of my life's experience, I have never seen a more potent bunch of brains gathered in one location than I inevitably see at exchange meetings, as pertaining to real estate. One of the activities normally included in a meeting of exchangors is a problem-solving or brainstorming session. The group intentionally looks for the most difficult problem, the nastiest, most tangled situation that presently exists among the attendees. For an hour or so, a discussion ensues wherein anyone who has an idea takes a turn at the microphone and offers their experience and possible solutions to the dilemma. The level of creativity and the depth of experience that exudes from some of the minds gathered there is nothing short of astonishing. I truly cannot put a price tag on the value of having such a brain trust to turn to with difficult situations. Perhaps even more surprising is the fact that no one in that circle ever asks for anything in return for a brilliant idea. Anything anyone can do is offered freely, as part of the camaraderie of the club, as it were.

WIN/WIN

Unlike traditional real estate sales, where competition for listings and buyers is brisk and often brutal, exchangors operate from a win/win mentality. Everyone is welcome to participate because the more people and the more properties present in the circle, the more potential transactions exist. Everyone who comes to an exchange meeting for the first time is assigned a mentor to make sure they get off to a good start. It is an environment where everybody supports everybody else. It is common to see arms around the shoulder of the new guy and to hear words of wise instruction and encouragement. Exchangors are a family, so to speak, and take good care of their own. Sponsoring, mentoring, and championing the new person is a way of life with exchangors. This concern for others is perhaps no more apparent than in the many charities that have been spawned by exchange groups. There are scholarship funds for college-bound kids of high aptitude and modest means. There is an educational fund that underwrites courses to be taught in the real estate community. And there are many more private charities directed to local recipients with health problems or other disabilities. Great good radiates from the generous hearts of the members of these professional groups. I, for one, am proud to be part of the exchange community.

JOINT VENTURES

It only follows that after finding such a capable, trustworthy group of professionals, who gather together to do business, that we would end up building investment teams within the group. Many exchangors are part of such teams that have in some cases been wildly successful in their investment activities by allocating each of their strengths to larger projects of which they each own a share. This is where it really gets fun. "Hanging out" with friends, while making millions together is about as good as it gets. Expect to pay your dues, to be tested, and to prove yourself before being invited to participate in any such ventures. Once you have demonstrated your character and capability, the quantity and quality of the opportunities for joint venturing with other exchangors increases dramatically.

EDUCATION

As I inferred previously, continuing education is a cornerstone of exchanging. Exchangors operate at such a high level of expertise and creativity that their skills are not easily acquired. There is a structure within each national exchange organization to preserve, catalogue, and teach all of the principles and practices that make exchanging such a powerful tool for building wealth. Every national exchange meeting includes at least one full day of education. The best instructors in the business teach topics in which they personally excel, to advance the collective competency within the exchange community.

Like professional athletes, those who make big money in exchanging pay a price to acquire the skills necessary to perform at peak levels. Nothing in this information is meant to give the impression that equity marketing is an easy business. Like everything else of value, it requires dedication, education, and a good bit of perspiration to succeed. However, the same effort spent learning and perfecting your practice of exchanging is apt to produce results beyond almost any other field in real estate where you might apply the same effort. As you embark upon your venture into exchanging, please keep this axiom in mind, "I didn't say it would be easy; I only said it would be worth it."

TIP The best of exchangors operate at the top of their game. By comparison, they have skills in real estate on par with any professional athlete in sports. They are the *crème de la crème* of real estate practitioners.

In addition, the groups teach a specific skill set known as "counseling" to all exchangors. Counseling is the art of communicating with exchange clients in a way that familiarizes the client with the new world of possibilities available through exchanging. Counseling educates the client in preparation for the client to begin approaching transactions in nontraditional ways. This grooms the clients to engage their equities in creating the mutual exchange of benefits outlined above. Counseling and the preparation of our clients to participate fully in the exchange process is one of the core tenets of the educational commitment of the equity marketing community.

Counseling courses promote high-level communication skills and one-on-one teaching skills. An exchangor expects to handpick a select few clients and to form a long-term mutual commitment to represent them. Lasting bonds of friendship are often formed with clients. To do the best job possible, an exchangor must know her client's finances as well as she knows her own. The exchange community offers dozens of examples of exchangors who have made tens of millions of dollars for themselves and their clients over a period of a few decades, while living an abundant life in the process, and enjoying beautiful friendships. Through the education offered by the equity marketing groups, wealth building through real estate becomes a fun and affluent way of life.

When I first began attending exchange meetings and heard how lucrative it could be for anyone who paid attention and worked hard, I wondered if it was true. As I looked around me, I saw people well into their seventies and eighties who were still working. I wondered how it could be so profitable if people who had been at it for so long couldn't afford to retire. As I got to know those grand folks with gray hair, I learned that most of them were indeed wealthy. I realized that they continued to come and to do deals because nothing brought them greater pleasure than making money while associating with their best friends. What are they going to do instead, go golfing, or boating? Most of them do plenty of both, and anything else they want to do. I can't think of any group that enjoys life more than exchangors because they have the means to live their dreams.

There you have it! While this chapter is only an overview of equity marketing, it gives you a starting point, a portal to which you can connect. Like my father, if you have a dream to control your own destiny, if you are a fan of the Rich Dad system and wish to set foot on a path that has been proven to build wealth during good times and bad, this is your invitation to do so.

On the wall of my private office at home hangs a painting of a Palomino stallion, an image of Dad's all-time favorite horse, "Old Yeller." On the back of it, scrawled in my dad's cowboy handwriting, are the words, "For Wayne, when I'm gone," penned there to make sure I received it after his death. For me, the painting is an emblem of the joys of my boyhood, spent at my dad's side, as we traveled up and down Utah, Idaho, and Nevada, trading horses and cows, hauling hay and learning to be entrepreneurs.

It has been a long and rewarding journey from horse trading to real estate exchanging. So much of my father lives on in me and in my sons and daughters. He died content and proud of his family. I love him. I miss him. I think he would be happy to know that his story may inspire others to strike out on their own. In his dichotomies, he was both my rich dad and my poor dad. In being both, he taught me great lessons. He gave me much to measure up to and a few things to strive to improve. His example presented me with choices similar to those that Robert Kiyosaki's rich dad and poor dad presented to him. I chose to go for it, to live my entrepreneurial dream! On a crisp January morning a few years ago, Robert Kiyosaki shared his vision with me of giving people a track to run on, as a means of acquiring real wealth and of accomplishing the Rich Dad mission, which is, "To Elevate the Financial IQ of All Humanity." Robert asked me to make available to his students the incredible opportunity inherent in equity marketing. Will reading this chapter be the gateway to your financial future? Will plugging into the vibrant exchange community I have described be a means of accelerating your personal accumulation of wealth? Now that you are armed with this information, it is entirely up to you and the choice is now yours. For me and for my family, I choose to grow old with my dear friends, being one of those gray-haired rich guys, still doing deals and living my dreams into my golden years. I choose to be rich in relationships, rich in finances, rich in health, and rich in wonderful experiences. I choose a rich life. Each of us has the power to choose for ourselves. What will you choose for yourself?

WAYS TO LEARN MORE

www.waynelpalmer.com
www.nce1031.com
A soon-to-be published book on real estate formulas, by Wayne Palmer

 **Wayne Palmer** is widely regarded as a master in the creative structuring of real estate acquisitions and financing, using notes and other forms of real estate paper together with 1031 Equity Marketing formulas. His skills come from thirty years of daily practice of his trade, as the owner and manager of National Note of Utah, LC, and several other companies. He has been involved in real estate development since 1978 in Utah, Idaho, Arizona, Hawai'i, and Minnesota. By way of industry credentials, Wayne is a Licensed Principal Real Estate Broker, a Certified Real Estate Note Appraiser, a Certified Cash Flow Master Broker, a Licensed Continuing Education Provider, and holds the Equity Marketing Specialist (EMS) designation with the National Council of Exchangors.

23

How to Create Retail Magic: A Tale of Two Centers

M*arty De Rito is an expert on retail real estate—shopping centers and retail properties. As you know by now, there is a difference between residential, commercial, office, raw land, and other niches of real estate investing. When I want information on retail real estate, Marty is the person I call.*

For years, no matter where I would go to in Phoenix, I would see Marty's company's signs—DeRito Partners—everywhere, but I had never met the guy. One of my bigger commercial properties is right next to a shopping center that Marty manages. I knew the owner of the property and some of the tenants, but still I had never met Marty.

After a while, my imagination began to take over. I pictured that De Rito Partners was an old firm and that Marty was some old guy who had started the firm but was no longer active in the business. Then one day, I met him in the gym and was surprised to meet a very young person! After talking to him, I realized that the reason I had not run into him was that he is a very busy, ambitious young man.

Today, Marty is taking on some of the biggest and most ambitious retail real estate projects in Phoenix. He's got guts. Talking to him is invaluable because he has insights into the world of business seen only from the world of retail. In other words, he focuses on what shoppers are buying and where, along with how well the shopper is doing financially. When I want to find out what is hot and what is not with shoppers, Marty is the guy. He has insight into the local economy and what parts of the city are growing and what parts are dying because he is on the front lines of consumerism—just by knowing how retailers in the area are doing. This is why Marty's knowledge is priceless.

—ROBERT KIYOSAKI

In your city or town, I'm sure there is one retail center that is simply the place to see and be seen. It is the center where people congregate, where people take their out-of-town guests, where they shop, and where they go for fun. And it is the center that you as an investor might be interested in owning one day, it is the center that you as a developer may want to emulate, and it is the center that you as a business owner would put at the top of your list when looking to lease space. No matter what your interest is in retail centers, this chapter will provide you with experiences and truths that you will want to know before entering the retail arena.

Generally speaking, centers like the one we are describing are no different from any other retail center; after all, retail centers are simply a collection of stores and eating places with parking spaces, signs, and landscaping. But somehow certain centers seem to be the ones that have won the popularity contest. They have become the winners in the battle for the shoppers' time, attention, and almighty dollar.

In the early days of my career, I admired the great minds who could pull together such amazing opportunities and then shape them into retail developments that didn't just hit the mark—they nailed the mark. Heck, they invented the mark, and then they nailed it! Now I admire those people even more because I know what it takes to make that kind of magic happen. Now I, along with the help of my team, have waved the magician's wand a few times. Experience has taught me, though, that it takes more than a wand, and there is little magic involved. Developing a premier shopping center takes three potent ingredients:

Great relationships
Great real estate
Great attention to detail

Now you may be thinking, "Marty, of course it takes those things. I've read a few other chapters in this book, and that seems to be what lots of successful real estate pros are saying." Good. I'm glad the other authors are reinforcing my message. Great relationships, great real estate, and great attention to detail are universal truths, and anyone who wants to achieve any level of success in real estate simply must put every ounce of effort into each one because any two without the other isn't good enough.

In my years, I've known real estate pros who have tremendous relationships with some of the biggest and best retailers. They can get the appointments when no one else can. They have their foot in the door. I've seen them have tremendous retail locations—at the proverbial corners of Center and Main with high traffic and plenty of customer potential. But then, I've seen them completely blow it when it came to the details. The architecture is off, or the economics of the center aren't right or the visibility is impaired or . . . the list goes on and on. It takes excellence in all three of these ingredients for success.

But what does excellence look like when it comes to retail centers? It's a very different animal when you compare it to other forms of real estate, and as you read further in this chapter, you'll come to see why. So whether you are considering venturing into the world of retail centers, thinking about buying a retail center, or even thinking about leasing space in one for a business venture, I'll show you what excellence means so you can recognize it when you see it.

It has taken me decades to learn what I am sharing with you. I was fortunate to handle the leasing and sales of hundreds of centers when I was a retail leasing agent at Grubb and Ellis Company and on my own at De Rito Partners, Inc., and the lesson has cost me plenty. About ten years into my real estate career, approximately seven years after I left Grubb and Ellis Company on good terms to start my own shopping center leasing and development company, I recognized a great piece of real estate—the 1-million-square-foot Christown Mall. It was more than thirty years old and needed a significant rehab to accomplish a drastic change in the tenant mix. My idea was simple. Add large power center retailers (Walmart, Costco, Target, etc.) into an enclosed mall setting. The previous standard department stores had either left or were leaving to go to the newer mall near the freeway. But my research showed Christown Mall still had significant traffic counts on the arterial street, there was a good density of customers who wanted discount stores, and the existing owner already had Walmart in the center but it wanted to expand to a supercenter.

It all sounded like I was well on my way. My mistake was in choosing a partner to purchase and redevelop the shopping center. The firm I chose had a net worth at the time that was equal to the size of the transaction. In development, nothing ever goes 100 percent right; working through a project takes time, persistence, and staying power, and by that I mean cash. The minute we hit some major obstacles, my partner wanted out. To make matters worse, when my partner entered the transaction, he sold a portion of his ownership to a "hard money" lender. I didn't know about it until it was already done. I knew if trouble were to occur, hard money lenders had no interest in giving me more time to work out the obstacles. Their business plan would be to push me out and force me to live up to the financial guarantees that I had given my partner, who I knew very well.

The lesson I learned was never enter a partnership if you are the sweat equity unless your financial partner has a significant net worth. Find a financial partner who has a net worth or financial means that is at least five times the opportunity. Additionally, never allow your partner to sell all or a piece of his ownership without your written approval and/or a first right of refusal. My little mistakes cost me $7 million dollars in cash.

That was eye-opening to me, and eyes once opened must never close again. I became far wiser after that, and so will you with every project. But my goal with this chapter is to make you wiser from the beginning *before* your money is on the line. I guarantee you'll never look at a retail center the same way again, whether you are looking at it as an investment or simply as a shopper. You'll see it in a whole new light.

I called this chapter "How to Create Retail Magic: A Tale of Two Centers" because I will be using two separate centers as examples throughout. The first center, called Casa Paloma, is one I built from the ground up, and it has been completed for about ten years. The second center, the Scottsdale Pavilions, is an acquisition, and we're in redevelopment right now, but the work was probably about ten years overdue. I chose these two centers for this chapter because in ways you will come to see, they are living, breathing examples of my three key ingredients for success: great relationships, great real estate, and great attention to detail. Let's dive in and define what these mean more specifically.

INGREDIENT NO. 1: GREAT RELATIONSHIPS

Years ago, I had the privilege of meeting Mel Simon, the largest owner of retail properties in the world (NYSE: SPG), and he said something I'll never forget: "Make a friend today and a deal tomorrow." Those were profound words, particularly in retail real estate where you may find yourself working with those same "friends" your entire career, particularly when it comes to leasing space to these tenants.

Unlike some areas of real estate—commercial office for example—where you may do a deal with a tenant company once and then never again, or at best maybe five or ten years later, retail real estate is often the opposite. You may find yourself doing one leasing deal, two, five, ten or more a year with a company like Subway, McDonald's, or a grocery store, for example. These companies and their real estate teams become regular customers, and, like anyone else in sales, I believe our product provides better value and adds to their bottom lines. In other words, almost on a daily basis, our reputation and our relationships go hand in hand. Weak performance is not an option.

Relationships, I've found over the years, come in a variety of flavors.

RELATIONSHIPS WITH TENANTS

I can't tell you how many times the great relationships I've earned with retailers on one project have helped me on another. For instance, at our Casa Paloma center—a wonderful upscale, mixed-use shopping area—our tenants there appreciated us because we created an exceptional property with significant retailer sales per square foot, and we worked to bring in the best of the best retailers creating a strong tenant mix.

TIP I can't tell you how many times the great relationships I've earned with retailers on one project have helped me on another.

Scottsdale Pavilions is a recent acquisition that we have always seen as a center with huge potential. It had been neglected by its previous owner, and currently it is about 20 percent vacant. The retail tenants didn't like the previous owner very much, but they are beginning to like us a lot because we are making a difference. We're infusing huge dollars into improvements that will make the center more desirable to both retailers and shoppers. And we are working with them to redefine the right mix of tenants and create significant customer demand so that everyone can make money. That's what relationships are all about.

This opportunity to completely redefine the tenant mix and remerchandise the Scottsdale Pavilions is good news for everyone. Guess where we will go to find new tenants? You got it, to the people and the companies who believe in us, who are partners with us in our other centers, and who are our friends. Of course, there will be retailers we've never worked with before in the Scottsdale Pavilions, too. Our existing relationships will even help us forge those new relationships. We have a ready, willing, and able group of friends who not only want their own brands to succeed, but they have us as well. And they know that partnering to create a great tenant mix is one of the ways success happens.

RELATIONSHIPS WITH SHOPPERS

Just as it is important to have great relationships with tenants, it's equally important to foster great relationships with shoppers. In retail, relationships come in the form of giving shoppers what they want. Later we'll get into the details of exactly what that is, but for now, let's focus on the relationship itself. When De Rito Partners, my Arizona-based company, bought the Scottsdale Pavilions, we knew it had a bad relationship with shoppers. How? Well for starters, business was dwindling year after year. It was an errand center, meaning it was a place where shoppers would come to stop at one store and then leave as quickly as possible.

In retail, the goal is to get the shopper to stay at your center as long as possible. Think about it; if you stay at a retail center an hour longer than you intended, you'll probably spend more money. We all do it, either on food or on some luxury that suddenly transformed into a necessity right before our eyes. That's the psychology of shopping (there's more, so keep reading), and each of us brings it to life every time we enter a Costco, a Saks, or any other retailer. But getting people to stay longer isn't as easy as it may seem. It takes the right combination of convenience, entertainment, and ambiance to make it happen.

TIP In retail, the goal is to get the shopper to stay at your center as long as possible. Think about it; if you stay at a retail center an hour longer than you intended, you'll probably spend more money.

That's where relationships come in. Call me a ladies' man, but I try to have great relationships with women. No, not in that way, but in the sense that women comprise two-thirds of all shoppers. With men making up 95 percent of retail center developers, it's critical that anyone in this business understand what women want. Before I began developing Casa Paloma, I asked my wife why she was traveling twenty miles north to shop at the retail centers in Scottsdale, rather than going to the ones closer to where we lived. She looked at me with an expression that seemed to say, "You don't know?" and then began to explain. "The centers here don't have the right stores. There's no Banana Republic, or Chico's or Ann Taylor. There are no good restaurants and no A.J.'s Fine Foods [a higher-end grocery store]. There's nothing upscale. It's just more fun to go shopping in Scottsdale and more convenient because there are lots of other stores nearby that I can stop in to pick up little things here or there."

"Oh," I replied, my wheels turning. I know she left thinking, duh, or some more adult equivalent of that expression, but the truth was I wanted to hear the truth from her. And then, I asked the same question of her friends. From them I got similar looks and similar answers. That led me to my lifelong relationship with female shoppers, and it's paid off in big numbers. Casa Paloma remains today one of the top-grossing centers in the state.

The Scottsdale Pavilions, by contrast, had forgotten about its shoppers. It was a hot property when it first opened up twenty years ago, before there was much competition in the area. But then the trade area began to grow. Other retail developers began forging relationships with shoppers where the Scottsdale Pavilions didn't bother. Business began to trail off, and before too long the Scottsdale Pavilions was in a downward spiral. When I bought the center, one of the first things we did was send a questionnaire to six thousand homes in the surrounding community. We told our neighbors that we were going to reinvigorate the center, and if they would kindly tell us what they would want there, we'd give them two free movie tickets. We had a flood of responses, not because of the free movie tickets alone, but because people were honored to have been asked their preferences. It was the beginning of our relationship with the shoppers in the trade area.

What Women Want

Women make up two-thirds of all shoppers, so it's a good idea to deliver what they want:

- convenience
- variety
- atmosphere
- fun—entertain me
- ample, easy parking
- security
- one-stop shop
- the right stores
- value for their dollar
- cleanliness

INGREDIENT NO. 2: GREAT REAL ESTATE

Ah, here it is again. You're thinking location, location, location. You've heard that before, but in retail, the word "great" means several things beyond just location, and they are critical. They are nonnegotiable. They are the differences between success and failure, between happy tenants and problem tenants. Here's my list:

GREAT MEANS VISIBLE

Let me say it again: great means visible. Shoppers can shop only in stores that they know are there, and that's all there is to it. A store that is hidden is a store that is empty. Or a restaurant or a newsstand or a health club or an oil and lube shop for that matter. Being seen from the street and visible to customers is *numero uno*!

TIP A store that is hidden is a store that is empty. Being seen from the street and visible to customers is *numero uno*!

One of the classic breaches of this rule happened a number of years ago in downtown Phoenix. The development was positioned on a busy corner a few blocks east of the city's main thoroughfare. It was an expensive center with beautiful Spanish Mission-style architecture and stucco walls. It was touted as a destination for shoppers downtown and the perfect venue for free community-building events. Add to the project that a very prominent, newsworthy group of investors were behind the development and you have the makings for a real success, right? Wrong.

The developers forgot two important rules: visibility and shoppers. Allow me to elaborate. The center was built in an open-air courtyard-style with its focus facing to an inner courtyard on all four sides. From the north/south and the east/west streets, drivers saw only the sides of the buildings. Sure there were some signs that faced outward, but they were not prominent and couldn't have been any more so without compromising the mission feel of the architecture. From inside the center, the feel was quite nice, with good intimacy and ambiance. But there were a few other problems. First, the center didn't have an anchor tenant to support its size and draw enough people to the destination. That was a big mistake. The second problem was that too few people ever actually experienced the courtyard ambiance because the center's design wasn't inviting. And the third problem was there simply weren't enough people living in the trade area to support the businesses that leased there. The economics didn't work.

The center struggled to attract retailers and shoppers, and within a few years it became office space and classrooms. It is a classic example of retail developers getting too focused on a vision for a retail center and forgetting the most critical rule of retail, which is visibility and shoppers.

I see the visibility and shoppers rule broken all the time, and I've seen retailers pay the price. Look around and you'll find otherwise successful retail brands and restaurant concepts unable to make their numbers work because there simply aren't enough customers walking through their doors. You'll begin to notice centers that just churn tenants every two to five years because no one can last. And you'll hear shoppers peg centers or specific storefronts as jinxed because nothing can ever survive there. I'm sure just as you have the winning centers in your city or town, you have the centers that just can't seem to get things going. Nine times out of ten, the problem is visibility.

I admit, the Scottsdale Pavilions has a visibility problem, but thankfully, it is one that can be corrected. When the center was first built, the front of it was designed to be along a soon-to-be constructed freeway on the center's west side. Large signs and landscaping water features, complete with the annual migration of Canadian geese, flank the west side of the center to this day. The signs are very visible, and anyone driving by can't miss the destination. Sounds great, right? The problem is that a few years after the Scottsdale Pavilions was built, the community had a change of plans and decided to build the freeway on the *east* side of the center, not the west. So now, the center's backside is facing the valuable freeway drivers. And let's face it, the backside doesn't have the water features, it doesn't have the landscaping, and it certainly doesn't have the geese. Our backside is not our best side. So part of the plan is to literally make over the center so that the back is no longer the back and the visibility from the freeway will be glorious, including new pylon signs.

GREAT MEANS THE RIGHT DENSITY
OF THE RIGHT SHOPPERS

But all the visibility in the world won't buy you anything if the right people—and the right quantity of the right people—aren't in the vicinity of the center. This is called demographics, and every center lives and dies by the density numbers. It takes the right number of people within your center's target demographic to create a winning project.

Retailers, restaurants, etc., are all interested in demographics. They count rooftops, they look at census numbers, and more, all to arrive at the ideal location profile for their stores. From the developer's perspective, density and demographics define which retailers will succeed in a center. For example, at Casa Paloma there was a high density of people who were perfectly suited to upscale retail. Our preliminary research showed that. So it made sense for us to skew the center that way. We were a fit for the higher-end retailers we targeted, and they were a fit for our shopper demographic. And the right density of those shoppers meant we could be confident that we would have enough traffic.

In some areas, density and demographics dictating the type of center is obvious. For instance, there is no point putting a check cashing service into a center that is sitting in the midst of million-dollar homes. But some areas are in transition, and the demographic makeup isn't always obvious. That's where research comes in and plays a critical role. In planning the Scottsdale Pavilions retail tenant mix, we know the higher-end customer density is there, and we have identified a number of demographic needs that are not being served. Our key priority will be matching those needs with the center, its retailers, and its customers.

GREAT MEANS CONVENIENT

My wife and her friends taught me this truth years ago when I was doing my research for Casa Paloma. Convenience is everything, and it came up over and over again in the list of what women want in a shopping center. If I sound sexist, I don't mean to be. Anyone getting into retail needs to always remember that most shoppers are women, so let's just say it: we are catering to women's needs, not the needs of men.

Convenience to women means several things. It means "on the way" to somewhere else. The center's location has to be on the way to or from work, school, the gym, the day care center, the salon, or some other destination. And better yet, if it is on the same side of the road she is traveling, all the better. Ask women and they will tell you that all things being equal, they are more inclined to stop at a store on the right side of the street than they are to stop at a store on the left side of the street. Crossing traffic is an inconvenience and can be dangerous.

TIP Convenience is everything, and it came up over and over again in the list of what women want in a shopping center.

Convenient also means easy and ample parking. Searching up and down rows of cars for a parking space is the last thing shoppers of any gender want to do when they are in a hurry; and who isn't in a hurry today? Shoppers tend to give a center a few chances when it comes to parking, but if the problem persists, shoppers will mentally label the center as "a hassle," and they won't come back.

There are simply too many other choices today, including "stores" on the Internet where parking is never an issue.

At Casa Paloma, we knew shoppers' feelings about parking, so we made sure it was plentiful by building more parking than a center typically requires. But how many times has plentiful parking been an inconvenience all its own? Sometimes an over abundance of parking can cause the parking to be so far away from the store entrance that it is all too easy for shoppers to think, "I'll do this another time." Parking that is too far away from the store is inconvenient. Knowing this, when we built Casa Paloma, we built it with a parking configuration that extends wide instead of deep in relation to the store fronts. In other words, the walk from a parking spot to the center is a matter of at most twenty yards versus fifty or more. The perception is we're convenient, and convenient means great real estate.

GREAT MEANS HAPPENING

Another important aspect of great real estate is that it happens to sit in an area that is vital and alive. That doesn't mean it needs to be in the nightclub district. What I mean is that great real estate has (or has had) other great real estate projects happening around it. Take for example the Scottsdale Pavilions. One of the reasons I acquired it is because it is sitting right in the middle of two huge development projects, both of which are compatible to retail. On the east side is a $450-million casino resort under construction. It will bring convention business to within a quarter of a mile of the center. On the west, less than two miles away, is the $1-billion Ritz Carlton Hotel and high-end community slated for development. Beyond that, commercial office space is springing up all around, and the center itself sits on a road currently under construction—translate that in the process of expansion—to carry a heavy load of east- and westbound traffic. Add this action all up and you have a happening location.

TIP Great real estate has (or has had) other great real estate projects happening around it.

This location with all its opportunity seems extraordinary. But sometimes happening locations are far less obvious. I've seen small neighborhood centers be very happening spots for the right tenant mix. They seem to be where people congregate or where people go to eat out or shop. It's all relative. Sometimes a happening center in a small town would be a failure in a bigger city. You can feel which centers are happening and why they are happening. The key is knowing which ones are going to become happening and which ones are going to stay happening.

We placed Casa Paloma in an area that had higher incomes, lots of families, strong high-tech employers, along with a strong and growing population density. The trade area wasn't providing places for these people, or others with similar demographics, to shop and eat. They wanted a high-end grocery store such as A.J.'s Fine Foods and upscale shopping for the family such as Gap, Banana Republic, and Talbots. Additionally, they wanted higher-end restaurants, which included Z Tejas Grill, Fleming's Prime Steakhouse, and Roy's Pacific Rim Cuisine. Casa Paloma delivered, and the center continues to be a success.

GREAT MEANS AFFORDABLE

Arizona has some of the most beautiful retail shopping in the world. I'm not biased about this; we simply do. We're a tourism state, and the Phoenix metro area is a tourism area, so my opinion stands to reason. We'd better cater to the tourists and provide great experiences, or they will simply take their travel dollars elsewhere. There are lots of wonderful travel destinations in this world.

But in an effort to create the most amazing shopping experience, it is easy for developers to overspend on a project, particularly with today's building costs. Elaborate building designs, costly façade work, expensive hardscapes and water features, high-maintenance landscaping, and high-dollar necessities like parking areas and garages can inflate the costs of a retail project very quickly, sometimes to the point where the economics just don't add up. Here's what I mean.

For the most part, all developers want to build the most beautiful shopping center that garners accolades from peers, family, and friends. However, your cost per square foot must be met by what your target retailers can afford to pay. A retailer whose rent factor, which is ideally less than 10 percent of sales, must have the appropriate sales volume from "their" customers. If the retailer can't justify the sales volume to meet the rent, they will not lease space at your shopping center. For us, we start with what we think the retailer can afford in rent, and then we back into what we can spend to develop or redevelop the shopping center.

If cash flow is king, as Robert talks about often in his books, then profitability is the king royale. Any center with economics that are so out of line that proven retailers cannot turn a profit will not stay in business long. Actually, when this pattern plays out, the center will go bankrupt and a second owner will buy it for cents on the dollar. Second owners do stand a better chance of getting the economics in line because their baseline costs are lower. But sometimes the damage is done, the shoppers' patterns have been established elsewhere, and there's no turning the center around.

As tempting as it is to want to build or even be a part of the most beautiful and best center in town, really examine the cost per square foot and sales per square foot spread. Even if you are looking to lease space, this rule applies. Affordability equals success.

TIP As tempting as it is to want to build or even be a part of the most beautiful and best center in town, really examine the cost per square foot and sales per square foot spread.

GREAT MEANS A SUPERIOR TENANT MIX

Way back at the beginning of this chapter, I asked if there was a center or two in your community that just seemed to be the winner. My guess is that at least one and maybe two came to mind. Well, while all these other great real estate requirements help make centers successful, the right tenant mix is a big part of the magic.

Is it an art, or is it a science? Creating the right tenant mix is as much about understanding the shoppers' psyches as it is about discovering the retail options, building the relationships, and knowing how to negotiate the deals. It takes being able to visualize a center before it comes out of the ground or before it is revitalized. That's the art part. I am fortunate to have great people around me, and we all work together to create a vision for a center. It is truly the most exciting part of my job and makes all the tough stuff worth it.

TIP Creating the right tenant mix is as much about understanding the shoppers' psyches as it is about discovering the retail options, building the relationships, and knowing how to negotiate the deals. It takes the right mix of stores that create the highest pedestrian traffic that lead to higher sales.

I mentioned earlier about the importance of keeping shoppers at your center longer. I always think of Las Vegas when this subject comes up. That's the key to success there. The casinos do everything in their power to keep people from walking out the door. They offer food, they offer drinks, they have shows, they have a variety of games to play, and many of the newer properties have spectacular attractions like elaborate gardens, water shows, and nightclubs. If a Las

Vegas casino were a retail center, what I just described would be called "the tenant mix."

So using a casino as a model, what does that example say about tenant mix in a retail center? To me, it means making sure we have the right "something" at the right time for our shoppers. It's not about having "something" for everyone; I don't want *everyone* at our centers. I want only the people the center is designed for. But when those right shoppers are there, I want to satisfy their every need. I want to feed them. I want to entertain them. I want to make them beautiful. I want to make their lives easier. I don't want them going to the next casino—or retail center—if I can keep them at mine.

A retail center is about more than just shopping, and a good tenant mix delivers it all with a blend of shopping, eating, dining, entertainment, and attractions so that even an errand can become a fun excursion. A great example is Casa Paloma. It has a fantastic tenant mix that satisfies shoppers' needs all in one location. There's no need to drive from center to center wasting time, fuel, and effort.

> ## Casa Paloma Tenant Mix
>
> Great real estate has a superior tenant mix that satisfies a shopper's every need.
>
> **Food**
>
> A.J.'s Fine Foods
>
> Cold Stone Creamery
>
> Z Tejas Grill
>
> Pei Wei Asian Diner
>
> Tomaso's Italian
>
> Fleming's Prime Steakhouse
>
> **Fashion**
>
> Ann Taylor
>
> Banana Republic
>
> Chico's
>
> Francesca's Collections
>
> Coffin & Trout Fine Jewelers
>
> Gap Woman/Gap Body/Gap
>   Kids/Baby Gap
>
> *CONTINUED*

GREAT MEANS ATTRACTIONS

Over the years I have learned I can't always address every shopper's need through my retail tenants. Sometimes it takes a bigger attraction to make that happen. And if we think about our Las Vegas casino example again, we know that big attractions have the power to keep people engaged longer, sometimes for hours, and sometimes for days.

TIP We know that big attractions have the power to keep people engaged longer.

Paris Paris

Talbots

White House/Black Market

Furnishings

Creative Leather

Ritz Camera

Showcase Home Entertainment

Sur la Table

Gifts and Accessories

Urban

Paper Soiree

Personal Services

Rolf's Salon

Alltel

Bath & Body Works

Cool Cuts 4 Kids

Philosophy

Postal Annex

American Laser Center

Valley Nails

I'm proud to say that our new Scottsdale Pavilions acquisition is the home of the longest-running auto show in the United States. Every Saturday, car enthusiasts come to the center and show off to other car lovers and spectators more than four hundred of their classics: Camaros, Chargers, Corvettes, Cobras, and more than a few Mustangs. It draws hundreds and hundreds of people every weekend. That's an attraction.

The show's beginnings were humble. The center's McDonald's franchisee, a car buff himself, started bringing his three collector cars to the center every week. They would attract attention, draw people to his restaurant, and in the process he would talk with other enthusiasts when the opportunity arose. Little by little, this passionate, enterprising franchisee began inviting others to bring their cars, too. Now the show is a landmark, and because of it, so is this center.

Alcohol can be an attraction. What do I mean? The Scottsdale Pavilions is part of a Native American community, which currently doesn't allow alcohol at retail shopping centers. This makes it very difficult to get sit-down family restaurants such as Chili's or Macaroni Grill. Eating is a form of entertainment and keeps people shopping longer. The community now recognizes this and recently voted in favor having alcohol served at these restaurants.

I've seen centers offer everything from merry-go-rounds to wade-in fountains (a big attraction in Arizona in July), and everything in between. The key is finding the right fit for your target shopper. Is the car show the right fit for a shopping center when it attracts mostly men? Especially since we know women do most of the shopping? At first glance, you may think not. But consider that a lot of those men bring the women in their lives along with them to the car show. Some of the women enjoy the car show, while others do their shopping as the men talk cars. The show is actually a terrific attraction for men and women shoppers alike. It certainly doesn't hurt McDonald's or other restaurant business either; the show practically surrounds the restaurant.

Another important kind of attraction is architecture. Exceptional design and architecture will draw people from all over if for nothing else than the experience. Of course, everyone knows a positive experience requires something to remember it by, so most people who visit will buy something, which is the point of all this. People like to shop, dine, and in today's world, even run errands in pleasant environments. That's one of the reasons why at the Scottsdale Pavilions, we are embarking upon a major renovation.

TIP Another important kind of attraction is architecture. Exceptional design and architecture will draw people from all over if for nothing else than the experience.

When the center was built twenty years ago, it was considered aesthetically pleasing. But after twenty years of neglect, when we bought it, it looked tired and out of date. The appearance absolutely affected everything, including leasing, customer count, and sales. Particularly when newer, more exciting competition popped up during the last boom real estate cycle.

Great architecture can stand the test of time. It can grow better with age, and it can help you establish your center or business as the place to go with shoppers. That was the case with Casa Paloma. Yes, we have a good tenant mix, but architecturally, the center is a winner. Not only does it look up to date in terms of style and color, but there are no flat storefronts. The center itself moves in, it moves out, and each store is separate and distinct architecturally. It is not a long box with window fronts. Why? Because in the science of shopping, when the eyes get tired, the eyes leave. We have to keep things interesting. And the more interesting the storefronts are, the more shoppers lose track of how far they have walked. If I can get a shopper to walk into one more store, they will buy something. Malls employ this psychology, so why shouldn't retail centers?

TIP Architecture to a shopping center developer is like store design to a retailer. Keep it interesting because when the eyes get tired, the eyes leave.

And speaking of malls, Casa Paloma was able to lock in concrete consumer shopping patterns before the big regional mall opened up, three years later, about eight miles away. Today, that mall has not impacted our business because we serve shoppers' needs in terms of offerings, and we are more convenient,.

So whether you are considering investing in a shopping center, looking to develop a new one, or lease a space for your business, find a center that fits the bill when it comes to this very important second ingredient: great real estate. You will make your life exponentially easier if you do.

INGREDIENT NO. 3: GREAT ATTENTION TO DETAIL

The business of real estate is a detail business. From the very beginning of a real estate deal to the very end of it and beyond into management and eventual sale, the best real estate is planned and managed to the very last detail all along the way. So what does that involve? Well, aside from a long to-do list, for me attention to detail is all about time management.

Yes, it is the ability to effectively manage your time, which will allow you the luxury to pay attention to the details, and there are lots of them. For example, if there are five thousand retailers out there, I can spend ten years meeting them all, or I can spend three. I choose to be efficient with my time and do it in three. That means I need to have more appointments, more meetings than others, and not waste any time.

Do you know why Napoleon won so many battles? Because, as historians recount, he "saw the value of one minute." For Napoleon it was all about operating more efficiently than his enemy operated, and he squeezed productivity out of every minute. If you can adopt this mind-set, then you will have time for the details. If you don't, you won't. Not because there aren't enough hours in a day, days in a week, and weeks in a year, but because in real estate, you are in a race against the clock with just about everything you do. Whether you're deep into your sixty-day due diligence period and must meet your contractual obligations, or you are completing construction on a center and are neck-and-neck with a competitor down the road, or whether you are working to get your spaces leased, the race is against the clock.

At De Rito Partners, we have a Monday morning development meeting that lasts three hours. You may say that doesn't sound like an efficient meeting, but allow me to elaborate. In that meeting we go over each and every development project we have underway, and we clearly define exactly what we must accomplish that week and who is responsible for doing it. There is no question about our path, and there is no hiding under a rock. Everyone steps up, and everyone is held accountable. But at the same time, everyone is allowed to do their jobs. It's a simple process, and it works.

I believe one of the reasons why the details are so important is that in real estate development—again, whether you are developing something from the ground up, buying an existing property, or searching for the right leasing opportunity—you must be thinking ten years out. You have to look at who the shopper is, what retailers that shopper will want now, and what they will want ten years from now. You have to understand the real estate cycle trends and be able to predict where they will go in the next five years and in the next ten years (see Craig Coppola's chapter in this book). Then you must have the guts to leap early enough to get the jump on your competition, solid plan in hand.

THE LIST

A book I read many years ago had a long list of everything a developer had to do when developing and managing any kind of real estate project. We have adopted it as our detail list. Of course, within each of the items on this list are sizeable lists of actions as well. But this will give you the start you need to understand the definition of the word *details*. We don't miss a single one of these as we plan and execute a retail center project. We talk about them at our Monday meetings, and we feel a tremendous sense of accomplishment when we can cross completed items off the list. I see the world in terms of goals, objectives, and accomplishments, and this list is the cornerstone of what we do. Here it is from A to almost Z.

The List

Consider this your to-do list for developing and managing a retail real estate project.

A. Establish your development criteria and objectives

B. Analyze and identify your market

C. Develop and prepare preliminary site plans, concept design, and strategies

D. Oversee the entitlement process, and prepare the legal documents required by your city or town

E. Establish a construction team, a construction manager, and consultants

F. Perform your preliminary feasibility studies and financial pro formas

G. Negotiate any joint venture agreements, development agreements, and construction loans

H. Set up your legal documents such as leases, utility contracts, easements, CC&Rs, etc.

I. Create and maintain your project schedules

J. Develop your construction and operating budgets

K. Negotiate construction contracts and manage the bidding

L. Hire your brokers and manage your marketing/leasing programs

M. Negotiate your consultant contracts

N. Manage your development team regularly

O. Organize and hold on-site construction meetings regularly

P. Manage project accounts payable and watch costs

Q. Approve all invoices and submit for payment through loan draws

R. Review your change orders and lien waivers

S. Develop your monthly joint venture reports complete with financials, marketing, and budgets

T. Establish your property management plan, and management guidelines/procedures if self-managing

U. Manage tenant turnover, punchlists, and occupancy

V. Select a mortgage company, and negotiate the terms and conditions of the first loan

W. Work with the utility companies and the city or town to secure a certificate of occupancy

X. Negotiate and manage any sale of the property to a new owner

Y. Be persistent, honest, positive, and work hard

THE RESULT

When you pay attention to detail, the result is a center that works. It's a center that feels good to be at and is an enjoyable experience from the moment shoppers drive in, to the moment they leave. Perhaps you have a center or two like that in your community. You know the ones that I'm talking about. They are the ones that are easy to get into. There is no driving five hundred yards past the entrance, making a U-turn to double back, and pulling in. Access is truly easy. Convenience is a given from the first turn of the wheel.

Another telltale sign that a developer paid attention to detail is good parking. I can drive into a center and within a moment know whether the developer got it right. Are there enough spaces so that shoppers aren't searching and searching, wasting time, and causing aggravation? Or is there too much parking, causing a center to lose its intimacy and for shoppers, particularly female shoppers, to feel insecure at night? These things matter. You can do everything else right, but botch the parking and you can be in trouble. I could cite pages of other signs.

Ultimately, the magic all comes from bringing everything together—design, architecture, shopper needs, tenant mix, convenience, feel, legal aspects, construction, parking, the list goes on and on—and ending up with something that is uniquely suited for the market and the moment. From there, magic becomes lasting by having the foresight and the plan to grow the center into maturity.

I love the complexities of retail real estate, and I love the challenge. This business taps into every aspect of who you are and every talent you have or think you have. It confronts your weaknesses head on and forces you to find solutions and resources to overcome them. It puts you in front of and beside some of the most amazing people in the world who possess talent and perseverance beyond compare. And in the end all the hard work produces a product that satisfies people's needs but, more important, provides the escape and enjoyment that makes life all it can be. For me, retail centers are more than just bricks and mortar; they can be and often are magic—a magic that requires hard work, integrity, dedication, and a healthy dose of life-long passion.

WAYS TO LEARN MORE

www.icsc.org

www.uli.org

www.ccim.com

Zeckendorf: An Autobiography of William Zeckendorf, by William Zeckendorf

Threshold Resistance: The Extraordinary Career of a Luxury Retailing Pioneer, by A. Alfred Taubman

Trump: The Art of the Deal, by Donald J. Trump

Trammell Crow, Master Builder: The Story of America's Largest Real Estate Empire, by Robert Sobel

Crossing the Road to Entrepreneurship, by Bert L. Wolstein

Sharing The Wealth: My Story, by Alex Spanos

Maverick Real Estate Investing: The Art of Buying and Selling Properties Like Trump, Zell, Simon, and the World's Greatest Land Owners, by Steve Bergsman.

Marty De Rito is the CEO of De Rito Partners, Inc., and De Rito Partners Development, Inc.—brokerage, management and commercial development companies based in Phoenix, Arizona. He has more than twenty years of commercial real estate experience, specializing in the sale, leasing, and development of retail properties, including shopping centers and automotive parks. De Rito has been successful in providing top-quality aggressive leasing and management expertise combined with conservative development expertise. The development company has developed over 5.5 million square feet and acquired 1.1 million square feet of retail and automotive properties. De Rito Partners, Inc., is the largest retail brokerage company in the state of Arizona based on the number of exclusive listings. The firm has thirty retail agents and exclusively represents and provides leasing services to sixty-two retailer accounts. The company has leased more than 11 million square feet, and has listed for lease approximately two-hundred- and-thirty shopping centers totaling more than 14 million square feet.

PART 4

Lessons Learned

Kim KIYOSAKI

24

What One Property Can Teach You

W*hat can I say? I got lucky. Kim is beautiful on the outside, and even more beautiful on the inside. On top of that she has courage and is very smart. She learns quickly. And I know she did not marry me for my money because when we met, I did not have any money. What we had was our love and a dream of becoming a rich couple together.*

In 1987, the stock market crashed. The savings and loan industry went bust, and the real estate market crashed. This is when I said to Kim, "Now is the time to invest."

She often states that, back in the 1980s, she had no idea what investing was, especially investing in real estate. On top of that, most people around us were crying the blues and complaining about the bad economy. Fear and pessimism were everywhere. In spite of that, she trusted me, and we began looking at distressed properties.

Our plan was simple. We would buy two houses a year for ten years, which meant we would have twenty homes to provide us income. She studied, did her research, and looked at house after house. Finally she bought her first property. That investment changed her life. Within eighteen months, she had achieved her ten-year goal of twenty properties. She has never looked back. She took to investing like a duck takes to water.

Today Kim is an investment partner in more than fourteen hundred rental units. Even as the economy crashed in 2007, her properties delivered positive cash flows while many other real estate investors were losing everything. In fact, her investment income went up as more people became renters.

She is, as the title of her book states, a rich woman. But more than money rich, she is financially smart. She is a financially independent woman who does not need me or any other man to take care of her.

That is why I am so proud of her and love her with all my heart.

—ROBERT KIYOSAKI

It is amazing the number of life lessons as well as the amount of hands-on knowledge you can learn from one single investment property. I'm not just talking about your first two or three investment properties as you're starting out; those almost always seem to deliver a steep learning curve. I'm talking about the lessons I continue to learn after years of real estate investing. Every property teaches me something new that I didn't know before. Here is the story of one property that to this day remains one of my greatest teachers.

MIAMI, FLORIDA

In 2003 my husband, Robert, and I were in Miami, Florida, attending an investment conference. At one of the breaks during the first day, a young real estate broker, Matt, introduced himself to us, and we spent a few minutes chatting. Being the good salesman that he was, he couldn't help but tell us about a real estate property that he had some inside knowledge of. The property was not on the market, but the two owners were entertaining offers if the buyers were serious. My first response was understandably skeptical. I didn't know this guy, and I didn't know if this was just a hyped-up sales pitch. In any event, it was a good pitch, and we had a couple of hours free that afternoon, so we drove with Matt to take a look at this property. Of course, according to Matt, it was the best deal he'd seen in years!

About twenty minutes later, we pulled into an attractive strip mall with a few shops and restaurants. The mall was less than two years old, and some buildings were still under construction. At one end of the mall was a large health and fitness club. The building was about thirty-eight-thousand square feet with parking spaces allocated for the club. The property for sale was the building occupied by the one tenant (known as a single-tenant property): the fitness club. This particular piece of property was a triple-net lease investment. This means that the tenant—the fitness club—pays the property taxes, insurance, and all repairs and maintenance. There is very little management on the owner's end. It is a very appealing type of investment, given the right terms. We wanted to know more.

THE FIRST, OF MANY, LESSONS

One of the first things that struck me on this visit was the potential risk. Since there is only one tenant, this means that all of our income on the property would be dependent on this one tenant. Therefore, the ultimate key to the success of a triple net, single-tenant investment property is, very simply, the quality of the tenant. Our income, our cash flow, and the value of our property would all depend upon the tenant's ability to pay us every month until the end of the lease. You can see the implications here. With any single-tenant building, you want to make sure that the tenant is financially strong and has a solid business foundation. In other words, Microsoft is a quality tenant, Martha's typewriter repair shop probably is not. The reason why you want an A-list tenant is that if the tenant leaves, so does all your income, and then you're left with an empty building that was designed for the tenant who is no longer there.

TIP One way to protect yourself from your only tenant vacating your property is to set up a reserve account. This is an account that you add to every month from the cash flow of your property. To sleep well at night, I'd recommend at least one year of reserves that allows you to pay the mortgage and any expenses associated with the property, while you look for your next better-quality tenant.

THE GOOD AND THE BAD

With any single-tenant property there is the risk of the tenant moving out early and leaving the property vacant with no income. However, associated with that risk we discovered another risk that was unique to this property. The mall where the fitness club was located was adjacent to a gated neighborhood community. Ordinarily, that might be a good thing, but in this case, an agreement between the owners of the fitness club building and these neighbors was in force. The agreement stated that any changes to the building must get approval from the neighbors. What would this mean for us? It meant that if the fitness club tenant moved out, then the neighbors would control what we were allowed to do with the property. They would control who and what could move in there. The neighbors, not the owner of the property, were in charge. This was a stumbling block. Of course, Matt, the broker, didn't see this as much of a problem. Robert and I did, though. If we were to move forward, we would want this agreement closely reviewed.

On the plus side, this property was in a prime location. It was just around the corner from a prestigious country club, and it was on a high-traffic main street. The property was newly built, and the financials, at first glance, made sense. Based on the numbers shown to us, we would receive a healthy cash flow of about 18 percent.

TIP Lesson Learned: The financials given to you by most brokers are *projected* numbers not *actual* numbers. Projected numbers are typically the best-case scenario, and they present a better picture than how the property is *actually* performing.

Matt drove us around so we could get a feel for the area. There was quite a bit of new construction going on, and the number of people moving into the area was on an upswing. All good signs. We gathered up all the information he had and flew home to Phoenix. On the plane trip home, Robert and I discussed the pros and the cons of the property, at least what we knew of it in the brief time we had. By the time the plane touched down in Phoenix, we had decided we would make an offer on the Miami property and pursue it further.

The next day, I phoned Matt and put in our offer. We went back and forth with the owners and fairly quickly came to an agreed-upon price. Now the work began, otherwise known as the due diligence period. This is when you perform a very thorough check of the property to make sure that what you think you're getting is what you're actually getting. And this is when my problems began.

FROM THE BEGINNING

From the outset, this property had challenges. First of all, I live in Phoenix, Arizona. The property is located in Miami, Florida. Phoenix is nearly two thousand miles from Miami—quite a distance. There was no way I could just drive down the street to check on the property. If a problem arose, I'd have to get on a plane, spend all day flying, rent a car, stay overnight in a hotel, and then spend another day flying home—a lengthy and costly affair.

Second, this was the first triple-net commercial property I had ever pursued. Most of the properties I owned were apartment buildings with many tenants. This was a whole new animal in a whole new area. I immediately started telling myself how much I *didn't* know about this type of deal. And my feet were already cool from the start. I heard these words repeated in my head, "What if I lose money? What if I make a mistake? Do I know what I'm getting into?" My self-doubt was strong and loud. Then someone suggested, "You should hire an attorney to review the agreement." "Aha!" I thought. "That will solve my problems." So I got a referral for an attorney in Tucson, Arizona, and I hired him.

That decision led to my next problem, which I didn't understand was a problem until later. The lawyer I had hired was not a real estate attorney; he was a business attorney. He understood contracts but didn't understand a real estate investment. There is a big difference.

So the due diligence continued on. Now my attorney was talking to their attorney. And neither attorney thought the other knew what he was talking about. They didn't like each other. They did not respect each other. Whatever my attorney suggested, their attorney rejected, simply because it was my attorney's idea. And whatever their attorney recommended, my attorney said no to for the same reason. We were getting nowhere quickly, and the fees were mounting.

My attorney, being from Arizona, began arguing on issues that were not relevant to this Florida property. It was as if they were bickering over what remedies we'd have in place if a blizzard hit Honolulu—highly unlikely. Our attorney wanted guarantees on absolutely every single thing that could possibly go wrong.

TIP Lesson Learned: Out of this ordeal came a real estate (and business) rule that I now follow closely: Do not allow an attorney to negotiate your deal for you. An attorney's job is to point out potential problems, and options to those problems, and then it's up to you to decide what to do. It's up to you to negotiate the deal.

ON A PLANE

My attorney lesson was a major one. This back-and-forth dogfight went on for three months, and we did not even have an agreement yet! All we had was an agreed-upon purchase price. That was all. My attorney would call me every day with a new wrinkle in the deal. Finally, after weeks and weeks of this, Robert and I decided we needed to get on a plane and go meet face-to-face with the owners to work out the final four or five issues that were still unresolved.

We flew to Miami, rented a car, drove to the property, and sat down with the owners to discuss the final points. Within thirty minutes, all issues were resolved and agreed to. It was that fast when we met buyer-to-seller (another lesson learned). The seller went back to his attorney to draw up the final contract. Robert and I flew home. I called my attorney and explained what we agreed to and that a new agreement was on the way.

The new agreement arrived, and every point we and the seller had agreed to in our conversation was different than we had discussed. Had the seller or the seller's attorney revised the deal points? I didn't know. The two attorneys went head-to-head once more. This whole process was not just frustrating, it was exhausting.

The PHONE CALL

We had been working on this deal for three months, and there was still no agreement. Just when we thought we had the final issue resolved, a new one would appear. We'd take one step forward and then two steps backward. Would we ever close this deal?

Then my answer came.

It was 10 p.m. on a Thursday, and Robert was out of town. The phone rang. It was Matt, the broker. "The deal is off the table," he said.

"What?" I responded. "What do you mean it's off the table?"

Matt went on, "The owner decided it's just been too difficult, and he's pulling the property off the market. He's going to hold on to it for now."

I was stunned. "But we've been working on this for months! How can he just walk away?"

"He just did." Matt said. "I'll stay in touch since I'm sure there's another good deal out there. Bye."

I hung up the phone, and I sat in silence for what seemed an hour. It was probably five minutes. "I know how I can save this deal," I said to myself. "I'll call the owner and talk to him directly." Not paying attention to the time difference I phoned the property owner; and thank goodness he was a late-night guy because he answered the phone. He graciously spoke with me about his decision for about fifteen minutes, but it became clear that I was not going to change his mind. We said our good-byes, wished each other well, and hung up the phone.

WHAT THE HELL HAPPENED?

Again, I was stunned, and now I could feel the anger building inside of me. I thought to myself, "I have spent months on this one deal. I've ignored every other deal that's come to me. What a waste of time! Flying back and forth, all the phone calls, all the arguments, all the time! And to end up with nothing!"

Then, still fuming, I started to ask myself some questions: "Why did I hire a Tucson attorney for a Florida property? Why didn't I call Dan and Steven, my two friends who understand this kind of deal? Why did I act as if I know nothing about real estate? I know how to put a real estate deal together. Why did I let it drag out for so long? Why didn't I just talk to the owner, instead of going through attorneys?"

"What was I so afraid of?"

My anger was now near explosion. At first, my anger was directed at the owner for pulling out of the deal. I was furious with my attorney. I was furious with their attorney. I was mad at Matt for not holding the deal together. But then the truth hit me. My real anger wasn't at any of them. My anger was with myself. The truth was, the owner, the attorneys, and the broker didn't cause this deal to fall apart, I let this deal fall apart. Why? Because I was afraid I would screw up. I was afraid I would make a huge mistake and I'd lose our money. This was the biggest deal I had done up to this point. We were going to put $1.5 million cash into this deal. "What if I lost it?" I kept asking myself.

The bottom line is that I didn't trust myself. I didn't trust what I knew to get this deal done. After fifteen years of doing real estate deals I *still* didn't trust myself. And that's what really set me off because I *did* know what to do. At that moment, I knew exactly what I should have done to get this deal closed, and I didn't do it. Why? Because I let fear take over. I let my own fear beat me. I stepped up to the line, and I quit. At that exact moment I knew that I quit, and I was furious with myself.

NOW WHAT?

By now it was about one in the morning. I don't even know if I was talking silently to myself or if I was yelling out loud. I was nearly psychotic by this time. I don't even know how I got from the living room of my house to my home office in a separate building, but there I was standing in my office. I glanced at my desk, and on the corner was a stack of real estate investment offerings. I began to calm down. One of the things that upset me so much was the amount of time I spent on this deal only to wind up with nothing, when there were probably several other investments I could have been pursuing. I picked up the pile of pro formas, each with a description and some financial information on a property, and I started to look through them. Most of the properties were apartment buildings since that is primarily what I invest in, and the brokers I dealt with knew what I was looking for.

Then I came across an offer that made me smile. Craig Coppola, a commercial real estate broker in Phoenix who has since become a very good friend and contributor to this book, had presented this particular property to me when he heard about the Miami property I was looking at. But I was too engrossed with that time-consuming deal to pay attention to what he was showing me. At the time, I figured he was just looking to make a commission. Now that my mind had cleared enough to see what was in front of me, I recalled some of his conversation: "You should take a look at this property. Better deal. In Phoenix." I spent the next hour with my calculator, reviewing this offering and writing down questions. I went to sleep that night with one all-important question on my mind, the answer to which had to be "yes."

THE MORNING AFTER

I knew that Craig was an early riser. He's very driven and is always one of the top commercial brokers in Arizona. At 7 a.m. I called his cell phone. "Hello, this is Craig." he answered.

"Hi Craig. It's Kim Kiyosaki," I replied.

"Hey Kim. What can I do for you?" he asked.

Then I asked the all-important question, "Craig, remember that property you talked with me about when I was looking to buy the Miami property?"

"Yes. I remember you weren't too interested," he reminded me.

I held my breath and asked, "Is it still available?"

Craig responded, "That was months ago. They never actively listed it. They only wanted to talk to truly serious buyers. Are you interested in it?"

"I am," is all I said.

"Seriously interested?" he asked.

"Very seriously," I replied.

"Let me call them and see what the status is. I'll call you back as soon as I talk with them," he replied.

"Thanks, Craig. The sooner, the better," I said anxiously.

The next thirty minutes seemed like forever. I had my cell phone by my side every second, glancing at it every few minutes. Finally, my phone rang, and I saw it was Craig. "Hi, Craig. Did you get ahold of them?" I impatiently asked.

"I did," he said.

"And?" I asked holding my breath.

"It's still available. It's not on the market, but they will consider a serious offer."

I took a deep breath, more of a heavy sigh of relief. "Are you still there, Kim?" Craig asked.

"I'm here," I answered. "How much are they asking?"

"Their price is $7.2 million," he replied.

"What's it worth?" I asked.

Craig laughed. "Honestly, I think it's worth at *least* $7.2 million. I still love this deal."

I was elated.

"Craig, tell them I'll give them full price, $7.2 million."

Craig asked, "Do you want any special terms such as subject to you obtaining financing or specific terms of the due diligence period?"

I replied with confidence, "No. Full price. We have our due diligence period, and if all is as they say it is, we'll close in sixty days."

Craig questioned, "That's it?"

"That's it," I said.

It's a New Deal

Craig called me back less than an hour later. "It's done," he said. "Now it's time to get to work. I have to ask you, though, when I first showed you this deal you wanted nothing to do with it. Why are you so confident about this property now? What changed?"

I explained, "Craig, for the past three months I have been pursuing this health club building in Miami. I know more than I ever wanted to know about this type of property. I've learned about the business itself, about what's important to obtain financing, as well as what's an issue and what's not an issue related to a health club property. So even though the Miami deal fell apart, I realized I was simply paying my dues."

I laughed and continued, "Craig, the beauty of this Phoenix property is that it is a health club, almost identical to the Florida property. The purchase price is less, and the amount of down payment is less than the Miami deal. Plus the cash flow is greater in percentage and in actual dollars. But the most ironic thing of all is that instead of being located in Miami, this property is four blocks from my house! I think I know this area pretty well."

Sometimes your best opportunities are, literally, right around the corner.

THE CLOSING

We spent the next two months going through our due diligence, putting together the financing, and drawing up the agreement. In sixty days, the deal was closed without a lot of effort. Today that Phoenix property is one of the best-performing properties I own. Had I not gone through the process—the drama, the headaches, and the learning—of the Miami property, I would have never noticed this Phoenix property, and I would not be enjoying the wonderful cash flow this property delivers.

The biggest win for me out of this entire process was learning that the reason I lost the Miami property was because of my own fear. It was my own fear that caused most of the stumbling blocks to getting this deal done. I could blame everyone else, but in reality it was my own fear that was to blame: fear of making mistakes, fear of losing money, fear of looking stupid, all of it. When I dug a little deeper, I came to the conclusion that, yes, I probably will make mistakes, and I may lose money, and maybe I'll look like an idiot if things go sideways. But the fact is, I know how to do a real estate deal, and if I do my homework, do my due diligence, get good terms and financing, and dot the i's and cross the t's, then my chance of success is pretty good.

My greatest win from the Miami deal is that it eliminated 95 percent of my fear regarding real estate investing. No longer would my emotions get in the way. I could now focus on the facts and the creativity often needed to make a real estate deal work. It reminded me of what I do know and that I will always learn more.

THE PROPERTY THAT KEEPS ON TEACHING

And, today, I have learned more. There are several other lessons this whole situation taught me. Here are a few more behind-the-scenes stories.

MONEY? WHAT MONEY?

Have you ever said to yourself, "That (*fill in the blank*) is too expensive. I can't afford it." And you walk away somewhat relieved that you don't have to put yourself in the uncomfortable position of buying something that will stretch your limits. I understand. I've done the same thing many times. The problem is, when it comes to real estate, if you automatically say, "I can't afford it," you take yourself right out of the deal . . . and it may be an exceptionally good deal you're walking away from.

One of many things I've learned from Robert's Rich Dad is that instead of saying "I can't afford it," ask yourself "How can I afford it?" By asking yourself that question, it forces your mind to think. And it's amazing the number of solutions you will come up with. So that's what I do with almost every real estate I pursue.

There was a time when I was just beginning in the world of real estate investing when I simply did not have the money because Robert and I were building our business, and we were broke. We barely had enough money to pay the bills—actually we didn't even have that much. So if we were going to purchase rental properties we *had* to get creative, we had to come up with inventive ways to finance our down payments.

Today, when I come across a good real estate deal, Robert and I rarely have the money we need—not because we're broke but because our money is always invested. It would be easy to say "I don't have the money" and pass on the property, but it's more challenging and makes me smarter if I have to figure out how to come up with the money that I need.

That was exactly the case with the health and fitness club property. I pursued the property first. Once I decided that I intended to purchase the property, only *then* did I begin to figure out how we were going to come up with the down payment. On the Phoenix property, the time frame was short from the time I said, "I'll take it!" to the day we actually closed. I had only about two weeks to create the cash funding needed.

TIP Lesson Learned: When it comes to a single-tenant commercial property, not only is the buyer concerned about the quality of the tenant, but the lender is even more cautious.

Fitness clubs, in general, at the time were not considered grade-A tenants simply because of the number of clubs that had gone out of business throughout the years. The industry as a whole had a lower ranking when seen through the eyes of a lender because they were viewed as a higher-risk tenant. Because of this, the lender required an even greater down payment than an apartment building lender might require. So not only did I not have the money for the typical down payment, but also I had to come up with an additional 10 percent to get this deal done.

The deal did get done. The down payment was a combination of cash we had on hand, a loan from our business, and a third party private loan. The loans were just that, loans paying interest. No equity in the property was given up for these loans. One of the two loans has since been paid back, and the other will be paid off shortly. The rent on this property has increased annually as per the agreement, so every year the cash flow has increased, the cash-on-cash return on our investment has increased, and the overall value of the property has increased. It is an outstanding performing property.

Yet, when all the papers were signed, the cash changed hands, and we took ownership of this property, I made one more unbelievable mistake.

THE *REALLY* BIG MISTAKE

As we were leaving the law office where the closing took place, Craig, the broker, reminded me of something I had forgotten. He said, "Just to let you know, I told you several weeks ago that the seller of this property you just bought owns the exact same property in a location up north. It's still on the market if you want to make an offer." After all I went through in the past few months, and then scrambling to find the funding for this property, I was just so relieved to get the deal closed that I laughed at him and without thinking said, "Not right now, Craig. I'm tapped out. *I can't afford it.*" And that was a very big and costly mistake.

Instead of taking a step back and looking at the opportunity in front of me, I fell into the "I can't afford it" trap and let a fantastic opportunity slip through my fingers. Had I taken the time and asked myself, "How can I afford it?" and put my mind to work, today instead of *one* great-performing health club property I could have *two* great-performing properties. It was a costly, but priceless, lesson.

AN ATTORNEY *CAN* BE YOUR FRIEND

Yes, we've all heard the countless lawyer jokes:

How can you tell when a lawyer is lying? His lips are moving.
What's the difference between a dead dog in the road and a dead lawyer in the road? There are skid marks in front of the dog.
Why don't sharks attack lawyers? Professional courtesy.

I've met my share of attorneys who are the cause of these jokes. They are the ones who give lawyers, as a whole, a bad name and reputation. The two attorneys handling the Miami property did absolutely nothing to give me a warm and fuzzy feeling toward attorneys. But out of every bad deal comes something good. And in this case the good was our Scottsdale attorney, Chuck Lotzar, who is also a contributor to this book.

Robert and I had met Chuck earlier through a mutual friend of ours. Chuck is a business attorney with a great deal of real estate experience. Because the fitness club property I was purchasing is a single-tenant property, the lease agreement between the property owner and the tenant must be very tight. For that reason, we brought Chuck on board to review and give us his expertise on the agreement.

Chuck made some necessary revisions in the agreement, and we all concurred, but then he brought up a crucial point that I was not aware of. Remember earlier when I mentioned that with a single-tenant commercial property the quality of your tenant is number one? As far as I could see, the tenant was a large, well-known, national fitness club chain. But that's not what the lease agreement stated. Chuck red-flagged this and brought it to our attention.

The tenant on the lease had a similar name to the national chain but was an Arizona entity. The lease we were looking at had listed a subsidiary of the national chain as the lessee, not the national chain itself. I asked Chuck what that meant and why it was important. He asked me, "This being a single-tenant property in a forty-four-thousand-square-foot building, sitting on 5.2 acres, what's your biggest concern?"

"Simple," I responded. "My biggest concern is that the tenant might move out before his lease is up."

"Exactly," he replied. "If your lease is with a small Arizona subsidiary and they wanted to break their lease, they could simply declare bankruptcy and walk away. Right?"

"Yes," I answered.

He continued, "For a national chain to walk away from this lease, they have to declare bankruptcy of their entire chain. They cannot say these five properties are bankrupt but these two hundred are not. They would have to walk away from *all* their properties. You want the national chain as the lessee for your protection against something like that happening."

"Lesson learned," I concluded.

Chuck had to untangle the original lease agreement and then rework it, all the while getting all parties to consent to the changes necessary to make this deal work for us. It wasn't an easy task, but he got it done . . . and in the short time allotted.

That's the benefit of having excellent legal advice and expertise. Chuck is not inexpensive, but he is worth his weight in gold. As a result of Chuck's diligence and know-how, he increased the value of our property well beyond what it would have been. So I'm happy to say that my respect and appreciation for the legal profession has been renewed. Yes, an attorney can be your friend.

TIP Lesson Learned: When legal advice is needed on a real estate transaction, seek out a well-qualified expert. And don't be afraid to pay well for it. Cheap advice is usually just that: cheap. And in my experience, whenever I go cheap it ends up costing me more in the long run.

PATIENCE, A VIRTUE . . . AND AN ONGOING LESSON

This same property, to this day continues to teach me lessons I have yet to learn. So even though this property was purchased in 2004, my learning continues in a very good way.

The latest is that this property is adjacent to three commercially zoned properties. They are all older buildings on land that could be added to our existing 5.2 acres to make a much larger property. So if any of these properties become available, we will naturally be interested in pursuing them. There is one property in particular that is of most interest to us.

Knowing that was our long-term plan from the start, we offered Craig an equity position in the property in exchange for managing any problems or issues that might arise and, more importantly, for keeping us abreast of what's happening with the adjoining properties.

People often ask why some of the best real estate deals seem to come to us first. My answer is pretty straightforward: We offer more to those we work with. It may be in the form of a higher commission, equity in the property, or solving a problem to help get the deal closed. Relationships, not the transaction, are the key to sound business. People who focus only on the transaction, getting the lowest price, paying the least in commissions, reneging on an agreement in order to get more money, etc., typically do not have strong relationships with those who have access to the best deals. If people are a pain to work with, otherwise known as "high maintenance," then sooner or later people will stop working with them, and the deal flow will dry up. Our brokers and real estate partners have become our good friends because we all trust one another, and we all want one another to succeed and make a lot of money. We are in the relationship for the longterm.

STILL PATIENT

Craig has patiently been building relationships with the owners of these adjoining properties. He's candidly shared our interest in their properties, and they have openly been keeping Craig up to date on their plans. Again, it comes down to relationships. Many business people think you have to keep all your plans and desires close to the vest, that it's best not to reveal too much and sneak up on them at the last minute. That's a lot of work, keeping things so secretive.

When it comes to real estate, it's not rocket science. The property has a certain value—the buyer knows it, and the seller knows it. Every property has various uses. For example, an apartment building can be turned into individual condominiums or a hotel. A two-story office building could possibly become a four- or eight-story office building. The building could be torn down and something new could be put up in its place. What exactly the buyer has planned may not be revealed, but both parties know what the options are. So I prefer to be up-front, when possible, and get to know the seller and what his or her needs are. It makes for a better negotiation and much less stress.

Because of Craig's work, Robert and I now have a very pleasant relationship with the owners of the adjacent property. There is no hidden agenda. They know we want to buy their property. We talk openly about it. They also know we're not emotionally attached to it, and we'll pay a price that makes good business sense. The owners have no need to sell right now. The property delivers a strong cash flow to them. We understand that. This is where patience comes in. We've been watching these properties for about four years, and we'll continue to do so until the opportune moment arrives.

TIP Lesson Learned: Sometimes the pieces have to come together, and you just can't force that. You must wait patiently.

THE PRESENT VS. THE FUTURE

Oftentimes, the key with real estate is not so much what's happening today but what you see coming in the future. This is where studying the market, watching and understanding the trends, and on-going learning gives you the upperhand. By not understanding these things, your real estate investment could become one big fat liability, instead of the asset you had intended.

Look at what happened to so many investors in the subprime 2007 and 2008 real estate fiasco. They weren't paying attention to the signs, and it ended up costing them dearly. Why? As the market was surging and prices were soaring, many people thought the prices would just continue up. So they paid well over value for the properties with generally one of these three scenarios in mind:

1. They would buy the property and turn around quickly and sell it for a higher price (also known as flipping property).
2. They would buy a rental property and assume that housing prices would get so expensive that people could not afford to buy a home and rentals would be very attractive. Demand for rentals would increase, and so would the rents.
3. They would buy a rental property, such as an apartment house, convert it to condos, and sell them off individually for a big profit.

Those strategies were all based on the then-present situation remaining the same with prices continuing to increase. They were dealing with the present knowledge and ignoring the signs of future trends and situations.

For example, my friend Ken McElroy, who is Robert's and my investment partner on several apartment buildings, said to me about two years before this current economical disaster came to be, "Kim, get ready for the market to turn. Housing prices are about to come down."

"Why do you say that?" I asked.

"Because," he said, "something just doesn't make sense when a husband and wife walk into our leasing office and fill out an application to *rent* an apartment. We turn them down because their income is too low to qualify for the rent they'd have to pay. But then they walk across the street to a condo complex, and with the same income figures they miraculously qualify to buy a condo with payments twice as high as our rent! This cannot go on for long." So Ken was already preparing for this mortgage crisis two years before it occurred because of a trend he saw occurring with his own properties.

THE THREE P'S: PATIENCE, PREPARATION, AND PROFITZ

Where patience pays off best is not to be patient just for patience's sake, but when you see the future trend unfolding and are preparing to take advantage of it.

My neighbor Peter in Hawai'i taught me about patience when he explained how he purchased a beautiful oceanfront house on the lot next to his residence. Peter understands real estate, and he understand trends. He's lived in Hawai'i all his life, and he's seen the ups and downs of the market there.

The house next door to his was purchased by a gentleman from Japan, at a time when the Japanese were buying up a lot of Hawaiian real estate. He paid top dollar for this house. The house sat empty for years. One day, Peter noticed a for-sale sign on the house and called the real estate agent. He discovered that the owner was facing some tough financial times and needed to sell the house. Of course, the house was listed for more than he paid for it. What the owner didn't realize, which Peter did, is that the Hawai'i market had started on a downturn, and prices were just beginning to fall. So he waited. Peter realized that by waiting he risked the possibility of losing the property to someone who was willing to pay the asking price, but knowing the values of Hawaiian real estate and foreseeing prices falling even further, he was willing to take that risk.

It wasn't long before he saw the words "price reduced" on the for-sale sign. He called the agent. The price was still too high. He waited. He watched. Another price reduction followed. He still waited. Finally, after about two years, the price came down to within striking range. He called the agent and made his offer. The offer was accepted. His patience paid off.

The Future of Our Property

I don't know if we'll end up purchasing any of the three properties adjacent to the property we own. That depends on the price, the terms, the market at the time, and the owner's wants and needs. But we are in position should that opportunity arise. Patience has already paid off to some degree simply because those properties are worth quite a bit less today than they were a couple of years ago. We prepare today for the future that we anticipate tomorrow.

In Summary

When it comes to real estate investing, the learning never stops. That's one of the beauties of being an active investor, hands-on, controlling the investment, closely involved, versus a passive investor whereby you simply turn your money over to a so-called financial experts and hope and pray they know what they're doing. The active investor is constantly learning, growing, and most importantly, getting smarter about money. The passive investor, by putting the money in someone else's hands and walking away, learns nothing.

When the real estate market changes, it forces us to get smarter and more creative in order to use the changes to our advantage. Every property is a teacher to me in some way. If I learn my lessons well, I get a high grade. If I don't, it's a low grade. And my grade is determined by my primary reason for becoming a real estate investor: *cash flow*—my two favorite words in the world of investing.

Kim Kiyosaki began her real estate investing career in 1989 with the purchase of a small, two-bedroom, one-bath rental property in Portland, Oregon. Today Kim's real estate holdings include over 1200 apartment units, commercial properties, and land, and she continues adding to her property portfolio. With a passion for educating women about money and investing, Kim draws on a lifetime of experience in business, real estate, and investing in her mission to support financial education. She is a sought-after speaker, television and radio talk show guest, the host of a PBS *Rich Woman* show, as well as a columnist for WomanEntrepreneur.com. She is a self-made millionaire and a happily married (but fiercely independent) woman. Her first book, *Rich Woman: A Book on Investing for Women*, hit the *BusinessWeek* best-seller list the month it was released and has held a spot there for the past eleven months. *Rich Woman* is a best seller in Mexico, South Africa, India, Australia, New Zealand, and across Europe. Kim has used the international forum of the Rich Dad brand to showcase the startling statistics related to women and money, and through *Rich Woman* and www.richwoman.com, she has created a community where women can learn and grow and seek their own financial security and independence.

In the Beginning . . .

*M*uch *of the world has heard or seen* The Apprentice, *Donald Trump's long-running television program. By writing a book together, I have had the benefit of being sort of an apprentice to Donald. Spending time writing* Why We Want You to Be Rich: Two Men One Message, *I learned a lot about him personally, his business philosophy, his real estate philosophy, and why he is as successful as he is.*

—ROBERT KIYOSAKI

MY FIRST BIG DEAL

I was still in college when I did my first big deal. I spent my spare time in college reading the listings of federally financed housing projects that were in foreclosure. I knew my colleagues might be reading the sports pages, but real estate truly was my focus even then, so I would devote my time to studying everything I could to learn about it.

One day I came across Swifton Village, which was in Cincinnati, Ohio. It was in big trouble with eight hundred, out of twelve hundred, vacant apartments. The developers had faltered. The government had foreclosed, and it wasn't looking too good. In fact, it was a mess. It was such a mess that there were no other bidders.

This did not discourage me because I saw it as a big opportunity. I presented the situation at Swifton Village to my father, and we bought it together for less than $6 million. The project had cost $12 million two years earlier. We got a mortgage for what we paid, plus about $100,000 that we used to fix up the property, which it badly needed. In translation, this means we got this project without putting down any of our own money, and it would be possible, from the rent proceeds, to cover the mortgage.

As a college student, I found this to be very exciting stuff. I knew it'd be a challenge, and it was, but my enthusiasm was there because I could so clearly see a success coming out of it. I had done enough research to know it had great potential—potential as well as immediate problems.

This complex had a reputation for having "rent runners"—tenants who would rent a trailer and in the middle of the night would pile their belongings into it and disappear. This happened on a regular basis, so I realized an immediate action would be for me to hire someone for 24/7 patrol, which I did.

The other thing that had to be addressed quickly was the state of the buildings themselves. Disrepair is one thing, dilapidation is another, and this complex had a high proportion of both conditions. We estimated it would require at least $800,000 to make an effective difference. One good thing is that we were allowed to increase the rents immediately, which we found much easier to do in Cincinnati than in New York.

The buildings were red brick, and we put white shutters on all the windows, which made a huge difference aesthetically. We fixed up the grounds. We replaced the very unattractive aluminum front doors on the apartments with white colonial doors, which, combined with the shutters, made a big difference. We didn't take shortcuts, but we made sure our improvements would be noticeable, and they were. Swifton Village had a new look, and people were impressed. We ran ads in the Cincinnati papers, and in less than a year it was completely rented.

We soon realized that we needed a permanent project manager. This was a big complex, and we'd already been through a few who hadn't worked out. I finally found a guy who has left a permanent impression on my memory. He was a con man from the inside out. He didn't try to hide that fact, and he had close to zero social skills. He was insulting, brash, and as politically incorrect as you could possibly be. But I noticed that he had the ability to get things done, to get them done quickly, and that he was effective as a property manager. The other guys I had might be more likeable or more honest, but they were not as competent when it came to their job. I had to keep my eye on this particular guy, but in the long run it was worth it to have the complex running well.

This property became a great success, and it didn't require me to be there very often. The property manager ran the place well, and there were no more rent runners. All was well until a few years later when I visited and spoke with a tenant who had become a friend. He told me that the neighborhood had changed, and that I should get out. Swifton Village was fully rented, and there were no complaints about the management, but I respected his insights enough to spend a few days in Cincinnati and check it out for myself.

I discovered that he was right. It was quickly becoming a very rough neighborhood. I decided to put Swifton Village up for sale, and it didn't take long to find a buyer. We sold it for $12 million—$6 million more than we had paid for it a few years earlier. For a first deal, it was a good one, and I learned some great lessons about human nature in the process. I also learned that foreclosures were not going to be my niche—but this first venture helped to fund my ultimate goal, which was to be a developer in Manhattan and to build my own buildings. I wasn't dabbling—my focus was intact.

Another lesson was the importance of delivering quality. I made sure the buildings were clean, safe, and well presented. We didn't have marble floors or gold fixtures, but the simple steps of making the grounds appealing, along with the addition of white shutters and attractive front doors went a long way to establishing my name with excellence. That's something to always keep in mind, whether your name is on the building or not. Learn to distinguish yourself in everything you do.

ARRIVING IN MANHATTAN

Starting out in Manhattan was definitely a challenge. One big New York real estate guy was quoted as saying, "Trump has a great line of s—t, but where are the bricks and mortar?" It wasn't exactly a warm welcome, but at least I knew what I was up against. Looking back, I think perhaps they didn't know who *they* were up against. I'm the guy who would eventually write *Never Give Up* and actually mean it. I'm still here and going stronger than ever.

That wasn't the case in the early 1970s. I was a newcomer, and the city was in debt. I even heard people talking about the city going bankrupt. It wasn't a nurturing environment for a budding developer. But my focus was so clear that I wasn't discouraged. I knew there were still opportunities even in a so-called

Quotable Quotes by Donald Trump

"Big problems can equal big opportunities."

"If you don't have major problems, you're probably not doing something major."

"Adversity is a fact of life. Accept that, and you will be prepared."

"Business is an art, whether it's real estate or anything else. Treat it that way by developing your technique, being tenacious, and remaining passionate."

"My father's four-step formula is one I've always used because it works: get in, get it done, get it done right, and get out."

"When you are confronted with a problem, ask yourself this question: Is this a blip, or is it a catastrophe? That will align your thoughts and your reactions to where they should be."

"Reaping and sowing are directly related, but you need to know which comes first."

"Resilience is part of the survival of the fittest formula—make sure you remain adaptable."

"Real estate has a way of evening itself out. There are always ups and downs, and that's a fact, not an aberration."

"Don't depend on anyone else for providing your financial security."

terrible market. In fact, it was a terrible market at that time. But my determination was such that I refused to give in to the facts and continued to work my way around them. There was no place like Manhattan—and I intended to stay.

My first real estate interests in the city were the abandoned railyards along the Hudson River, at 34th Street and 60th Street, which was about one hundred acres. I then tried to convince the city that the site for the new convention center (now known as the Jacob Javits Center) should be built where it is on West 34th Street, instead of where the city wanted to build it, all the way downtown in Battery Park. As I said in my first book in 1987, *The Art of the Deal*, "We won by wearing everyone else down. We never gave up . . ." in referring to this 1977 battle. In 1978, the city finally decided to build on West 34th Street, which was a victory for me.

However, the city and state decided they would oversee the job. My offer to manage it was rejected, and as a result they went close to $700 million over budget. A lot of money was wasted, and today we are seeing how quickly the center has deteriorated. But at the time, I focused myself on the far more exciting prospect of the 60th Street railyards that I had. I wanted to make it a residential haven that faced the Hudson River. I knew I'd face a lot of opposition there, between zoning and the adjacent community, as well as from a city that was in financial crisis. It was in 1979 that I allowed my option on the 60th Street railyards to expire—but somehow I knew I'd be involved with them again later, which has proven to be true. Trump Place now proudly stands on those former yards, and is still being completed, almost thirty years later. But that's another story.

During this time with the railyard property, I was still looking around at other opportunities in Manhattan. The old Commodore Hotel, which was situated next to Grand Central Station, was having a hard time of it. The whole area was having a hard time, in fact, and it looked like it. It had become a crummy neighborhood that everyone tried to avoid—certainly much different than it is today.

I set out to try to acquire the Commodore Hotel and change it for the better. Once again, I wasn't met with great enthusiasm. Even my father said, "Buying the Commodore at a time when even the Chrysler Building is in bankruptcy is like fighting for a seat on the Titanic." He was well aware of the risk involved.

While I was aware of the risk, I also saw it as a way to get the city back to a flourishing condition, not just limping along, which is what was happening. The neighborhood had become dilapidated, and this was a good way to get it back on track again, along with providing some jobs. There are always several ways to view a situation, and it's a good idea to have your vision intact enough to withstand opposition.

At the time that I was interested in going into negotiations for the hotel, they owed $6 million in back taxes, had recently spent $2 million in renovations (which was obviously not enough), and they wanted out. In order to purchase the hotel for $10 million, I would need a tax abatement from the City of New York, financing, and a commitment from an experienced hotel company. In addition, I would have to structure a deal with other interested parties, and that was certain to be complex. Complicated is an understatement for this situation, and it took several years of negotiating to work it all out.

One of the first things I did was to find a designer who knew what I wanted to do and had the same enthusiasm for the project. I found a young architect named Der Scutt who was a perfect fit—he understood what I wanted to do, which was to wrap the building and make it a reflecting façade for the buildings surrounding it. It might have been premature to find a designer before I knew the deal would even go through, but I'm a strong believer in following your vision and working from there. I also had a compatriot in vision who believed in my plans as vividly as I did.

I also needed to find an operator, one with a lot of experience. I realized that a lot of big hotel chains had a presence in New York, but the one that I liked the most, the Hyatt, didn't. I called to see if they were interested, and they were. We made a deal quickly and announced it to the press in May of 1975. So I had a hotel partner.

What was left was still monumental—I needed to get financing and a tax abatement from the city. I decided to hire a real estate broker who was in his sixties and had a lot of experience. I was twenty-seven at the time, and I thought having a broker on board would look good, which it did. With an architect, a hotel partner, and an experienced broker lined up, I was ready to go for it.

We hit a brick wall, and fast. Without financing, the city wasn't about to consider a tax abatement. Without a tax abatement, the banks weren't very interested in financing. It was a classic catch-22 situation. While discussing this, we decided we'd bring up the obviously hurting and decaying city and hopefully make the bankers feel guilty for looking the other way when we were obviously trying to do something constructive. Well, that didn't work. But we kept trying, and we finally found a bank that appeared to be interested.

After spending many hours of time and effort with them, one guy suddenly just changed his mind. He brought up ridiculous and unimportant issues and was obviously trying to kill the deal. We tried everything, but he was set in a negative groove and couldn't be convinced to change his mind.

It was at this point that I wanted to give up. Literally, I was worn out. It was my lawyer, George Ross, who convinced me to keep trying, and he made it clear that I'd already spent so much time on this project that I shouldn't just walk away from it. So I decided to approach the city, even without financing, to explain the situation. It was clear that the Hyatt Hotel organization was enthusiastic about coming to New York, and they'd do a great job, but the costs were just too high. We needed a break on property taxes or nothing would be done. I also pointed out how the new hotel could work as a catalyst for sparking up the whole Grand Central area into renovation and rejuvenation.

It worked. The city agreed, and it was a deal that would make us partners, and a deal that would benefit everyone. I would receive a property tax abatement for forty years, and I would buy the Commodore for $10 million, with $6 million going to the city for back taxes. Then I would sell the hotel to the city for one dollar, and they would lease it back to me for ninety-nine years. As a result, we got financing from two institutions.

None of this was easy, and when I look back I realize I had great fortitude to hang in there for so long. But it was worth it. The Hyatt at Grand Central started the revitalization of the whole area, and today it's a thriving and beautiful hub of New York City. The hotel itself reflects the architecture of the area in the four exterior walls of mirrors that replaced the formerly dingy façade of the Commodore. This project did not have my name on it, but I can tell you that every detail mattered. The quality was there, the vision was there, and the results are still there.

Ten Small Steps to Big Success

1. Find out what you love to do. Trust yourself enough to find out what is best for you, and what you're best at doing. For great success, you need great passion, but make sure it's well directed.

2. Learn everything you can about what you're doing: Be an expert.

3. Ask yourself questions. For example, ask yourself, "Is there anyone else who can do this better than I can?" It's another way of saying know yourself, and know your competition. That can simplify things quickly.

4. Know the world. See the world as an emerging market. Study it—daily. That's a requirement, not an elective.

5. Focus, and make sure it's a 100 percent focus—nothing less.

6. Know your own blind spots. Ask yourself, "What am I pretending not to see?"

7. Set the bar high—do the best you possibly can.

8. Think positively. Zap negativity immediately. Focus on the solution, not the problem.

9. Be persistent, tenacious, and alert—every single day. Get this momentum going daily and don't let up.

10. Never give up. Never, never give up—that is the best advice I can give you.

Donald Trump is the chairman and president of the Trump Organization, a privately held company in New York. The Trump Organization encompasses global real estate development and global licensing, sales and marketing, property management, golf course development, entertainment, product licensing, and brand development. In a departure from his real estate acquisitions, he is a best-selling author; produces and stars in the television reality show *The Apprentice*; and partners with NBC Television Network in the ownership and broadcast rights for Miss Universe, Miss USA, and Miss Teen USA pageants. He is the archetypal businessman—a deal maker without peer and an ardent philanthropist.

26

What Is the Most Important Thing You've Learned from Your Father About Real Estate?

DONALD TRUMP JR.

Don Trump Jr.'s father and I are the same age. The famous Donald Trump, one of the greatest celebrity real estate developers in the world, is a valued friend and mentor to me. Having Donald Trump as a coauthor and friend has been one of the greatest blessings in my life. Another blessing has been getting to know Donald's two sons, Don Jr. and Eric.

One night, Donald Trump and I were guests at the Quill Awards, an evening similar to the Academy Awards, but rather than recognizing Hollywood stars, the Quill Awards recognizes great authors. Donald Trump and I were there to present the award to the best business author.

At the awards dinner, I got to sit next to Don Trump Jr. and his gorgeous wife. For some reason, our discussion got around to the subject of big game hunting. At that dinner, I found out that Don Jr. along with his brother, Eric, is not only a hunter, but a gun collector, just like me. Now I know that guns and hunting are not politically correct subjects. So it was refreshing to find a young man, actually two, who shared the same passion in life, a subject I tend to be secretive about—even to my wife, Kim, who is an animal rights activist and person who is not particularly fond of guns. Kim, like Donald Trump, prefers the golf course to the wilds.

Over the years, I have gone hunting with Don Jr. and Eric a number of times and have gotten to know them personally. They have it all. They are rich, famous, good looking, and perfect gentlemen. They are not spoiled brats as many rich kids are. They are driven, smart, experienced, and market savvy. I learn a lot about real estate and life on every hunting trip we take together.

Their father and mother can be very proud of these two young men.

—ROBERT KIYOSAKI

This simple statement seems so obvious, but I am always amazed by the number of people who miss out on incredible opportunities because they're too afraid to simply ask. Ultimately, these people fear rejection. They are afraid of the word "no." They are either shy, weak, or too proud to ask for something or to negotiate the things they want in life. The world of real estate is no place for people who fit this description. So here's your chance to buck up.

TIP **In life and in business you never get anything you don't ask for: always negotiate!**

Shrinking from the task of negotiating, by being afraid of simply asking for what they want, people from all walks of life, not just real estate, miss a fundamental opportunity to do what all great business people try to do: buy goods or service at a better price. I learned from my father at a very early age that in business you must take advantage of every easy opportunity. He didn't sit me down and explain this lesson. Rather it was one that took me two summers of very hard work to figure out.

My first job was as a dock attendant at a marina we owned as part of what was at the time Trump's Castle Casino in Atlantic City, New Jersey. I was fourteen years old and living away from home for two months tying down boats, and hooking up electrical and water systems and anything else that I could be persuaded to do for minimum wage plus tips. Everyone should work for tips at some point in their life. Nothing puts life, service, and work ethic into such clear perspective as that. Working for tips was a great lesson in and of itself.

After two summers of dock work, it was time for me to start working as a landscaper at one of our properties. The position had a lot more responsibility and required more skill. I ran tractors, I operated chainsaws, and I performed the hard labor required to keep the property looking pristine. I was making minimum wage at this job, too, but there were no tips from the drunken boaters who occasionally let a twenty slip through their hands. My salary was minimum wage and nothing more.

At first, I said nothing about the pay structure of this job. I didn't want to seem greedy, and I suppose I was too proud to ask for more money. But toward the end of summer, I finally went to my father and asked him why I had not gotten a raise when I took this more skilled position. Especially since the tip component of my salary was now nonexistent. His answer was very simple, "You did not get a raise because you did not ask for one. Why would I pay you more than you were willing to work for?" Well, that did it for me. It was a hard lesson, and one that in hindsight seems so obvious. But the bottom line was that I had let my emotions, my fears, and my pride get in the way of what I wanted to achieve.

Since then, I always make a conscious effort to never put myself in the same position again. The hard work that summer didn't bother me, but I felt like I had wasted an entire summer working a job that paid minimum wage when I could have been earning more if I had only asked for it. That lesson has stuck with me to this day.

As is often the case, the hardest lessons are the best lessons, and my summer as a minimum wage landscaper certainly drove the message home. Thankfully, I learned it before the stakes got too high. If you're going to lose income, it's always better to do it when playing with low numbers. Learn your lessons like I did, before too many zeros get into the mix.

I no longer let the fear of "no" overpower me. Instead, I make a game of negotiations. Here's how I play it, and you can do it, too. At every opportunity, I ask for, negotiate, and almost always get something above and beyond where I started. To me anytime I save a few dollars or get an extra "something" thrown in—whatever that "something" may be that I am asking for—I have created additional value. And here's a universal truth: Creating value is what business is all about!

When it comes to real estate and life in general, don't be afraid to ask. The worst that can happen is that the person you ask says, "No." And in that case, you're no worse off than you were when you started. Asking is quick, it takes two seconds, and believe it or not, good businesspeople expect it. By simply asking, you give yourself and everyone else the time and the opportunity to put themselves in a better financial position and add value. Even if you get the dreaded "no" at first, it's not so bad. Sure, you may not get exactly what you wanted, but often you can split the difference and end up somewhere in the middle with each side giving a little and getting a little. That's the power of negotiation. Even in that scenario, you end up ahead.

The reality that I learned all too well is to just keep asking and pushing. No one in his right mind will refuse to sell you something at his original price simply because you tried to buy it cheaper. The worst case scenario is that you end up exactly where you started. Eventually, you will come to realize that hearing "no" is not the worst thing in the world after all. It becomes part of the game, and hearing "no" actually makes it easier for you to ask in the future.

Eventually, you'll get bolder. You'll discover when you ask for something egregious that you think the other person can't possibly deliver, often the compromised position ends up more in your favor than you could have ever hoped for. In some cases the person may agree to your crazy question and take the bait, hook, line, and sinker. When playing the game, try not to fall out of your chair when this happens (and it will) because the last thing you want is the other person to realize is that he made a mistake. He may try to renegotiate for a better deal, leaving you snatching defeat from the jaws of victory.

The same holds true if a seller gives you a quote that you find completely thrilling. Don't accept the proposal as is. Go through the exercise of back-and-forth negotiation. Even after the back-and-forth seems to be over, ask him to do a bit better just so he feels he got the most out of you. It's how the game is played, and it will ensure the deal closes. There will be time for exuberance, but it is not when you are at the table. Practice restraint so the other person feels they got the best of you, not the other way around. Do that and you set the tone for future negotiations, and you set yourself up to win again and again and again.

Finally, the more you ask, the easier it becomes to ask in the future. Hearing "no" becomes no big deal. You'll find the habit of asking and the skill of pushing creates a positive cycle of circumstances that can create benefits for you and the projects you apply the techniques to. Try to negotiate at every opportunity, I mean every opportunity. You'll be surprised where you'll find results. I even try negotiating at retail stores. When the regular clerk who is checking me out says, "No," I ask to speak to his manager. Do this and you're almost guaranteed a 10 percent break if you push a bit. Sounds crazy? Try it and see. A 10 percent savings is 10 percent earned.

When you build up confidence in your negotiation techniques, become flexible in how you argue your points, and can adjust your style, you'll find the negotiating game becomes easier. Give it a go; you have nothing to lose and a lot to gain.

Donald Trump Jr. is an innovator and leader in today's young business world. As an executive vice president at the Trump Organization, Donald Jr. works in tandem with his siblings Ivanka and Eric to expand the company's real estate, retail, commercial, and hotel interests nationally and internationally. His extensive real estate development experience, rigorous education, and inherent business sense add a level of detail and depth to the management of all current and future Trump projects. In addition to his real estate interests, Donald Jr. is an accomplished and sought-after speaker and has been featured as an advisor on the highly acclaimed NBC show *The Apprentice*.

ERIC TRUMP

I am afraid to say my wife, Kim, is in love with Eric Trump. While she is very fond of Ivanka and Donald Trump Jr. Eric has a special place in her heart. She loves him because he is an especially kind person—just like her—and good-looking. He is the youngest of three children, just like Kim who is the youngest of three daughters. While all three Trump children have that celebrity magic, to Kim, Eric is special.

One of the most memorable times in my life was when Don Jr. and Eric invited me to hunt pheasants at their club, an hour out of New York City. At the time, I did not really know the two young men. Spending the day in the mud and the cold, slogging through knee-high water, and chasing pheasants with dogs, let me know how truly special and unique they are. I got to see them outside of the high-rise offices next to the Plaza Hotel and Central Park on Fifth Avenue.

One of the first things I noticed is both young men shoot and collect the same antique shotguns I collect. They are old shotguns—about seventy-five years old—from Belgium made by Francotte, a family of gunmakers few people have heard of.

The next thing I noticed was how kind and respectful Eric and his brother were to everyone. They were not snobbish or arrogant. They were not even phony gentlemen. They were truly kind and respectful. It did not matter if the people were members of the club or workers of the club, all people were treated with the same warmth and respect.

Later, as we drove back to New York City, we stopped by an old village inn, possibly two hundred years old, to have a meal. Again, both young men went out of their way to greet and say hello to the staff of the restaurant. While the patrons gawked and stared at the two young celebrities, Eric and his brother went behind the counter into the kitchen to say hello to the kitchen staff. I gained a new level of respect for each of them on that day. Their kindness is extraordinary.

In 2008, I invited both young men to a private island in the chain of Hawaiian Islands for a hunt. As we drove to the helicopter pad, Eric was texting his sister, Ivanka, a special family recipe. When I asked him if he knew how to cook, he and his brother chimed in saying, "Of course." When I asked them how they learned to cook, both young men explained that they saw their family service staff as servants for their mom and dad, not servants for them. Rather than become spoiled kids who expected to be waited upon by their parents' servants, they learned to cook and take care of themselves and each other. I can say that all three children truly love each other.

Today, I see all three kids as incredible role models for the next generation, just as their dad and mom were role models for my generation. It is with personal gratitude that my life's work has put me in contact with the Trump family and the people of the Trump Organization.

—Robert Kiyosaki

For as long as I can remember, every morning started out the same way. I would make my way to my father's bedroom before school and kiss him goodbye. As I was leaving, he would always say, "And remember, Eric, never trust anyone." These certainly are not the words you typically hear a father say to a son who is heading off to kindergarten, and the true meaning of the words didn't quite resonate until adulthood. Today, however, as I grow our business, my father's lesson is more relevant than ever.

I first learned the meaning of my father's words from my older brother, Don, who is not only my best friend, but also a mentor to me to this day. After school, Don would always suggest that we trade the coins in our piggybanks: I would happily exchange my quarters for several of his shiny pennies, thinking that the quantity I was receiving far outweighed the actual value of my coins. One day, I walked into my father's room with my pile of pennies to show him what a great investment I had just made. Noticing how Don was conning his little brother, my father looked at me, explained the concept of value versus quantity, and exclaimed, "Eric, what did I tell you? Never trust anyone!" Suddenly, I remembered his daily admonition.

Today, as executive vice president of Development and Acquisitions for the Trump Organization, I encounter situations on a daily basis that make me reflect on my father's words and advice. I've realized that self-reliance is a businessperson's most essential tool. Take one particular instance. I was negotiating a mutual partnership to bring an ultra-exclusive restaurateur into one of our projects. After months of tedious negotiations, the night before we intended to sign the deal, I learned, through a slip-up made by one of the restaurateur's architects, that they had been instructed to build a restaurant far exceeding all our agreed-upon budgets.

Shocked by the dishonesty and fraudulent intentions exhibited by my would-be partner, I immediately cut off all negotiations and ended the deal. I am a firm believer that everything happens for a reason, and despite being upset over months of wasted efforts, today I have a smile on my face knowing we made the right decision, went with a different restaurateur, and now own the most successful restaurant in the city.

In a similar instance, my father knew a successful businessman who pledged to donate $40 million, to be paid in four equal installments, to his alma mater. After paying the first two installments, the businessman ran into severe financial difficulties and asked the college for additional time in which to pay the remaining $20 million. Instead of being grateful for the $20 million that it had received, the college sued this man for both nonperformance and breach of his contractual obligations. Eventually, this individual was forced to file for bankruptcy and, though he ultimately made a full financial recovery and was able to come back even stronger than before, he vowed to never give another cent to the college.

I have been fortunate to have lived a privileged life and am sincerely grateful for my family, education, and upbringing. However, make no mistake that with this lifestyle I also faced difficult challenges. It is human nature to be envious of what other people have, however oftentimes such envy creates a variety of rationalizations for bad behavior. As a child, you do not necessarily see or know that you are privileged or underprivileged, and therefore you can be an easy target for people who may have ill intentions. That was me. But my father's words helped me to see the world as it is and learn that people usually act in their own self interest, even to the detriment of others at times.

This belief is a fine line to walk because I typically like to give people the benefit of the doubt but, as I grow older, I often tend to expect the worst from people so I can avoid being taken by surprise or being disappointed. It is an unfortunate, but necessary stance. However, it gives me a new appreciation and insight into what my father was trying to instill in me as a young child: Discernment comes with experience.

In business and in life there is simply one reality: There are good people and bad. There always have been and always will be. The simple lesson to learn is trust yourself, not others, keep your head out of the clouds, and you will always succeed.

As an executive vice president of Development and Acquisitions for the Trump Organization, **Eric Trump** is actively involved in all aspects of real estate development, both nationally and internationally. From the initial acquisitions and development partnership to the final design, construction, sales, and marketing functions, he plays a pivotal role in Trump projects around the world. Eric appears as a keynote speaker for real estate conferences nationwide, as well as in various press outlets such CNBC, Fox, NBC, and the *New York Post*. Along with his work with the Trump Organization, he works fervently to aid children in need, having started the Eric Trump Foundation for St. Jude Children's Hospital.

27

● Robert KIYOSAKI

Overcoming the Fear
of Failing

For years I have traveled the world, speaking on entrepreneurship and investing. My intent is to highlight the importance of financial education and how financial education is essential to financial freedom and financial security. When asked what I personally invest in, I say, "I became financially independent investing in real estate."

Regardless of where I am—the United States, Australia, South Africa, Europe, or Asia—or to whom I am speaking—rich or poor—what I hear back are similar responses to the idea of investing in real estate. Here are a few choice comments:

"I don't want to fix toilets."

"I don't have any money."

"I don't have the time."

"Real estate is risky."

"What if I lose money?"

"You can't do what you do here."

It is my opinion these responses are simply excuses. Excuses that mask a deeper, darker, hidden, unexpressed reality. In my opinion, most people who use these excuses are:

1. Not educated in real estate.
2. Lazy.

466

3. Afraid of failing.

4. All of the above.

I say this because most people want to be financially free. Most people would love to have financial security. Most people would love to have money coming in regardless of whether they worked or not. Many people would love to stop working and do something they really wanted to do.

To me, real estate represents freedom. Real estate means control over my life and my future. I am not depending upon a retirement plan filled with stocks, bonds, and mutual funds—investments that someone else manages. I want control of my financial destiny.

This is why when I hear such excuses as "I don't have any money" or "I don't want to fix toilets." I know these excuses are just that. I know people are looking at the journey, not the destination. A friend of mine has two sayings about this human failing. His first saying is, "Everyone wants to go to heaven, but no one wants to die." His second, "Many people will not start the journey until all the lights are green."

TIP Unfortunately, too many people allow their excuses to get between them and the life they would love to live.

Unfortunately, too many people allow their excuses to get between them and the life they would love to live. Rather than look beyond real estate, looking at what becoming a real estate investor can do for their lives, most people are blinded by their own excuses. They see what they are afraid of rather than what they want in life. Fear and laziness blur their vision, limiting the boundary of their lives.

The following are my points of view regarding the four excuses.

EXCUSES OF THE POOR

EXCUSE NO. 1: NO EDUCATION

Most people are smart enough to invest in real estate. Investing in real estate is not that tough. Anyone who has bought a home or rented a place to live has invested in real estate. So investing in real estate is not tough. Making money in real estate is another matter. Making money in real estate takes real, real estate education.

When I speak of making money in real estate, I am speaking of *cash flow*. Cash flow is income coming in every month, regardless of whether I work or not. I am not talking about *capital gains*. When people say their house has appreciated in value, or they flipped a property—buying low, fixing it up, and selling it—they are speaking of capital gains. There is a tremendous difference between cash flow and capital gains. In my opinion, capital gains are easier to achieve than cash flow. Achieving sustainable cash flow requires a higher degree of financial education. The good news is you do not have to go to college for four years to get this education. A three-day seminar is sufficient, if it is a good seminar. The Rich Dad Company offers beginning and advanced courses in real estate investing.

In 1997, when *Rich Dad Poor Dad* was published, I wrote about the difference between *assets* and *liabilities*. My rich dad's definitions were simple: *assets put money in your pocket* and *liabilities take money from your pocket*. In the book I stated, "Your house is not an asset. It is a liability." In other words, for most people, their biggest real estate investment, their house, cash flows out, not in. I received hate mail for years because of this one point. After the subprime mess, massive foreclosures, and declining home values, millions of people now realize that real estate can be either an asset or liability.

For most people, their home is a *liability*, even if the mortgage is paid off. Most homes are liabilities because most homes do not produce any income. Most homes cost money: for insurance, property tax, repairs, and other expenses. If a person sells his or her home and the sale puts money in that person's pocket, at that moment the home is an asset. Until then, it is a liability.

TIP To be financially free, your real estate must produce income in good or bad economies. Once you learn to do that, you are free for life. This is why a little financial education is important.

EXCUSE NO. 2: LAZINESS

Laziness is a personal matter. I know I am lazy. I battle the lazy boy inside of me on a daily basis. For example, when I wake up, I know I should go to the gym, but the lazy boy says, "Oh, you can exercise tomorrow. Why not make a cup of coffee and read the paper." By the age of two, most people are experts at making excuses.

When I hear people say, "I don't want to fix toilets" or "I don't have enough money," I know these are excuses from a lazy person because I use the same excuses. When I hear someone repeat to me the same excuses I use myself, I want to say, "What makes you think I want to fix toilets?" or "What makes you think I have money?" But what I really want to say is, "It's because I don't want to fix toilets, and it's because I want to have a lot of money, that's why I invest in real estate."

Rich dad often said, "Many lazy people are hard-working people." At first, I did not understand what he meant. As I got older, I began to understand his words more clearly. Growing older, I also found it easier to be busy at work than it was to do what I needed to do. Today, I still use excuses such as, "I'm busy" or "I have too much work to do" or "I need a break." Today, I meet many hard-working people, hiding behind the curtain of hard work, yet deep down, they are too lazy to get rich. So they invent an excuse.

When I was in high school, my poor dad often said to me, "I can't go to your football game because I've got work to do." He never attended a game in the three years I played high school football. He also said the same thing about becoming rich or at least financially free. He was always busy. In my opinion, he often used hard work as an excuse to hide from life. He was a good, hard-working, high-income, poor man.

My rich dad was a rich man because he did not work hard for money. Instead, he worked hard at having his money work hard for him. The harder his money worked, the more money he made, and the more free time he had. The more free time he had, the more money he made.

This drove my poor dad crazy. My poor dad often called people like my rich dad, "The idle rich." Rather than have his money work hard, my poor dad put his money in the bank. My poor dad believed in saving money. This drove my rich dad crazy. He would say, "Your father works hard because his money is lazy. All your dad's money does is sit in the bank. I come along, borrow your dad's money, buy a piece of real estate, and put your dad's money to work for me."

TIP Professional education is all about learning to work for money. Financial education is all about learning to have money work for you. So the question is, "Who works harder? You, or your money?"

EXCUSE NO. 3: FEAR OF FAILING

Fear is often a combination of lack of education and laziness. The acronym F.E.A.R. stands for *False Evidence Appearing Real*. Because of fear, many people see only what can go wrong. Due to lack of education, they cannot see what can go right.

When I am asked, "How does a person overcome the fear of failing?" I simply reply, "Get some education, gain some experience, find a mentor, and get off your butt." In other words, improve your vision. See what most people cannot see. See the opportunities most people cannot see because of fear. See the destination and the journey.

TIP One of the reasons I have a team of advisors when I invest is simply that each person sees something different. After listening to what each person has to say, I then make up my mind.

Most great investments are right in front of you. The problem is seeing them. The reason most investments are hard to see is that great investments are seen with your mind, not your eyes. Years ago, I wanted to buy a piece of ranch-land. My dream was to build a remote mountain cabin in the woods. I also wanted it for free. After challenging my mind, I went looking for my dream. A few months later, I came across a spectacular piece of property. It was approximately eighty acres, including an old rock house built in the 1880s. The asking price was $115,000. I believe I put $10,000 down—with the terms of no interest and no payments—and asked for one year to pay off the balance. After fixing the house, I subdivided the property, sold thirty acres with the house for approximately $215,000. I put some money, about $75,000, net in my pocket and still have the fifty free acres today.

After the transaction was completed, a neighbor who lived in a remote cabin a few miles away came by and was upset that I made money and got fifty acres for free. She had watched the property for years, but did nothing. She had a similar idea but failed to buy the property because she was afraid of failing. "What would you have done if you had failed?" she asked. "What if the property had not sold?"

"I still would have had my dream," I replied. "It would not have been for free, yet I would still have my dream."

"But what if you had failed?" she demanded.

Taking a deep breath I replied, "I knew that if things did not work out, I would have been creative and tried something else. Every failure would have made me smarter and eventually more successful. You can fail only if you do nothing."

She looked back at me and said, "And I did nothing, so I failed."

Shrugging my shoulders, I said softly, "I leave that decision up to you."

The Deadliest Word

One of the most deadly words in the English language is the word "try." When someone says they will "try" to do something, I know they will probably not do it. There is a world of difference between the statements, "I will try to do it" and "I will do it." The difference between the two statements is the word "commitment."

My favorite way of describing the word commitment comes from the following question and answer:

Question: What is the difference between bacon and eggs?
Answer: The chicken is involved but the pig is committed.

If you want to become financially free, don't be a chicken. Get committed. Forbid yourself from using the word "try." You either will or you won't.

THE POWER OF EDUCATION

About twenty years ago, I took a simple two-day course on creative financing. I believe I paid about $350 for the program. I think lunch was included. If it hadn't been for that course, I would not have seen the free land opportunity. My neighbor, who did not take the course, could not see what I saw. All she could see was failure.

As most of us know, we are in the Information Age. The problem is, there is too much information. The reason education is important is that education trains our brains to selectively take in information and turn information into meaning. Due to a lack of real estate education, my neighbor was overwhelmed with information, most of it negative. Her brain was not trained to focus, process information, and turn it into positive meaning. That is why a little real estate education can be priceless.

RICH PEOPLE AND COWARDS

Fear is a very powerful human emotion. How we handle fear determines if we become rich people or cowards. When it comes to money, *fear* turns most people into cowards.

Is it okay to have fear? While fear causes most people to do nothing, fear causes other people to take action. Since I do not want to fail and lose money, I take real estate education classes and read books on real estate. I did it twenty years ago, and I am still learning today. That is why I could ask my brain to find me a piece of land that I didn't have to pay for, and why I continue to invest today. Buying the eighty acres, or any investment, I still have fear. I still fear losing. I just use my fear to take action and get smarter. I know that if things do not go right, I will use my creative mind and gain wisdom in the process. Many people use the fear of failing as a reason to do nothing.

TIP Fear causes most people to do nothing; fear causes other people to take action. I still have fear. I still fear losing. I just use my fear to take action and get smarter.

Then there are people who attend real estate classes, study hard, and they still let fear stop them. One reason is due to analysis paralysis. That means they study too much. When it comes time to put their money on the line, the coward in them chimes in and gives them all the reasons why the deal will not work. Just before they sign the papers, Chicken Little pops into their head and begins to shout, "The sky is falling! The sky is falling!"

Just as I battle the lazy boy in me, I also do battle with my own resident Chicken Little. One of the beauties of real estate is that you have time to think. There have been many times that I have found a piece of property, put in an offer, had the offer accepted, and then I began my research—a process known as due diligence. It is during this due diligence period, a period that can be as short as a week or as long as six months, that I bring in my team of advisors and mentors. When I make the final decision either to buy or back out, I make it as a member of a calm, rational, educated, and experienced team—like the team who contributed to this book.

Due diligence periods do not guarantee success. There can still be unforeseen problems. If a problem arises, again I call on a team to assist me with problem solving, and it is that problem solving that increases my wisdom, wisdom that I can use on the next investment. At minimum, even if I lose some money, I will be smarter than someone who did nothing. It is with this philosophy that I invest, in spite of my fear.

EXCUSE NO. 4: ALL OF THE ABOVE

All of us are human. All of us need more education. All of us can be lazy. All of us are afraid of failing. The difference between all of us begins with all of the traits that make us human. The difference between all of us begins with how we address our excuses.

The following are some of the ways I personally address the four excuses.

ADDRESSING EXCUSE NO. 1: NO REAL ESTATE EDUCATION

My financial education began with the game of Monopoly. Rich dad would play that game with his son and me, over and over again. When I asked him why we played the game so often he said, "Because the formula for great wealth is found in this game." Most of us know the formula, which is this: Four green houses turns into one red hotel. At the age of nine, I realized that I could be rich if I followed this simple formula and turned a game into real life.

To show us the game being played in real life, rich dad took his son and me to see his green houses. Ten years later, when I was nineteen, rich dad bought his red hotel on Waikiki Beach.

When I returned to Hawai'i from the Vietnam War, I asked my rich dad how I could get started in real estate. His reply was, "First get educated. I've taken you as far as I can go. You need to take the next step." A month later, I was watching television and saw an infomercial for a real estate course. I purchased the course for $385, which was a fortune at the time, since I made only about $600 a month as a Marine Corps pilot.

It was after the course ended that my real education began. Everything the instructor taught us came true. He said, "The first problems you will run into are real estate agents. Most real estate agents are salespeople, not investors. They would not know a good investment from a bad one." This is true today. For months, all I heard from real estate agents is, "You can't do that. Those deals do not exist."

The next thing the instructor said was, "Find a mentor, someone who did invest in real estate." Since my rich dad was already my mentor, I went immediately to him. Rich dad's first words were, "How can I teach you something until you do something?"

TIP "How can I teach you something until you do something?"—RICH DAD

For the next few months, I drove around in my spare time, looking at properties, talking to real estate agents, finally doing something as my rich dad had suggested. After I finally put an offer in on a property, I ran back to rich dad and proudly showed him the offer. As you can already guess, he ripped it to pieces. Although it was painful to find out how little I knew, that experience was priceless because I was finally doing something.

The deal I brought him was a low down payment deal. The problem was I lost money every month; it was a negative cash flow investment. Rich dad's lesson was, "How many investments can you afford if you lose money every month?"

Obviously, my reply was, "Not many."

His next question was, "Why do you want to pay money to lose money?"

"Because the real estate agent said the price would go up and I would make my money back," I replied.

"Will the real estate agent guarantee that?" rich dad asked.

"I don't know," I replied. "He just said I would make a lot of money when I sold it."

"Will he guarantee that?" asked rich dad again.

"I don't know," I replied again.

He then said, "Rather than lose money, how many investments can you afford if you make money every month?"

Thinking for awhile, I replied hesitantly, "As many as I can find?"

Rich dad smiled and said, "Go out and find investments you can make money on. Never bring me an investment that you pay to lose money on. Never bet on a property going up in value."

It was back to the streets. As rich dad said, "How can I teach you something until you do something?" I was beginning to learn something.

My next lesson was learning to handle discouragement. As time dragged on, I became more and more discouraged. Everything was too expensive or would have cost too much money in repairs. Dragging my tail between my legs, I went back to rich dad for some sympathy, and as you can guess, he gave me none.

When I complained about not having enough money, rich dad just laughed. His lesson was, "When you find an investment that makes money, you will find the money."

A month later, I found a one-bedroom, one-bath condominium on the island of Maui, one block from a gorgeous white sand beach. I was excited that I finally found a great investment. I bought three of them, with credit cards and seller financing. Each month, I made a net $25 per unit. I was making money, not losing money. Rich dad was correct. When you find a great investment, you will find the money.

TIP When you find a great investment, you will find the money. —RICH DAD

For your information, even if $25 does not sound like much, it is one of four sources of income. In real estate, the four sources of income are:

1. **Cash flow.** In this example I was making $25 a month.
2. **Amortization.** Each month, a little bit of my loan was being paid off. If I held the property to the end of the mortgage, technically my tenants would have paid off my mortgage.
3. **Depreciation.** Accounting and tax rules allow me to depreciate my property, which means I am making money but it looks like I am losing money. I am making money because I am legally allowed to pay less in taxes. So this is money coming in because less money is paid out in taxes. It is also known as *phantom cash flow.*
4. **Appreciation.** This is the price of the unit going up in value. Appreciation is also known as capital gains. Most people invest for appreciation. During the last real estate boom, flippers were buying and then selling for a profit. This is investing for appreciation (capital gains).

These four sources of income are also known I.R.R.—an internal rate of return. Being able to see these four different incomes gives me a lot more confidence.

As I said earlier, I don't invest for appreciation, I invest for cash flow. In fact, one of the reasons why I do not like to flip property is that I like all four of these income opportunities and it takes such a long time to find a great property.

Another reason why I do not like to flip a property is that I can gain access to my appreciation without selling the property. For example, let's say I buy a property for $200,000 and a few years later it goes to $300,000. Rather than sell the property, I would rather borrow out the equity and continue to let the tenant pay for my second mortgage. Obviously, I borrow only if my rent can cover the increase in monthly payments.

I learned the hard way about selling or flipping a property. Here's the story.

More Than Fixing a Toilet

I wish I could say my education was complete after I bought the three units. Little did I know that the next phase of education was about to begin, an education in property management. After owning the three condos for a few months, the septic system on the entire development burst, and the sewage run-off ran into one of my condos. Next on my real estate education curriculum was how to deal with developers, homeowners associations, lawyers, and a smelly rental unit.

My first plumbing problem was a much bigger than fixing a toilet.

SELLING OUT OF THE PROBLEM

The good news is, even though I was losing money because the tenants moved out, the Maui real estate market was taking off. A real estate agent, the very type of person I was warned to be wary of in my real estate course, offered me $48,000 per unit. Since my base cost was only $18,000 a unit, my gross capital gains would be about $30,000 a unit. The money and the septic system went to my head. I sold.

Immediately after I sold and put the money in my pocket, the real estate agent sold the units for $65,000 a unit a few weeks later. The lessons were piling up. I made money, but I was really losing money. The septic system caused me to think emotionally rather than rationally.

In real estate investor terms, the septic system made me a perfect candidate for another investor. I became known as a "don't wanter." A don't wanter is someone who does not want their property. They want out. They are emotional and irrational. Soon after the subprime mortgage mess hit in 2007, the market was filled with don't wanters. Great investors love don't wanters. If you want to become rich, look for don't wanters, and then look at the real estate they don't want.

THE BIGGER PROBLEM AND BETTER LESSON

Another lesson I gained from that first experience is this: "If just starting out, make sure the real estate is less than an hour's drive away." Since these properties were on another island, when there was a problem I had to take time off from work, drive to the airport, park my car, take a flight, rent a car, drive an hour to the property, work on the problem, and then hurry back home, missing a day's work. That was expensive. Today, I can handle properties far away, but when I was just starting out, I should have found a property as close to home as possible, less than an hour's drive away. After you have purchased at least ten properties, because each property will have a new lesson, then you can start expanding your operational radius.

MORE PROPERTIES—MORE PROBLEMS— MORE MONEY

Next on my educational curriculum were capital gains taxes. Selling the three units put a lot of money in my pocket, and I spent it. The next year, I found out what capital gains taxes were. I had made money, and now I had tax problems. I found out that the government tax collectors do not like excuses.

Every property comes with different problems and different lessons. Each lesson caused me to seek further education and gain more real life experience. This is how I got smarter, wiser, and richer. I got richer by failing. I found out that people who do not fail also do not succeed.

TIP I got richer by failing. I found out that people who do not fail also do not succeed.

Today, my wife, Kim, and I own approximately fifteen hundred apartment units and earn more money in a month than most people earn in years. While the education and experiences have not stopped, the financial rewards have gone up. Even during the subprime mortgage crisis, our properties have continued to do well. No matter how tough times get, most people want a roof over their heads.

As far as mentors go, the real estate professionals in this book are our mentors. Whenever Kim and I have a question, these are the people we call. Simply said, our education never ends because the problems and challenges we face never end.

So how does one overcome the fear of failing? My answer is grow up. Since failing is part of learning, start with baby steps. Babies crawl before they walk and walk before they run. Babies fall many times during the learning process. That is why it is good that babies are short when they start out. They do not have far to fall.

Our educational system makes two big mistakes when teaching people. The first mistake is that it punishes students for making mistakes. If you make no mistakes, you are an A student. If you make too many mistakes you are labeled a failure. This is why so many people who did well in school do not do well in real life. The second mistake is that in school, you have to take tests on your own. If you cooperate with your classmates during test time it is called cheating. One of the reasons I make more money than many A students is because I make more mistakes and I cheat—meaning that I cooperate. This book is written by the people I cooperate with at test time.

How to Find Great Advisors and Mentors

A question I am often asked is, "How do I find great advisors and mentors?" My reply is, "In fairy tales and in real life, you kiss many frogs before you find a prince or princess, so start kissing."

One valuable lesson I have learned is, "In every bad deal I meet good people." For example, I was working on a deal with a person who talked like and looked like he knew what he was doing. "Joe," (not his real name), had the credentials and the diplomas. Then the deal we were working on went bad, and his true personality, his dark side, came out. The good thing was that I met Ken McElroy through the process. I do not know where "Joe" is today, but Ken and I have become great friends and have gone on to make millions of dollars together.

Today, I am not afraid of deals going bad because I know that through bad deals I meet good people. In other words, when deals go bad, the true character—the good or the bad in a person—comes out from behind the curtain.

How Do You Overcome the Fear of Failing?

Here are ten things you can do right now:

1. **Take classes or read books before starting.** If you have no money, go to the library. Remember, your mind is your greatest asset. Invest in that first.
2. **Avoid taking advice from losers.** Stay away from people who say that something cannot be done. Be aware of real estate sales people who give investment advice but who do not invest in real estate.
3. **Find mentors, people who have already gone to where you want to go.**
4. **Look at a minimum of one hundred investments before buying anything.** Take a new route home from work and look at different neighborhoods. Jog or ride a bike in new neighborhoods. Observe if neighborhoods are changing, going up, or going down. Talk to people who live in the area to find out what is going on. Once you find an area you are interested in, become a five-block expert. Become the smartest person in one square mile. When you begin to see investments that make money, the money will find you.

5. **Start small.** Know that you will make mistakes. My rich dad often said, "When someone does something to make a killing, they get killed." Invest in property less than an hour from where you live.

6. **Stay humble.** When people make money, they often get cocky. When people get cocky, they make foolish mistakes. It is through humility and humor, being able to laugh at our successes as well as our failures, that we learn best. In other words, don't take yourself too seriously. The septic system blowing up and flowing into my first condo still causes me to laugh. Today, I am cautious about investing in anything that is downhill from something else. Today, I do know exactly what rolls downhill!

7. **Dream big.** The only difference between my first investment and my investments today are zeros. My dream was not real estate. My dream was financial freedom, and each property, good or bad, was a stepping-stone to that dream.

8. **Remember, the world is filled with hard-working poor people.** Many people today are slaves to money. Today, many people will have to work for money all their lives. So, every day, remind yourself not to be one of them. Work hard at having your money work hard for you so you do not have to work hard for money.

9. **There are no perfect investments.** Each investment comes with problems. Each investment will challenge you. Each investment will teach you something new. If you *do nothing*, you *learn nothing*. If you learn nothing, you remain poor. So remember, the only way you can fail is to fail to do something.

10. **And no, I do not fix toilets.** If I knew how to fix toilets, I would, so I never learned how to fix them. Instead, I learned how to hire and fire professionals such as real, real estate agents, accountants who know the tax advantages of investing in real estate, mortgage bankers who personally invest in real estate, lawyers who understand real estate law, property managers who love taking care of property, contractors whose passion is building or fixing real estate, and other specialists whose business is to be the best at the business of real estate. So I do not know how to fix toilets, or how to do accounting or real estate law, but I do know who does.

As the years go on, you will get smarter and so will your team of professional advisors. Ultimately, real estate is not your asset. Real estate alone does not make anyone rich. Investing in real estate offers you the opportunity to get smarter. It is your education, good and bad experiences, lessons learned, wisdom that comes with time, and your team, a team like my team that contributed to this book, that will ultimately become your greatest assets.

TIP If you do not have enough money for an investment, remind yourself that if you *do not* solve that problem, you will have money problems all your life. My rich dad said, "If you can solve the problem of *not having money*, you will *have more money* for life." Henry Ford said, "Thinking is the hardest work there is. That's why so few people engage in it."

Real Life Story: Why Waste a Priceless Mistake?

During this last real estate bubble, a friend bought one property, flipped it, and made some money. That first easy success went to his head. He now thought he was Donald Trump's long lost brother. As the property bubble continued to inflate, he went on a buying spree, buying properties in Las Vegas, Miami, San Francisco, Mexico, London, and Phoenix. Today he is bankrupt and blames real estate for his problems. His problem was he knew only one type of market, a market bubble. He now knows what a real estate bust looks like. Since he blames real estate rather than himself, he has not learned much. He has wasted priceless mistakes. He fails to learn that it is after the bubble bursts that the real, real estate investors come out, and the real killings are made. The killings are made from foolish investors who got killed.

TIP The reason there are more poor people than rich people is that it is easier to say, "I can't afford it," rather than ask the question, "How can I afford it?" The moment you ask yourself the question, "How can I afford it?" your most important asset, your mind, goes to work. If you use the excuse, "I can't afford it," your mind goes back to sleep and you get back to working hard as a slave to money.

So please do not allow the *fear of failing* to come between you and your *financial freedom*. Failing is essential to success.

TIP If you *do nothing,* you *learn nothing*. If you learn nothing, you remain poor. So remember, the only way you can fail is to fail to do something.

Index

Credits